BRITAIN AND IRISH SEPARATISM

BRITAIN AND IRISH SEPARATISM
FROM THE FENIANS TO THE FREE STATE 1867/1922

THOMAS E. HACHEY

Marquette University

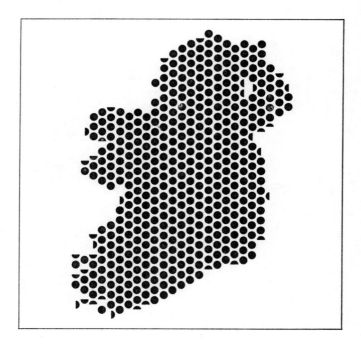

RAND McNALLY COLLEGE PUBLISHING COMPANY/CHICAGO

Current Printing (last digit)
77 78 79   15 14 13 12 11 10 9 8 7 6 5 4 3 2 1

To

My father and mother: Leo and Margaret Hachey

and

May, Helen and Tom

Contents

Preface • ix

Acknowledgments • x

Introduction • 1

Chapter

1. British Liberalism and the Irish Home Rule Movement (1867–1900) • 11

2. We Are Not British: The Varieties of Separatist Sentiment in Ireland (1890–1911) • 37

3. Union Forever: Britain's Most Dangerous Hour (1911–1914) • 67

4. Other Portraits of Protest: Nationalist and Labourite Dissent in Ireland (1914) • 96

5. The Ascendancy of Revolutionary Separatism in Ireland (1914–1916) • 130

6. The Easter Rising: Rebellion and Reprisal (1916) • 162

7. Reaction to the Rising: The Growth of Sinn Fein (1916–1918) • 183

8. Dail Eireann and the Irish Separatist Appeal to the Peace Conference (1919) • 201

9. Irish Separatism and American Politics: The British Response (1919–1921) • 232

10. War for Independence and the Partition Compromise (1919–1922) • 259

Epilogue • 274

Appendices • 311
Bibliography • 321
Index • 331

Preface

The purpose of this book is to examine Irish separatism in its constitutional, cultural, and revolutionary contexts from the aftermath of
the Fenian rising to the establishment of the Irish Free State. In the
period between these events constitutional separatism was given
new direction by the inception of the Home Rule movement in
1870 and the subsequent development of the Irish Parliamentary
Party; cultural nationalism enjoyed a renaissance of unequaled ac-
complishment; and revolutionary nationalism suffered a temporary
eclipse, only to emerge again with renewed fury. Recently opened
British Government archives provide an instructive perspective by
revealing the American dimensions of the Anglo-Irish conflict, particularly in the years immediately following World War I. Arranged
topically, but also chronologically, the chapters in this volume focus
upon the events and circumstances which ultimately determined
the direction and destiny of Irish separatism from 1867 to 1922.

THOMAS E. HACHEY

August 1976
Higgins Beach
Scarborough, Maine

Acknowledgments

I am grateful to the Marquette University Committee on Research for the generous grant which provided welcome support during the preparation of this book. My task was considerably facilitated by the competent and amiable assistance which I received from the respective staffs of the National Library of Ireland, the Scottish Record Office, the Public Record Office, London, the British Museum, the Beaverbrook Library, the Plunkett Foundation, the American Irish Historical Society, New York, and the National Archives, Washington, D.C. For their expert advice and efficient service I am heavily indebted to the library personnel at both Marquette University and at the University of Wisconsin.

It would be difficult to credit adequately the generous assistance accorded me by Leslie Seed, Assistant Keeper, Public Record Office, London, who aided me in the expeditious retrieval of documents recently opened to public inspection. I should also like to thank Her Majesty's Stationary Office for permission to reproduce Crown copyright materials for use in this work and in a related documentary study.

In the editing and preparation of this manuscript for publication, I was particularly fortunate to have the services of Rand McNally editor Kevin Thornton. His patience, understanding, and professional skill simplified my work considerably. Kevin's empathy and enthusiasm for this study was a source of special inspiration. I should also wish to acknowledge with gratitude the editorial services of Margaret Boberschmidt, who edited a draft of the earlier chapters, and indeed I must thank Editor-in-Chief Lawrence Malley for his unfailing support and encouragement from the very outset of this project.

Special thanks is owed to two loyal friends and professional colleagues, Alan Ward of the College of William and Mary, and Lawrence McCaffrey of Loyola University of Chicago, for their useful suggestions and constructive criticisms. I am equally indebted to two other anonymous readers for their comments and advice. For her formidable effort in typing and proofing the manuscript I am, as always, most obligated to my wife Jane.

Note on Usage

In this study, the words "nationalist" and "nationalism" are spelt with a small "n" when referring either to the demands or to the diverse elements of Irish nationality. Wherever feasible, however, a capital "N" is employed when the referent is either the Irish Parliamentary Party, or its particular constituency and/or political viewpoint. Moreover, the terms "Southern Ireland" and "Twenty Six Counties" are used interchangeably for the Irish Free State, Eire, or the Republic of Ireland; and "Northern Ireland," "the Six Counties" and "Ulster" are used synonymously throughout the book. Whatever imprecision which some of these usages may contain, it is hoped that their net effect will serve the purposes of clarification and identification.

T. E. H.

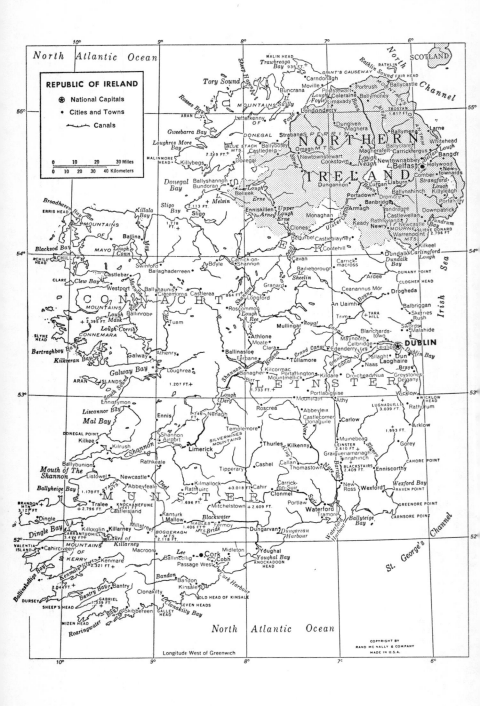

Introduction

Ireland's troubled and frequently tragic relations with England over the past 800 years have been substantially influenced by two elements: geography and religion. It was perhaps inevitable that the geographical proximity of the two island countries would lead the more populous and powerful England to expand her interests at the expense of her Irish neighbor. English colonizers and adventurers began settling and plundering Ireland in the twelfth century, shortly after the Norman conquest of England, but it was not until the reign of Henry VIII (1509–1547), however, that all Ireland was brought under English control. In the Protestant Reformation which convulsed much of Europe, a cruel twist of fate created further tensions for future Anglo-Irish relations when England became Protestant while Ireland remained Roman Catholic. England's emergence as a dominant maritime power in an age of colonization and mercantilism doubtlessly would have forced Ireland into a dependent status in any circumstance. But Ireland's sympathy for and cooperation with the Catholic Powers of Spain and France in their religious wars with England in the sixteenth and seventeenth centuries had lasting consequences. The English determined that the security of their country required a totally subjugated Ireland. In 1601, an English army dispatched by Queen Elizabeth achieved that objective with a ruthless determination which included destroying crops in order to reduce the Irish peasants to starvation.

Ireland's present religious division dates from the land settlement which followed. Since Ulster clan chiefs had raised the most effective resistance to religious and political Anglicization, their province was singled out by the wrathful conquerors. Under James I in 1608 scores of choice Ulster plantations were forfeited for treason and given to Scots and English settlers. The town of Derry was awarded to a company of Londoners who promptly renamed it Londonderry, a name Ulster Catholics refuse to recognize even today. Besides the estates confiscated by the largely English nobility, thousands of Presbyterian farmers from Scotland were settled throughout Ulster as tillers of the soil. These Scots received comparatively small plots of land, but they took a much stronger hold than the absentee English landlords who lived handsomely in England off the rents paid by Irish tenants. The plantation policy left Ulster the only province in Ireland with a significantly large Protestant garrison. It was also during this period that the Irish Parliament in Dublin was enlarged with a majority of Protestants in order to check the power of the Catholic nobility, Anglo-Irish as well as Irish, in the other three provinces of Leinster, Munster and Connaught.

Fearing further property confiscations and religious persecution, Irish Catholics turned to violence in 1641 and massacred thousands of native Protestants. England was horrified but helpless, for she was trembling on the brink of her own civil war between Puritans and royalist supporters of Charles I. Fearing the Puritans more, the Irish vainly attempted to aid King Charles, but Oliver Cromwell's Puritan army defeated the Stuart forces and executed the King. Puritan fury then turned upon Catholic Ireland as Cromwell's veterans descended upon that country not only for conquest, but for revenge. After Catholic Ireland had been subdued, however, Puritan ferocity diminished and comparatively few were executed for their part in the rebellion. The poor were left unmolested and, under the terms of a general pardon, were permitted to return to their ordinary lives without fear of punishment. Severe penalties were reserved for the wealthy. Catholic landowners in Ireland were divided into two groups: those who had participated in the rebellion and those who had not. The former promptly lost their estates and all their property rights. The latter were allowed to retain land but were forced to settle in the western provinces of Connaught. Their former holdings were then divided among the officers and men of Cromwell's army, a policy which all but completed the destruction of the Irish gentry.

Another tragic chapter in Irish history resulted from Ireland's support of James II, the Catholic King of England who was deposed in the "Glorious" Revolution of 1688. James landed in Ireland with French money and arms in 1689. William of Orange, the new King of England and leader of the Protestant forces, arrived in Ulster the following year, setting the scene for an epic battle between English kings fought on Irish soil. Although the Catholics were not finally defeated until the signing of the treaty of Limerick in 1691, the psychological turning point and most memorable event of the war was the battle of the Boyne River where William's army defeated the Catholic forces under James. The victory all but assured the ultimate triumph of the Protestant cause. The Battle of the Boyne is fondly remembered among the Protestant community of Northern Ireland where it is annually celebrated on July 12, Orangeman's Day, with parades and festivities.

Neither the Tudor plantation policy nor the Cromwellian settlement had as devastating an effect upon Ireland as did the Penal Laws which were passed in the last few years of the seventeenth century and in the early decades of the eighteenth. Protestant ascendancy was maintained by an Irish Parliament controlled by agents of English absentee landlords. Presbyterians as well as Catholics suffered from the economic exploitation. A flourishing wool industry was destroyed when export from the country was forbidden. The resultant poverty forced many Presbyterian merchants and craftsmen to emigrate. It also reduced the vast majority of the Catholic population into demoralized and impoverished tenant laborers.

During the late eighteenth century, Irish Protestants,

more confident of their position, less frightened of the beaten Catholic masses, resentful of British mercantilist restrictions, and anxious to free the Irish Parliament from English domination, developed a patriotism of their own. Active opposition was made possible by French assistance to the American Revolution which provided an excuse for the formation of a supposedly defensive volunteer Protestant army. With these volunteers behind him, Irish nationalist Henry Grattan, a constitutional separatist, demanded and obtained trade concessions and an independent Irish Parliament. But middle-class Protestants were still unhappy with a parliament which served primarily, if not exclusively, the interests of the landed gentry. The Society of United Irishmen, founded in Belfast in 1791, moved the reform movement to the political left. Its leader, Theobold Wolfe Tone, a revolutionary separatist, was a Dublin Protestant; but the heart of this national movement was in revolutionary Ulster. United Irishmen saw themselves as culturally distinct from other British ethnic groups. Finding their inspiration in the ideals of the French Revolution, they hoped to unite Catholics and Protestants under the banner of liberty. Their goal was a democratic republic, and they regarded the exploited Catholic peasantry as natural revolutionary allies of the Nonconformist Ulster middle-class in achieving that end. In the ill-prepared and disastrous United Irishmen uprisings of 1798, Protestants in Armagh died no differently from Catholics in Wexford.

A major factor contributing to the failure of the United Irishmen movement was that most Irish Protestants preferred keeping the system of ascendancy, with all its shortcomings, rather than extending political equality to the Catholic majority. Limited Catholic gains toward equality, the fear of a French invasion supported by an Irish conspiracy, and the impact of the Evangelical movement in Britain and Ireland revived militant Protestantism and provided Anglicans and Presbyterians with a common no-popery position. The success of the Orange Order in the late 1790's was a manifestation of this new Protestant spirit. Orangeism was the outgrowth of an Ulster Protestant tenant farmer secret society, the Peep O'Day Boys, rivals to the Defenders, a Catholic agrarian secret society. Protestant farmers resented Papist competition for the limited land available, particularly in Ulster communities with large Catholic populations. Beginning in 1795, the Orange Order rapidly grew in size and was soon terrorizing Catholics in southern Ulster counties, driving some of them into the wild and sparsely settled regions of Connaught. Recognizing the anti-revolutionary potential of the Orangemen, members of the gentry class took command of the movement, armed its membership, and persuaded government authorities that no-popery was an effective tool of law and order. Orangeism spread throughout Ireland into Britain where it won adherents in the highest quarters, including members of the Royal family.[1]

After the United Irishmen rising of 1798, England and Ireland were joined in 1800 in a legislative union which abolished the Dublin Parliament and gave the Irish representation in the British Parliament at Westminster. Irish separatism on a national scale did not advance beyond the humble strides made in the last two decades of the eighteenth century. The constitutional separatism symbolized by Grattan's parliament died among the upper classes; the nonsectarian revolutionary separatism of Wolfe Tone had no leadership and little following among a population which found expression for its resentments in local agrarian agitation and crime. Robert Emmet attempted to revive the United Irish spirit for a new rising in 1803, but his effort met with dismal failure. Emmet, the younger brother of one of the radical leaders of the 1790's, hoped to secure help from Napoleon who was at war with England at the time. But such aid was not forthcoming, and what was supposed to have been a revolution ended as a Dublin street scuffle on the night of July 23, 1803. Robert Emmet was captured and

---

[1]Lawrence J. McCaffrey, "The Catholic Minority in the North" in *Divided Ireland*, ed. Francis William O'Brien (Rockford, Illinois, 1971), pp. 48–49.

brought to trial. After making a dramatic declaration of his nationalist faith to the court, he was executed. Although his name was entered among the pantheon of Irish martyrs by the separatists of future generations, few of his contemporaries were moved by his example. In the next few decades, Irish dissent would take the form of agrarian disturbance and Catholic agitation.

Ulster Protestants originally were the most bitter opponents of the Act of Union, for they feared a remote British Parliament might be more responsive to Catholic grievances and agitation. It was indeed British Prime Minister William Pitt's intention to remove the remaining disabilities of the Penal Laws against Catholics. King George III denied Pitt royal assent, however, and Catholic emancipation was delayed until 1829 when it was accomplished largely through the efforts of Daniel O'Connell. O'Connell also succeeded in creating modern Irish nationalism on the foundations of Catholic civil rights. His achievements changed the attitudes of nineteenth century Ulster Protestants who now became the most militant champions of maintaining the Union. Orange leaders came to view British power as the best guarantee of Protestant ascendancy in Ireland. Furthermore, since Ulster was the only section of Ireland to participate in the Industrial Revolution, linen factories and Belfast shipyards were assimilated into the British urban industrial complex. Protestant merchants and industrialists were convinced that a revived Irish parliament dominated by a priest-ridden Catholic peasantry would destroy Ulster's economy and persecute their religion.

Beginning in 1845, Ireland's eight and one-half million people (twice the present population) either witnessed or suffered the ravages of famine caused by a potato crop blight and aggravated by one of the most severe winters ever. During the next six years approximately one million people died of starvation and disease; and from 1847 to 1854 nearly two million others emigrated, most of them to the United States, where they perpetuated their Anglophobic sentiments in often radical Hibernian organizations.

Irish separatist sentiment, inspired by Daniel O'Connell's ultimately unsuccessful campaign to restore the Irish parliament and to repeal the union between Ireland and Britain, found new expression in the 1840s. Young Ireland, a youthful and heterogeneous group of constitutional, cultural, and revolutionary separatists, collaborated to produce the *Nation,* a weekly newspaper founded in 1842 to aid O'Connell in his campaign to repeal the Act of Union. But the alliance was short-lived; the Young Irelanders grew critical of O'Connell in 1844 and became his active opponents shortly thereafter. The issue upon which they most sharply disagreed was essentially a sectarian one. Some of the Young Irelanders were Protestant, and all of them believed that religion was a matter of private conscience which had no place in politics. Accordingly, these men supported Prime Minister Robert Peel's university plan for Ireland which chartered non-sectarian "Queens Colleges" in Belfast, Cork, and Galway in 1845. These colleges were linked by the establishment of a federal university in 1850, the Queen's University in Ireland, which charged low tuition fees, offered generous scholarships, and rendered university education more accessible in Ireland than in contemporary England. Archbishop John MacHale of Tuam led the Catholic hierarchy in condemning these "godless" schools because they provided for the secular education of Irishmen of different religious persuasions at the same institution, and in spite of the fact that the various denominations were at liberty to arrange for the pastoral care and religious instruction of their own students. When Daniel O'Connell joined MacHale in denouncing the Queens Colleges, the Young Irelanders rebuked the champion of Catholic emancipation for his religiously partisan and politically illiberal stance.

Young Irelanders next took to quarrelling among themselves which was perhaps inevitable given the wide disparity of political views which they embraced. Thomas Davis, a Protestant barrister from Dublin and the acknowledged leader of the group, espoused Wolfe Tone's conception of Irish nationality as including anyone who lived in Ireland, irrespective of creed or origin. Charles Gavan Duffy, a Catholic journalist from county Monaghan who edited the *Nation,* anticipated the creation of the Irish Parliamentary Party which would function independently of the two English parties at the Westminster Parliament. Duffy's views influenced the later political thought of Charles Stewart Parnell in much the same way as James Fintan Lalor, another Young Irelander from a farming community in county Leix, would influence Michael Davitt on the supreme importance of the land question in Ireland. Lastly, John Mitchel, a unitarian solicitor from county Down, advanced the revolutionary separatist vision of complete independence from Britain, as well as the use of physical force to accomplish that end.

On May 23, 1848, the Young Irelanders launched a poorly conceived and totally unsuccessful insurrection. The original scheme had called for the seizure of Dublin, thereby paralyzing the government, and risings throughout the country. Nothing went as planned, however, and only in county Wexford did the rebels make a notable stand. The rising in Wexford did not begin until May 26, and the last insurgent stronghold did not surrender until June 21. It was a farcical performance, and nearly all of the Young Irelanders ended up as convicts or as refugees.

Two of the younger refugees of the 1848 insurrection, James Stephens and John O'Mahony, settled in Paris among a community of European political exiles. From that sanctuary they began plans for the creation of a revolutionary society which would be dedicated to the overthrow of British rule in Ireland. O'Mahony travelled to New York in 1858, and found that the Irish emigrants there constituted a receptive popular following whose support might be enlisted for another rebellion. Stephens journeyed to Dublin the same year and, shortly after his arrival, founded an oath-bound secret society called the Fenian Brotherhood (the name Fenian was derived from the Gaelic "Fianna," a military force led by a legendary Celtic warrior). The Fenians, also known as the Irish Republican Brotherhood (I.R.B.), developed from two small charter groups in Dublin and New York to a sizeable organization of many thousands by 1865.

Fenianism was distinct from all previous separatist movements in that it drew its support from both the Irish at home and the many Irish emigrants who had settled abroad. The Fenian movement repudiated constitutional methods and urged the forcible overthrow of British power in Ireland at the earliest possible date. Although uncompromisingly committed to the establishment of an independent republic, the Fenians never formulated any specific national reform program. They were, however, in universal agreement with Thomas Davis's definition of a non-sectarian nationality and generally favored the separation of church and state.

Other veterans of the 1848 rising, including John O'Leary, Charles Kickham, and Thomas Clarke Luby, followed the example of Young Ireland and helped sustain a weekly newspaper, the *Irish People*, which was founded in Dublin by James Stephens in 1863. But less fortunate precedents were also followed and fratricidal feuding, the nemesis of Irish separatism, was soon in evidence. Another Young Irelander who had returned from exile, William Smith O'Brien, condemned the conspiratorial character of the Fenian organization in the pages of the *Nation*. More serious attacks were mounted by the Roman Catholic episcopacy which disapproved of all oath-bound secret societies and quite gratuitously accused the Fenian nationalists of being communist. These recriminations did not, however, prevent Fenianism from attracting an ever increasing number of followers whose numbers included Irish-American military veterans and Irish soldiers serving in regiments garrisoned in Ireland.

Upon the conclusion of the American Civil War in April, 1865, hundreds of combat experienced Irish officers from the American armies returned to Ireland in the expectation of participating in a military effort against British forces. By this date London had some evidence of a Fenian conspiracy to launch a rebellion, and government officials at Dublin Castle were authorized to raid the editorial office of the *Irish People;* O'Leary, Kickham and Luby were arrested, tried, and sentenced to long terms of imprisonment. James Stephens was also captured a short time later, but he soon escaped. The police responded by taking elaborate precautions to foil any impending rising: thousands of suspects were detained without trial as the government temporarily suspended the *habeas corpus* act; arms were seized; and British army regiments thought to include any number of Fenian sympathizers were relocated outside of Ireland. James Stephens' equivocation was as much responsible for the subsequent Fenian debacle as were these government precautions, since he had repeatedly postponed the rising until it was too late to act from even a modest position of strength.

Stephens quarrelled with colleagues who had grown impatient with his indecision, and he eventually left Ireland. An insurrection was then arranged for March, 1867. When it finally occurred, the armed rising was suppressed in a single night with scarcely a shot being fired. Even more so than the Young Ireland rising of 1848, the Fenian rebellion was an unqualified fiasco. It was a crippling blow for revolutionary separatism, but not a mortal one. For almost forty years, revolutionary separatism would be in eclipse, while cultural and constitutional separatism would engage the national imagination of Ireland.

Chapter 1

British Liberalism and the Irish Home Rule Movement (1867–1900)

The violence and terrorism which marked the Irish War for Independence from 1919 through 1921, and the enduring enmity which unregenerate republicans have felt toward England ever since have led some students of this period to assume that the war was the unavoidable consequence of hostile attitudes long held by two implacable adversaries. In truth, however, the bitter conflict was not inevitable and, in the decades immediately preceding World War I, the political leaders in both England and Ireland were at least agreed upon the necessity for a constitutional solution to their differences.[1] There had always been those Irish nationalists who

---

[1] The Irish Parliamentary Party, which enjoyed the support of the majority of Irishmen, and the British Liberal Party, which governed the United Kingdom from 1905 until 1915 and shared power in a coalition government thereafter until 1922, were both committed to a constitutional resolution of what was generally referred to as "the Irish question."

favored driving the English from their country by physical force, as was demonstrated in the abortive uprisings of 1798, 1848, and 1867.[2] Correspondingly in England, the mingled horror and anger which these events produced had two different effects: they reaffirmed the belief of those who felt that a repressive government was what Ireland deserved or needed, but they also prompted thoughtful men to wonder if the time had not come to provide Ireland with constructive alternatives to the desperate path of political terrorism. That one of those men beginning to think in this way was William Gladstone was one of the more positive legacies which the Fenian uprising of 1867 bequeathed posterity.[3] Gladstone, who became prime minister of Britain in 1868, later became a champion of Irish home rule.

THE FOUNDING OF THE FENIANS

The Fenian movement, also called the Irish Republican Brotherhood, was founded simultaneously at Dublin and New York in 1858. It never abandoned its commitment to the development of a secret military organization and the violent overthrow of the British administration in Ireland.[4] But after the miscarriage of their 1867 revolution in Ireland, the Fenians on both sides of the Atlantic were compelled to wait nearly fifty years before the insurrection of 1916 offered another opportunity to challenge the British by force of

---

[2] While none of these uprisings ever approached the proportions of a major insurrection, they did unmistakably demonstrate that Ireland presented an urgent political problem for Britain.

[3] F. S. L. Lyons, *Ireland Since the Famine* (New York, 1971), p. 127.

[4] For an excellent biography of the Fenian leader James Stephens, see Desmond Ryan, *The Fenian Chief* (Dublin, 1967). Recommended studies of the Fenian movement are T. W. Moody, ed., *The Fenian Movement* (Cork, 1968); Desmond Ryan, *The Phoenix Flame. A Study of Fenianism and John Devoy* (London, 1937); A. M. Sullivan, *New Ireland* (London, 1877); John Devoy, *Recollections of an Irish Rebel* (New York, 1929).

arms. Indeed, one of the Irish Republican Brotherhood's most notable accomplishments was its ability to sustain itself for so long a duration. The official British policy toward the I.R.B. was naturally hostile, even if often benign in practice; the Unionists regarded the Fenian organization as a seditious body infested with alien revolutionary influences; the overwhelming sentiment of Irish parliamentarians at Westminster toward the I.R.B. was one of repugnance; and the Catholic Church, probably the most powerful influence in Irish affairs, was strongly opposed to the Fenian militants as it was to all organizations which required the taking of a secret oath.[5] Despite these adversities, the I.R.B. survived and endured as new men joined to replace those who were imprisoned following the 1867 fiasco. A supreme council was formed to harmonize I.R.B. policies and strategy, and the small but stalwart group began its long vigil during which it nearly always refused to cooperate with moderate Irish nationalists who were seeking home rule for Ireland through constitutional methods. In America, the reorganized I.R.B., which called itself the Clan na Gael, was often willing to aid Irish parliamentarians seeking the more limited goal of self-government under the British Crown.[6] But the majority of the former Fenians in both Ireland and America were quite convinced that any meaningful freedom for Ireland would only come when Britain was sufficiently preoccupied with other matters to permit a successful armed rebellion in Ireland.

---

[5] Beginning in 1861, Irish Roman Catholic bishops issued pastoral letters warning their flocks that excommunication was the automatic penalty incurred by those subscribing to the Fenian oath. Edward Norman, *A History of Modern Ireland* (Coral Gables, Florida, 1971), p. 163. For a more extensive study of the Church's position, see Edward Norman, *The Catholic Church in Ireland in the Age of Rebellion, 1859–1873* (London, 1965), and Donal McCartney, "The Church and Fenianism," *University Review* 4 (Winter, 1967). pp. 203–215.

[6] For a treatment of the Fenians in America, see William D'Arcy *The Fenian Movement in the United States, 1858–1868* (Washington, 1947); see also Leon O Broin, *Fenian Fever. An Anglo-American Dilemma* (London, 1971).

THE POLICIES OF PRIME MINISTER GLADSTONE

Fenians accomplished more by their defeat in 1867 than they perhaps realized. Acts of terrorism or rebellion by Irish insurgents invariably had resulted in retaliatory measures by England, but the emergence of Britain's new Liberal Prime Minister William E. Gladstone was fortuitous for the future of Anglo-Irish relations.[7] Gladstone recognized that the nationalist sentiment in Ireland, of which the Fenian movement was but one manifestation, represented a dangerous alienation from Britain on the part of ever-increasing numbers of Ireland's Catholic majority.[8] Accordingly, the prime minister sought conciliation through reform. In 1869, his church act disestablished and disendowed the Anglican Church of Ireland whose privileged position, supported by tithe or state subsidies, had long been an object of Irish Catholic resentment.[9] Gladstone's land act of 1870 was intended to guarantee the security of tenant farmers by forcing their landlords, in all cases of eviction (except for nonpayment of rent) to compensate them for equity in or improvements on the landlord's property. While this initial effort to check the abusive power of landlords did not prove successful, it was a significant departure from the traditional policies of London governments in that it was the first attempt of the British Parliament to intervene on the side of the Irish tenants.[10]

[7]Gladstone, in a letter to his wife early in his political career, affirmed that England would be compelled to help resolve the social and religious injustices in Ireland. J. L. Hammond, *Gladstone and the Irish Nation* (London, 1964), p. 51.

[8]Gladstone felt that aggressive separatists like the Fenians were the product of Britain's neglect of Irish problems, and of Britain's failure to redress legitimate Irish grievances. Ibid., pp. 79–80.

[9]For an instructive analysis of the Irish Church Act of 1869, see J. C. Beckett, "Gladstone, Queen Victoria and the Disestablishment of the Irish Church, 1868–9," *Irish Historical Studies*, 13 (March, 1962), pp. 38–47. See also P. J. Corish, *A History of Irish Catholicism: Political Problems, 1860–78* (Dublin, 1967), pp. 23–36.

[10]Even this modest step was taken with evident misgivings as is demonstrated by the remarks of one member of Parliament who, while agreeing to vote for Gladstone's land bill, professed to find the proposed legislation "revolutionary" in the way in which it dealt with property. *Parl. Debates*, Commons, 3rd Series, 11 March 1870, Vol. 199, col. 1761.

When, however, Gladstone sought to redress still another grievance, Irish Catholic complaints that they were denied facilities and opportunities for higher education, his party suffered the first of several electoral reversals which the Irish Question would render the Liberals over the next few decades.[11]

THE UNIVERSITY QUESTION

Prime Minister Gladstone's university bill would have expanded Dublin University in a bold and imaginative manner; his plan was, in fact, later adopted by several Canadian universities. British Liberals hoped to answer Catholic demands for higher education without compromising the principle of separation of Church and State in Ireland, so recently affirmed through the disestablishment of the Church of Ireland, by converting Dublin University into a national institution with affiliated sectarian colleges. Under this scheme the university would not offer lectures or examinations in such potentially controversial disciplines as theology, history, or moral philosophy. Instead, each of the adjunct colleges was to be allowed to provide courses and certificates in these areas. But the idea, still widely discussed though not yet adopted in Ireland to this day, was too progressive for its time. Irish Protestants, proud of the academic distinction achieved by Trinity College, were hostile to Gladstone's scheme for a heterogeneous institution of Protestant and Catholic colleges. Moreover, the Irish Catholic hierarchy had consistently opposed nondenominational higher education since the Queen's Colleges controversy of the 1840s. They now argued that the manifest advantage of tradition, pres-

---

[11]The opposition of Irish Liberals, together with that of the Irish Catholic bishops who were insisting upon the government's giving them a denominational university, contributed to the defeat of Gladstone's university bill and to the downfall of his ministry. P. Corish, *A History of Irish Catholicism*, pp. 55-57.

tige and endowment enjoyed by Trinity College would render any Catholic affiliate of the Dublin University inferior and unable to attract quality faculty or students. At the urging of their bishops, Irish Catholic Liberal M.P.'s voted against the university bill in the House of Commons, thereby forcing Prime Minister Gladstone to call for a general election in January 1874.[12] The complexity of the Irish problem in Anglo-Irish affairs is further illustrated by the results of this election. The Liberals were defeated on the Irish reform issues, with Benjamin Disraeli and the Conservative Party assuming power in Britain. The new Irish home rule movement did succeed, however, in winning fifty-nine seats for its adherents in the House of Commons.

ISAAC BUTT

British statesmen like William Gladstone had not been the only ones impressed by the circumstances and personalities which dominated the Fenian rising of 1867, or the equally fateful Young Ireland rising of 1848.[13] Indeed, Isaac Butt, the founding father of the Irish Home Rule movement, was profoundly influenced by the courage and integrity of the participants in each of these revolts and was doubtlessly inspired by their example in the formulation of his political activities.

---

[12]Ever since the Roman Catholic bishops had declared their opposition to the non-sectarian Queen's Colleges in the 1840s, there had been a "university question" in Irish politics. Although a Catholic University had been established in Dublin, in 1854, with John Henry Newman as its first rector, it had no endowments and its degrees were not recognized. Accordingly, the bishops had continued to demand that the government provide, at public expense, a recognized denominational university system. See J. C. Beckett, *The Making of Modern Ireland, 1603–1923* (London, 1969), p. 380.

[13]Like the Fenians, the Young Irelanders accomplished much in defeat since no other group probably has had so great an influence on the thinking of later generations of Irishmen. For the writings of contemporaries to the Fenian movement see L. Fogarty, ed., *James Finton Lalor* (Dublin, 1947) and Charles Gavan Duffy, *The League of North and South* (London, 1886). A good history of the movement is Denis Gwynn, *Young Ireland and 1848* (Cork, 1949).

Butt was a Trinity College trained Irish Protestant whose varied avocations included lecturing in political economy at Trinity, serving for a time as editor of the unionist *Dublin University Magazine,* and conducting a law practice. By the late 1840s Butt had concluded that Britain's economic policies worked to the serious disadvantage of Irish interests, and he soon rejected his unionist political philosophy in favor of a nonsectarian nationalist creed. Butt served as a legal counsel to many of the Young Irelanders in the 1848 sedition trials and, as a part of their defense, argued that the cruel and capricious politico-economic policies of the British government were responsible for the ripening seeds of revolution in Ireland. He also warned that future uprisings were inevitable unless London instituted programs of government relief as a means of blunting the impact of the horrific famine which ravaged Ireland in the late 1840s. Butt further recognized the wisdom of permitting an Irish parliament which would serve the best interests of both Ireland and the British Empire.[14]

THE FOUNDING OF THE IRISH PARLIAMENTARY PARTY

Isaac Butt gained new prominence in Ireland following the abortive Fenian insurrection of 1867 as he eloquently defended the Fenian prisoners at their trials, at great personal expense and sacrifice. His work in subsequent years when, as president of the Amnesty Association, he worked with some success to have the Republicans freed from prison, won Butt the respect of the Irish Catholic masses. The major contribution of his public career, however, was his work on behalf of Irish federalism. This ideal gave the title to his book, pub-

---

[14]Lawrence J. McCaffrey, *The Irish Question, 1800–1922* (Lexington, Kentucky, 1968), pp. 89–91.

lished in 1870, and was the all-consuming objective of his life after that date. Butt perceived the differences between industrial Britain and agrarian Ireland as too extreme to be reconciled by a common parliament. He also feared that the social, economic, and political radicalism advancing in Britain might spread to Ireland. Indeed, Butt felt that the demagoguery of radical republicanism evidenced by the Fenians, whose political rights he had defended, was a warning that Ireland was becoming increasingly susceptible to revolutionary extremism. It was Butt's purpose therefore, to rally Conservatives into assuming the leadership of Irish nationalism by organizing the Home Government Association in 1870 and later, in 1874, the Irish home rule Parliamentary Party.[15] There was little support or sentiment for physical force advocates in Ireland during the 1870s, and the growth and development of Butt's Irish Parliamentary Party provided Irish nationalism with a constitutional alternative to Republican schemes for terminating the union with Britain.

BUTT AND THE FEDERALIST IDEAL

While Isaac Butt may rightly be remembered as the founder of the Irish home rule movement, his cause was to be advanced by others more politically dexterous than he. Butt's political conservatism inhibited the conduct, objectives, and strategy of the parliamentary party which he, as chairman, proposed to lead. He rejected Charles Gavan Duffy's concept of a completely independent, strongly disciplined Irish party which would vote as a block on all legislation related to Irish interests. Butt, however, had insisted that Irish representatives to the Westminster Parliament should have the free-

---

[15]Butt's concept of Irish federalism and his influence in shaping the Irish home rule Parliamentary Party are comprehensively examined in Lawrence J. McCaffrey, *Irish Federalism in the 1870s: A Study in Conservative Nationalism* (Philadelphia, 1962).

dom to support either Whig or Tory policies and that only on the home rule question would Irish M.P.'s be expected to render a unanimous vote. It was Butt's hope that a policy of conciliation might woo British M.P.'s into seeing the logic of his federalist plan which would permit Ireland home rule under its own parliament, while preserving the authority of the Parliament at Westminster over all matters of common interest: colonial affairs, foreign policy, and Imperial defense. Although personally popular with British politicians, Butt's conciliatory approach won him few converts at Westminster, and his reluctance to enforce party discipline diminished his effectiveness as an Irish Nationalist leader. There soon emerged within the Irish party a small group who rejected Butt's strategy of conciliation and called instead for obstructionist tactics designed to frustrate both British parties in the House of Commons. Two Fenians, Joseph Gillis Biggar and John O'Connor Power, began this militant policy. They were joined in 1875 by a newly elected M.P., Charles Stewart Parnell, whose nationalist zeal had been inherited from his father, an Irish Protestant landowner, and his American mother who was of Irish descent.[16]

CHARLES STEWART PARNELL

Parnell quickly became a prominent figure on the Anglo-Irish scene as he exasperated his opponents in the House of Commons by his brilliant orchestration of obstructionist tactics. Isaac Butt loathed such methods no less than did British Unionists and, as a result, the Irish party only found itself

---

[16]McCaffrey, *The Irish Question,* pp. 99–109. For a detailed analysis of the Butt-Parnell power struggle, see David Thornley, *Isaac Butt and Home Rule* (London, 1964), pp. 300–378. In assessing the influence of Butt upon Irish politics, Thornley writes, "It is not then, perhaps, too much to say that by his achievement Butt had made possible the political phenomenon of the party of Parnell." Ibid., p. 387.

further divided than before. Moreover, Parnell was far more disposed than Butt to accept assistance from any quarter which seemed likely to advance the interest of Irish home rule, even if such aid was tendered by radical and anticonstitutional groups. Without abandoning his own commitment to change through parliamentary means, therefore, Parnell accepted support from the Fenian movement in America, as organized in the Clan-na-Gael. And although the Supreme Council of the I.R.B. condemned all participation in parliamentary activities, the new party continued to make converts among Fenians even in Ireland. Among this latter group, Michael Davitt clearly exercised the greater influence upon Parnell. Davitt had served seven years of a fifteen year penal servitude sentence for his participation in Fenian activities when, in December 1877, he was freed in response to the agitation in Ireland for amnesty for the Fenian prisoners. His unrepentent hatred of British landlordism was, if anything, reinforced by his years spent in jail and he promptly became active in an effort to forge a coalition between Fenians and Parnellites. Parnell was already the most influential force in Irish parliamentary politics and, even before the death of Isaac Butt in 1879, was generally acknowledged to be the future leader of the home rule movement. But Parnell declined to join the I.R.B. and Davitt, who then travelled to America and consulted with John Devoy's Clan-na-Gael, turned his attention to establishing a common front of constitutional and revolutionary nationalists on such issues as the land question and self-government. The Clan approved of this alliance, but Parnell did not, nor did the Supreme Council of the I.R.B.[17] An unexpected development, however, soon gave these dissident Irish groups a new sense of unity.

---

[17]T. W. Moody and F. X. Martin, eds., *The Course of Irish History* (Cork, 1967), pp. 283–285. For an excellent analysis of Parnell's cautious relationship with revolutionary Nationalists see T. W. Moody, "The New Departure in Irish Politics, 1878–9," in H. A. Cronne, T. W. Moody, and D. B. Quinn, eds., *Essays in British and Irish History in Honour of James Eddie Todd* (London, 1949).

Exceptionally wet weather, crop failures, and falling prices in the winter of 1878–79 threatened the rural population of Ireland with the worst economic disaster since the great famine of the 1840s. Many small farmers were faced with the immediate prospect of bankruptcy and eviction, and the ultimate peril of starvation confronted their families. Davitt, who had been born to poverty in 1846 at the height of Ireland's epic famine, and Parnell, born the same year in a luxurious mansion in county Wicklow, both realized that the economic problems of their countrymen took precedence over political strategies. It was for the purpose of providing a nationwide outlet for agitation and for the promotion of self-defense among tenant farmers that Davitt founded the Irish Land League in 1879. Parnell agreed to serve as its president. The league afforded a common cause to moderate home rulers and to extreme republicans alike and produced reverberations which extended beyond Ireland to the Westminster Parliament.

THE IRISH LAND LEAGUE

The Land League was generously endowed by Irish-American contributions, enjoyed widespread nationalist support in Ireland, and even won the official approval of a number of the country's Catholic bishops and nearly the entire parish clergy.[18] A good deal of the credit for averting another great

---

[18]Parnell travelled to the United States late in 1879 to raise funds and win support for the Land League. During his visit, from January to March, 1880, he journeyed over 16,000 miles and spoke in sixty-two cities, in addition to addressing a joint session of Congress. His tour was instrumental in raising over $300,000 for famine relief and Land League agitation. Thomas N. Brown, *Irish-American Nationalism, 1870–1890* (Philadelphia, 1966), p. 103. Thomas William Croke, Archbishop of Cashel, unreservedly committed himself to the Land League and thereby ". . . prevented the alienation of the people from the clergy, and preserved to the Irish Church then and for the future its very considerable power and influence in Ireland." Emmet Larkin, *The Roman Catholic Church and the Creation of the Modern Irish State* (Philadelphia, 1975), pp. 52–53. For a thorough analysis of the Catholic bishops' reaction to the Land League, see Ibid., pp. 24–53.

famine following the winter of 1879 was owed to the extensive volunteer relief work of the Land League.

British authority was seriously challenged in Ireland during the so-called land war of 1879–82. The league's primary purposes, however, were to halt evictions and to obtain a reduction of rents, and ultimately to make tenant farmers the owners of their land. Members of the Royal Irish Constabulary and other officers of the law who were a part of the legal eviction process, together with their families, often found themselves socially ostracised by members of the Land League and their growing number of supporters. Exploitative landlords and those tenant farmers who cooperated with them were also subjected to a boycott. Occasionally the passions generated by these tactics erupted into violence as militant tenant farmers burned the hayricks and maimed the cattle of unpopular landlords. Agents of offending landlords, as well as tenant farmers who rented the farms of evicted friends of the Land League, sometimes suffered physical reprisals.[19]

Violence and physical retaliation were not, however, Land League policy. The organization often made evictions the occasion for noisy demonstrations; it sheltered and supported families evicted for nonpayment of rent; and it paid for the defense of persons prosecuted because of their league involvement. But these activities were not illegal, nor was the Land League an unlawful organization. The British government, therefore, was initially uncertain as to how it would contend with the movement.

GLADSTONE'S LAND BILL

A general election held in April 1880 resulted in a defeat for Disraeli's Conservative government and returned Gladstone

---

[19]These tactics were "... developed into an effective policy and first applied to an estate in county Mayo where Captain Boycott was an agent. Boycott became the name for the new tactic." McCaffrey, *The Irish Question,* p. 114.

as prime minister. Determined to make another attempt at Irish reform, Gladstone introduced a bill in 1881 which provided for a fixed period of tenure at fair rents and for free sale of the tenant's interest in the farm. Partly because of the prodding of Queen Victoria and partly because Gladstone coupled this conciliatory bill with coercive measures against agrarian violence in Ireland, the House of Lords passed the measure in August 1881.[20] The new legislation, however, did not extend to those tenants already in arrears, and Parnell seized upon this fact when he rejected the Liberals' bill and continued to lead agrarian agitation. An exasperated Prime Minister Gladstone responded by using the powers provided by the coercion bill to imprison Parnell and a few of his lieutenants in Kilmainham Gaol, Dublin. Agrarian violence increased rather than diminished following Parnell's arrest, and the potential danger posed by the absence of responsible leadership among Irish militants was in the interest of neither the government nor the incarcerated Land League leaders. Accordingly, under the terms of the so-called Kilmainham Treaty, which won Parnell and his associates release from prison in May 1882, Gladstone promised to settle the arrears question and to end coercion. Parnell, in turn, consented to issue a public endorsement of the Land Act and to cooperate with the Liberals in advancing further Irish reform.[21]

By 1882, British politicians, both Conservatives and Liberals, were generally convinced that the landlord system in Ireland was no longer tenable. Under Gladstone's scheme, by which land courts fixed fair rents for tenants, Irish landlords after 1881 were increasingly forced to consider the advan-

[20]Lord Spencer, the Irish Viceroy, consented to a scheme that limited the powers of the British Government in Ireland on the condition that certain clauses of the Crimes Act be renewed. Lord Harrington, the Secretary for War, and Sir William Harcourt, the Home Secretary, objected to Gladstone's making any major concessions to Parnell. L. P. Curtis, Jr., *Coercion and Conciliation in Ireland, 1880–1892: A Study in Conservative Unionism* (Princeton, 1963), p. 17.

[21]For an authoritative account of the negotiations which culminated in the Kilmainham Treaty, see R. Barry O'Brien, *The Life of Charles Stewart Parnell*, Vol. 1 (London, 1898), pp. 258–269.

tages of selling out to their tenants on favorable terms or to accept the eventual prospect of sharing ownership with them. Since dual ownership held little appeal, the inevitable consequence was a sharp rise in peasant proprietorship.[22]

THE NATIONAL LEAGUE

Parnell was still in prison when the Land League was outlawed in 1881, and the Irish leader did not lament its passing. He had watched with mounting concern as the influence of the Fenians and other radicals grew within the league, for their very presence posed a threat to the parliamentary methods of the home rule movement.[23] With the passing of the agrarian crisis, Parnell helped promote a new organization, the National League, to fill the void created by the demise of the Land League. An aggressive policy was needed to win the attention and loyalty of the Irish masses, and Parnell felt that his tightly knit party could be most effective as a balance of power in the House of Commons.[24] When the votes of his Home Rule M.P.'s forced the Liberals out of office

[22]Between 1903 and 1920 nearly nine million acres of land changed hands in Ireland, and an additional two million acres were in the process of being sold. The Wyndham Act of 1903, together with the Amending Act of 1909, paved the way to peasant proprietorship in Ireland. For the details of these two acts, see F. S. L. Lyons, *John Dillon: A Biography* (London, 1968), pp. 229–235, and pp. 307–308.

[23]The abandonment of the land war in favor of the constitutional struggle for home rule was decidedly agreeable to the membership of the Irish Parliamentary Party. Conor Cruise O'Brien, *Parnell and His Party* (Oxford, 1957), p. 77.

[24]By the early 1880s, when tenant right had triumphed in Ireland, Parnell's commitment to constitutional nationalism in the form of home rule enjoyed the support of the Irish at home and in America. While the Clan-na-Gael financed the I.R.B.'s futile bombing campaigns designed to intimidate British politicians into conceding Irish self-government, most Irish-Americans were contributing their dollars to the Parnell-dominated National League. Lawrence J. McCaffrey, *The Irish Diaspora in America* (Bloomington, Indiana, 1976), pp. 132–133.

in August 1885, Parnell supported a minority Conservative government under Lord Salisbury who promised to initiate a land purchase program for tenant farmers in Ireland.

LAND REFORM

It is one of the many ironies in this era of Anglo-Irish history that it should have been a Conservative administration which, by the Ashbourne Act of 1885, established a program authorizing the Government to lend tenants five million pounds at four percent interest, over a forty-nine year repayment period, to purchase their farms. This, together with successive legislative rulings like the Wyndham Act of 1903, eventually did abolish the old system of landlordism and helped transform Ireland into a land of peasant owners.[25] While the tenants were primarily concerned with the possession of their land, Parnell saw such ownership only as a further step toward the ultimate goal of home rule for Ireland. Although the Liberals won the general election of November–December 1885 in Britain, Parnellites carried eighty-six seats in Ireland and thus assured the Conservative minority of continued control if the coalition were sustained. While the Conservatives' ambitious imperialistic program earned them the support of the recently enfranchised British masses, Lord Salisbury, however, offered Irish nationalists little more than token gestures of conciliation. Gladstone was quick to recognize that the Liberal Party needed the support of the Irish party in the House of Commons. He was further convinced that the impressive showing by home rule candidates in Ireland made their cause impossible to ignore any

---

[25]There were landlords who welcomed the land purchase by peasants because the land war and the home rule agitation had made investment in land a nonpaying proposition. Curtis, *Coercion and Conciliation in Ireland,* pp. 346–347.

longer. In December 1885, William Gladstone gave open
support to Home Rule for Ireland.[26]

THE HOME RULE BILL OF 1886

Gladstone's endorsement of home rule had an immediate
impact upon the power alignment in the House of Commons.
Since Disraeli could scarcely win support for such a measure
from his Tory constituency, he abandoned all effort at concili-
ating Irish nationalism and instead introduced an Irish coercion bill in Parliament. In openly embracing unionism as a
central plank in their party platform, the Conservatives diminished some of the ideological ambiguities which had
plagued the Irish question in nineteenth century British politics. Aristocratic Whigs of the landed gentry tradition, whose
commitment to political, social, and economic reform had
won them over to the Liberals, were no less hostile to the
prospect of home rule for Ireland than were their Conservative counterparts. The Whigs seceded from the Liberal Party
and called themselves Liberal Unionists. Although the Liberal Unionists remained essentially opposed to the Tory program of imperial policy abroad, both Liberal Unionists and
Tories agreed that there should be no devolution of political
authority within the United Kingdom. Since their common
viewpoint on issues relating to home affairs overshadowed
differences on foreign policy, it was only a matter of time
before the Liberal Unionists were absorbed into the Conservative fold.[27]

When Gladstone declared for home rule, he won the im-

---

[26]Gladstone's motive in supporting Irish home rule was not simply a
pragmatic or political one. He believed it to be the moral or Christian
solution, and it was a central tenet of his faith as a Liberal that enlightened
self-government was the highest stage of political evolution that man could
reach. Lyons, *Ireland Since the Famine,* p. 176.

[27]Although the Liberal Unionists tried for a time to maintain their separate identity, in moments of crisis it was their Unionism rather than their
Liberalism that they were obliged to emphasize. Ibid., p. 292.

mediate support of the Irish Parliamentary Party and in January 1886, at the age of seventy-seven, he displaced Disraeli and formed his third administration. On April 8, Gladstone introduced the first home rule bill into the House of Commons which proposed a devolution of authority from the imperial Parliament to an Irish parliament which was comparable to that later created for Northern Ireland in 1921. The bill also provided for control of local affairs by an Irish executive and parliament in Dublin. Matters pertaining to foreign and imperial policy, the crown, peace and war, customs and excise, the post office, coinage and legal tender, and trade and navigation would, however, continue to be administered by Westminster. Irish M.P.'s would sit at Westminster only in the eventuality of any future revisions of the home rule bill. Irish magistrates were to be selected by the Irish government, and paid by the Irish Exchequer which was also obligated to contribute to the costs of the empire. The act stipulated that the rulings of Irish courts were subject to appeal to the Privy Council in London, and that the Privy Council would retain its power to determine the constitutionality of bills passed by the Irish parliament.

Parnell's reaction to the 1886 home rule bill resembled Michael Collins' response to the terms of the Anglo-Irish treaty in 1921 (See Chapter 10). Both men reasoned that the terms offered by the British were, in each instance, the best that could be achieved at that time, and both fully intended to exploit the concessions granted by London to further the ends of Irish nationalism. So, while Parnell accepted Gladstone's bill in principle, he reserved the right to amend the details of its application. The bills' proposals fell considerably short of the national independence so long demanded by a substantial part of Irish opinion. It did, however, recognize Ireland's claim to nationhood and it was therefore positively received by most of nationalist Ireland and by the majority of the Irish in America and in the Dominions.[28]

---

[28]Moody and Martin, eds., *The Course of Irish History* pp. 289–290.

THE DEFEAT OF THE 1886 HOME RULE BILL

Yet the bill's ultimate fate was decided not by the endorsement of the Irish party in the House of Commons but rather by the vote of dissident Liberals who simply could not reconcile themselves to Irish home rule. It was they who effected the defeat of the bill on June 8, 1886, and it was they who contributed to the subsequent rejection of Gladstone's Government at the general election held the following month. That polling returned 316 conservatives and seventy-eight anti-home rule liberals, soon to be known as Liberal Unionists, while Gladstonian liberals in the House of Commons now numbered only 191, with the 85 Irish home rulers no longer possessing any potential to affect the balance of power at Westminster. Gladstone resigned and Lord Salisbury returned as prime minister for the Conservative Party which, with the exception of one brief interlude, would hold power and thereby exercise control over Ireland for the next twenty years.

Despite the rejection of the home rule bill by the House of Commons in 1886, Irish nationalists did not gravitate toward the more militant physical force philosophy of the Irish Republican Brotherhood but sought instead to express their opposition through constitutional means. Irish faith in the parliamentary system in those difficult days was a tribute to the respect and confidence which Gladstone and Parnell inspired. The electoral defeat for the home rulers had not been as overwhelming as the July 1886 returns would suggest. In addition to the eighty-five Irish Nationalist M.P.'s, three-fifths of the Scottish members and five-sixths of the Welsh members in Commons had supported Gladstone. Although the most entrenched opposition to home rule, apart from the Protestant sections of Ulster, had come from English constituencies, Gladstone continued to gain converts to his position in the course of the next few years.[29] Indeed, by 1890, Glad-

---

[29]"In England, almost from the close of the general election of 1886, voters began to go back to Liberalism." P. S. O'Hegarty, *A History of Ireland Under the Union, 1801–1922* (London, 1952), p. 599.

stone had good reason to expect that both his party and program would triumph in the next general election.

PARNELL: RISE AND FALL

By the 1880s, Charles Stewart Parnell was at the pinnacle of his popularity in Ireland, and he was gaining greater prestige and respect in England too. The latter circumstance was most notably due to the egregious effort undertaken by *The Times* of London which, in 1887, sought to implicate Parnellites in the outrage and murders which had occurred in Ireland during and after the land war. In one of its defamatory articles, the *Times* reproduced a letter with Parnell's alleged signature condoning the murders in 1882 of Lord Frederick Cavendish, Chief Secretary for Ireland, and his Under-Secretary, T. H. Burke. In the most notorious atrocity of this period of agrarian agitation in Ireland, these men had been ambushed and killed while strolling in Phoenix Park, Dublin, by a group of fanatical physical force nationalists who called themselves "the Invincibles." The murders of Cavendish and Burke, which were unanimously condemned by the leadership of the Irish Parliamentary Party, caused Parnell such despair that he considered abandoning politics altogether. A special commission of three high-court judges was appointed to inquire into the charges following the *Times'* publication of still more seriously incriminating letters supposedly signed by Parnell.[30] During the hearing it was revealed that the *Times* had purchased the letters in good faith from the Dublin journalist, Richard Pigott. Under cross-examination in court, Pigott, a man of unsavory reputation in Irish nationalist circles, admitted to having forged the letters. This disclosure produced a feeling of revulsion in England toward the

---

[30]The special commission had undertaken to investigate not the letters but the various charges which had been made by *The Times* against Parnell and others in his party. This was tantamount to putting the whole nationalist movement on trial.

shoddy journalism of an esteemed newspaper, and the standing ovation given Parnell when he entered the House of
Commons following the inquiry reflected the sympathetic
sentiment that prevailed throughout much of Britain.

It was, therefore, both a personal and a national tragedy
when Parnell's private life brought his public career to such
an inglorious close a short time later. In December, 1889,
approximately ten months from the date of Parnell's triumphant vindication over charges carried by the *Times,* he
became the focal point of yet another scandal. William O'-
Shea, a one-time friend of Parnell and a former Irish M.P.,
sued his wife Katherine for divorce and named Parnell as
correspondent. Many in Ireland, and not a few in England,
believed the case to be another libel intended to discredit the
Irish Nationalist leader. When the trial concluded nearly a
year later, however, the details of the ten-year affair between
Parnell and Kitty O'Shea were commonly known, and neither contested the judge's ruling in favor of William O'Shea.
British nonconformist opinion, which embodied the zeitgeist
of the Liberal Party, had supported Gladstone's campaign for
home rule as a moral issue after the secession of the Whigs,
and was indignant and uncompromising in its determination
that Parnell should resign. Victorian England could tolerate
immorality on the part of its statesmen if they exercised
proper discretion and circumspection, but public revelation
was awkward, and admission of guilt was unredeemable.
Prime Minister William Gladstone probably would have had
difficulty in admonishing a party leader on the subject of
sexual morality,[31] and it was with a sense of genuine anguish
that he reached his painful decision regarding Parnell's political fate.

Ulster Unionists and British nonconformists were not the

---

[31] Beginning in 1845, Gladstone participated in social work directed toward the rehabilitation of London prostitutes. It is impossible to determine
Gladstone's exact relationship with these women, but his diary contains
entries which, while guarded, suggest activities which caused him to suffer
serious moral recriminations. M. R. D. Foot and H. C. G. Matthew, eds., *The
Gladstone Diaries,* Vol. 3 (Oxford, 1974), pp. xliv–xlvii.

only parties petitioning Gladstone to repudiate Parnell. In London, Henry Edward Cardinal Manning, the Catholic Archbishop of Westminster, urged Gladstone to call for the Irish leader's resignation. Manning had never deemed the Protestant aristocrat a suitable spokesman for Irish nationalism. When Gladstone publicly demanded on November 26, 1890, that Parnell accept at least temporary retirement from leadership of the Irish party, the latter refused. In his "manifesto to the Irish people," published on November 29, Parnell disavowed his own strategy of courting alliances with British parties which would support the cause of Irish home rule, and specifically denounced Gladstone's schemes to promote that end as having been hopelessly inadequate. This public break between the two men created divided loyalties amongst the members of the Irish Parliamentary Party, but Gladstone's expressed desire to avoid a ruinous split in the Liberal ranks convinced a majority of Irish M.P.'s that their leader was indeed a liability. Parnell, however, was stubbornly convinced that he could appeal to the people and carry the country over the heads of the party. He embarked on a public speaking tour of the Irish countryside which was lost before it began since the Catholic bishops and parish priests immediately threw their weight against the tainted leader. Parnell drove himself at a feverish pitch until his health was ruined and he collapsed completely on October 2, 1891, while campaigning for candidates loyal to him in three separate by-election contests.[32] Parnell died four days later, at the age of forty-five.

THE HOME RULE BILL OF 1893

Parnell's fall deprived Irish nationalists of a charismatic political genius who was without equal in either his country or his

---

[32]In those desperate final days, Parnell cryptically hinted that he had so lost patience with British Liberalism as to wonder whether constitutional methods were any longer viable. For an interesting analysis of the implications of Parnell's remarks, see Michael Hurst, *Parnell and Irish Nationalism* (London, 1968), p. 96.

party. But Gladstone continued to make converts in Britain to the Liberal pledge for Irish home rule. He won the general election of 1892 on a home rule platform and became prime minister and head of government for the fourth and final time. After careful preparation and long deliberations with colleagues in Parliament, Gladstone introduced a second home rule bill in 1893 which differed from the first most essentially in permitting Irish representation at Westminster during discussion of Irish and imperial questions. This bill passed the House of Commons only to be defeated in the House of Lords. An exasperated Prime Minister Gladstone concluded that the only alternative was to dissolve Parliament and to fight an election on the issue of the veto power of the House of Lords. That view, however, was not shared by other Liberal leaders, and Gladstone, now eighty-four years of age, resigned as prime minister and leader of the Liberal Party. He was succeeded by Lord Rosebery whose tepid support for Irish home rule, coupled with the demoralized and disillusioned spirit of the post-Parnell Irish party, made the once promising prospect of political self-determination for Ireland appear more remote than ever.

SCHISM WITHIN THE IRISH PARLIAMENTARY PARTY

While the fortunes of the Liberal Party had been laid low by the defection of its two extreme wings, the Whigs under Lord Harington on the right and the radicals under Joseph Chamberlain on the left, the solidarity of the Irish party had been shaken even more profoundly. The schism in the Irish Parliamentary Party was a direct outgrowth of Parnell's refusal to accept the inevitable political consequences of the public disclosure of his liaison with Mrs. O'Shea. Instead of displaying the instinctive pragmatism which had marked his career, Parnell permitted pride and passion to dictate his choice of action. He believed that he had earned the leadership of Irish nationalism and he was not willing to surrender it in order to comply with the sham conventions of Victorian society, nor was he inclined to capitulate to the ultimatum of the British Liberal Party leader.[33] Michael Davitt was one of the first prominent Irish nationalists to call for Parnell's resignation, and two prominent members of the Irish party, John Dillon and William O'Brien, who at the time were in the United States on a fund raising campaign, also urged resignation in the interest of the party. When Parnell refused, the Irish Parliamentary Party split over the issue at a meeting held in a committee room in the House of Commons on December 6, 1890. Justin McCarthy, vice-chairman of the Irish party, was elected as the new leader by the forty-four members who then broke with both Parnell and the twenty-seven Irish M.P.'s who remained loyal to him. For the next ten years the cause of Irish nationalism was hindered by the feuding factions in the Parliamentary Party. John Redmond assumed the leadership of the Parnellite minority after the death of Parnell, while John Dillon, in 1896, became the leader of the anti-Parnell Irish M.P.'s. Dillon proved himself a more selfless, if not more dedicated, patriot than Parnell when, in 1900, he negotiated a reconciliation with the tiny Parnellite faction and accepted Redmond as the chairman of a re-united Irish Parliamentary Party.[34]

THE UNIONIST GOVERNMENT

Britain enjoyed a period of modest prosperity and expansion during the 1890s, and preoccupation with the Irish question diminished at Westminster as foreign and colonial affairs filled the public mind. Lord Rosebery, who had served as

---

[33]Parnell had become "... the romantic hero, dazzled by his own myth, preferring a tragic ending to self-effacement and the continuation of his policy." Conor Cruise O'Brien, *Parnell and His Party*, pp. 348–349.

[34]Dillon was strongly opposed to Redmond's being elected in his place, but he accepted the decision of his party with grace and generosity. Denis Gwynn, *The Life of John Redmond* (London, 1932), pp. 94–95.

Gladstone's foreign secretary and later succeeded him as prime minister in March 1894, was an imperialist who had serious reservations about home rule for Ireland. Similarly, Irish M.P.'s, upon whom Rosebery depended for his majority in Commons, were less than enthusiastic about the prime minister and, after sixteen months of leadership in this climate of mutual distrust, he resigned in June 1895. Lord Salisbury returned to power at the head of a coalition ministry of Conservatives and Liberal Unionists which, in the general election held the following month, won an impressive majority of 152 seats at Westminster. What came to be known as the Unionist Government would remain in office for the next ten years—first under Salisbury, who served as prime minister until 1902, and then until 1905 under his nephew, Arthur J. Balfour, who had formerly served as Lord Salisbury's chief secretary for Ireland. Both men were committed Unionists who regarded the Irish masses as not only unready or unfit for self-government, but also as a threat to property interests everywhere. Moreover, they feared that a Catholic dominated Irish parliament might be anti-British, as well as anti-Protestant, and might pose a danger to the security of Britain and the stability of the empire. Balfour particularly perceived the growth of Irish nationalism as merely a regional phenomenon of economic origin which would collapse once the obstacles to greater peasant proprietorship of the land were removed. Even Karl Marx had once lamented that the rural peasant class was hopelessly conservative and immune to socialism or radical democracy once their quest for land had been met. Balfour very probably would have agreed.

THE UNIONIST GOVERNMENT AND IRELAND

British policy toward Ireland under the Conservative-Unionist coalition was one of conciliation and coercion, a carrot and stick approach, which was more notable for its reform than for its repression. As chief secretary for Ireland from 1887 to

1891, Arthur Balfour restrained agrarian agitation and violence by the vigorous enforcement of the Crimes Act which earned him the approbation "Bloody Balfour" in Ireland; but he was also to be remembered as the man who attempted to "kill home rule with kindness." For example, in 1887 Balfour introduced a land act which lowered rents to match costs and provided further protection against eviction. In 1891, the chief secretary established a board to provide relief and to stimulate the growth of the Irish economy. The work of that agency resulted in substantial progress being made in some of the most depressed areas of the country.[35] Moreover, the Local Government Act of 1898 gave Irishmen the same control over local affairs and appointment to local office as Englishmen enjoyed in England. A final Unionist land scheme was passed by Parliament in 1903 which encouraged landlords to sell and receive a cash bonus for their holdings from the government and permitted Irish tenants to buy with low interest rates and granted them a sixty-eight and one half year repayment period. Similar legislation over the next six years resulted in nearly a quarter of a million peasant proprietors gaining control of nearly half the arable farmland of Ireland. Landlordism had not been totally destroyed, but its demise was fast approaching. When the Unionists left office in 1905, only the university question remained of all the major social, economic and political grievances which Irish nationalists had so often enumerated in their demand for home rule. But behind the appearance of seeming tranquillity in Ireland there was a new militancy fomenting in the national soul.

THE INFLUENCE OF THE BOER WAR

Ever since Parnell's November 1890 manifesto, in which he had repudiated the liberal alliance and the Gladstonian pro-

---

[35]Curtis, *Coercion and Conciliation in Ireland*, pp. 174–215, and 331–374.

posals for Irish home rule, there had been no alternative policy advanced by an Irish leadership to capture the mind or imagination of the people of Ireland. The reconciliation between the Parnellites and anti-Parnellites in 1900 failed to restore the once significant influence of the Irish Parliamentary Party at Westminster, and the majority given the Conservative-Liberal Unionist coalition by the general election of July 1895 left John Redmond with far less political leverage than Parnell had enjoyed. Meanwhile, the British were preoccupied with a more immediate threat to the empire in the form of the South African Boer War. The majority of Irish nationalist opinion sympathized with the Boers and that armed conflict encouraged "physical force" ideas in Ireland. Those who had scorned "the new departure," the cooperation of some Fenians with the Parliamentary Party, and who had rejected constitutional methods in the struggle for Irish freedom applauded the victories of the Boers and identified with their cause. But there was also a sizeable minority of Irish nationalists who served the crown in the British Army, in the police, and in the civil service; and among these and their families there were differing loyalties.[36] Ambivalencies such as these were a natural by-product of the Anglicization of Ireland which nearly three centuries of British administration had achieved. At that very moment, however, an effort by Irish intellectuals to awaken their country to an appreciation of its unique cultural identity provided an inauspicious and nonpolitical beginning to what would inspire the most profoundly revolutionary period in Ireland's long and turbulent history.

---

[36]For the Irish nationalist reaction to the Boer War, see Conor Cruise O'Brien, *States of Ireland* (New York, 1973), pp. 65–69.

Chapter 2

We Are Not British: The Varieties of Separatist Sentiment in Ireland (1890–1911)

Much of the enthusiasm for home rule which Parnell had generated in Ireland died with the vanquished leader, and the spectacle of internal strife within the Irish party during the following decade further contributed to the populace's disenchantment with politics. To many young Irishmen, the Irish party's leadership was as uninspiring as were its doctrines of political nationalism. Some of these disillusioned Irishmen retreated from the petty parochialism of local politics in order to fulfill their emotional and psychological needs in a more meaningful, if somewhat mystical, haven. They turned to a more romantic world, where poetry seemed more important than politics and where ideals were valued more than votes.[1] There are, therefore, two Irish histories for

---

[1] Donal McCartney, "From Parnell to Pearse," in T. W. Moody and F. X. Martin, eds., *The Course of Irish History* (Cork, 1967), p. 294.

the decades 1886–1916. One, the history of the Parliamentary Party, focuses upon land and local government reform, and upon the unrelenting ebb and flow of the fortunes of Irish home rule. The other is the revival of the spirit of Young Ireland, which had fostered the cultural nationalism of the 1840s and which was insisting once more in the 1890s that political independence was not the country's most critical need. The men of this latter tradition asked what it would profit a nation if it were to gain its freedom at the price of its soul. They warned that it would be a hollow victory if Ireland won her own parliament in Dublin, only to have Irishmen remain British in culture and values. To be truly free, Ireland would have to be de-Anglicized and restore her own language, culture and traditions. Affirming that they were not British, the cultural nationalists inspired the inception and growth of three significant movements: the Gaelic Athletic Association, the Gaelic League, and the literary revival.[2]

THE AWAKENING OF ROMANTIC NATIONALISM

The spirit of romantic nationalism which awoke or resurrected a sense of nationality amongst the subject peoples of central and eastern Europe in the nineteenth century had had an impact upon Ireland too, as was demonstrated by the Celtic and Ossiani Societies of the 1840s and 1850s. With much the same defiance which typified the reaction of other oppressed peoples against an alien civilization, Irish writers and intellectuals attempted to revive the ancient language and literature of their native land. That effort faltered and, after the futile Fenian uprising of 1867, Irish nationalist leaders emerged who perceived their struggle with Britain in political rather than cultural terms. The rebirth of cultural

[2]Lawrence J. McCaffrey, *The Irish Question, 1800–1922* (Lexington, Kentucky, 1968), p. 136.

nationalism in Ireland during the 1880s derived first from a rather improbable source: the athletic field. Although the Irish language had become all but extinct in many parts of the country, Irish games, particularly hurling, had retained their popularity since they constituted one of the few forms of entertainment for the rural population. Michael Cusack, an Irish speaking native of county Clare, founded the Gaelic Athletic Association at Thurles, in county Tipperary on November 1, 1884.[3] The G.A.A. was formed for the purpose of fostering native games and sports, and also as a challenge to the Irish Amateur Athletic Association, an Anglo-Irish body which sponsored the country's major athletic meetings under the rules of that organization. Hurling and Gaelic football soon initiated a passionate enthusiasm which ultimately generated an uncompromising hostility toward foreign games. The Gaelic Athletic Association also instilled a feeling of pride on the part of Irish people for their cultural heritage. And although the G.A.A. was organized for the promotion of sports and not politics, it contributed notably to the revolutionary climate which was again on the ascendancy amongst some Irish nationalist groups.[4]

THE GAELIC LEAGUE

Another movement which helped provide an intellectual foundation for the cause of Irish cultural nationalism was the Gaelic League. Just as the Gaelic Athletic Association had brought the new emphasis on Irish heritage to the towns, villages, and rural parishes through recreational pastimes which extolled Gaelic football and hurling while engender-

---

[3] For further details on Cusack, see David Greene, "Michael Cusack and the Rise of the G.A.A.," in Conor Cruise O'Brien, ed., *The Shaping of Modern Ireland* (London, 1960), pp. 74–84.

[4] It might also be noted that at least four of the seven men who attended Cusack's meeting on November 1, 1884, were Fenians. See F. S. L. Lyons, *Ireland Since the Famine* (New York, 1971), p. 221.

ing hostility toward "foreign" games, the Gaelic League appealed to the more educated middle class in the cities and large towns. Founded in 1893, the league was conceived as an apolitical and nonsectarian organization solely concerned with the nurturing and expansion of the Irish language. Douglas Hyde, the son of a Protestant rector from an Irish speaking region of county Sligo, was its dominant personality. Hyde was a graduate of Trinity College, and he devoted his life to the language movement. It was he who originated the slogan "the de-Anglicization of Ireland," and, in 1889 he published the first of several volumes of translations of Gaelic stories and poems.[5] Hyde also encouraged the development of a contemporary literature of the Irish language while the Gaelic League, which by 1908 had as many as six hundred branches throughout the country, helped promote the speaking of Irish, the writing of Irish literature, and the playing of Irish music. Hyde failed in his effort to immunize his movement from politics, partly because militants infiltrated it and used it for their own purposes, and partly because it essentially encouraged the notion of a separate people. The League actually helped foster separatism and, instead of binding Irishmen of all creeds and opinions together, it drove the wedge between north and south–unionist and nationalist–deeper than ever.[6]

THE IRISH LITERARY REVIVAL

A third movement which represented still another dimension in the growth of Irish cultural nationalism was the Irish literary revival of the 1890's. Like the Gaelic League, it originated among members of the Protestant Ascendancy and was similarly resolved at its inception to remain apolitical.

[5]For a new and insightful study of the works of Douglas Hyde, see Gareth W. Dunleavy, *Douglas Hyde* (Lewisburg, Pa., 1974).
[6]Oliver MacDonagh, *Ireland* (Englewood Cliffs, N.J., 1968), p. 64.

Anglo-Irish writers of this distinguished generation were, with few exceptions, from established families whose means had been diminished by the Act of Union and the Industrial Revolution. Feudal Ireland had suffered an eclipse during the nineteenth century and Dublin, once the proud capital of the Anglo Irish aristocracy, had been reduced to a provincial city. For the Ascendancy, it was a cruel new world which not only caused them economic loss, but also one which favored the machine, commerce, slums, and the growth of cities and empires. There seemed to be no viable outlet for the imaginative capacities of people of ability. In recoiling from urban and industrial blight, Anglo-Irish writers turned for inspiration to the rural peasant life which recalled the golden days of the integral community, romanticized previously in the writings of William Wordsworth. Yeats yearned for that earlier time when there was no mob of shopkeepers to come between the big house and the hut; when literature was a tale told by a warm fire, rather than a sixpenny novel; when a dwelling was a humble thatched roof cottage; and business was a form of barter for the peasant and an understanding between aristocratic gentlemen.[7] But Yeats denounced Irish nationalism whenever it defamed art in the name of politics and led to shoddy literary standards. Despite Yeats's own standards, however, a nativist literary movement which preached social forms distinct from and antagonistic to those predominating in Great Britain encouraged more than separatism; it fed the flames of Anglophobia, and almost surely inspired the imaginations of some of those who later led the 1916 Easter Rising.[8] Yeats, in old age, pondered his part in the literary revival's culpability for the bloodshed of that event when he wrote:

> Did that play of mine send out
> Certain men the English shot?[9]

[7]William I. Thompson, *The Imagination of an Insurrection* (New York, 1967), p. 41.

[8]MacDonagh, *Ireland*, p. 65.

[9]A. N. Jaffres, *W. B. Yeats: Man and Poet* (London, 1949), pp. 137–138.

THE NATIONAL LITERARY SOCIETY

William Butler Yeats and Douglas Hyde founded the Irish Literary Society in London at the end of 1891 for the expressed purpose of producing a whole new school of literature which would owe its inspiration to the Irish past. In May 1892, they founded the National Literary Society in Dublin. It was to this group that Hyde gave his memorable address, "The Necessity for de-Anglicising Ireland," in which he urged his fellow countrymen to reject all trappings of English culture before they lost irretrievably the sense of a separate nationality. The movement was joined by a galaxy of literary talent: George Russell, T. W. Rolleston, Standish O'Grady, James Stephens, J. M. Synge, George Moore, and others. Collectively they revived and romanticized the early legends and history of the country, characterizing Ireland as a poor old woman who would become queen only when men became chivalrous again and thought her worth dying for. Indeed, that theme was reflected in Yeats's *Cathleen ni Houlihan,* the 1902 play about which he later agonized, "Did words of mine put too great a strain on that woman's reeling brain?" Cathleen ni Houlihan, a traditional allegorical personification of Ireland, appears in the guise of an old woman and summons a young man to what the audience might assume was the rebellion of 1798. The young man, who is to be wed that day, is implored to sacrifice all for Ireland. "It is a hard service they take that help me," spoke Cathleen ni Houlihan, dramatically played by Maud Gonne, as she praised the many who had helped her in the past and might yet die for her in the future.[10] The play had an intense emotional impact on contemporary audiences. Irish republican revolutionaries like P. S. O'Hegarty and Countess Markievicz would later recall the indelible impression which it had upon them, just as Stephen Gwynn, a Protestant consti-

---

[10]W. B. Yeats, *Nine One-Act Plays* (London, 1937), p. 36.

tutional nationalist, was moved to wonder whether such plays should be produced unless "one was prepared for people to go out to shoot and be shot."[11]

IDEALS OF THE IRISH LITERARY REVIVAL

It was not political revolution, however, but a cultural identity distinct from Britain's which the members of the Irish literary revival sought for their country. Repudiating the religious and political prejudices of their Protestant Ascendancy class, they condemned British rule in Ireland because it denied the opportunity for growth to an indigenous and significant Irish culture; and because the materialism of the Anglo-Saxon world threatened what they perceived as the wholesome simplicity of rural peasant life in Ireland. But the avowedly apolitical sentiments of the Irish literary revivalists did not mean that politics had no influence upon them. The considerable effect of the fall of Parnell on the writers of the generation who came after him is a widely recognized fact of Irish literary history.[12] Parnell was easily identifiable with a classic Celtic hero, Cu Chulain, and he also symbolized a political messiah who was crucified by the people he came to liberate. Through their use of the Parnell legend, the Anglo-Irish writers attempted to prepare the way for some future messiah—possibly from their own group—who would lead the nation to a fulfillment of its cultural destiny.

Precisely how that goal was to be achieved was not a matter of common agreement among the writers themselves. Yeats, who had become emotionally involved with republicanism during his early years, soon recoiled from the restraint which it sought to place upon the expression of art. Lady Gregory, George Russell, and Douglas Hyde preferred

---

[11]Conor Cruise O'Brien, *States of Ireland* (New York, 1973), p. 70.

[12]It is perhaps even more manifest in the writings of James Joyce than in the works of the Anglo-Irish group.

conciliation to confrontation and saw no merit in Ireland's physical force tradition. George Moore, though strongly attracted by the country of his birth, was bitterly critical of blind adherence to revolutionary nationalism.[13] J. M. Synge supported home rule but refused to prostitute his art, or to compromise his talent for the sake of romantic nationalism. James Joyce, a product of urban middle-class Catholic Ireland, withdrew from the literary and language movements, and left the country to live in self-imposed exile saying: "A nation which never advanced so far as a miracle play affords no literary model for the artist, and he must look abroad."[14] Unsympathetic to both cultural and political nationalists, this youthful and relatively unknown writer irreverently spurned an invitation to join the literary revival by telling Yeats it was a shame he was too old to be influenced by the work of James Joyce.[15]

REACTION TO THE IRISH LITERARY REVIVAL

There was ample justification for Joyce's low esteem of his fellow countrymen's capacity to appreciate good art. In 1898, Yeats and Lady Gregory undertook an ambitious scheme to provide an appropriate medium for Irish drama in the form of the Irish Literary Theatre, recreated as the Abbey Theatre in 1904. Yeats's play *The Countess Cathleen* and Edward Martyn's *The Heather Field* were chosen as the experiment's premier productions. Martyn's Ibsenite play was

---

[13]George Moore, *Hail and Farewell,* vol. 1 (London, 1937), Ebury edition, pp. 220–221. For a recent and authoritative study of the complex mind of George Moore, see Janet Egleson Dunleavy, *George Moore: The Artist's Vision, the Storyteller's Art* (Lewisburg, Pa., 1973).

[14]For an illuminating commentary on Joyce's alienation from the Irish literary revival, see James Joyce, "The Days of Rabblement," in Ellsworth Mason and Richard Ellman, eds., *The Critical Writings of James Joyce* (New York, 1959), pp. 68–72.

[15]See Joyce's own account of this rebuff in James Joyce, *Finnegans Wake* (New York, 1959), p. 37.

all but forgotten in the rage and indignation with which contemporary audiences and critics responded to *The Countess Cathleen.* That play depicts two devils descending upon Ireland to tempt the starving peasants to sell their souls for gold. The Countess Cathleen trades all of her possessions and, in desperation, expresses a willingness to sell her soul to save the poor from famine. The verdict of Catholic and nationalist opinion was swift and uncompromising: Yeats's play was deemed repugnant, for no Irish man or woman would be so morally craven as to barter his or her soul with the devil. That inauspicious response to the experimental debut of the Irish Literary Theatre anticipated the future outcry against other playwrights.[16]

The next artist to suffer the wrath of the intolerant Dublin theatrical audiences was J. M. Synge. His play, *In the Shadow of the Glen,* was first produced in 1903 by what now was officially known as the Irish Literary Theatre. Synge portrayed the loneliness and frustrations of a young wife married to an old man and condemned to the monotony and isolation of a remote Wicklow cottage. The play ends with the wife running off with a traveling man. Critics were quick to label the character of Norah Burke, the faithless wife in Synge's play, as a slander against the nation and the virtue of Irish women.[17] Yeats, writing in the *United Irishman,* warned about the danger of permitting a sense of misplaced patriotism to translate into a hatred of ideas. Yet this furor was mild compared with the reaction to Synge's 1907 production, *The Playboy of the Western World.* Once again Irish peasant life was presented in less than idyllic scenes, and the purity of Irish womanhood was once more an issue. Audiences at the Abbey Theatre hooted until the actors became inaudible, and critics railed about the calumny perpetrated against "the people." Writing for his nationalist publication *Sinn Fein,* Arthur Griffith pronounced Synge's play as "a vile

---

[16]Lyons, *Ireland Since the Famine,* p. 234.
[17]That was essentially the thrust of ardent nationalist Arthur Griffith's criticisms of the play.

and inhuman story told in the foulest language we have ever listened to from a public platform."[18]

With the death of Synge in 1909 and George Moore's departure from Dublin two years later, the Irish literary revival's fading influence signaled the displacement of the Anglo-Irish effort to establish a cultural nationalism, which Yeats called "a spirituality," by the more narrow and parochial cultural nationalism of republicans and other political separatists. Douglas Hyde's play, *The Twisting of the Rope*, was more readily appreciated by some of these militant patriots because it was written in Irish. But Hyde himself was enough of a realist to recognize that the creation of an entire body of literature in Irish would have to await some future date. He further believed that English could be used in the meantime to promote Ireland's indigenous culture.

Perhaps the estrangement of the Anglo-Irish cultural nationalists from the new emerging political forces, led principally by men of the Catholic middle-class, was all but inevitable. Except for Edward Martyn, who was a Catholic, and George Moore, who was a lapsed Catholic, all of the Irish literary renaissance figures were Protestant. Moreover, with the exception of Yeats, Synge, and George Russell (AE), all were from the gentry. The Anglo-Irish writers were aliens in their own land. They never abandoned their cosmopolitan life style or vision, remained serenely loyal to the political union of Ireland with Great Britain and, despite their genuine empathy for the Irish peasant, understood neither the dynamics of the Celtic historical experiences nor the complexities of the Gaelic soul.

THE INFLUENCE OF THE LITERARY REVIVAL

But the influence of the literary revival, however muted it may have appeared at the time, had a notable effect upon the

---

[18] *Sinn Fein*, February 2, 1907. In a cable to Yeats, Lady Gregory reported how the audience broke up in disorder at the word 'shift,' [woman's under garment] because they thought it inconceivable that any Irish girl would use an indelicate expression in the presence of a man.

future course of Irish political history. The quality of the creative work which it produced was unsurpassed in any country in the world. Through the works of the writers of the revival, educated and influential people were brought to a keener understanding of Ireland's culture, traditions, history, and grievances. Most importantly, Ireland's demand for freedom was better understood and more sympathetically appreciated by sophisticated people in Britain, throughout the empire, and in the United States. When Ireland fought her War for Independence between 1919 and 1921, world opinion was with her, and it was world opinion which ultimately converted British politicians to the view that they would have to extend some measure of independence to nationalist Ireland.[19]

SIR HORACE PLUNKETT AND AGRICULTURAL REFORM

Another dimension to the growing self-assertion of Ireland, which differed in kind but not in intensity from the de-Anglicization effort of most cultural nationalists, was the modernization of the Irish economy and social practices. The most significant of these ventures was the cooperative movement initiated by Sir Horace Plunkett in 1889. Although he was of the Ascendancy class and served for a time as a Unionist M.P. to Westminster, his schemes were vilified by militant Irish Unionists and nationalists alike. His goals were moral and economic, and were as devoid of sectarian taint as was Hyde's language program. Plunkett sought to make the Irish farmer self-reliant and technically skilled, and called upon the state to support deserving individuals who had taken the initiative to help themselves.[20] To many nationalists, such

---

[19]McCaffrey, *The Irish Question,* p. 141.

[20]Plunkett also thought co-operative action more productive than agitation in obtaining a better life for agrarian Ireland from the British Parliament. See Sir H. Plunkett, *Ireland in the New Century* (London, 1904), p. 82.

proposals bordered perilously close to socialism. For many Unionists, the whole idea was repellent, for it touched upon too many entrenched positions and established interests.

Born in Ireland in 1854, the third son of the sixteenth Baron Dunsany, Horace Plunkett was educated at Eaton and Oxford and, shortly thereafter, spent ten years (1879–89) living as a rancher in Wyoming where he hoped the change of climate would help combat the early stages of a tubercular condition. He returned to Ireland in 1889, where, in the wake of his father's death, he assumed the responsibility of managing the extensive family properties in England and in Ireland. Plunkett was a perceptive and humanitarian landlord who recognized that the British government's assistance to peasant proprietors in Ireland would soon resolve the old and bitter issue of tenure. It was Plunkett's belief that agrarian Ireland should turn its attention next to the questions of production and distribution, examining the best ways to cultivate the soil and stabilize the rural economy in the face of potentially ruinous foreign competition. But years of coercion and eviction, as well as idle flirtation with nationalistic demagoguery had, in Plunkett's view, sapped the moral fiber and self-reliance of the tenant farmer. Cooperation, rather than pointless agitation, would yield a more efficient utilization of the country's resources and, more importantly, restore the Irishman's self-respect.[21] While Plunkett's Unionist political views would eventually evolve to the point where he accepted dominion status for Ireland, he exhibited little patience with the provincial partisanship of Unionists and nationalists alike.[22] He lectured his fellow Unionists for their recalcitrant attitude toward the task of regenerating the nation's economy and condemned their adherence to short-term interests, maintaining that Unionist policy in Ireland had been "to uphold the Union by force rather than by a

---

[21]Lyons, *Ireland Since the Famine*, pp. 202–203.
[22]For a useful study on Plunkett's career, see Margaret Digby, *Horace Plunkett* (Oxford, 1949).

reconciliation of the people to it."[23] Plunkett accused nationalists of being so negative toward all things British that they
seemed willing to sacrifice the benefits of any economic reform prior to home rule in the name of misplaced principles
which bred the very sort of conformity and lethargy which
he felt accounted for much of the country's ills.

Plunkett felt more comfortable with Anglo-Irish intellectuals than he did with politicians for he neither liked nor
understood politics. He applauded the success of Douglas
Hyde's Gaelic League and declared that it had invigorated
every area of Irish life, and had contributed substantially to
the intellectual, social, and moral improvement of the people.[24] When he required the services of a gifted writer to
convince Irish farmers of the merits of his plan for cooper-
atives, based upon a Danish model which had much impressed him, Plunkett turned to William Butler Yeats. The
task which Sir Horace had in mind involved bicycling all over
Ireland to give speeches, attend important functions and
dinners, and help in the establishment of rural banks for the
Irish Agriculture Organizational Society.[25] Yeats declined
Plunkett's offer, but suggested George Russell (AE) as a substitute. Russell accepted with some misgivings, but was told
by Yeats that such close communion with the people of the
countryside would afford insights into the tragedy and poverty of rural Ireland and thereby heighten Russell's artistic
sensitivities, rendering him a more powerful mystic and poet
because of the experience.[26] Plunkett and Russell were not
always in harmony, for the latter remained suspicious of government assistance on the grounds that cooperation meant
self-help, but governmental assistance meant state domina-

---

[23]Plunkett, *Ireland in the New Century*, p. 68. Similar statements can be
found in Sir Horace's private correspondence with such figures as George
Bernard Shaw, Woodrow Wilson and Colonel House. See *Plunkett MSS.*,
Plunkett Foundation for co-operative Studies, London.
[24]Moody and Martin, eds., *The Course of Irish History*, p. 297.
[25]Thompson, *The Imagination of an Insurrection*, pp. 172–173.
[26]Allan Wade, ed., *Letters of W. B. Yeats* (London, 1954), p. 291.

tion. Their differences, however, did not prevent Russell from dedicating his 1916 book, *The National Being*, to Sir Horace Plunkett with whom he still disagreed but of whom he remained genuinely fond.

Plunkett's ideas were not nearly so unsound as was his grasp of politics or, occasionally, his judgment of men. He diagnosed the problem of the Irish agrarian economy as being more than a depression caused by the importation of cheap food from abroad; it was, he thought, rather a case of poor packing and grading in the marketing of Irish eggs and butter. Expensive but efficient new methods and machinery, such as the mechanical cream separator and churn, were already available. His problem lay in persuading farmers to agree to pool their resources in order to reduce costs. Dairies, or creameries as they were called in Ireland, were a rarity when Plunkett undertook his cooperative movement. By 1894 there were over thirty cooperative societies in Ireland, and Plunkett sought to give his growing experiment national cohesion that year by establishing the Irish Agricultural Organization Society. In 1892, he was elected to Parliament from the largely Unionist constituency of South Dublin, and after his own re-election in the Unionist Conservative coalition's electoral victory of 1895, Plunkett participated in programs which were a part of that government's "kill home rule with kindness" approach to the problem of Ireland.[27]

With the British Parliament's 1899 passage of the act which created the Department of Agriculture and Technical Instruction for Ireland, Plunkett's career ambition of revitalizing the Irish economy through a program of state aid and self-help seemed more achievable than ever. Plunkett assumed the vice-presidency of the department and directed its activities in such areas as agricultural and technical instruction for Irish farmers and rural shopkeepers. He somewhat naively believed that cooperative methods would reach

---

[27]The Irish Local Government Act of 1898 gave Ireland a system of local government on the British model. Plunkett hoped this important political reform would help divert Irish nationalist energies from home rule agitation to economic improvement in Ireland.

fruition through a harmony between individual initiative and state aid. Plunkett, however, lost his parliamentary seat to a more orthodox Unionist in the general election of 1900, and a year after the Liberals were returned to power in 1906, he lost his vice-presidency in the department. Thereafter, the Department of Agriculture and Technical Instruction no longer worked in partnership with Plunkett's Irish Agricultural Organization Society which survived largely on its founder's resources until 1913 when it began to grow in size and prosperity. His legacy perhaps fell short of his vision, for he made little impact on the economic or social life of the country beyond systematizing the dairy industry through an organization which survives to this day.[28] Plunkett's failure to accomplish more is partly explained by his poor understanding of the influence which politics exerted at this time in the national life of Ireland. Unionists' suspicion of and disenchantment with Plunkett was evident from the vote of his South Dublin constituency in 1900. Although Irish Parliamentary Party nationalists had joined Plunkett and other Unionist parliamentarians to investigate the implications for Ireland of a Royal Commission report, they were not inspired by any feeling of national commonality in the apolitical, nonsectarian sense embraced by men like Plunkett, Hyde, or Yeats.[29]

D. P. MORAN AND ECONOMIC REFORM

The hope of furnishing Ireland with a twentieth century economy was not limited to Plunkett's dream of a second

---

[28]For a critical assessment of Sir Horace Plunkett's contribution to Irish history, see J. J. Byrne, "AE and Sir Horace Plunkett," in O'Brien, ed., *The Shaping of Modern Ireland,* pp. 152–163.

[29]A Royal Commission examining the financial relations between Britain and Ireland produced a survey in 1896 which appeared to support those who had charged that Ireland had been seriously overtaxed since the 1801 Act of Union. Despite the common interest which this finding held for nationalists and Unionists alike, the two groups failed to agree in 1897 on any method of response to the Commission survey.

Denmark. A more intensely nationalistic version of the same desire was the "Buy Irish" campaign which was promoted by such influential journals as the *Leader*.[30] Founded in 1900 by D. P. Moran, who was its editor and proprietor for the next thirty-six years, the *Leader* consistently advocated a policy of "voluntary protectionism" by urging its readers to purchase Irish goods and to support Irish industry. Moran, an Irishman by birth and a London journalist by profession, was a representative example of how complex and diverse the anti-British, or at least the separatist, movement in Ireland really was. He was well known to the members of the Irish Literary Society and to those in the Gaelic League, and was more especially celebrated as the author of a series of articles on what he himself called "the philosophy of Irish Ireland." A strong supporter of Douglas Hyde's Irish language revival, Moran was nonetheless hostile to Hyde's Anglo-Irish literary friends whom he contemptuously referred to as those "West Britons" who aped the English. D. P. Moran was equally cynical toward the revolutionary Fenians of 1867, and every Irish home rule leader after that date, since their efforts, in his estimation, had been directed towards the dubious goal of political independence without regard to the more important end of creating Gaelic nationalism.[31] With his emphasis upon industrial and economic self-sufficiency for Ireland, Moran should have been the natural ally of Arthur Griffith and his Sinn Fein (ourselves) organization since both of these separatists were instrumental in undermining the whole constitutional movement. But while Moran agreed with Griffith's economic objectives, he ridiculed the Sinn Feiners as the "Green Hungarians" and thought their goal for a dual monarchy, using the Austro-Hungarian monarchial model while retaining an essentially British political system, was a betrayal of the concept of an Irish Ireland.

[30]MacDonagh, *Ireland*, p. 67.
[31]Donal McCartney, "Hyde, D. P. Moran, and Irish Ireland," in F. X. Martin, ed., *Leaders and Men of the Easter Rising: Dublin 1916* (New York, 1967), pp. 47–54.

GRIFFITH'S SINN FEIN

Sinn Fein, however, did prove to be the most important of several cultural nationalist organizations. The Gaelic words, meaning simply, ourselves, but sometimes translated, we–ourselves or ourselves alone, accurately reflected the political viewpoint of the organization's founder. Arthur Griffith was, by personal conviction, a separatist, even a republican, but he was enough of a realist to sense that Irish public opinion did not share his convictions. Moreover, he was aware that an Irish republic could scarcely be established by force of arms because of Britain's substantial military power. Instead, Griffith advocated a dual monarchy modeled vaguely on the precedents of the eighteenth century Irish parliament and the Austro-Hungarian arrangement of 1867.[32]

Born in Dublin in 1871, Griffith was a printer by training whose economic difficulties required him, as a young man, to emigrate to South Africa. He returned to Ireland at the request of his friend, William Rooney, to edit a weekly newspaper, *The United Irishman*.[33] Rooney and Griffith, together with a small group of like-minded cultural nationalists, organized the Cumann na nGaedheal in 1900 to advance Irish independence by supporting Irish industries, history, literature, language, music, art, and the cultivation of Irish games. They also advocated resistance to all things which contributed to the Anglicization of Ireland. Rooney's premature death in 1901, at the age of twenty-seven, deprived Griffith of his closest and most gifted collaborator.[34] It was at the 1902 convention of Cumann na nGaedheal that Griffith first

[32]Joseph Lee, *The Modernisation of Irish Society, 1848–1918* (Dublin, 1973), p. 156.

[33]The first issue of *The United Irishman* appeared in March, 1899.

[34]Rooney was also a close friend to Douglas Hyde and a leading supporter of the Gaelic League. But Rooney agreed with Hyde that Anglo-Irish literature, while not a perfection of Irish thought, was an acceptable and necessary substitute until the Irish language was spoken once more by the people of the nation. William Rooney, *Prose Writings* (Dublin, 1909), pp. 230–232.

launched his dual monarchy scheme. He held up the Aus-gleich of 1867, which made Austria and Hungary two sepa-rate entities linked by the emperor, as a model for Britain and Ireland. Insofar as Arthur Griffith was a firm nationalist, who for a time even belonged to the uncompromisingly na-tionalistic Irish Republican Brotherhood, he very probably was unaware of how Hungarian autonomy was seriously di-minished by the Ausgleich arrangement which provided for Austrian control of the ministries of war, foreign affairs, and certain economic activities within that empire.

Griffith proposed a plan calculated to achieve maximum results with only a minimum risk of precipitating armed hos-tilities with Britain. The first step was for the Irish home rule M.P.'s to leave Westminster and establish a parliament in Dublin. An Irish government, Griffith thought, would re-ceive the support of local governmental boards and agencies and would thereby present the British with a de facto situa-tion. Lastly, he anticipated a movement of mass civil disobe-dience, passive resistance, and voluntary adherence to the native system which would isolate and idle British adminis-trative power. Forced to choose between conflict and com-promise, London would concede Irish independence if Britain and Ireland continued to swear allegiance to a com-mon monarch.[35] Thereafter, Griffith thought, Ireland could proceed with legislation protecting native industries, since economic self-sufficiency was as important as cultural and political considerations in safeguarding the nation's sover-eignty.[36]

Griffith's policies held a natural attraction for several sepa-ratist societies like Cumann na nGael, the National Council,

---

[35]T. M. Kettle, a member of the Irish Parliamentary Party and a professor of national economics at the Royal University of Dublin, called Griffith's proposal the "largest idea contributed to Irish politics for a generation." P. S. O'Hegarty, *A History of Ireland Under the Union, 1801–1922* (London, 1952), p. 130.

[36]In this respect, Griffith admitted to being profoundly influenced by the economic protectionist theories of Bismarckian Germany's Friedrich List who wrote *National System of Protection.*

organized in 1903 to protest the visit of King Edward VII to Ireland, and the Belfast republicans who founded the Dungannon Clubs. In order to stem the proliferation of overlapping societies, Griffith outlined a common policy for all at the National Council's annual convention in 1905. It was given a Gaelic christening and became known as the Sinn Fein policy, with most of the representative groups joining in 1908 to form the body known simply as Sinn Fein. The purpose of the organization was to work for the reestablishment of Irish independence, and the language of the Sinn Fein constitution was expressly separatist but sufficiently ambiguous to appeal to Gaelic Leaguers and Dungannon Club republicans alike. The organizational weekly paper, known after 1906 as *Sinn Fein* rather than *The United Irishman*, successfully supported a few candidates for local elections, but Griffith's party failed in its bid to defeat the Irish Parliamentary Party's nominee for the North Leitrim seat in a 1907–8 by-election. Sinn Fein never exceeded many more than one hundred clubs and societies during its heyday, between 1908 and 1910, and its political fortunes dwindled thereafter until its phenomenal regrowth in the final years of World War I.[37]

SINN FEIN'S LIMITED SUCCESS

There are, of course, a number of reasons which account for the very limited success of Sinn Fein's early initiatives. The financial cost of providing an alternative to the Irish Parliamentary Party on a national level was prohibitive and exceeded the organization's meager financial resources. Moreover, the British Government's budget crisis of 1909

---

[37]Donal McCartney, "The Sinn Fein Movement," in K. B. Nowlan, ed., *The Making of 1916* (Dublin, 1969), p. 38. From 1910 to 1913, the Sinn Fein movement was virtually moribund. See R. M. Henry, *The Evolution of Sinn Fein* (Dublin, 1920), p. 88.

proved propitious for John Redmond's Irish Parliamentary
Party by giving it a new leverage in demanding home rule
and thereby rendering constitutional nationalism viable
again. Sinn Fein was also being outflanked by the increasingly active Irish Republican Brotherhood whose paper,
Irish Freedom, espoused a more militant course of establishing an Irish republic by physical force, as opposed to the plan
of gradual nation building by passive resistance which
Griffith advocated.[38]

Perhaps another Sinn Fein liability was the personality of
Arthur Griffith himself. He was too much of an individualist
to be an effective organizational leader. A silent and reserved
man in the company of the few whom he allowed to be close
to him, Griffith could be obstinate, narrow, opinionated, and
suspicious of others and their ideas. He was a talented journalist who labored with intensity, but he was capable of lash-
ing out against real or imagined enemies in brutally sharp
editorials. In Griffith's writing it is possible to perceive the
provincialism and intolerance generic to cultural nationalism. He lauded the work and goals of the Gaelic League and
the Gaelic Athletic Association, but he was ever skeptical of
the writers associated with the literary movement. Like the
Young Ireland nationalists of the 1840s, Griffith believed that
writers and intellectuals must subordinate their talents to the
aims of Irish nationalism. Indeed, he thought the sacred mission of literature was to create a sound nationalist opinion,
publicize Irish grievances, and justify the noble cause of self-
government.[39]

Because Sinn Fein preached self-reliance, its doctrines included ignoring the services or forces of the enemy. Accordingly, when Yeats called in the police on the mob that rioted
at the Abbey Theatre during Synge's *Playboy of the Western
World,* Griffith's outrage was directed at more than a pro-

---

[38]The I.R.B. was revitalized by the return of the veteran Fenian Tom
Clarke from America in 1907. See Sean O Luing, "Arthur Griffith and Sinn
Fein," in F. X. Martin, ed., *Leaders and Men of the Easter Rising,* p. 60.
[39]McCaffrey, *The Irish Question,* p. 142.

duction which weakened the national effort by its vile portrayal of Irish life. In Griffith's eyes, "an Irish playwright had sought the help of the English forces at Dublin Castle in maintaining order within the theatre and thus had given strength to the enemy by recognizing and using his forces of occupation."[40] That bitter observation in 1907, only five years after Yeats had dedicated *Cathleen ni Houlihan* to the memory of Griffith's dearest friend, William Rooney, suggests how rapidly things were changing in Ireland.

LIBERAL VICTORY IN BRITAIN

Changes were also underway in Britain at that time which were eventually to favor the prospects of constitutional nationalists in the Irish separatist movement. Liberal leaders were encouraged by the victories of their party in by-elections following the Boer War and by the dissension within the ruling Conservative Party which, by 1905, had been in power for ten years. The imperialist wing of the Liberal Party, however, had been offended by the pro-Boer position of Irish nationalists who had, naturally enough, supported the Boers in their fight with Britain for their independence.[41] Former Liberal Prime Minister Lord Rosebery had even broken with his party over Ireland, and the new leader, Sir Henry Campbell-Bannerman, adopted a policy which retained the commitment to home rule but de-emphasized Irish self-government as an immediate objective of Liberal policy. In December 1905, when Prime Minister Arthur Balfour resigned because he could no longer provide effective leadership, Campbell-Bannerman was asked to form a new government. He named a cabinet that included a number of

---

[40]Thompson, *The Imagination of an Insurrection*, p. 69.
[41]Two small Irish brigades, commanded by John McBride and Arthur Lynch, actually fought on the Boer side in that war.

exceptionally talented men and focused upon the demand for radical social reform which had been growing in Britain since the economic decline in the 1870s.[42] In the general election of 1906, the Liberals won their greatest victory since 1832 by capturing 400 seats to only 157 for the Conservative Unionists. The recently formed Labour Party won 30 seats while the Irish Nationalists claimed 83.[43] Home rule had played no part in the electoral campaign and the question of social and economic reform was seen to be the issue of greatest urgency to British voters. Having won such an overwhelming mandate, the Liberals were in a position to formulate a policy for Ireland without Unionist or Irish nationalist dictation.

THE IRISH COUNCIL BILL

Reconciliation between John Dillon's anti-Parnellites and John Redmond's Parnellites had given the Irish Parliamentary Party an appearance of unity in 1900. But political nonconformists like T. M. Healy and William O'Brien denied party chairman Redmond control of a truly cohesive party. The overwhelming Liberal electoral triumph in January, 1906 caused further problems for Redmond as the Campbell-Bannerman government waited more than a year before proposing the Irish Council Bill which pleased virtually no one in Ireland. Under its provisions, an Irish Council, partly elected and partly nominated, would be empowered to control certain Irish departments and would be funded by a grant from the imperial exchequer. At the Irish party's 1907

[42]His Cabinet included Sir Edward Grey as Foreign Secretary; David Lloyd George as President of the Board of Trade; Richard Haldane as Secretary of State for War; John Burns, a socialist, as President of the Local Government Board; and intellectuals like John Morley and James Bryce.

[43]David Butler and Jennie Freeman, eds., *British Political Facts, 1900–1967* (New York, 1968), p. 141.

national convention, John Redmond rejected the council proposal as totally inadequate. Yet he urged his party to continue its support of the alliance with the Liberals, arguing that the Council idea had been advanced as an interim step and that the Liberal Party remained committed to Irish home rule.[44] Redmond also pointed to the social reforms which had been passed, with evident benefit to Ireland, and warned against strengthening the hand of the nation's republican or Sinn Fein extremists.[45]

JOHN REDMOND

A few Irish Parliamentary Party members, notably Healy and O'Brien, actually proposed temporary withdrawal from the House of Commons, which is what Arthur Griffith had been seeking, although they did not support the Sinn Fein plan for civil disobedience or unilateral action in establishing a native parliament. John Redmond's determination to retain his party's alliance with the Liberals prevailed in part because of his own political skill and also because of the Irish party's satisfaction with the constitutional reforms already accomplished. Redmond was a man of moderate temperament and, unlike Parnell, he had full confidence in the essential justice of the British parliamentary system. It was his oratorical ability, his competence as a parliamentarian, and his willingness to indulge differences of opinion for the sake of compromise which brought the Irish party a stability it had not known for years.[46]

---

[44]For a highly useful discussion of this subject, see H. W. McCready, "Home Rule and the Liberal Party," *Irish Historical Studies,* 13 (September, 1963), pp. 316–348.

[45]Acts were passed between 1906 and 1909 to improve the housing of the working-class in the countryside and in the towns, and to remedy the defective finances of the Wyndam Act.

[46]Still the most authoritative study of Redmond's life and career is Denis Gwynn, *The Life of John Redmond* (London, 1932).

BIRRELL AND THE IRISH UNIVERSITIES ACT

Augustine Birrell, who became chief secretary for Ireland in 1907, worked successfully toward strengthening the financial provisions of the Wyndam Act and thereby lent further credence to Redmond's contention that the Irish Parliamentary Party's alliance with the Liberals was in Ireland's best interest. Perhaps Birrell's greatest achievement in Ireland was the Irish Universities Act of 1908, which at long last put an end to the university question. While it did not resolve the differences between the University of Dublin (Trinity College) and the Catholic majority in Ireland, the act did abolish the Royal University of Ireland which had been established in 1879 as a temporary compromise.[47] In its place two new universities were established: Queens University, Belfast, and the National University of Ireland, a federal body incorporating University Colleges Dublin, Cork, and Galway. The latter, though technically nondenominational, was intended to fulfill the standards of a Catholic university, and Nationalist Ireland generally accepted it as such.[48]

THE GENERAL ELECTION OF 1910

While the Universities Bill was before Parliament in 1908, Prime Minister Campbell-Bannerman resigned and died shortly thereafter. His successor, Henry Herbert Asquith, promptly gave a public assurance that the Liberal Party still regarded home rule as the only solution to the Irish question.

---

[47]The Royal University of Ireland was purely an examining body empowered to grant degrees to all who passed the necessary examinations. No attendance at any college was required except for degrees in medicine. The students of the Catholic University which, from 1882 onwards, was known as University College, Dublin, now were eligible for government sponsored fellowships and university degrees.

[48]For an account of Birrell's role see Leon O Broin, *The Chief Secretary* (London, 1969), pp. 21-24. Cf. Lyons, *Ireland Since the Famine*, p. 262.

Conservatives, meanwhile, contented themselves with delaying or defeating government measures through their permanent majority in the House of Lords. In 1906, that chamber consisted of 602 peers, of whom 480 called themselves Unionist, 88 declared themselves Liberals, and 34 had no affiliation. A crisis situation evolved in 1909 over the budget of that year. Chancellor of the Exchequer Lloyd George proposed to increase income and luxury taxes, to introduce a series of land taxes, and to raise duties on alcoholic beverages and tobacco.[49] These, he said, were drastic but necessary steps if the government were to find more money for old age pensions, expanding social services, and defense. The Irish party was unhappy with a budget which threatened the interests of distillers and publicans, upon whom the party depended so heavily for financial contributions and local support. Conservatives were outraged at what they regarded as an assault against property interests. Redmond adopted the strategy of seeking concessions on the details of the budget while supporting it as a whole, hoping to goad the Conservatives into a precipitous action which might result in diminishing the veto power of the House of Lords. It was a case of taking the bitter with the sweet: much as the Irish party disliked the budget, they disliked the House of Lords even more. When that chamber rendered its almost predictable veto, by a vote of 350 to 75, Asquith called for a general election in January 1910.[50]

In the subsequent polling, the Unionists gained 116 seats, effecting a near balance between the major parties of 275 Liberals to 273 Unionists. But the Liberals still had a majority vote in Commons, and with it the government, because they had the support of forty Labour and seventy Irish home rule

---

[49]Specifically, Lloyd George sought to increase taxes on unearned income, death duties, and establish new taxes on land, especially on land used only for hunting purposes.

[50]The House of Lords had not interfered with a finance bill passed by the House of Commons for 200 years, which suggests that the upper chamber did indeed view Lloyd George's budget as an attack on the structure of society.

M.P.'s. The Irish party had been split once more, partly over the question of supporting the budget, resulting in eleven Irish independent Nationalists being returned to Westminster. This was more than compensated for, however, by the fact that Redmond's bloc of seventy votes now held the balance of power in the House of Commons. But Redmond also knew that if he brought the Liberal Party down he would simultaneously postpone home rule indefinitely. His confidence in the good faith of the Liberal Party had been strengthened by its successful grant of self-government to the Transvaal in 1906.[51]

Although some contemporaries had anticipated that the Liberal majority might be sizeably reduced in the January 1910 election, no one could have foreseen the stunning results which created an entirely new balance of power. Why did the same electorate which had given the Liberal Party a 224-seat advantage over the Unionists in 1906 reduce that margin to two seats only four years later, particularly in light of the Liberals' vigorous program of social reform? The evidence suggests no single answer but rather that a variety of issues and interests influenced the voters. Some members of the working-class resented paying more pennies for their pints and smokes; the trade unions regarded the government welfare programs as inadequate (which accounts for Labour winning forty seats, a remarkable feat for a party not yet four years old); many middle-class and rural Liberal voters objected to the collectivist character of the government's social welfare services and the means of financing them through taxes on property; and Britons generally were apprehensive over German naval and military power, but were divided over what sums should be spent on defense. Beyond these and other considerations, however, there is little doubt that the Irish question played a significant role in the revival of the Unionist party. Although the Liberals had again deemphasized the home rule issue in their electoral campaign,

---

[51]J. C. Beckett, *The Making of Modern Ireland, 1603–1923* (London, 1969), p. 423.

their opponents had argued that a successful assault on the
veto of the House of Lords would be followed by a Liberal
attempt to terminate the union with Ireland.[52]

The Liberal government's ultimate weapon against the
House of Lords was to request the king to create new peers.
With 480 opponents to be outvoted, however, the number of
peers that might have to be created was likely to compromise
seriously that royal prerogative. Redmond warned Asquith
that the eleven independents returned from Irish constituencies in the recent election reflected a growing hostility
toward the budget in Ireland. And it was the sort of divisive
issue which T. M. Healy and William O'Brien were likely to
exploit at the expense of both the Liberal and Irish parties.
Accordingly, Redmond demanded that the Lords' veto
power be limited and that a home rule bill be placed on the
agenda as the price for the Irish party's support of the budget.[53]

CONFLICT OVER THE HOUSE OF LORDS

A Parliament Bill was introduced in the House of Commons
which limited the number of times the House of Lords could
veto an act passed in Commons to three sessions, which
meant a time period of approximately two years. Further
action was delayed by the death of King Edward VII in May
1910. His son, George V, assumed the throne amid a widespread feeling that the young and inexperienced monarch
ought not to be subjected at once to the trauma of a full-scale
constitutional conflict. It was this consideration which
prompted the Liberal and Conservative leaders to enter into
a private conference in the hope of breaking the deadlock.[54]
Their meetings proved fruitless, but they did agree that to

---

[52]McCaffrey, *The Irish Question,* pp. 147–148.
[53]F. S. L. Lyons, *John Dillon: A Biography* (London, 1968), pp. 292–298.
[54]For further details on the participants and particulars of this conference, which included more than a dozen meetings between representatives
of both parties, see Roy Jenkins, *Asquith* (New York, 1966), pp. 214–217.

make the will of the electorate absolutely clear another general election would be held in December 1910. This time the Liberals and the Unionists emerged with total parity, 272 seats each, while Labour rose to forty-two and the Irish Nationalists numbered eighty-three, of whom seventy-three were followers of Redmond. For the House of Lords, it was the moment of truth.

A growing sense of near hysteria swept the houses of Parliament as the Liberals and their allies prepared to pass the most momentous piece of legislation to affect the English constitution in centuries. Prime Minister Asquith drew up a list of 249 men who would be created peers, should the situation so require, while at Buckingham Palace, the king fretted over his dilemma with his secretaries. On July 23, 1911, the debate on the Parliament Bill began amid a scene of unprecedented chaos. As the prime minister rose to speak, Lord Hugh Cecil, from a corner seat below the gangway, began to scream "Traitor! Traitor!," a refrain which scores of Unionists promptly took up. The Speaker of the House attempted to restore order without success. Will Crooks of the Labour Party shouted to Lord Cecil that many a man had been certified (declared mentally incompetent) for less than half of what the noble lord had done that afternoon. Thus rebuked by one of his social inferiors, Cecil nearly collapsed. Unionist Sir Edward Carson then rose to move adjournment to which the Speaker replied, with icy politeness, that the debate had not yet begun. Redmond implored the Irish M.P.'s not to behave like "bloody fools," but a capricious Irish minority, led by William O'Brien, began to taunt the screaming, howling Unionists which resulted next in the Irish fighting among themselves. For three-quarters of an hour Prime Minister Asquith attempted to deliver his address but failed to progress beyond an opening sentence as the disturbances continued unabated. Other speakers were also hooted down, whereupon the Speaker adjourned the House on the grounds that a state of "grave disorder" had arisen.

Never before in the history of Parliament had a prime minister been denied a hearing.[55]

Even the more recalcitrant Unionist M.P.'s recognized, however, that they could not prevent the passage of the Parliament Bill by such obstructionism. When the bill did pass Commons, its presentation to the House of Lords in August 1911 provoked an exchange of recriminations in that otherwise sedate, aristocratic assembly almost as distasteful as the one that had occurred in the lower chamber. With a notable number of lords abstaining, the vote was only 131 to 114 in favor of the bill. Victory for the Liberals had been accomplished by the thirty-seven Tory peers and thirteen prelates who supported eighty-one Liberal peers. The House of Commons had triumphed.[56]

THE PARLIAMENT ACT OF 1911

The Parliament Act subsequently received royal assent and, with Redmond still holding the balance of power at Westminster, it was generally accepted that Irish home rule could not be delayed beyond two more years. Irish separatism was a dream about to be fulfilled, or so it appeared, and the prestige of those who had sought that end through constitutional means was never higher in Ireland. But many of the nation's cultural nationalists, and most of its republicans, viewed the imminence of home rule as an unwelcome arrangement. More important, and far more ominous, was the fact that the Protestant Unionists in Ireland, particularly those who resided in Ulster and who constituted the majority

[55]George Dangerfield, *The Strange Death of Liberal England* (New York, 1961), pp. 56–58.

[56]Peter Stansky, *England Since 1867: Continuity and Change* (New York, 1973), pp. 86–87. The motive of the Tory lords who supported the bill was simply their desire not to see their beloved House of Lords diluted with "instant peers."

of the population of that region, were uncompromisingly opposed to home rule. Britain had survived a crisis, but she was about to encounter her hour of gravest peril.

Chapter 3

Union Forever: Britain's Most Dangerous Hour (1911–1914)

British Prime Minister Herbert Asquith introduced the third home rule bill before the House of Commons on April 11, 1912. He thereby set in motion powerful forces which had been gathering in anticipation of the bill, and which possessed a considerable potential for fateful consequences. Asquith did not recommend a separatist scheme, but rather a mild federal proposal which offered a decidedly narrow measure of autonomy. Under the provisions of this home rule bill, local affairs would be administered by a Dublin parliament consisting of a popularly elected lower house, the membership of which would be drawn from an established number of representatives from each of the four Irish provinces; and a senate, whose members were to be nominated by the crown and subsequently by an Irish executive. Ireland would retain forty-two members in the imperial Parliament at Westminster who would be free to participate in all parliamentary business whether or not such business was of Irish concern. The imperial Parliament, however, would reserve for itself legislative power and/or authority over questions involving foreign affairs, finance, and religion.[1] Even control of the Irish police force was not immediately to be conferred upon the new Irish government.

THE IRISH PARTY AND THE HOME RULE BILL OF 1912

Despite the substantial qualifications in this Liberal offer of self-government, Redmond and most Irish Nationalists reacted with surprising enthusiasm. The Irish party leader actually disliked the limitations imposed upon the Irish parliament, but felt that the prospect of Dublin's eventual control over finance and internal order amply exceeded Gladstonian nineteenth century proposals. Moreover, unlike Parnell, Redmond was prepared to accept a subordinate parliament, and to pledge loyalty to the British Empire without insisting upon dominion status. He was aware of the increasingly militant Ulster Unionist opposition to any form of home rule, and of the danger that Irish Nationalist demands for further concessions might prompt the Liberal cabinet to postpone the bill's implementation, or to exclude Ulster from the bill's sphere of influence.[2] Arthur Griffith, of course, denounced the home rule bill as hopelessly inadequate, but Sinn Fein did not engage in any form of violent protest.[3] The sentiment of most Irish separatists was reflected in the triumphant reception accorded Redmond at the National Conven-

[1]Ulster was guaranteed an overrepresentation in the lower house of the Irish legislature, and the senate was expected to include a substantial number of Protestants. Moreover, the Irish government would not be permitted to fund or to show partiality toward any religious sect.

[2]Oliver MacDonagh, *Ireland* (Englewood Cliffs, N.J., 1968), pp. 57–58.

[3]In response to the home rule bill Griffith wrote, "If this be liberty, the lexicographers have deceived us." See Sean O Luing, "Arthur Griffith and Sinn Fein," in F. X. Martin, ed., *Leaders and Men of the Easter Rising: Dublin 1916* (New York, 1967), p. 61.

tion which met subsequently in Dublin. The Irish party received messages of congratulation from the leaders of the self-governing Dominions of Canada, South Africa, and Australia. What many of the celebrants overlooked and underestimated, however, was the determination of Irish Unionists to resist home rule even to the extent of imperiling the British constitutional system.

IRISH UNIONISM

Ever since the general election of 1885, Irish Unionism had become more stridently sectarian and more narrowly regional until 1912, when it became virtually synonymous with Ulster Unionism. Unionism, nonetheless, was never entirely monolithic; there were some Catholics to be found among its ranks, just as there were Protestants who were prominent in Irish Nationalist circles. Most of the tiny Protestant population which lived in the predominantly Catholic counties of Ireland's three southern provinces were as committed to Unionism as were their co-religionists in Ulster, but the isolated position of these southern Protestants was destined to exclude them from any active role in resisting home rule.[4] It was the heavily Protestant areas of Ulster that produced a backlash movement following Gladstone's conversion to home rule in 1885. In the general election of that year, Ulster's nine counties returned seventeen Irish Nationalists to the imperial Parliament, as against sixteen Conservatives. Equally ominous from the Unionist's view was the fact that, excepting the two seats allotted to Dublin University, the Conservatives failed to win a seat in any other constituency in Ireland. These electoral returns were to have two significant effects; first, Irish home rulers and their British Liberal

[4]Catholics constituted the overwhelming majority of the population in the counties of Ireland's three other historic provinces of Leinster, Munster, and Connaught.

allies tended thereafter to underestimate the strength and tenacity of Ulster Unionism since the political loyalties of that province were so evenly divided; and secondly, Unionists themselves were driven to exaggerate the siege mentality to which, for historical reasons, they were already prone, and to resist home rule with even greater vigor.[5]

ULSTER UNIONISM

Protestant Unionists in Irish counties outside of Ulster were often of the more prosperous middle- and upper-classes, but within Ulster they formed a more heterogeneous group. Ulster Unionism was a popular movement, as fervently embraced by farmers and farm laborers, shopkeepers and factory workers, as it was by landlords and professional men, and by merchants and industrialists. The population of Ulster's nine counties was rather evenly divided between Roman Catholics and Protestants, but the wealth of that province was largely in the hands of the latter. Among the lower classes there was, in some regions, a long tradition of sectarian rivalry in which Protestant and Catholic farmers and laborers competed for land and jobs. But until 1885, most of the affluent Protestants had felt that their position of superiority was secure. The results of the 1885 general election, however, shook them out of their complacency and into an activist role in the effort to defeat home rule.[6]

Faced with a common danger which threatened the survival of the Protestant Ascendancy in Ireland, old rivalries were forgotten as Anglicans and Presbyterians, landlords and tenants, and employers and employees promptly closed ranks after 1885. The Orange Order was resurrected as the

---

[5]F. S. L. Lyons, *Ireland Since the Famine* (New York, 1971), pp. 285–286.

[6]Unionists had neglected to anticipate the impact which the franchise act of 1884 would have upon the outcome of the general election in the following year. J. C. Beckett, *The Making of Modern Ireland, 1603–1923* (London, 1969), p. 399.

organizational instrument of militant Protestantism.[7] Founded in 1795, the Order had managed to survive its own formal dissolution in 1836 since many small farmers and agricultural laborers had retained its spirit in a social, if not political, context. Once again, however, it emerged as a symbol of Protestant patriotism and provided a common ground where men of different social backgrounds could meet on a basis of equality, and plan a strategy in their mutual interest. Ulster, of course, was the only province in Ireland where a pronouncedly militant Protestant organization like the Orange Order could function effectively. Unionists in other parts of Ireland had lost every one of the more than fifty constituencies which they had contested in the general election of 1885. Thereafter, they channeled their efforts through the Irish Unionist Alliance, founded in 1891, and attempted to propagandize British voters on the evils of home rule. The Alliance, which never exceeded more than seven or eight hundred members, took steps in 1907 to harmonize its activities with those of the Ulster Unionist Council. Protestants in southern Ireland were as opposed to a Dublin parliament as were their co-religionists in Ulster because of a widely held belief that home rule would result in their financial ruin.[8]

British statesmen were surprised by the passions which the home rule issue provoked among Irish Unionists, and some Conservatives promptly sought to exploit that sentiment for their own ends. As early as 1886, Lord Randolph Churchill, following a visit to Belfast, coined a phrase which soon gained wide currency: "Ulster will fight and Ulster will be right." A year earlier he had written to a friend, "The Orange card is the one to play. Please God! It may prove the ace of

---

[7]For a comprehensive study of the Orange Order during the first four decades of its existence, see H. Senior, *Orangeism in Ireland and Britain, 1795–1836* (London, 1966).

[8]For a more complete analysis of Irish and Ulster Unionism, see D. C. Savage, "The Origins of the Ulster Unionist Party, 1885–6," *Irish Historical Studies,* 12 (March, 1961), pp. 185–208; and P. J. Buckland, "The Southern Irish Unionists and British Politics, 1906–14," *Irish Historical Studies,* 15 (March, 1967), pp. 228–255.

trumps."[9] Such unscrupulous manipulation of an intensely emotional and potentially dangerous issue was due in part to Conservative frustration over the Liberal-Irish Nationalist alliance. Irish Protestants were also used as pawns by the no-popery wing of British Toryism which opposed Irish home rule more for theological than economic reasons. The Conservative victory of 1895, and that party's subsequent ten year stay in power, diminished for a time the anxieties of Irish Unionists. The Liberal electoral victory in 1905, however, revived the expectations of Irish Nationalists and the apprehensions of home rule opponents. British Unionism was particularly strong in the House of Lords and in the Conservative party. Its adherents viewed the Irish Unionist Alliance and the Ulster Unionist Council as allies in the defense of landed interests and the preservation of empire. The close relationship between British Unionism and the various branches of Irish Unionism was underscored in 1906 when Walter Long, an English country gentleman and an M.P. from South Dublin, succeeded Colonel E. J. Saunderson as leader and spokesman of the Irish Unionists at Westminster.[10]

ULSTER UNIONIST SIR EDWARD CARSON

It was not until the 1910 budget crisis, and the subsequent assault on the veto power of the House of Lords, that Unionist activity began to reach a fever pitch. That was the year in which Sir Edward Carson was chosen to succeed Walter Long, following the latter's election to a London seat, as leader of the Irish Unionists at the imperial Parliament. To all appearances, Carson seemed a curious choice. He was a

---

[9]Nicholas Mansergh, *Ireland in the Age of Reform and Revolution* (London, 1940), p. 108.

[10]Walter Long served as chairman of the Ulster Unionist Council, the purpose of which was to form an alliance of all Unionist Associations, and to keep them in touch with the parliamentary representatives at Westminster.

southern Unionist, a Dubliner, who did not share the typical Ulster Protestant's hatred of "popery," and who, earlier in his career, had supported Irish Catholic claims regarding university education. As a southern Unionist, Carson's opposition to home rule was unqualified. While some Ulster Unionists openly discussed the possibility of excluding the northeast from the jurisdiction of any future Irish Nationalist government, Carson categorically rejected any such compromise. Nonetheless, this improbable chairman of the Ulster Unionist Council recognized that Ulster provided an indispensable power base for the Irish Unionist fight against home rule, and the fervor and dedication which distinguished his efforts toward that end won him the unreserved admiration and loyalty of his Ulster Protestant followers. The irony was that, in 1910, Carson was unable to foresee how such activity would ultimately lead to Ulster separatism and to the abandonment of Irish Unionism.

Born in Dublin in 1854, Carson was of Scot Presbyterian ancestry, and his mother was from an established family in county Galway. He was educated at Trinity College and was accepted to the Irish bar in 1877. His success as a crown prosecutor led to his appointment, in 1892, as Irish Solictor-General. A few years thereafter, Carson transferred his law practice to London where he became a celebrated leader of the English bar. His technique of cross-examination was formidable, his mastery of a brief meticulously complete, and his oratory compelling. These were the traits which would prove useful to him in politics as well as in the law, and he fascinated contemporaries as much by his personality as he did by his ability.[11] Carson's success at the bar was in part due to his ability in convincing the court of the merits of his case, for he believed so passionately in his client's cause that he made believers of the judge and jury.[12] It was precisely this manifest trait of total commitment which overcame a Dublin accent and won the trust of Ulster Unionists.

---

[11] Lyons, *Ireland Since the Famine* p. 298.
[12] H. M. Hyde, *Carson* (London, 1953), p. 1.

Faced with the imminence of home rule once the 1911 Parliament Act had been entered into the statute-book, Carson switched his base of operations from Westminster to Belfast. He appeared there in September 1911, to address a rally sponsored by the Ulster Unionist Council at which he told his audience, "We will yet defeat the most nefarious conspiracy that has ever been hatched against a free people."[13] Carson's motive in urging Ulster to resist home rule, whatever the cost, was inspired by his belief that the plan would not prove feasible unless it encompassed the whole of Ireland. Accordingly, he intended to defeat the entire scheme for an Irish government by rendering it economically impractical through the exclusion of the country's northeastern industrial region. That strategy, although quickly endorsed by both the Ulster Unionist and Conservative parties, was based upon a faulty assumption. Ireland, without Ulster, was still a viable economic unit. But in 1911, Carson, if not his supporters, seemed quite unaware of the potential consequences of his strategy. In encouraging Ulster's defiance of a parliamentary decision, he unwittingly deserted his fellow southern Unionists and unsuspectingly strengthened the prospects for some future political partition of the country.[14]

ULSTER UNIONIST JAMES CRAIG

If Carson was the leader and spokesman of the Ulster resistance, the master organizer of the movement was Captain James Craig. Born at Sydenham, near Belfast, in 1871, he was the sixth son of a millionaire whiskey distiller. Craig was educated in Edinburgh and later pursued a business career which took him first to London, and then to Belfast. Upon the

---

[13]Ian Colvin, *The Life of Lord Carson*, Vol. 2 (London, 1934), p. 76.

[14]Convinced of the wisdom of his strategy, Carson told Irish Unionists "Believe me, any Government will ponder long before it dares to shoot a loyal Ulster Protestant, devoted to his country and loyal to his King."

outbreak of the South African war, he was given a commission with the Royal Irish Rifles and, before being taken prisoner, fought with such bravery and valor that he won the admiration of his men and his Boer captors alike. Upon his return from the war he entered politics and, in 1906, was elected to Parliament as a member for East Down. His record in the House of Commons was not particularly distinguished, but he was soon recognized as a skillful parliamentary tactician who could make a fine art of filibustering.[15] Craig was a man obsessed with one idea: to preserve the character and integrity of the Ulster community he knew and loved. He identified completely with the attitude of militant Ulster Unionists who were prepared, if necessary, to resort to armed rebellion in pursuit of that end. Craig, the master organizer, interpreted this sentiment for Carson, the inspired leader who mesmerized his Ulster following with fiery rhetoric. It was therefore appropriate that Carson's first address to a mass audience of Unionists should have been delivered on the grounds at Craigavon, Craig's home outside Belfast. Denouncing the Liberal government that was preparing to bring in another home rule bill, Carson declared: "We must be prepared ... the morning home rule passes, ourselves to become responsible for the government of the Protestant province of Ulster."[16]

Liberals and Irish Nationalists were inclined to dismiss such oratory as a bluff, and indeed even some Conservatives who supported Carson would have been horrified had they thought his statements were intended to do more than intimidate home rule advocates. The Ulstermen were not bluffing, however, and two days after Carson's speech, a five man commission under the leadership of James Craig was appointed by the Ulster Unionist Council to prepare a constitution for a Provisional Government of Ireland which would

[15]St. John Ervine, *Craigavon, Ulsterman* (London, 1949), p. 135.
[16]Ronald McNeill, (Lord Cushendun), *Ulster's Stand for Union* (London, 1922), p. 51. For a brief but informative study, see also Hugh Shearman, *Not an Inch: a Study of Northern Ireland and Lord Craigavon* (London, 1942).

respond to the interests of Ulster and to those of "loyalists in other parts of Ireland."[17] The bold assertion on behalf of southern Unionists was, however, pure sham. The southern allies would have to be abandoned and native Ulster Unionists knew it. Even the fanatical Carson was eventually reconciled to that inevitability which only intensified his determination to preserve the Union for as much of northeastern Ireland as possible.

ULSTER UNIONISM AND BRITISH STATESMEN

Meanwhile, British statesmen further exacerbated the Irish problem. The most important of these statesmen was Andrew Bonar Law who, in November 1911, succeeded Arthur Balfour as leader of the Conservative Party. Bonar Law had been born in Canada, but was of Ulster Presbyterian stock. He made his fortune in the iron trade, entered politics and, by virtue of his forensic skill and his instinctive political pragmatism, soon became a prominent figure among Conservatives. Addressing a Conservative rally at Blenheim in July 1912, Bonar Law called Britain's Liberal government a "Revolutionary Committee" which had seized despotic power by fraud and, he further asserted, "I can imagine no length of resistance to which Ulster can go in which I should not be prepared to support them."[18] Having thus recklessly accorded militant Ulster Unionists with a blanket endorsement, the leader of the Conservative Party next journeyed to Belfast where, only two days before the home rule bill was to be introduced in the House of Commons, he gave an incendiary speech to an audience of 100,000 Ulstermen. He proclaimed to the cheering throng: "The government by their Parliament Act have erected a boom against you, a

---

[17]Hyde, *Carson*, p. 291.
[18]Robert Blake, *The Unknown Prime Minister* (London, 1955), p. 130.

boom to cut you off from the help of the British people. You will burst that boom."[19]

F. E. Smith, a Conservative from a Liverpool constituency and a close friend of Sir Edward Carson's, made similarly inflammatory remarks both in England and Ireland. In retrospect, what seems all the more remarkable about Smith's utterances is that not only was he, like Carson, a prominent member of the English bar, but also, as the Earl of Birkenhead, he later served as Lord Chancellor of the Realm and was a signatory to the 1921 Anglo-Irish treaty.[20] In England, Smith publicly declared that he would accept the consequences of war in Ulster even if "the whole fabric of the Commonwealth be convulsed."[21] At a later address before an Ulster audience at Ballyclare he spoke openly of the possibility of civil war throughout the United Kingdom. Smith told his listeners that their Unionist comrades in England so opposed home rule as to be ready "to risk the collapse of the whole body politic to prevent this monstrous crime."[22]

British Liberals had little occasion, and perhaps less inclination, to present the government's position on home rule to Irish audiences, particularly in Ulster, since that party had lost its traditional constituency to Nationalists, Conservatives, and Unionists. But an Ulster Liberal Association still survived and, in early 1912, its leadership invited Winston Churchill to speak to a home rule meeting at Ulster Hall in Belfast.[23] Churchill, who had recently left the Home Office for the Admiralty, had a penchant for provoking controversy equal to that of any Unionist demagogue. Craig and Carson

---

[19] *Ibid.*, p. 129.

[20] Smith was appointed Attorney General in Prime Minister Asquith's coalition government on November 3, 1915 and, as Lord Birkenhead, was made Lord Chancellor on January 10, 1919.

[21] Nicholas Mansergh, *The Irish Question, 1840–1921* (London, 1968), p. 201.

[22] Dorothy Macardle, *The Irish Republic* (New York, 1965), p. 90.

[23] Two leaders of the Ulster Liberal Association who supported the home rule meeting in Belfast were Lord Pirrie and James Armour, a Presbyterian clergyman. For a biography of the latter, see W. S. Armour, *Armour of Balleymoney* (London, 1934).

were outraged when the Liberal Association announced that Irish Nationalist party leaders John Redmond and Joseph Devlin would appear on the same platform with Mr. Churchill, and the Ulster Unionist Council quickly sought to deny them the use of their meeting site in Belfast. Such a blatant suppression of free speech embarrassed some Unionist supporters in Britain, but Ulstermen countered protests by replying that Churchill was at liberty to express his opinions anywhere except in the building which his father had consecrated to the loyal cause.[24]

Tensions began to mount in Belfast as the appointed date for the home rule meeting approached. Unionists next announced that they had hired Ulster Hall for the evening of February 7, the day prior to the home rule gathering, and that they intended to pack it with a solid mass of men who would resist all effort to eject them on the following day. The Ulster Liberal Association demanded that more police and troops be stationed in Belfast, and in London the Liberal government suffered its by now usual uncertainty over how to deal with Northern Ireland.

If Unionists defied the police and soldiers there would be bloodshed, but the Unionists knew submission to force would lend credibility to the argument that home rule could be imposed on Ulster by bayonets. Churchill did little to ease the crisis, and he declined the advice of friends and colleagues who urged him to alter his plans. Alarmed by the prospect of serious rioting in Belfast, British authorities at Dublin Castle ordered police reinforcements into the troubled city, together with five battalions of infantry and two companies of cavalry. These were more than precautionary measures, for a short time earlier two thousand Catholic workers had been driven from the Belfast shipyards amid scenes of considerable brutality. Doubtlessly, his desire to prevent harm to the Belfast citizenry, rather than concern

---

[24]Ulster Hall was the very place in which Churchill's father, Randolph Churchill, had preached the crusade against home rule. A. T. Q. Stewart, *The Ulster Crisis* (London, 1967), pp. 50–51.

for his personal safety, finally dissuaded the First Lord of the Admiralty from giving his home rule address at Ulster Hall. Churchill was insufferably stubborn, but cowardice was never his failing. A carefully orchestrated boycott prevented Churchill's sponsors from procuring any other suitable facility in Belfast. Ultimately, they were forced to settle for a portable shelter, imported for the occasion from Scotland, and erected on the Celtic Football Ground in a Catholic Nationalist sector of the city.[25]

THE ULSTER VOLUNTEER FORCE

Because the Ulster Unionist leadership preferred, for tactical reasons, to avoid a confrontation on this occasion, Churchill's appearance at the home rule rally in Belfast was uneventful. But if his departure from Ireland, when compared to the eve of his arrival, was very much an anticlimax, it was not because the Orange lodges had grown more passive. In January 1912, members of the Orange Order had begun openly to raise and train paramilitary groups which, under the direction of the Ulster Unionist Council, were united a year later into a single body known as the Ulster Volunteer Force. When the Council discovered that justices of the peace could authorize civilian drilling in their respective jurisdictions, a concerted effort was made to increase the size and efficiency of the U.V.F. Retired British Army general Sir George Richardson was brought to Belfast in July 1913, and was asked by the Council to recruit a general staff and assume command of the Protestant force. The Unionist leadership desired the U.V.F. for two reasons: to enforce the authority of the Provisional Government should it ever become operational; and

---

[25]The Ulster Unionist Council instructed its membership not to interfere with the football field meeting for fear of further alienating the British press. George Dangerfield, *The Strange Death of Liberal England* (New York, 1961), pp. 92–93.

to impose discipline upon the Orange rank and file, for the sectarian riots in Belfast during the summer of 1912 had demonstrated how quickly civil demonstrations could lead to uncontrollable disorder. By the end of 1913, the U.V.F. had become a formidable force with its own communication system and the capability to seize and control the harbors, roads, and railways of Ulster, and establish the authority of the Provisional Government. An indemnity fund was even launched to provide for casualities and their dependents. There was little doubt that superior organization equipped the Unionists to deal with their Nationalist neighbors, but weapons would be needed if armed resistance against the British Army were ever required. And as early as 1913, the U.V.F. had begun preparations for the secret importation of arms into Ulster.[26]

THE ULSTER COVENANT

Despite the growing martial fervor in Northern Ireland, the Ulster Unionist movement was never in any real danger of having its civilian leadership displaced by U.V.F. military officers. Sir Edward Carson, James Craig, and the Ulster Unionist Council were always in total control. On August 17, 1912, the Council announced that September 28 would be designated in Ulster as Ulster Day, when loyal Orangemen would pledge themselves to a sacred Covenant. The Unionist leadership intended the occasion to provide a safety-valve for popular emotion, while simultaneously demonstrating the solidarity of Ulster Protestants. The term "covenant" was deliberately chosen by Unionist leaders in imitation of the considerably different Scottish covenant of 1580.[27] Indeed, the phrasing of the "Solemn Covenant" assumed the charac-

---

[26]A. T. Q. Stewart, "Craig and the Ulster Volunteer Force," in F. X. Martin, ed., *Leaders and Men of the Easter Rising*, pp. 72–73.
[27]Beckett, *The Making of Modern Ireland*, p. 428.

ter of a religious oath as it pledged its signatories to resist the conspiracy of home rule whose subversive threat to civil and religious liberty had imperiled the unity of the empire. "In sure confidence that God will defend the Right . . ." the covenanters further promised to resist any Irish parliament which might be created. In the presence of leading ministers of the Church of Ireland, Presbyterian clergymen, and representatives of other Protestant denominations, Sir Edward Carson signed the Covenant at a ceremony in the Belfast City Hall on the proclaimed holiday. In an obvious appeal to sectarian patriotism, Carson made his appearance beneath a faded yellow silk banner which was adorned with a black star in its center and bore a scarlet cross on a white ground in one corner. It was the very same banner which had accompanied William of Orange at the Battle of the Boyne 222 years earlier.[28]

In Dublin, the Covenant was signed by two thousand men who gave proof of their birth in Ulster, and similar signatures were collected in Edinburgh, Glasgow, London, Liverpool and, of course, in every town and hamlet throughout the Protestant regions of Ulster. Women signed a separate but similarly worded declaration and ultimately almost 500,000 signatures were gathered.[29] The military preparations of the Ulster Volunteer Force left little doubt as to the determination of those who had pledged to resist the execution of any British act of parliament which sought the establishment of Irish home rule. The Ulster Unionist Council announced a campaign to enlist 100,000 men who had signed the Covenant and were between the ages of seventeen and sixty-five. Meanwhile, the Council's military committee prepared to mark off the nine counties of Ulster into divisions and districts, each of which was to raise a determined number of regiments or battalions.[30] Apparently, the signatories, who in their Covenant had described themselves "as loyal subjects of His Gracious Majesty King George V," saw no contradic-

[28]Dangerfield, *Strange Death of Liberal England,* p. 114.
[29]Liam de Paor, *Divided Ulster* (Baltimore, 1970), p. 80.
[30]Stewart, *The Ulster Crisis,* p. 70.

tion between that claim and their preparations for armed rebellion against the King's government.

THE ESTABLISHMENT OF THE IRISH VOLUNTEERS

It is worth noting that, while the Irish Republican Brotherhood and Irish nationalism's physical force tradition had survived to the eve of World War I, the parliamentary and/or constitutional forces had commanded the loyalty of most Nationalists in Ireland since the 1870s. The immediate cause of the return to militarism in the south was the formation of the Ulster Volunteers which directly inspired the establishment of the Irish Volunteers in November 1913. The latter was conceived as the counter-organization to Carson's force and was, from its inception, infiltrated and, to a significant degree, controlled by the Irish Republican Brotherhood. Using prominent members of the Gaelic League, especially Eoin MacNeill, as "front men," the Brotherhood intended to manipulate the new body for its own purposes through Sean MacDermott and an important new convert to republicanism, Patrick Pearse. What all this really signified was that for the first time in over forty years, the advocates of violence in Ireland were in a position to influence, and possibly capture, the mass movement of Irish Nationalism.[31] Paradoxically, the I.R.B., the most rabidly separatist group among all Irish Nationalists, owed its sudden good fortune to its most implacable enemies, the Ulster Unionists.

CONFLICT OVER THE 1912 HOME RULE BILL

Meanwhile in parliament, the debate over the home rule bill which Prime Minister Asquith had introduced in April 1912,

---

[31]MacDonagh, *Ireland,* pp. 70–71.

produced threats, recriminations, and scenes seldom seen before in the House of Commons. Asquith had hoped to allay what he thought to be the exaggerated apprehensions of intractable Unionists by emphasizing how an Irish parliament would in no way impair the supremacy and absolute sovereignty of the imperial Parliament.[32] Following a number of stormy sessions in which Conservative and Ulster Unionist leaders alternated in leveling verbal attacks against home rule, a Liberal member of Commons, W. G. Agar-Robartes, raised the controversial question of partition. He proposed the complete exclusion from the bill of the four predominantly Protestant counties of Antrim, Armagh, Londonderry, and Down. Irish Nationalists condemned this scheme since it would have meant a permanent partition. Asquith and the Liberal leadership could not support it if Redmond's party did not. And the Unionists, who were demanding even the exclusion of the three heavily Catholic Ulster counties of Cavan, Monaghan, and Donegal, would never have considered surrendering the mixed counties of Tyrone and Fermanagh.[33]

Tensions in the House of Commons finally reached the breaking point on November 13 when, while speaking on the Irish home rule bill, Prime Minister Asquith was interrupted by Sir William Bull who screamed at him from across the floor, "Traitor." When Asquith demanded a formal retraction, Bull refused and left the chamber. Chants of "resign, resign" and "civil war, civil war" created such a cacaphony that members of the government were prevented from being heard and the speaker adjourned the House. When it reassembled an hour later, the shouting began anew and the Speaker left the chair after ten minutes. As the government ministers began to depart, Winston Churchill waved his handkerchief tauntingly at the opposition members. Ronald

---

[32]*Parl. Debates*, Commons, 5th Series, 15 February 1911, Vol. 21, col. 1097.

[33]Roy Jenkins, *Asquith* (New York, 1966), pp. 280–281.

McNeill, an Ulster Unionist, became so enraged that he picked up a leather bound book, which happened to be a manual containing rules and advice for observing good behavior in parliament, and threw it with some force at Churchill, who was struck on the side of the head. Churchill was with difficulty restrained from retaliation and prevailed upon to leave the premises. The next day, apologies were offered and accepted, but from that incident onwards many Liberals and Conservatives no longer attempted even the pretense of polite conversation with one another.[34]

Early in January 1913, Sir Edward Carson moved an ammendment to the home rule bill proposing the total exclusion of Ulster's nine counties. The motion was defeated, as Carson had expected, by a margin of ninty-seven votes; but it served its intended purpose as an apparent demonstration to the British public that Unionists were at least willing to compromise. Irish party leader John Redmond subsequently declared that Nationalists could not and would not give their consent to the mutilation of the Irish nation.[35] On January 16, the third reading of the home rule bill was passed by the House of Commons by a majority vote of 110. It was then submitted to the House of Lords which on January 30, rejected it by a vote of 326 to 69. This meant that the bill would return to the House of Commons, pass through all its stages again, and would ultimately be forced through both Houses by the operation of the 1911 Parliament Act. It was thus bound to become law by the summer of 1914. Observing these developments from the American Embassy at No. 6 Grosvenor Square, Ambassador Walter Hines Page wrote his brother Robert in North Carolina that he believed the United Kingdom to be on the verge of civil war.[36]

---

[34]Stewart, *The Ulster Crisis,* p. 67; see also Dangerfield, *Strange Death of Liberal England,* p. 116.

[35]F. S. L. Lyons, *John Dillon: A Biography* (London, 1968), pp. 332–334.

[36]Burton Hendrick, *The Life and Letters of Walter H. Page,* Vol. 1 (New York, 1922), p. 158. Page wrote on December 22, 1913, "I asked the Prime Minister the other day how he was going to prevent war. He didn't give any clear answer."

Having lost the battle at Parliament Square, Conservative leaders began making confidential representations at Buckingham Palace in the hope that King George V would exercise the prerogative of the royal veto, or dissolve parliament and force another election on the question of home rule, or even convince the Liberal government to exclude Ulster from the bill. Lord Lansdowne, Arthur Balfour, and Andrew Bonar Law were among those tendering this sort of advice to His Royal Highness. George V, while new to the throne, was faultlessly circumspect about constitutional matters involving the affairs of state. He did summon Prime Minister Asquith to the Palace on August 11, and expressed his keen concern over the impending danger of widespread civil disorder in Ulster. The king further inquired if Asquith might not consider a broader devolution scheme, as had been advocated by Lord Dunraven, which would provide for a federal system of separate parliaments for southern Ireland, Ulster, Scotland, and Wales. These bodies would be given local autonomy but would remain subordinate to the imperial Parliament. Asquith did not oppose the plan for a general devolution, but he knew that the Irish Nationalists would never accept the creation of two Irish parliaments. Moreover, he recalled that the veto of the crown had not been exercised in 200 years, and that its application in this instance was more likely to imperil the monarchy than to mend the Irish problem. Lastly, the Prime Minister refused to agree to an election before the home rule bill became law because an election would vitiate the whole purpose of the Parliament Act and might possibly incite revolution in southern Ireland. He did accept, with reservations, the King's invitation to meet with the Conservative, Unionist, and Irish Nationalist leaders for an arbitration conference to be held at Buckingham Palace.[37] But nearly a year would pass before that meeting ever took place.

Asquith, who by early 1914 was laboring under enormous

---

[37]Harold Nicolson, *King George V* (London, 1967), pp. 298–302.

pressures from all sides, at last persuaded Redmond and his Nationalist colleagues to agree to the proposal that individual Ulster counties be given the option of remaining apart from home rule for six years, after which they would automatically come under the Irish parliament. Conservative leader Bonar Law had previously responded to proposals for protecting Ulster's interests by saying "nothing could be worse for us than we should be put in the position of having to refuse an offer which the people of this country would regard as fair and reasonable."[38] Ulster Unionist leader Sir Edward Carson reacted quite differently. When the Prime Minister proferred his proposal to the House of Commons on March 9, Carson sneeringly replied that Ulster would not accept a death sentence with a stay of execution for six years. A week later Carson stalked indignantly out of the House and left for Belfast where, many believed, he had gone to establish an Ulster provisional government.[39]

PORTENTS OF VIOLENCE IN ULSTER

At long last the Liberal government began to take the necessary naval and military steps to strengthen its position in northern Ireland. The Home Office had received evidence sometime earlier that weapons and ammunition were being smuggled into Ulster. The government had acted to prohibit the importation of arms into Ireland in December 1913, but that was after the rabidly Unionist Ulsterman, Major Fred Crawford, had succeeded in acquiring several thousand rifles and a few machine guns for the U.V.F. Subsequently, the

---

[38]D. G. Boyce, "British conservative opinion, the Ulster question, and the partition of Ireland, 1912–21," *Irish Historical Studies*, 17 (March, 1970), pp. 92–93. Bonar Law's moderation, however, was more evident in his private correspondence than in his public remarks.

[39]"Incomprehensibly, no one pointed out that the whole point of the six years was that it gave a new British Parliament a chance to review the situation and thus grant a virtually permanent reprieve." Robert Kee, *The Green Flag* (London, 1972), p. 483.

Ulster Unionist Council sponsored Crawford's trip to Germany for the purpose of purchasing an additional 20,000 guns. On March 17, 1914, a special committee appointed by the British Cabinet recommended moving troops from camps in both southern Ireland and England to reinforce the guards stationed at Ulster armories and weapon depots. The First Lord of the Admiralty also undertook to send several additional destroyers to Ireland. Bonar Law viewed these developments with alarm and called for a vote of censure against the government for turning Ulster into "a new Poland."[40]

These were indeed grave decisions and they were made all the more fearful by the rumors which abounded regarding the alleged disaffection among military commanders. It was, of course, true that the officers class as a whole was Unionist in its sympathies, and that many of them were from Irish Protestant backgrounds. Still more ominous was the fact that Unionist leaders were at this very time contemplating whether or not to cause the House of Lords to veto the annual Army Act. Such a step would have denied the government the means to keep a standing military force. That the Conservative Party should have even considered such a tactic, at a time of deep international tension in Europe, was an appalling indication of how deeply the Irish crisis had corroded all the ordinary decencies and conventions of constitutional government.[41]

THE CURRAGH INCIDENT

On March 20, Adjutant General Sir Arthur Paget, commander-in-chief of British military forces in Ireland, informed his

---

[40]Jenkins, *Asquith,* p. 306.

[41]Lyons, *Ireland Since the Famine,* p. 307. In a letter to Carson, dated December 9, 1913, Lord Milner hinted darkly that the military would have to be paralysed in order to assure the success of Ulster's rebellion. Colvin, *The Life of Lord Carson,* Vol. 2, p. 241.

subordinate officers that the country was likely to be "ablaze" within twenty-four hours. Since impending military operations could possibly involve coercive measures in Ulster, officers who were residents of that province were to be excused from service. All others were expected to execute their duties as ordered or face dismissal. Paget had received his instructions from the War Office, but he unintentionally communicated them to his staff officers in such a manner as to confuse them about both the operations and the expectations of their superiors in London. Consequently, fifty-eight of the cavalry officers stationed at the Curragh camp in Ireland submitted their resignations rather than face the prospect of having "to coerce" Ulster. Although the press was quick to label the affair a "mutiny," it was really a misunderstanding which was quickly reconciled, and the officers involved retained their commissions. All the same, the incident shocked Britain and doubtlessly affected public confidence in the Liberal government.[42]

In a scenario reminiscent of the Truman-MacArthur confrontation, two British Generals of Anglo-Irish background next attempted to use the Curragh "mutiny" for what were indisputably political purposes. Sir Herbert Gough and Sir Henry Wilson left Ireland and travelled to London where they extracted from the Secretary of State for War, Colonel J. E. B. Seely, a commitment that the government would not seek to use the Army to suppress political opposition to the policy or principles of the home rule bill. For Asquith, such insubordination was the final straw. Seely and the two generals were obliged to resign and Asquith, who personally administered the War Office for the next four months, immediately repudiated Seely's pledge. But nothing could conceal the fact that the Unionist claims to having support in the Army had some foundation, and that the government

---

[42]For a detailed account, see A. P. Ryan, *Mutiny at the Curragh* (London, 1956), pp. 128–169. See also James Fergusson, *The Curragh Incident* (London, 1964), and Sir C. E. Calwell, *Field-Marshall Sir Henry Wilson: His Life and Diaries,* Vol. 1 (London, 1927), p. 138.

could not depend on the loyalty of the military in any coercion of Ulster.[43]

ULSTER GUN-RUNNING

Even before the controversy over the Curragh incident had subsided, Major Crawford was in Hamburg arranging the purchase of some 20,000 German and Austrian rifles, together with 3,000,000 rounds of ammunition. The purchase was subsidized by the Ulster Unionist Council's defense fund, which consisted of contributions made both by English and Irish Unionists. Some members of the Council's arms committee had opposed giving Crawford these funds because they judged him to be a dangerous fanatic who might damage their cause. Crawford's daring scheme for smuggling arms into Ulster by sea won James Craig's endorsement, however, and Crawford was given the money and sent on his mission. Several high-ranking Conservative leaders knew of the plot and Crawford, while enroute to Germany in February, even conferred with Carson at the latter's London home.[44]

Following several misadventures, the impetuous Crawford succeeded in landing a shipment of German arms on the east coast of Ulster, at the ports of Larne, Bangor and Donaghadee, on the night of April 24–25. Everything thereafter was conducted with remarkable speed and efficiency: the Antrim division of the U.V.F. surrounded and occupied Larne, and a large convoy of vehicles, which had been discreetly assembled during the day, converged upon the port and expedi-

---

[43]Lyons, *Ireland Since the Famine*, p. 307. After Seely's resignation, Asquith declared "the army will hear nothing of politics from me and, in return, I expect to hear nothing of politics from the army." Ryan, *Mutiny at the Curragh*, p. 159.

[44]Frank Gallagher, *The Indivisable Island* (London, 1957), p. 97. Carson, though not without misgivings, had given his consent to the plan in January 1914.

tiously transported the bundles of rifles to hiding places in different parts of the province. Within twenty-four hours the task was completed while the British authorities, who had been diverted to Belfast by the arrival there of a decoy ship, made no other effort to interfere.[45]

BRITISH REACTION TO CURRAGH AND GUN-RUNNING

The Curragh incident and the Ulster gun-running had a double effect upon the situation in Ireland. On the one hand, the importation of the German guns had restored the military supremacy of the Ulster Volunteers over the Irish Volunteers (with the inevitable result that the latter were induced to imitate the northern example). On the other hand, the heightening crisis demanded resolution more than ever and, since Carson could not be budged, the government's inclination was to bring further pressure upon Redmond to compromise.[46] Publicly, however, the Liberal government condemned Unionist extremists and the cabinet considered arresting a few of the men who were known to have been involved in the gun-running, but in the end nothing was achieved except a belated strengthening of the naval shore patrol off the Ulster coast. When the House of Commons next assembled on April 27, 1914, Prime Minister Asquith defiantly pronounced: "His Majesty's Government will take, without delay, appropriate steps to vindicate the authority of the law."[47] Still, no action was instituted against either the

---

[45]Stewart, "Craig and the Ulster Volunteer Force," in F. X. Martin, ed., *Leaders and Men of the Easter Rising,* pp. 76–77; for a comprehensive account by Stewart, see *The Ulster Crisis,* pp. 176–212.

[46]Lyons, *Ireland Since the Famine,* p. 308. The Irish Volunteers had by this time exceeded the U.V.F. in numbers, but until they could procure a similarly large quantity of weapons the balance of power would lie with Ulster.

[47]*Parl. Debates,* Commons, 5th Series, 27 April 1914, Vol. 61, col. 1348.

U.V.F. or the Ulster Unionist Council members who had publicly pledged to create a provisional government for the nine county province if Parliament allowed the home rule bill to become law. Rather, on May 4, the Prime Minister wrote to Sir Edward Carson, the leader of that overtly seditious group, and secretly invited him to a conference regarding the Irish question. Asquith apparently had been encouraged to believe that Carson's moderate, even conciliatory, manner in the House of Commons following the gun-running episode was a signal of hope for possible compromise.[48]

When Asquith on May 5 did meet Carson, who was accompanied by Bonar Law, their conference was kept secret from the general public and, indeed, from the Irish Nationalists. Beyond asserting to the need for attaching an amending bill to the home rule legislation as it might apply to Ulster, the three men could not agree to anything more specific. At the urgent prodding of King George V, the cabinet considered the subject and, on June 23, introduced an amending bill first to the House of Lords, in order to see what the peers would do before wasting the time of the House of Commons upon it. The cabinet's plan provided for county option for six years, the very proposal which Carson had earlier characterized as a "stay of execution." Within a week the Tory-dominated House of Lords re-fashioned the amending bill to Unionist tastes. All the nine counties of Ulster were to be excluded, without reference to any plebiscite or time period.[49]

It was with an air of resignation that Prime Minister Asquith agreed to accept the king's invitation for a conference to be held at Buckingham Palace between leaders representing both sides of the home rule dispute. The first meeting was held on July 21, with Asquith, Lloyd-George, Redmond, and

---

[48]Asquith wrote Carson further on May 28 saying that he would be "proud and pleased" if he, Carson, found it possible to attend a birthday dinner for the King which the Asquiths were hosting on June 22. See Colvin, *The Life of Lord Carson,* Vol. 2, p. 399.

[49]Jenkins, *Asquith,* p. 318.

Dillon providing the home rule delegation, and Bonar Law, Lord Lansdowne, Carson, and Craig representing the opposition.[50] The conference ended inconclusively on July 24, but the King was convinced that it had contributed to a more friendly understanding between all parties. At a private audience which he accorded to each of the participants, the king was told by John Redmond that the Irish Nationalist party would be able to do many things to meet the views of Ulster once the home rule bill was on the statute book.[51]

JOHN REDMOND AND THE IRISH VOLUNTEERS

John Redmond, however, no longer had the confidence of the overwhelming majority of Irish nationalists which he had enjoyed a short time earlier. Two days after the Buckingham Palace Conference the Irish Volunteers, without Redmond's prior knowledge or consent, conducted a gun-running operation which differed notably from the Ulster model in that it was conducted in broad daylight. Technically, Redmond was in control of the southern Volunteers but in fact, as this event illustrated, he had little influence in that organization.[52] His options for political negotiation on the home rule bill were further reduced by the consequences which resulted from the Irish Volunteers' gun-running. The greater part of the weapons had been landed at Howth, on the north side of Dublin Bay, in the belief that they could be distributed quickly and to best advantage from that location.[53]

---

[50]The King limited his own role to giving a brief welcoming address at the start of the conference.

[51]Denis Gwynn, *The Life of John Redmond* (London, 1932), p. 342.

[52]Redmond's success the previous month in packing the Provisional Committee of the Irish Volunteers with his political lieutenants proved a superficial victory.

[53]Not unlike the Ulster gun-running episode, this operation also had its measure of misadventures. For an account by a contemporary, see Darrell Figgis, *Recollections of the Irish War* (London, 1927).

THE BACHELOR'S WALK INCIDENT

From the outset, the Irish Volunteers encountered more difficulties and enjoyed less success in their gun-running than had the Ulster Volunteers. The German Government, preoccupied with the growing specter of a European war and anxious not to antagonize England, forbade its citizens to sell arms to Irishmen. It was only after representing themselves as Mexicans that the Irish nationalist agents were able to purchase some 1,500 rifles and 45,000 rounds of ammunition from a Hamburg firm. When, however, the Under-Secretary at Dublin Castle heard of guns being landed at Howth, he dispatched a battalion of troops to seize the contraband. Recalling how 30,000 rifles had been landed at Larne without any visible sign of concern from the police or military, the Dublin populace was enraged to witness the government's response to the importation of 1,500 rifles by nationalists. Although the Irish Volunteers succeeded in secreting their modest arsenal, an unruly crowd of rock-pelting civilians attacked the British soldiers as the latter were returning from their futile march to Howth. In the narrow confines of Bachelor's Walk along the Liffey River, the battalion's rearguard first fixed bayonets, and then fired indiscriminately into the jeering, stone-throwing mob. Three people were killed and thirty-eight were injured.[54]

THE OUTBREAK OF WORLD WAR I

"Remember Bachelor's Walk" immediately became the slogan of Ireland's angry and increasingly restive nationalist population. Prime Minister Asquith knew that their fury was not likely to be mollified by the Royal Commission which, after investigating the incident, made Assistant Dublin Po-

[54]Leon O Broin, *The Chief Secretary* (London, 1969), pp. 102–103.

lice Commissioner W. V. Harrell, who was compelled to resign, its scapegoat. Winston Churchill later recalled how the British Cabinet, in their preoccupation with the menace of civil war in Ireland, had been startled to learn of the Austrian ultimatum to Serbia on July 24, less than four weeks following the assassination of the Archduke Ferdinand at Sarajevo. Indeed, even the outbreak of war with Germany on August 4, found King George V, in common with the majority of his subjects, still distracted by the unresolved Irish problem.[55] British Foreign Secretary Sir Edward Grey had informed Parliament on the previous day, August 3, that Germany's threat to Belgium's neutrality and Britain's commitment to France made probable a war against the Central Powers. John Redmond, in an emotional address to the House of Commons, subsequently pledged Ireland's support for the war, and requested the government to leave the defense of Irish shores to the Volunteers from north and south. Redmond thought Germany represented authoritarianism, militarism and contempt for the integrity of small nations. His emotions were deeply involved in the fight for the survival of the ideals which he shared with English statesmen and in the defense of France and Catholic Belgium, a country even smaller than Ireland which had become the victim of an aggressive, imperialist power. He also perceived the war as an opportunity for common purpose to triumph over sectarian and regional prejudice, a potential solder through which the north and south of Ireland might be joined once more. Redmond could not, however, allow the war to be used as an excuse to abandon the home rule bill since that would entirely destroy the nationalist support which he still enjoyed in Ireland. Accordingly, the Irish party leader continued to urge the Prime Minister to delay no longer in placing the measure on the statute book.

---

[55]Nicolson, *King George V,* pp. 325–329.

PASSAGE OF A QUALIFIED HOME RULE BILL

Ulster Unionists responded to the war with equal patriotic fervor, but they were also determined not to accept home rule. In September 1914, the Government of Ireland Act became law by an act of parliament but it contained two important qualifications. One was a suspensory provision delaying the operation of home rule until after the conclusion of the war; the other was that home rule would not become operative until Parliament had allowed some provision for Ulster by special amending legislation. Royal assent was given on September 18, and there was much jubilation in Redmond's Irish Nationalist camp, for it appeared that the long and bitter struggle for self-government was over, and would be finally won at the war's end. In Ulster, however, Carson told his followers that they had little to fear for the Act was but a scrap of paper which would alter nothing for them at the conclusion of hostilities. British Liberals, believing that the vexing Irish question had finally been put to rest, felt relieved and gratified.

Indeed, to many contemporaries, the conflict appeared to have resolved itself with an almost Shakespearian reconciliation. But, in fact, "all's well that ends well" could not apply to this tempestuous drama. The curtain was about to rise upon a new struggle in which bitterness and tragedy would obliterate this early scene of apparent resolution.

Chapter 4

Other Portraits of Protest: Nationalist and Labourite Dissent in Ireland (1914)

On September 20, 1914, two days after royal assent had been accorded to the amended home rule bill, and seven weeks following the outbreak of the Great War, John Redmond reversed his earlier position when he publicly and unconditionally committed nationalist Ireland to the Allied cause. His previous policy had been to endorse the use of Irish Volunteers for the defense of Ireland's shores, without requiring any oath of allegiance to the crown. The latter stance had won him the support of many, including some extreme nationalists; but, in an address to a county Wicklow audience on September 20, he suddenly and substantively shifted his policy and called on the Irish Volunteers not only to defend Ireland but also to fight the enemy at the front lines. What induced Redmond to do this is not at all certain. Perhaps he was swayed by a sense of gratitude over the fact that home rule had at last been placed on the statute book, or he may have thought an Irish Nationalist demonstration of loyalty to the empire necessary since Sir Edward Carson already had urged the Ulster Volunteers to fight in France. Whatever Redmond's motive, his declaration had the immediate consequence of splitting the Irish Volunteers into two rival factions. The prestige and solid organization of Redmond's Parliamentary Party prompted about nine-tenths of the Volunteers, some 170,000 men, to stand behind the home rule leader, and they subsequently renamed themselves the "National Volunteers." Some 11,000 others, however, retained the name "Irish Volunteers" and formed their own independent organization in October 1914.[1]

THE NEW IRISH VOLUNTEERS

Although nominally led by a moderate nationalist, university professor Eoin MacNeill, this new splinter group of Irish Volunteers was in fact controlled by the Irish Republican Brotherhood and the more militant elements of Irish separatism.[2] The militants represented a faction within a faction and, as the events of Easter week, 1916, were to illustrate, they succeeded in planning and executing strategy without the knowledge of MacNeill and other moderates in the organization. Meanwhile, the overwhelming number of National Volunteers supported recruitment for the Allied military effort and so impressed southern Unionists that it led to a *détente* between these two groups during the early period of the war.[3]

---

[1]Denis Gwynn, *The Life of John Redmond* (London, 1932), pp. 384–392.

[2]F. X. Martin, ed., *The Irish Volunteers, 1913–1915* (Dublin, 1963), pp. 144–155.

[3]For a wider discussion of the *détente* between southern Unionists and Nationalists, see Patrick Buckland, *Irish Unionism: One. The Anglo-Irish and the New Ireland, 1885–1922* (Dublin, 1972), pp. 42–44.

THREE CRISES

Unionism and its defiant Tory supporters were not the only peril confronting Britain on the domestic front in 1914, however. As George Dangerfield convincingly demonstrated in his masterful book, *The Strange Death of Liberal England,* there were three separate forces which converged at that time to destroy the traditional foundations of English Liberalism. Indeed, had World War I not occurred when it did, the United Kingdom's constitution and its democratic institutions might not have survived the mortal dangers posed by the burgeoning social and political unrest. In addition to the Unionist rebellion, the two other great crises of that day were the suffragette agitation and conflicts within the labour movement.[4]

It cannot be argued that either of these forces had an impact upon Anglo-Irish relations which even approximated that exerted by the Unionist crisis. Both, however, did have some connection with Irish separatism. That connection was scarcely notable in the instance of the suffragette movement, but was rather considerable in the case of labour. The suffragettes in Ireland were never as numerous nor as politically influential as they were in England where Emmeline Pankhurst's Women's Social and Political Union organized reasonably effective and widely publicized demonstrations. Countess Markievicz, soon to emerge as a prominent Irish revolutionary, was nonetheless active in the Irish suffragette movement. Mrs. Francis Sheehy-Skeffington, whose husband was the editor of the feminist *Irish Citizen,* picketed with other Irish suffragettes when British Prime Minister Asquith visited Dublin in July 1912. The suffragettes did not confine themselves solely to picket lines and peaceful demonstrations. Arson and vandalism had become almost standard tac-

---

[4]For the classic study of how these three forces dealt a lethal blow to Liberalism, see George Dangerfield, *The Strange Death of Liberal England* (New York, 1961).

tics for the suffragettes in England and not surprisingly, women demonstrators set fire to the Theatre Royal in Dublin where Asquith was to speak.[5] With the outbreak of war against Germany, most suffragettes followed the example of Mrs. Pankhurst who suspended her campaign to enfranchise women and turned her energies toward supporting the war effort.

THE BACKGROUND OF THE LABOUR CRISIS

In order to better understand the significance of the Irish labour movement in 1914, as well as its relationship to Irish separatism, it is useful to examine the circumstances and personalities which helped shape its development. Class conflict in nineteenth century Ireland had been essentially confined to the agrarian sector because, with the exception of the industrialized northeastern region, the country itself was predominantly agricultural. But even then, grievances were ultimately redressed through such constitutional devices as the 1903 Wyndham land purchase act, rather than through the more radical designs of Michael Davitt who had hoped to substitute collectivization (land nationalization) for the feudal tenant system. Socialist influences were also evident, even if not very pronounced, in urban areas. Branches of Karl Marx's International Workingmen's Association existed briefly in Dublin, Cork and, Belfast in the late 1860s and early 1870s. Irish workers, however, were no more likely to ignite a social revolution than were British labourers. When the Dublin United Trades Association was formed in 1863, its declared objectives were the protection of trade and the promotion of native industry. Its successor, the Dublin

---

[5]Jacqueline Van Voris, *Constance de Markievicz* (Amherst, Massachusetts, 1967), p. 94. The fire was set by two English suffragettes. It earned them the admiration of their Irish sister comrades and five years' penal servitude at Mountjoy prison.

Trades Council, founded in 1880, was principally concerned with protecting the interests of skilled workers and was equally apolitical. Rank and file members of Irish trade unions usually supported the home rule campaign of the Irish Parliamentary Party even though the unions, as organizations, did not endorse political programs.[6]

It was not until 1894 that the Irish labour movement revolted against the second-class status accorded it by British labour leaders and established the Irish Trades Congress in Dublin.[7] Its stated purpose was to supplement the work of the parent Trade Unions Congress in Britain, but the formation of an independent Irish body was to prove the first step toward the eventual separation of the two movements. For the next two decades of its existence, except for an invitation in 1900 to merge with the British organization, the Irish body was virtually ignored by the British Trades Union Congress.[8]

JAMES CONNOLLY

One of the dominant personalities to appear on the Irish labour scene at this time was James Connolly. Born in Edinburgh in 1868 of Irish parents who were forced to emigrate to survive, Connolly's early life had been one of abject poverty. In 1896, he arrived in Ireland where he worked for a time as a paid organizer for the Dublin Socialist Society.[9] For

---

[6]"Parnell clashed with Davitt over the latter's scheme for an alliance of the home rule forces and the British labour movement." See Arthur Mitchell, *Labour in Irish Politics* (Dublin, 1974), pp. 14–15.

[7]A British Trades Union Congress had been formed in 1868, and many Irish trade unionists belonged to amalgamated unions whose headquarters were in Britain. After 1894, however, Irish labour leaders took little part in the proceedings of the parent British T.U.C. For a useful study of the early British labour movement, see Henry Pelling, *The Origins of the Labour Party, 1880–1900* (London, 1954).

[8]J.D. Clarkson, *Labour and Nationalism in Ireland* (New York, 1925), pp. 181–189.

[9]Socialist bodies in Dublin at this time included former members of Karl Marx's First International. See John W. Boyle, "Ireland and the First International." *The Journal of British Studies*, 2 (May, 1972), p. 62.

the next seven years Connolly attempted to support his wife and children while simultaneously working to wean the unresponsive Irish worker from his passive acceptance of the status quo and toward the ideals of the socialist state. Connolly succeeded in founding the Irish Socialist Republican party and a newspaper, the *Worker's Republic,* both of which proved to be rather modest enterprises. Despite his eloquence as a speaker, his talent as a writer, and a wisdom born of personal privation which afforded him an instinctive empathy for and sensitivity to the plight of Dublin's slum dwellers, Connolly was unable to generate enough income from his efforts to support himself and his family. In 1903, he left Dublin for America where he became an organizer and propagandist for the Industrial Workers of the World.[10]

It was in the United States, while working for the I.W.W. in the vanguard of American industrial unionism, that Connolly first encountered and then subscribed to the syndicalist ideas which would influence so much of his later thought. He wrote articles and published pamphlets in which he predicted that the workers would one day seize the industries, and that this seizure would ultimately lead the workers to possess all political power.[11] Connolly recognized, however, that nationalism was a formidable tradition in Irish life, and he proposed to reconcile the international character of his own ideology to the more parochial views of his countrymen through a manifesto which called for the establishment of an Irish Socialist Republic. In that same manifesto, he insisted upon: the nationalization of railways and canals; a graduated income tax to subsidize pensions for widows, orphans, and the aged; the institution of a forty-eight hour work week and a minimum wage; and public control of national schools which would be free up to and including the university level. For entirely different reasons, Connolly concluded, as had the former Chief Secretary for Ireland, Arthur Balfour, that

---

[10]For an instructive account of Connolly's early life, see Desmond Ryan, *James Connolly* (London, 1924).

[11]C. D. Greaves, *The Life and Times of James Connolly* (London, 1961), pp. 176–177.

the Irish question was essentially an economic question. For Connolly, the precise method by which Irish political liberation should be accomplished was far less important than the achievement of his economic goals; political freedom, he felt, inevitably would be attained by the socialization of the means of production, distribution and exchange.[12]

Connolly used this rationalization as a justification for his unorthodox syndicalist ideas. While other syndicalists spoke of overthrowing the capitalist state by means of a general strike, Connolly felt that some sort of political action would be required to establish the Socialist Republic in Ireland. Like William Walker, the Belfast delegate who became president of the Irish Trades Union Congress and who perceived no contradiction in combining Ulster Unionism with international socialism, Connolly apparently saw no danger of a socialist movement's being swallowed by a nationalist revolution. It was a miscalculation on his part, but he was destined never fully to appreciate that fact before going to his untimely death before a British firing squad in 1916.[13]

JAMES LARKIN

If Connolly was Ireland's leading socialist theorist and propagandist, James Larkin was that nation's master polemicist and organizer of industrial unionism. Except for his Liverpool birth in 1876, Larkin's background was remarkably similar to Connolly's. Poverty had driven Larkin's parents to emigrate to England, and his childhood years were harsh and difficult ones spent in a wide variety of menial jobs.

James Larkin was a physically powerful man whose thunderous oratory and strong presence made him a most impressive speaker for the huge working-class audiences he so often

---

[12]Ibid., pp. 60–62.

[13]For an impressionistic view of James Connolly by a contemporary and co-worker in the Irish Socialist Republican Party, see William O'Brien, *Forth the Banners Go* (Dublin, 1969), edited by Edward MacLysaght.

addressed. After several years as a dock worker, he became a member of the National Union of Dock Labourers and, in 1906, was appointed the union's general organizer. He was sent to Ireland the following year to organize the dockers in Belfast, Dublin and in other Irish ports. It was first in Belfast, and later in Dublin, that Larkin achieved success in organizing the carters and dockers and, at the end of 1908, Larkin broke with the English-based Dockers Union over a conflict of policy and founded his own Irish Transport and General Workers Union.[14]

THE I.T.G.W.U.

The new organization was the first Irish union to adopt a socialist program which had as its ultimate object a new economic order involving, not only the nationalization of all means of transport, but also "the land of Ireland for the Irish people." Moreover, it proposed the organization of all workers, skilled and unskilled, in one union, and sought to achieve that goal through militant union tactics, such as the boycott and the sympathetic union strike, and by the use of class-oriented propaganda.[15] Larkin's union was, of course, resented by English trade union leaders who claimed to see in its nationalist orientation a divisive influence upon working-class interests, while the Irish Nationalist party was angered by Larkin's re-establishment of the Dublin branch of the Independent Labour Party in 1908.[16] His enemies extended even to the Irish Trades Union Congress whose more conser-

---

[14]James Sexton, General Secretary of the Dockers Union, thought Larkin was inclined to call too many Irish strikes which had to be financed from English and Scotch pockets. Emmet Larkin, *James Larkin: Irish Labour Leader, 1876–1947* (London, 1968), pp. 55–56.

[15]Mitchell, *Labour in Irish Politics,* p. 26.

[16]Sinn Fein leader Arthur Griffith was also hostile to Larkin. Griffith opposed anyone who disrupted Irish industry, upon which rested the hope for Irish prosperity, and he denounced Larkin for attacking capitalism rather than the abuses of capitalism. Padraic Colum, *Ourselves Alone!* (New York, 1959), pp. 109–110.

vative members expelled Larkin from that organization in 1909. But when, in the following year, Larkin was imprisoned for his part in a Cork strike, his fellow-unionists rallied to his cause, and both he and his Irish Transport and General Workers Union were formally affiliated with the Congress in 1911. Larkin's insistence upon "industrial unionism"—the extension of trade unionism to the hitherto unorganized ranks of unskilled labourers—and the imbuing of these masses with militant class-consciousness, actually anticipated in Ireland the great wave of syndicalist-styled strike action which swept over Britain in 1911 and 1913.[17]

By 1910, James Connolly, disillusioned with the feuding between factions of the American industrial unionists, was ready to come home. His return to Ireland was prompted by an invitation from the newly formed Socialist Party of Ireland to conduct a lecture tour designed to reawaken socialist interest in the country. When the movement lost the support of some middle-class sympathizers and was unable to pay him a salary, Connolly found himself in the very situation which, in 1903, had forced him to emigrate to the United States. He was contemplating emigrating again in 1911, this time to England, when he was given an appointment in Belfast as an organizer for Larkin's Irish Transport and General Workers Union. At this juncture in his life, Connolly was neither a member of the Irish Republican Brotherhood, nor was he greatly interested in the nationalist physical force movement. He was committed to the establishment of a Socialist Republic of Ireland and, for the moment, to the goals of Larkin's I.T.G.W.U. which, by the spring of 1911, was the most militant union in the British Isles.[18]

Connolly and Larkin were men of widely differing temperaments, which accounted for their occasionally less than cordial relationship in the labour movement, but neither was

---

[17]F. S. L. Lyons, *Ireland Since the Famine* (New York, 1971), pp. 276–277.
[18]J.W. Boyle, "Connolly, the Citizen Army and the Rising," in K. B. Nowlan, ed., *The Making of 1916* (Dublin, 1969), pp. 51–53.

doctrinally inflexible. Before his return from America, Connolly had published *Labour in Irish History,* an essentially Marxist interpretation which portrayed Ireland's past experience within a social and economic context, and predicted that the resolution of the country's problems would be achieved through class warfare.[19] Political realities, however, gradually forced Connolly into a succession of ideological compromises which ultimately led him to endorse and participate in the fundamentally nationalist revolution of 1916. Like Connolly, James Larkin was capable of pragmatism. His biographer has explained how Larkin could be at once a convinced socialist and a dedicated trade union official:

> As a Socialist, every day was denunciation day with the promise of a better tomorrow. As a trade union official, every day resulted in another compromise with a system that was dedicated to the frustration of a better tomorrow. Would the Socialist, diluted by the spirit of the trade union compromise, eventually come to terms with the despised system? Or would the system purge itself because of the pressure applied by the Socialist and become less despised? . . . James Larkin's Socialism became his faith, and his trade unionism became his work. Essentially a Catholic, Larkin believed that both the faith and the work were necessary to the social salvation of the working classes.[20]

THE LABOUR CRISIS

Britain was rocked by a succession of labour strikes in 1911, the largest being the seamen's and docker's in July, and the railway worker's in August. Larkin's Irish Transport and General Workers Union was soon heavily involved in work-stoppages and in sympathetic strikes which included a num-

[19]James Connolly, *Labour in Irish History* (Dublin, 1956). The first edition of this work was published in 1910 while Connolly was still in the United States.
[20]E. Larkin, *James Larkin,* p. 19.

ber of skilled and unskilled labourers.[21] During 1912, with
the volume of trade increasing and business eager to recoup
its losses of the previous year, Larkin accomplished some of
his most effective peaceful bargaining. While the concessions
made by employers to the union's demands for better wages
and to improved working conditions were minimal for the
most part, the degree of control which Larkin's I.T.G.W.U.
exercised over the port of Dublin, as well as over other Irish
ports, made that organization a force to be reckoned with. It
is therefore not surprising that the numbers joining Larkin's
union rose dramatically from 4,000 in 1911 to 8,000 in
1912.[22]

Between January and July 1913, Larkin won additional
concessions for his dock workers from the leading Dublin
shipping companies, and even extended his union to include
the agricultural labourers of the surrounding countryside.
But in August 1913, Larkin undertook the most formidable
challenge of his trade union career. He turned his attention
to the Dublin United Tramway Company which was a part
of the commercial empire belonging to William Martin Murphy. Murphy was perhaps the wealthiest and most successful
businessman in Ireland. In addition to his extensive railway
and business interests in Ireland, Britain and the empire,
Murphy also owned the *Independent,* a newspaper which he
often used as a powerful propaganda weapon. When Murphy
refused to recognize Larkin's union, the latter retaliated by
organizing a strike by tramwaymen on August 26, during the
Horse Show week, at the height of the Dublin social season

---

[21]In Belfast, Connolly succeeded in gaining higher wages for I.T.G.W.U.
members who worked in the deep-sea docks, and he organized unskilled
workers, many of them women, who were employed in the linen industry.
Larkin, meanwhile, won some wage increases for dockers, carters, coal-men
and, eventually, railway men in Dublin and other Irish ports.

[22]Membership continued to increase in 1913, but there is some disagreement as to how much. F. S. L. Lyons estimates there were approximately
10,000 members that year while Emmet Larkin, citing the Report of the
Twentieth Irish Trades Union Congress, puts the figure at 14,000. See Lyons, *Ireland Since the Famine,* p. 279; see also E. Larkin, *James Larkin,* p.
98.

and, therefore, at the moment of greatest inconvenience. In September 1913, Murphy, together with some 400 fellow members of the Employers Federation Limited, launched a counter-offensive in which 25,000 workers were locked out of their jobs.[23] Tensions between workers and employers mounted, tempers flared, and street demonstrations led to ugly confrontations and riots. After the arrests of Larkin and Connolly, the resistance to the employers was organized and directed by two able trade unionists, William O'Brien and P. T. Daly. They immediately appealed to the British Trades Union Congress which responded with substantial grants of money and food. The British T.U.C., however, refused to support sympathetic strikes or to assist the Dublin workers in any but a voluntary way. Inevitably, it soon became a question of how long British trade union contributors would be willing to subsidize their Irish comrades.[24]

Perhaps as many as 100,000 men, women, and children were affected by the strike and lockout. That winter, with cold, hunger and destitution threatening thousands of Dublin families, a group of well-intentioned English people organized a plan for Dublin slum children to be placed in English homes for the duration of the dispute. Archbishop William Walsh of Dublin, together with other members of the Catholic hierarchy, condemned sending the children to England where they might lose their faith and be proselytized by socialists.[25] Clerical fears that socialism was a plot by the evil forces of the secular world against the spiritual and temporal interests of Irish Catholics prompted some priests to behave in an unbecoming manner toward the English social workers involved in the foster home plan. There were, for instance, bands of priests who physically intervened to detain "kid-

---

[23]The Federation had been formed in June 1911, following the first wave of strikes in Ireland.

[24]Lyons, *Ireland Since the Famine*, pp. 280–281.

[25]Archbishop Walsh's condemnation took the form of a letter published in the Dublin daily papers on October 21, 1913. See E. Larkin, *James Larkin*, p. 124.

napped" children as the youngsters were departing for England from harbor quays and railway platforms.[26] In the face of such virulent opposition from the Catholic clergy, the rescue operation was abandoned and the slum children were preserved from the "fate" of exposure to theological impurity.

Sectarian bigotry of this kind moved Larkin, who had been released after a brief detention in prison, to make a fiery speech in which he predicted that those who had sought to divide the working-class by encouraging religious intolerance had lit "a fire in Ireland they will never put out."[27] Larkin next went to England in October 1913, where he denounced the British trade union leaders for failing to support the Irish struggle with sympathetic strike action. He appealed to the rank and file union members, over the heads of their leaders, with manifestoes and speeches which were so intemperate as to alienate the very people whose contributions had sustained the Irish workers since the early days of the lockout. As funds from England dwindled to a trickle, the strikers began to return to their jobs, often on the stringent anti-union terms of the employers, in the months of January and February 1914. The death-knell of the Larkin strike movement sounded when the Builders Labourers Union agreed, on February 1, to the humiliating condition that none of its members should remain, or become in the future, a member of the Irish Transport Workers Union.[28]

One historian has concluded that Larkin's defeat in 1914 demonstrated that national prejudices were stronger than class loyalties. This view supposes that the decision of the British Trades Union Congress to limit its support of the strike was evidence that the British proletariat was unwilling

---

[26]The Catholic Protection and Rescue Society was established in 1913 to combat this activity by English social workers, all of which was consistent with the Irish Catholic hierarchy's traditional opposition to the legal adoption of Catholic children by persons of other faiths. See J. H. Whyte, *Church and State in Modern Ireland, 1923–1970* (New York, 1971), pp. 190–191.

[27]E. Larkin, *James Larkin*, p. 125.

[28]Ibid., p. 141.

to sacrifice for Irish workers in the cause of class solidarity.[29] Another historian has contended that the British trade union leaders reacted as they did, not because of Larkin's abuse, but rather because they could not have agreed to his demand for sympathetic action in support of the Dublin men without involving themselves in a general industrial war in Britain.[30] There is considerable merit to each of these arguments, for the Dublin strike and lockout of September 1913 to January 1914 was perceived by contemporaries within the larger context of Anglo-Irish relations. Larkin's movement was an Irish movement which had revolutionary overtones. British trade union members who would otherwise have supported workers against employers were, in this instance, influenced by their Ulster partisan sentiment in the Unionist versus nationalist struggle which then dominated Irish affairs. Also, the conservative British Trades Union Congress leadership disliked Larkin and his tactics, and feared that labour might be drawn into a dispute in Ireland when that country appeared on the verge of a civil war which could spread to every part of the Kingdom.

CONNOLLY EMERGES AS LABOUR LEADER

On January 30, 1914, Larkin himself publicly admitted, "We are beaten, we will make no bones about it; but we are not too badly beaten still to fight. ...."[31] Larkin's courage, if not always his judgment, was widely respected in the Irish labour

---

[29]Lawrence J. McCaffrey, *The Irish Question, 1800–1922* (Lexington, Kentucky, 1968), pp. 144–145. McCaffrey further argues that the indifference of British labour opinion to economic and social injustice in Ireland forced the Irish worker, who became more nationalistic and revolutionary, to see the need for the complete destruction of British influence in Ireland if Irish society was to be truly reformed.

[30]E. Larkin, *James Larkin,* p. 142. Larkin also notes that British labour leaders rightly suspected that the British worker would not respond to a declaration of industrial war, especially if the issue was purely Irish.

[31]Ibid., p. 141.

movement, and he was the popular choice for the presidency of the Irish Trades Union Congress in 1914. He remained as intemperate as ever, however, and even threatened to resign from his own union in June. The collapse of international socialism following the outbreak of war, together with the patriotic response of trade union members to the nationalist cause, left Larkin isolated and disillusioned. In late October, he went on a lecture tour in the United States for the purpose of raising money for his union. While he very probably intended to return after a year or so, his preoccupation with the antiwar movement and his work in organizing the American Communist Party extended his stay. Larkin was later charged with advocating "criminal anarchy" and was subsequently sentenced to a five to ten year term in New York's Sing Sing Prison. He did not return to Ireland until 1923, and he never regained the dominant position which he had once held in the Irish labour movement. The vacuum left by Larkin's 1914 departure not only allowed James Connolly to emerge as the leader of Irish labour, but it also permitted closer ties between Sinn Fein's Arthur Griffith and Connolly who were equally opposed to Ireland's involvement in the war. Such cooperation between Irish labour and Sinn Fein nationalists had been previously precluded by the hostility which Griffith and Larkin felt toward one another.[32]

THE CITIZEN ARMY

Connolly would grow to share many of the views of militant nationalists respecting political revolution, and the creation of the Citizen Army took him further in that direction. At its inception in November 1913, the Citizen Army's purpose was the training of workers for self-defense in clashes with the police, as well as the bolstering of morale amongst those

---

[32]Connolly was accepted by Griffith, while Larkin was not. See Greaves, *Connolly*, p. 219.

idled by the strike and lockout. Captain J. R. White, an ex-British officer and veteran of the Boer War, first suggested the formation of a Citizen Army after police and picketers had clashed on the Dublin quays over the "scab labourers" whom the Irish employers had imported from England. Since the Irish Volunteers were founded at the same time, with far superior organization and facilities, the tiny Irish Citizen Army attracted scarcely 200 men. The Volunteers were organized primarily as a counter-force to the para-military Ulster group, and Connolly and Larkin felt the need for a separate "Labour Army" as a response to the use of police and soldiers on the employers' side in industrial disputes.[33] When the strike collapsed in the early months of 1914, however, the Citizen Army declined to the point where it nearly ceased to exist.

It was in March 1914, that a general labourer and future playwright, Sean O'Casey, together with a handful of others including Captain J. R. White and Countess Markievicz, helped reorganize and rebuild the Irish Citizen Army. Membership was open to all who were committed to the concept that the ownership of Ireland, moral and material, should be vested in the people of Ireland; and to the proposition that public ownership required the sublimation of all differences of birth, privilege, and creed in the common name of the "Irish people". At the insistence of James Larkin, a further clause to this new constitution and declaration of purpose of the Citizen Army required inductees, whenever possible, to be members of a trade union recognized by the Irish Trades Union Congress.[34]

The conflict of personality and temperament between Sean O'Casey and Countess Markievicz illustrates the sort of factionalism which was endemic, and often disabling, to the

---

[33]Larkin felt that since the government had not suppressed the Ulster Volunteers, workers too had the right to drill and train a force for their own purposes. Ibid., p. 263.

[34]Boyle, "Connolly, the Citizen Army," in Nowlan, ed., *The Making of 1916*, pp. 54–57.

various Irish separatist movements.[35] Born in London in 1868, Countess Markievicz had been christened Constance Gore-Booth. She was raised at Lissadell in county Sligo and, as the daughter of a prominent Anglo-Irish ascendancy family, she was presented to Queen Victoria in 1887. But shortly after her marriage to a Polish Count, Casimir Markievicz, with whom she shared an interest in theatre and painting, the Countess became engaged in cultural and political associations which would draw her ever closer to the more militant Irish separatists and farther away from her society friends and family. Yet, Countess Markievicz was as far removed from a trade unionist as it was possible to be, and Sean O'-Casey, a product of the Dublin slums, viewed her involvement in the Irish Citizen Army with deep suspicion. She had joined the Volunteers because that organization appealed to her Irish and revolutionary interests and, although she shared Larkin's dislike for Arthur Griffith, she also became a member of Sinn Fein. The egalitarian character of the Citizen Army was perhaps its principal attraction for the Countess who had a deep and genuine compassion for the poor.[36]

Simultaneous membership in the Citizen Army and the Volunteers was unthinkable to O'Casey who thought the latter, at least before that organization split into rival factions, to be the tool of Irish Parliamentary Party men who had little empathy for the Dublin workers. The Countess, O'Casey told his fellow council members, should be required to resign from one group or the other. While his hostility to the Volunteers was real, O'Casey almost certainly was looking for a pretext to oust the Countess, whom he personally resented, from the Citizen Army. O'Casey's recommenda-

---

[35]For an autobiographical account of O'Casey's tenure as Secretary to the council of the Irish Citizen Army, and of the reasons which compelled him to resign that organization, see P. O' Cathasaigh [Sean O'Casey], *The Story of the Irish Citizen Army* (Dublin, 1919).

[36]Three good biographies of the Countess are: Sean O'Faolain, *Constance Marciewicz* (London, 1934); Jacqueline Van Voris, *Constance de Markievicz* (Amherst, Massachusetts, 1967); and Anne Marreco, *The Rebel Countess* (London, 1967).

tion posed an embarrassment to the Army's council, for the Countess had donated food and had toiled in the soup kitchens during the lockout. It was her friend, Captain J. R. White, who had started the Citizen Army with fifty pounds of his own money. And it was the Countess who had sheltered James Larkin when the authorities were seeking his arrest during the Dublin strike agitation. When Larkin asked O'-Casey to apologize to the Countess, O'Casey resigned from the Citizen Army. After the outbreak of the war and Larkin's subsequent departure for America, Connolly became the major driving force behind both the Army and the Transport and General Workers' Union. Because of the collapse of international socialism, Connolly concluded that British rule in Ireland would have to be overthrown by an armed insurrection as the first step in the fulfillment of his own goals, and he was willing to work with nationalists toward that end. Countess Markievicz supported this view, but Sean O'Casey remained alienated and his constant squabbling with his comrades in the Irish Republican Brotherhood led to his resignation from that organization also.[37] O'Casey did not participate in the 1916 Rising and in his play, *The Plough and the Stars,* produced ten years after that event, he mocked the pretensions of both bourgeois and proletarian Irish separatists who took part in the Easter Rebellion.

THE RENAISSANCE OF THE I.R.B.

While the Irish Citizen Army and the Irish and National Volunteers were doubtlessly the more visible exponents of Irish separatism at the outset of the war in 1914, the Irish Republican Brotherhood was experiencing a renaissance

---

[37] In the judgment of one of her biographers, Countess Markievicz never really understood what James Connolly was seeking to accomplish. See O'Faolain, *Constance Marciewicz,* p. 207. For Sean O'Casey's rather sentimental reminiscences of this period, see Sean O'Casey, *Autobiographies,* 2 Vols. (London, 1963).

which was soon to make it the preeminent force in Irish nationalism. Committed to the forcible overthrow of British rule in Ireland, the I.R.B. had just barely survived several decades of eclipse during which the constitutional methods of the parliamentary nationalists had left the Fenian ranks isolated and depleted. The possibilities afforded by Britain's preoccupation with the war, together with the emergence of a new generation of talented leaders, accounted for the change in the I.R.B.'s fortunes.[38] Three young men who best represented the new leadership in this period of organizational transformation were: Denis McCullough, Bulmer Hobson, and Sean MacDermott.

DENIS McCULLOUGH

McCullough was born in Belfast in 1883. His father, the owner of a public house, was a Fenian who spoke reverently of that body as "the organization." But like so many of his contemporaries, he talked more of the real or imagined glories of the past than he did of the future. Young McCullough grew up with a very romanticized view of the I.R.B. and, upon being admitted to membership at the age of eighteen, he was disillusioned to find that secret, oath-bound organization subsisting on the dreams of old men. Denis McCullough soon recruited a number of young idealists who shared his impatience over the inactivity of the old guard in the Irish Republican Brotherhood. They established two new I.R.B. "Circles" in Belfast and insisted that members agree to be sober, disciplined, and active. Those who were not were soon purged, including McCullough's own father. The Supreme Council of the I.R.B. in Dublin, which was initiating similar reforms, named Denis McCullough director of the I.R.B. for Ulster in 1909 and in December 1915, he was elected presi-

---

[38]For an informative account by a contemporary, see Diarmuid Lynch, *The I.R.B. and the 1916 Rising*, edited by F. O'Donoghue (Cork, 1957).

dent of the Supreme Council with total authority over the I.R.B. in Ireland and Great Britain.[39]

BULMER HOBSON

Bulmer Hobson was recruited by McCullough in 1904 and rapidly became one of his most able lieutenants. Although the two men were born the same year and in the same city, Hobson was from an entirely different family background. His father was a Quaker in religion, a businessman by trade, and a Gladstonian home ruler in politics. At an early age Hobson joined the Gaelic League and the G.A.A. and worked to promote causes which were pronouncedly nationalist and nonsectarian. After his induction into the I.R.B., Hobson collaborated with McCullough in forming the militantly separatist Dungannon Club whose ultimate aim was to establish an Irish Ireland, discourage recruitment into the British Army, and promote enlistment into the I.R.B.

SEAN MACDERMOTT

Of all the eager young men who were attracted into the movement, Sean MacDermott was by far the most impressive. Born in 1884, MacDermott, the son of a small farmer in county Leitrim, had drifted from Ireland to Glasgow and then back to Belfast in search of gainful employment. He was an ardent nationalist who found an outlet for his restless energies first in the Dungannon Club and later, in 1906, in the I.R.B. MacDermott's demonstrable abilities prompted the Supreme Council to appoint him national organizer for

[39]F. X. Martin, "McCullough, Hobson and Republican Ulster," in F. X. Martin, ed., *Leaders and Men of the Easter Rising: Dublin 1916* (New York, 1967), pp. 97–98.

the I.R.B. at the end of 1908, a post he filled with remarkable success until the 1916 Rising.[40]

As a secret society, the I.R.B. was unwilling to move into the open until the right psychological moment. The censure of the Roman Catholic hierarchy and the popularity of constitutional nationalism in Ireland were formidable obstacles for the organization to surmount, but these did not prevent the I.R.B. from secretly and successfully infiltrating nearly every Irish separatist movement of consequence. At the beginning of the twentieth century, the I.R.B. had a tiny membership with active centers in the larger cities of Ireland and Britain, and close ties with the Clan-na-Gael in the United States. A new generation of dedicated young republicans entered the Gaelic League and the Gaelic Athletic Association and moved into responsible positions. They also controlled a number of the Dungannon Clubs and, after the latter merged with Arthur Griffith's Sinn Fein in 1907, men like Bulmer Hobson and Sean MacDermott quickly assumed influential roles in Griffith's organization.[41] Indeed, it was Hobson who, together with Countess Markievicz, founded the Fianna Eireann, the republican boy scouts. Although Hobson and the Countess undertook that effort independently of any instruction from the I.R.B., the Fianna produced a number of recruits who later served the republican cause.[42] Few in numbers but strong in conviction, the Irish Republicans were on the move and by 1914 they were advantageously positioned to determine the course of Irish nationalism—if the Irish Parliamentary Party stumbled in its own strategy.[43]

---

[40]Ibid., pp. 99–102.

[41]The I.R.B. members in Sinn Fein persuaded Griffith to drop Dual Monarchy as his organization's official political objective and, in 1917, a revised Sinn Fein constitution endorsed a Republic as the goal of Irish Nationalism.

[42]For further details respecting the training given these Irish youths, see Bulmer Hobson's recollections (1947), in F. X. Martin, ed., *The Irish Volunteers*, pp. 19–20.

[43]McCaffrey, *The Irish Question*, p. 143.

OTHER I.R.B. MEMBERS

There were others, of course, besides the above-noted triumverate of McCullough, Hobsen and MacDermott, who played an important part in priming the I.R.B. into a high state of preparedness. One such member was Thomas Clarke, an Irish nationalist who, in 1883 and at the age of 26, had been sentenced to life imprisonment by a British court for his part in a dynamiting campaign in England. After serving fifteen years of his sentence Clarke was released in poor health, and looking considerably older than a man of forty because of his brutalizing prison experience. He next traveled to America where he worked closely with John Devoy and the Clan-na-Gael. Following Clarke's return to Ireland in 1907, he was elected to the Supreme Council of the I.R.B. and served as a vital link between that body and the Clan in America.[44]

Tom Clarke was an uncompromising advocate of an independent and sovereign Irish republic, and his militancy was shared by P. S. O'Hegarty, a brilliant journalist and contemporary historian who, together with Bulmer Hobson, wrote for the I.R.B.'s official paper, *Irish Freedom,* which first appeared in 1910.[45] Patrick McCartan, an Ulster nationalist who was a physician by profession, served as that newspaper's nominal editor and in 1914 numbered among the activists on the I.R.B. Supreme Council.[46] Another activist was Major John MacBride, who had fought for the Boers in the South African War where, in the Transvaal, he had become close friends with an Irish journalist named Arthur Griffith. MacBride, who had married the nationalist-minded

---

[44]Clarke and Devoy were in constant communication after Clarke's return to Ireland in 1907. See Florence O'Donoghue, "Ceannt, Devoy, O'Rahilly, and the Military Plan," in F. X. Martin, ed., *Leaders and Men of the Easter Rising,* p. 195.

[45]See P. S. O'Hegarty, *The Victory of Sinn Fein* (Dublin, 1924); and *A History of Ireland Under the Union, 1801–1922* (London, 1952).

[46]The *Irish Freedom* newspaper was suppressed by the British Government in 1914.

actress Maud Gonne (See Chapter 2),[47] complained in a letter
to John Devoy that the older I.R.B. men were "sitting on
their back sides and criticizing and abusing one another."[48]
Gradually the older members were eased out; P. T. Daly was
expelled from the Supreme Council in 1910, and Fred Allen
resigned two years later. Despite the influx of new blood, the
total membership of the I.R.B. in 1912 was approximately
2,000 and, aside from the modest subscriptions afforded by
these men, the organization's only other outside support was
the three hundred pounds which it received as an annual
subsidy from the Clan-na-Gael.[49] All the dedication and discipline imaginable would have little availed the I.R.B. had it
not been for the welcome but unexpected change in the
mood of nationalist Ireland. With the Ulster Unionist signing
of the Solemn League and Covenant in 1912, and the launching of the Ulster Volunteers, the Irish struggle was unmistakably moving out of the sphere of parliamentary legislation
and into the sphere of physical force. Moderate nationalists
had no choice but to support the creation of a rival para-
military force, the Irish Volunteers, and the I.R.B. began
almost immediately to exploit that new force for its own
ends.

MacNEILL SPARKS A NEW I.R.B. MILITANCY

The spark which served to ignite a new militancy in the
hitherto moderate ranks of Irish nationalists was an article by

[47]Writing for William Rooney's and Arthur Griffith's *United Irishman,* on
the occasion of a royal visit to Dublin in 1900, Maud Gonne described Queen
Victoria as the "Famine Queen." *United Irishman,* April 7, 1900. McBride's
marriage to the actress earned him the enmity of W. B. Yeats that lasted
until MacBride's execution before a firing squad. Thereafter, Yeats revered
rather than maligned this Irish "martyr."
[48]W. O'Brien and D. Ryan, eds., *Devoy's Post Bag,* Vol. 2 (Dublin, 1953),
p. 347.
[49]B. Hobson, *Ireland Yesterday and Tomorrow* (Tralee, 1968), p. 104. This
was a far cry from the 1860s when the numerical strength of the Fenians
was estimated to be 80,000 members. See Kevin B. Nowlan, "Tom Clarke,
MacDermott, and the I.R.B.," in F. X. Martin, ed., *Leaders and Men of the
Easter Rising,* p. 109.

Eoin MacNeill entitled "The North Began." Writing in the November 1, 1913 issue of the Gaelic League publication,[50] MacNeill, who had been active in the Irish language movement but had been a moderate home ruler in politics, made a strident appeal for nationalist action. The Protestant movement in the north was, he reasoned, actually a home rule movement since the Ulster Volunteers had demonstrated a determination to be masters of their own fate no matter what the British parliament decided. Indeed, the Ulster Volunteers recalled for MacNeill the heroic precedent of the Volunteers of the 1780s, and he further noted how the disbandment of that earlier body had led ultimately to the loss of Ireland's own parliament. The historical parallel may have been misplaced, but insofar as it was advanced by a man who held the chair of Early Irish History at University College, Dublin, it was excellent and persuasive propaganda. Sir Edward Carson, claimed MacNeill, had shown the way by appealing to force. MacNeill's response was to summon Irish Volunteers in a defense of the constitution and to suppress the "rebellious attitudes" of Ulster Orangemen and British Tories.[51]

Bulmer Hobson, who had succeeded Patrick McCartan as editor of the I.R.B. publication *Irish Freedom*, read MacNeill's "The North Began" in the Gaelic League's weekly and immediately contacted its managing director, Michael Joseph Rahilly. Rahilly, or The O'Rahilly as he preferred to be called, in order to attract a wider readership had solicited MacNeill to write an article on a subject which would transcend the otherwise narrow focus of the Gaelic League publi-

---

[50]*An Claidheamh Soluis* was the League's weekly publication which was operating at this time under the managing directorship of Michael Joseph Rahilly.

[51]T. Desmond Williams, "Eoin MacNeill and the Irish Volunteers," in F. X. Martin, ed., *Leaders and Men of the Easter Rising*, pp. 138–139. In fact, "MacNeill hoped to emulate the Volunteers of 1782 who without using force had by merely standing firm achieved their objectives of legislative independence." Donal McCartney "MacNeill and Irish-Ireland," in F. X. Martin and F. J. Byrne, eds., *The Scholar Revolutionary* (Shannon, 1973), p. 95.

cation.[52] The O'Rahilly, who was not a member of the I.R.B., was surprised but pleased by the interest which MacNeill's article generated. After Hobson met with The O'Rahilly, the two men asked MacNeill if he would head a committee to initiate and organize the very Volunteer organization which MacNeill had proposed. MacNeill agreed, and invitations were extended to a handful of nationalists, chosen principally by Hobson and The O'Rahilly, to a meeting at a Dublin hotel on November 11, 1913. Of the ten who were present for that initial gathering, four were members of the I.R.B. But the physical force men kept a low profile, and even Hobson did not attend that meeting for fear of deterring the moderate separatists whose support would be essential to the new organization.[53]

Two weeks later, on November 25, a huge public rally was held at the Rotunda Rink in Dublin to launch the new movement. A committee of thirty, more than a third of whom were members of the I.R.B., coordinated what proved to be an enormously successful meeting despite the confusion caused by Jim Larkin's supporters, who were demonstrating in the streets as part of their bitter struggle with the Dublin employers. Over 3,000 enthusiastic recruits were enrolled after MacNeill delivered an eloquent address in which he expanded on the points he had made in "The North Began." MacNeill reassured moderate nationalists by affirming that the purpose of the Irish Volunteers would be defensive and protective, and that that body would not contemplate either aggression or domination.[54]

The Gaelic title of the Volunteers was *Oglaigh na h-Eireann,* Army of Ireland, and the uniform cap badge was to bear the letters F F, standing for Fianna Fail, a mythical

---

[52]The O'Rahilly was born in 1875 to a prosperous Kerry family. He was first attracted to Irish separatism by Arthur Griffith's Sinn Fein organization. For further background on his life and career, see Marcus Bourke, *The O'Rahilly* (Tralee, 1967).

[53]For the names of those who did attend, see F. X. Martin, ed., *The Irish Volunteers,* pp. 95–96.

[54]For the text of MacNeill's remarks, see Ibid., pp. 98–101.

warrior band of Celtic legend. Under the governance of the Provisional Committee, with MacNeill as chairman, The O'-Rahilly as Treasurer, and Bulmer Hobson as Secretary, the Irish Volunteers increased rapidly in number until there were some 75,000 members by May 1914, and future recruitment would more than double that figure. Despite the existence of the loudly defiant Ulster Volunteers and the compartively moderate tone of the Irish Volunteers, however, the leadership of the Irish Parliamentary Party was clearly uneasy over the phenomenal development of a nationalist movement which the party did not control.[55]

ULSTER GUN-RUNNING

With the appearance of yet another private army on the scene in Ireland, the prospect of civil war was stronger than ever. But although the formation of the Irish Volunteer movement horrified John Redmond, particularly since it included known I.R.B. members, he felt unable to utter any public discouragement to the Nationalists in light of the military preparations in Ulster.[56] The British Government was also alarmed by these developments and on December 4, 1913, issued a proclamation prohibiting the import of arms into Ireland. On the night of April 24–25, 1914, the Ulster Volunteers demonstrated that the British proclamation, enforced by lethargic authorities, posed no hindrance to a determined and disciplined organization. Major Fred Crawford and his Unionist comrades not only succeeded in smuggling a substantial amount of arms and ammunition into Ulster (see Chapter 3), but they also escaped the legal consequences of

---

[55]Irish Parliamentary Party leaders John Redmond, John Dillon and Joseph Devlin were displeased by the formation of the Irish Volunteers. See John J. Horgan, *Parnell to Pearse* (Dublin, 1949), p. 229. See also F. S. L. Lyons, *John Dillon: A Biography* (London, 1968), p. 350.
[56]Gwynn, *The Life of John Redmond,* p. 245.

that undertaking because the London Government dared not touch them. The Chief Secretary for Ireland, Augustine Birrell, and the Lord Lieutenant, Lord Aberdeen, recommended to the British Cabinet the arrest of known or suspected ringleaders involved in the gun-running. While the evidence against them was not conclusive, Birrell and Aberdeen were of the opinion that London should not appear indifferent to those who had flaunted the law with impunity. The Cabinet, however, instructed Birrell to do nothing. King George, Prime Minister Asquith, and even Irish party leader John Redmond, all shared the opinion that prosecutions would only aggravate the situation in Ulster. In a letter to Asquith, in which he reported the view of a senior army staff officer who had described the morale of the army in Ireland as gloomy, Birrell noted that Lord and Lady Aberdeen were giving a dance that night and that, to him, everything seemed like an early chapter in Thomas Carlyle's *French Revolution.* [57]

ROGER CASEMENT

What the Irish Volunteers required, if they also were to procure arms, was money.[58] Surprisingly, it was not the I.R.B.-related Clan-na-Gael in America which ultimately provided the funds for weapons purchases at this time, but rather English Liberals and home rule sympathizers. Alice Stopford Green headed a small London committee which, alarmed by the government's inaction toward the Ulster Volunteers and sympathetic to the moderate Irish nationalists, quickly raised the sum of 1500 pounds to buy guns for the Irish Volunteers. It was another instance of people with an Anglo-Irish background aiding the nationalist cause. Mrs. Green, formerly of county Meath, was the daughter of a Church of

---

[57]Leon O Broin, *The Chief Secretary* (London, 1969), pp. 95–97.

[58]The O'Rahilly, in a letter to John Devoy in America, made clear that lack of money, and not the government proclamation, was the organization's major problem. See W. O'Brien and D. Ryan, eds., *Devoy's Post Bag,* Vol. 2, p. 426.

Ireland Archdeacon and the widow of the historian J. R. Green.[59] After his death, she had researched the history of her native people and the separatist cause to which her book, published in 1908 and entitled *The Making of Ireland and its Undoing*, was clearly sympathetic.[60] The man who persuaded her to undertake the fund raising was Roger Casement, who was also Anglo-Irish. Casement was born near Dublin in 1864 but, after being orphaned at an early age, he was reared in the Protestant stronghold of county Antrim. He entered the British Foreign Service in 1892 and won an international reputation for his work in exposing the exploitations of natives by European employers in the Congo and in South America. Mrs. Green, a patron of humanitarian movements, had been corresponding with Casement since 1904 when he had first written her on behalf of the Congo Reform Association. Casement was later knighted for his work and in 1913 had retired from government service. He had, however, become deeply involved in Irish affairs. Casement had known Bulmer Hobson since 1904 and was an admirer of Griffith's Sinn Fein. By the end of 1913, he was a member of the Provisional Committee of the Irish Volunteers, and it was in that capacity, in the following spring, that he solicited Mrs. Green's financial assistance for the Volunteer organization.[61]

---

[59]According to one contemporary, Mrs. J. R. Green and other Ulster Protestants were anxious to take some action which would dispute Sir Edward Carson's pretense that he spoke for all Ulster Protestants. See James R. White, *Misfit: An Autobiography* (London, 1930). Correspondingly, Mrs. Green was anxious that MacNeill not be exploited by the extremists in the Irish Volunteers. See R. B. McDowell, *Alice Stopford Green: A Passionate Historian* (Dublin, 1967), pp. 100–101.

[60]For another of her works on the character of the historically distinctive Irish identity, see A. S. Green, *Irish Nationality* (London, 1912).

[61]Other supporters of the fund-raising included Mary Spring Rice, daughter of Lord Monteagle and cousin to Sir Cecil Spring Rice, the British Ambassador to the United States; Conor O'Brien, who was also a cousin of Mary Spring Rice and a grandson of the Smith O'Brien of 1848 fame; Erskine Childers, an Englishman born in Ireland, and his American wife, Mary; and Darrell Figgis, a literary journalist who lived in London. All were admirers of Sinn Fein and shared the belief that home rulers should be in a position to defend their constitutional rights.

Early in May 1914, Casement had gone to London with Eoin MacNeill to meet with John Redmond and to discuss the latter's participation in the Volunteer movement. To their dismay, Casement and MacNeill found Redmond determined to acquire complete control over the organization, and suspicious of some of its Provisional Committee members, most notably Patrick Pearse.[62] Meeting the next afternoon at Mrs. Green's Westminster home, Casement and MacNeill conferred with Darrell Figgis, an Anglo-Irish journalist with a good knowledge of the Continent. It was agreed that the best way to counter Redmond's otherwise inevitable dominance of the Volunteer movement lay in the independent securing of a supply of desperately needed weapons. At the time, the Irish Volunteers were drilling with wooden rifles and broom handles. Darrell Figgis volunteered to go to Europe and purchase what guns and ammunition he could with the money which had been raised by Mrs. Green's committee. Since, however, the whole venture was illegal, plans were conducted in strictest secrecy. Among the members of the Volunteer Provisional Committee, only Casement, MacNeill, Hobson and The O'Rahilly knew what was contemplated; and in London, only those on a need-to-know basis were apprised. Besides Mrs. Green and Darrell Figgis, this included Erskine Childers who offered his yacht, the *Asgard*, for the arms shipment.[63]

ERSKINE CHILDERS

Erskine Childers was an English Liberal who had been born in Ireland, was educated at Cambridge University, and had worked for fifteen years as a clerk in the House of Commons. He was an accomplished yachtsman and had served in the British Army during the Boer War. Doubtlessly, the intrique of arms smuggling appealed to him for, as early as 1903, he

---

[62]Darrell Figgis, *Recollections of the Irish War* (London, 1927), p. 15.
[63]F. X. Martin, ed., *The Howth Gun-Running, 1914* (Dublin, 1964), p. 38.

had spent a great deal of time sailing along the German North Sea coastline while gathering material for his famous espionage novel, *The Riddle of the Sands.* But he did regard his family's house in county Wicklow as home, and his dedication to the principle of self-government for Ireland was indeed genuine even though the purist, Arthur Griffith, would later revile him as "that Englishman."[64] Despite Griffith's bitter comment, the fact remains that it was members of the English gentry and the Anglo-Irish, including three women, who constituted the two crews of the yachts employed in the Irish Volunteers' gun-running. According to plan, Figgis and Childers purchased 1500 Mauser rifles and 45,000 rounds of ammunition from a firm in Hamburg and the arms were then transported by tug to two waiting yachts in the North Sea. One landed safely at Kilcoole in county Wicklow while the other, as part of a scheme almost flawlessly arranged by Bulmer Hobson, made a daring daylight landing on July 26 at Howth Harbor on the north side of Dublin Bay. The latter vessel was Childers' yacht, the *Asgard,* and it carried the bulk of the weapons which were then distributed to a thousand Volunteers gathered at the dock. The unloading was accomplished in a half-hour. The coast guards had spotted the landing but, being hopelessly outnumbered, had not interfered.[65]

IRISH VOLUNTEER GUN-RUNNING

As the Volunteers triumphantly marched away with their arms, they were suddenly confronted and halted by a body

[64]Erskine Childers was a committed home ruler at least as early as 1908. Moreover, he later served the Irish nationalist cause with valor during the Anglo-Irish War of 1919–21, and died in defense of his beliefs during the Irish Civil War. His son, Erskine Childers, was President of the Irish Republic from June 1973 to his death in November 1974.

[65]For excerpts from the accounts by contemporaries, and further details on the specifics of the gun-running, see F. X. Martin, ed., *The Howth Gun-Running, 1914.*

of police reinforced by a military detachment of the King's Own Scottish Borderers. While the authorities argued with the Volunteers' leaders, the rank and file slipped away with their weapons and escaped seizure. This whole episode might have proven a victory for the moderate Irish nationalists, had it not been for the tragedy at Bachelor's Walk later that same afternoon (See Chapter 3). But despite the fact that a government commission conducted an immediate inquiry and ultimately censured the troops involved for lack of control and discipline,[66] the contrast between the Ulster Volunteer's experience at Larne and that of the "massacre" at Bachelor's Walk was loudly trumpeted by militant Irish separatists. Constitutional nationalists had good reason for concern because the mood of the country was becoming ugly.

REDMOND AND THE IRISH VOLUNTEERS

Irish Parliamentary Party leaders John Redmond, John Dillon, and Joseph Devlin had begun in early May to prod Eoin MacNeill into amending the composition of the Volunteers' Provisional Committee in their favor. They felt that with the home rule campaign approaching its climax, and with the likelihood that the bill would not reach the statute-book without the special problem of Ulster being dealt with separately, it was imperative that the Nationalist party leader have behind him the same kind of disciplined force that Carson had at his disposal. Redmond rejected a compromise suggestion for an elected executive and, taking the Volunteer leadership entirely by surprise, published an ultimatum in the Irish press on June 9, 1914. In it he demanded that twenty-five persons nominated by his party should be added to the Volunteers' Provisional Committee which, of course,

---

[66]*Report of the Royal Commission on the circumstances connected with the landing of arms at Howth on 26th July 1914*, Parliamentary Papers, 1914–16, Vol. 24, pp. 805–892.

assured him virtual control. The Volunteer leaders were faced with a painful choice. They could spurn Redmond, who still possessed the allegiance of the vast majority of nationalists and who could wreck the Volunteer organization if he called upon his followers to boycott it, or they could submit to his demand and alienate the militant nationalists at the very moment when, unknown to them, weapons were enroute by sea and unanimity was more important than ever.[67]

HOBSON'S GUN-RUNNING SCHEME

Eoin MacNeill, who was still a moderate nationalist, disliked Redmond's conditions, but took the pragmatic view that the organization's compliance was necessary if a divisive, and possibly ruinous, split was to be avoided. The Provisional Committee accepted this decision, not without misgivings, after Roger Casement and Bulmer Hobson supported it.[68] Hobson was particularly emphatic that the unenviable choice be made since he was fearful of anything that might imperil his carefully prepared gun-running scheme which was then already in progress. His advocacy involved him in bitter recriminations with his I.R.B. colleagues. Tom Clarke accused him of being in the pay of Dublin Castle and never spoke to him again. And his old friend Sean MacDermott was also permanently alienated. Even John Devoy, in America, dismissed Hobson as a correspondent for the Clan-na-Gael newspaper, the *Gaelic American.*[69] Although he remained a

---

[67]Lyons, *Ireland Since the Famine,* pp. 325–326; for the text of Redmond's June 9 ultimatum, see Gwynn, *The Life of John Redmond,* pp. 317–318.

[68]Redmond received letters from Roger Casement welcoming the Irish party leader's participation in the Volunteers and urging him to provide vigorous leadership. Redmond, however, distrusted Casement as he did most newcomers in Irish politics. See Gwynn, *The Life of John Redmond,* p. 318.

[69]W. O'Brien and D. Ryan, eds., *Devoy's Post Bag,* Vol. 2, p. 456.

member of the I.R.B., he resigned from the Supreme Council and ceased to edit *Irish Freedom.*[70] Eventually, thanks to Casement's intervention on his behalf, Devoy reappointed him as a correspondent, and Hobson returned to the inner circles of the I.R.B., only to clash once again with his colleagues in a crisis of far greater consequence two years later. Meanwhile, the guns were successfully landed at Howth and, though they remained inwardly divided, the Volunteers had avoided, for the moment, the humiliation of a public split. Membership even soared to an unprecedented 180,000 by September 1914.[71]

REDMOND SPLITS THE IRISH VOLUNTEERS

Redmond was delighted with his triumph and expected the remaining militant nationalists on the Provisional Committee to resign in short time. As he confided to an American correpondent, he preferred to await that eventuality rather than to expel them from the body since the latter course would inevitably lead to the establishment of a counter-organization which, no matter how small or unrepresentative, would harm the cause of Irish nationalism at that moment.[72] When, however, on September 20, 1914, only seven weeks after Britain had declared war against Germany, Redmond called on the Volunteers to fight not just for Ireland, but for the empire too, he precipitated the very schism which he had once attempted to avoid.

As wa.: noted earlier, the effect of Redmond's declaration

---

[70]F. X. Martin, ed., *The Irish Volunteers*, pp. 43–53; Hobson, *Ireland Yesterday and Tomorrow*, pp. 48–56.

[71]After Redmond took charge of the Irish Volunteers in July 1914, enlistments increased to over 15,000 a week and the United Irish League of America promised the Irish party leader that the Volunteers would receive all the money required to defend the home rule cause. See McCaffrey, *The Irish Question*, p. 157.

[72]O Broin, *The Chief Secretary*, p. 99.

was to split the Volunteers in two. About 170,000 stayed with Redmond to form the Irish National Volunteers, or simply National Volunteers, which made the distinction clearer; and approximately 11,000 declared their allegiance for MacNeill and retained the name Irish Volunteers although, because they included the more extreme section of the nationalist movement, they were popularly dubbed the "Sinn Fein" Volunteers.[73]

While John Redmond and the National Volunteers began preparations to promote recruitment for the British army, the Irish Volunteers substituted a fifty member General Council for the now defunct Provisional Committee. The Council, which included members from each of the counties throughout Ireland, in turn elected a nine member Central Executive. Both the Executive and the General Council, unknown to MacNeill, contained a majority of I.R.B. members.[74] To all appearances, the split in the Volunteers, far from weakening Redmond and the bulk of the Volunteer body, had rendered them greater harmony and solidarity than ever. MacNeill's splinter organization, which became involved in an embarrassing altercation with James Larkin and members of the Citizen Army at an October 11 ceremony commemorating the twenty-third anniversary of Parnell's death, appeared almost pathetic. What was not apparent in those autumn weeks, however, was that the sands of time were running swiftly through the hourglass of constitutional nationalism. The winds of a world war were about to scatter the flickering embers of the physical force tradition until its raging flames would consume the Irish separatist movement.

---

[73]Some estimate the number of National Volunteers to have been close to 188,000, with the Irish Volunteers numbering 13,500. For further comment, see Breandan MacGiolla Choille, ed., *Intelligence Notes, 1913–16* (Dublin, 1966), p. 175.

[74]F. X. Martin, ed., "Eoin MacNeill on the 1916 Rising," *Irish Historical Studies,* 12 (March, 1961), p. 228.

Chapter 5

The Ascendancy of Revolutionary Separatism in Ireland (1914–1916)

World War I may have spared Britain from civil strife, and perhaps civil war, over the Irish home rule issue, but the war also complicated and compounded Anglo-Irish differences. John Redmond, chairman of the Irish Parliamentary Party, pledged Nationalist Ireland to the defense of the British Empire because he believed such a commitment would allay the apprehensions of those in the United Kingdom who were distrustful of home rule, and would prove to the world Ireland's allegiance to the principles of freedom and her worthiness for self-government. Meanwhile, Ulster Unionist leader Sir Edward Carson spoke and acted in a manner entirely calculated to destroy the effort of Redmond's appeal for cooperation among Irishmen and for a cessation of domestic strife. "Ulster Day" was celebrated with much fanfare on September 28, 1914, and both Carson and Bonar Law assured Unionist audiences that the wartime emergency and the need for Ulster Volunteer recruits in the British Army would in no way weaken the Irish Protestants' resolve or ability to resist home rule.[1] Equally intransigent were the Irish Volunteers who had broken with Redmond over the issue of Irish Nationalist support for the war and, under the leadership of Eoin MacNeill, loudly opposed recruitment while demanding immediate implementation of the home rule bill. And within that splinter group was the secret I.R.B. organization which welcomed the war on the principle of "England's danger, Ireland's opportunity."[2]

IRELAND AND THE WAR EFFORT

Indeed, in her hour of danger, England missed or mismanaged a splendid opportunity both to promote the war effort and to foster goodwill among the nationalist population in Ireland. During the early weeks of the war, Irish Parliamentary Party leaders John Redmond and John Dillon had sought to advise the British Cabinet on the way in which recruitment in Ireland could be most effectively accomplished. They implored the government to consider the creation of Irish brigades, complete with their own uniforms and officered by leaders chosen from the National Volunteers. Noting that similar concessions had been accorded to Australia and New Zealand, where they had proven hugely popular, the Irish leaders reminded the British ministers that the need for special symbols was even more imperative in Ireland where old prejudices against the British Army had to be overcome.[3] But the War Office, under Lord Kitchener, refused to consider these proposals. Secretary of State for War Kitchener, like so many other high-ranking soldiers in the British Army, was an Irishman by birth who nonetheless distrusted Irish

---

[1]Denis Gwynn, *The Life of John Redmond* (London, 1932), pp. 389–395.
[2]Joseph Lee, *The Modernisation of Irish Society, 1848–1918* (Dublin, 1973), p. 154.
[3]Gwynn, *The Life of John Redmond*, p. 388–389.

nationalism and typified the military mentality that had earlier supported Ulster and the Curragh officers.[4] Adding insult to injury, Kitchener, moreover, authorized the formation of a special division from the ranks of the Ulster Volunteers, the 36th, with its own officers and its own emblem, the Red Hand of Ulster.[5]

British Prime Minister Herbert Asquith was appreciative of Redmond's support in the war effort, and he was anxious to accommodate the Irish party leader's desire to placate nationalist opinion. Asquith agreed, therefore, to visit Dublin on September 26 to help celebrate the passing of the home rule act. After five hundred National Volunteers marched through the streets of Dublin with rifles and bayonets, the Prime Minister and the Irish Parliamentary Party chairman addressed a capacity audience of several thousand in the Round Room of the Mansion House. John Redmond was cheered when he declared that in proportion to population Ireland had a larger quota serving in the front lines than had any other part of the United Kingdom. And John Dillon was greeted with applause when he affirmed that the war would prove to the people of Britain and of Britain's Empire that the friendship of Ireland was "worth the price [of granting home rule]."[6] The most enthusiastic response, however, was generated by Prime Minister Asquith who promised that the same conditions which had enabled Carson to raise the Ulster Division would be granted to the new Irish formations. A few days later, on September 30, Asquith wrote Redmond: "I have spoken to Lord Kitchener on the subject of your letter, and he will have the announcement made that the War Office has sanctioned the formation of an Irish Army Corps."[7]

That announcement was never made and the Prime Minis-

---

[4]Giovanni Costigan, *A History of Modern Ireland* (New York, 1970), p. 305.

[5]Lord Kitchener even allowed these troops the further concession of receiving their initial military training at camps located in Ulster.

[6]For a full account of the parade, the speeches, and the reaction of the Dublin audience to this recruiting rally, see *Freeman's Journal*, September 26, 1914.

[7]Gwynn, *The Life of John Redmond*, p. 394.

ter, who did in fact remind Kitchener of this matter on at least one other occasion, was soon preoccupied with the many urgent demands of the war. Redmond conducted his own unrelenting campaign of prodding British Army authorities into permitting Irish nationalist brigades the use of badges and emblems, such as a gold harp on a green field, which would be distinctively their own. Thanks to Redmond's pressure, there was formed, in addition to the 10th Irish Division stationed at the Curragh, a third Irish Division (the 16th) with headquarters in Tipperary and Cork. By November, 1914, the Ulster Division was already up to strength, and nothing but the hostility of Kitchener and his friends at the War Office stood in the way of the immediate combination of the three divisions into an Irish Army Corps. Meanwhile, General Sir Lawrence Parsons, a Unionist Irishman who commanded the newest Irish Division, the 16th, authorized the adoption of an Irish insignia. But he did so only after Lord Kitchener, who had himself relented on the issue in the hope of bolstering recruitment in Ireland, gave the order that it be done. This did not, however, prevent Parsons from refusing John Redmond's son a commission,[8] or from transferring Irish units to English, Scottish and Welsh regiments in direct defiance of what Asquith had previously promised Redmond. Nor did it enhance the Irish Parliamentary Party's recruiting efforts when not a single Catholic was admitted to the Ulster Division in those early months of the war, while qualified Catholic Nationalists were routinely denied commissions in the two other Irish divisions whose senior officers were almost exclusively Protestants.[9]

---

[8] Young Redmond was a barrister and had been, since 1910, an M.P. for a Nationalist constituency in county Tyrone. He gained a commission with the Dublin Fusiliers of the 10th Division at the Curragh and in 1917, while fighting in France with the Irish Guards, he won the D.S.O. for his conduct in battle.

[9] General Parsons even denied Redmond's request to give Gavan Duffy a commission. Duffy had returned to Ireland from Australia in order to join the new Irish Brigade. He was the grandson of Sir Charles Gavan Duffy, who had been the ablest figure in the Young Ireland movement of the 1840s. An overseas Irishman with a famous name, Gavan Duffy was an ideal person for Redmond to present at recruiting meetings as evidence of the enthusiasm which Irishmen abroad and in the dominions had for the war.

In spite of such provocations, Redmond and most of Nationalist Ireland continued to give their unstinted support to the war effort. By the autumn of 1915, there were 132,454 Irishmen serving in the British Army, 79,511 of whom were Catholics and 52,943 of whom were Protestants. Irishmen won seventeen Victoria Crosses during the first thirteen months of the war, and the mounting casualty lists teemed with the names of great Irish regiments: Royal Irish Fusiliers, Munster Fusiliers, Dublin Fusiliers, Inniskilling Fusiliers, Royal Irish Rifles, the Leinster Regiment, the Irish Guards, and the Connaught Rangers. At Gallipoli, in what was one of the most costly and disastrous Allied campaigns, the War Office was typically reluctant to identify the 10th Division as an Irish unit despite the fact that it had distinguished itself with great gallantry.[10]

There were two principal reasons why, with few exceptions, Irish public opinion rallied to the aid of Britain in the early part of the war. First, there was the feeling that with the passing of the home rule act the Liberal Government had kept its pledge to Nationalist Ireland; although the statute had been accompanied by a second one, postponing the act until the end of the war, nearly everyone believed the war would be terminated soon. Secondly, there was the inspiration of Belgium and its heroic primate, Cardinal Mercier, who had defied the Germans. Southern Irishmen, or at least Catholic Nationalists, were understandably sympathetic to the plight of a small Catholic nation which had been attacked by the strongest Protestant power in Europe. Moreover, it cannot be denied that rural Ireland's sudden prosperity, which produced demands for Irish dairy products in the English market, contributed to a more tolerant view of the war on the part of many Irishmen.[11]

---

[10]Robert Kee, *The Green Flag* (London, 1972), p. 525.

[11]Costigan, *Modern Ireland*, p. 304. Police reports sent to Dublin Castle during this period described the sudden rural prosperity, owing to higher prices and record sales, which extended from Tyrone and Cavan in the north, to Wexford and Cork in the south. See Breandan MacGiolla Choille, ed., *Intelligence Notes, 1913–1916* (Dublin, 1966), pp. 201–211.

IRELAND'S GROWING DISAFFECTION WITH THE WAR

But these responses were quite temporary. As the casualty lists mounted the new sentiment of the country may have been best expressed by the reported response of one young Irishman to a female recruiter who called at his home: "Enlist? Is ut me enlist? An' a war going on!"[12] Indeed, the war was being waged for a longer duration, and at a more frightening cost to human life, than had been generally expected. The unrealistically optimistic expectations concerning the war's end which were held by many, both in Britain and in Ireland, are reflected in the evolution of the home rule act. In September 1914, the home rule act had been suspended for a period of twelve months or in the event of continued hostilities, for a further period to be fixed by the king in Council but in no case lasting longer than the end of the war. When in September 1915, this initial twelve month time period did expire, the suspension of home rule was continued only for another six months, or until the end of the war if that were to come sooner.[13]

It was only natural that the early enthusiasm which the recruiting efforts had generated would begin to wane once the attrition of the war began to take its toll. The insensitive treatment accorded the Irish by Kitchener and the War Office also had its effect in diminishing the number of National Volunteers who might otherwise have joined the British Army. Even the passage of the suspended home rule act had left, in the vague language of an amending bill, the Ulster problem unresolved, and some Irishmen who earlier had been concerned for Belgium's independence began now to contemplate their own liberties. More and more there developed among the population a sense of detachment

---

[12]Edgar Holt, *Protest in Arms: The Irish Troubles, 1916–1923* (London, 1960), p. 68.
[13]Kee, *The Green Flag*, p. 523.

from the war, a feeling that the conflict, however good for business, was not truly Ireland's affair.[14]

This, of course, was precisely what the militant Irish separatists had been arguing since the beginning. From the earliest weeks of the war, Irish Volunteers and the Citizen Army had drilled in the countryside, held public reviews, and conducted anti-British demonstrations in the towns and cities. Republicans and Sinn Feiners organized antirecruiting campaigns, and the separatist press emphasized the need for neutrality in the conflict between the Allies and the Central Powers. British authorities, anxious to avoid violent incidents like Bachelor's Walk, permitted the drilling and parading, but occasionally jailed or deported republicans and Sinn Feiners for "seditious activities." Three of the more extreme nationalist newspapers were suppressed before Christmas 1914, but soon reappeared under new names.[15] Nearly everyone in Britain and Ireland underestimated the potential capabilities of the tiny minority of determined dissenters who comprised the ranks of the militant separatists.

A controversy between British Government ministers over the shortage of shells and munitions, and a disagreement over tactics between the First Sea Lord and his superior in the British Cabinet, prompted Prime Minister Asquith, in May 1915, to form a coalition government in the hope of avoiding any further ruptures. On May 18, Asquith offered Redmond an unspecified Cabinet post and informed the Irish Parliamentary Party chairman that the opposition forces in the House of Commons were demanding that Sir

---

[14]Another notable fact was the change in attitude of the ever influential Roman Catholic hierarchy. "Whatever enthusiasm the clergy may have had for the war effort at the outset was largely dissipated before the end of 1915." David W. Miller, *Church, State and Nation in Ireland, 1898–1921* (Dublin, 1973), p. 312.

[15]Lawrence J. McCaffrey, *The Irish Question 1800–1922* (Lexington, Kentucky, 1968), p. 164. After the suppression of Connolly's *Irish Worker*, he published the *Worker's Republic*. Griffith's *Sinn Fein* was succeeded by *Scissors and Paste*; and *Nationality* was substituted for *Irish Freedom* when that I.R.B. publication was banned. See Holt, *Protest in Arms*, p. 69.

Edward Carson should also join the coalition ministry. Redmond declined, explaining that his position with Irish Nationalists would be hopelessly compromised in accepting such an appointment. He further warned the Prime Minister that the inclusion of Carson in the coalition government could only have the most undesirable consequences in Ireland. Once more, the British Government manifested its capacity for insensitivity, if not indifference, to the plight of Irish home rule advocates who had demonstrated their own loyalty to the empire since the outset of the war. Asquith not only selected Carson, but also filled half of his reconstructed Cabinet with Unionist politicians whose leaders had pledged themselves unconditionally to the repeal of the home rule act.[16] In a letter to John Redmond on June 3, 1915, Bishop Michael Fogarty of Killaloe wrote prophetically, if perhaps somewhat prematurely, "home rule is dead and buried and Ireland is without a national Party. . . ."[17]

Antiwar sentiment in Ireland, with its corollary anti-British overtones, did not, however, reach a significant level until the end of 1915. The Unionists, north and south, were not the only ones who regarded the Sinn Fein and republican opposition to recruitment as disloyal. There were more than 100,-000 Irishmen on active service by this date, two-thirds of whom had joined the British Army since August 1914, and their families and friends naturally supported these soldiers, if not always the Allied or empire interests for which they were fighting. Moreover, the separation allowances and other remittances received by the tens of thousands of Irish families with men in service were a welcome influx to the country's economy.

---

[16]For the Redmond-Asquith correspondence, see Gwynn, *John Redmond*, pp. 423–432. Some of Asquith's new Cabinet appointees included Andrew Bonar Law as Colonial Secretary and Sir Edward Carson as Attorney General. Asquith's only noteworthy concession to Redmond was his withdrawal of Unionist James Campbell's name from consideration for the post of Lord Chancellor of Ireland. See Leon O Broin, *The Chief Secretary* (London, 1969), pp. 144–145.

[17]Miller, *Church, State and Nation in Ireland*, p. 315.

The initial enthusiasm in Ireland for the war was doubt-lessly diminished by Asquith's Cabinet appointments of Unionists who, before the European conflict, had threatened to plunge the kingdom into civil war rather than accede to an act of Parliament. But it was the mounting casualty lists in the wake of the disastrous Gallipoli campaign, and the bloodbaths at Neuve, Chapelle, and Loos on the Western Front, which were most responsible for the growing sense of revulsion toward the war and for the ascendancy of neutralist sympathies. Republicans and Sinn Feiners, who were re-solved to establish Irish independence by physical force, were emboldened by this dramatic shift in sentiment, even though they themselves were divided over both the timing and the method by which they hoped to accomplish their goal.

THE I.R.B.

As early as August 1914, shortly after the outbreak of war, the Supreme Council of the Irish Republican Brotherhood had met and had agreed in principle to the armed overthrow of British authority in Ireland and to the establishment of an Irish republic.[18] Undeterred by its inability to implement such a decision at that time, the I.R.B. was quick to recognize that the October 1914 schism in the Volunteer movement could be used to good advantage.[19] Redmond's renamed National Volunteers, who pledged themselves to the support of the war, may have represented nearly ninety-five percent of the Volunteer organization, but the approximately 11,000 Irish Volunteers who remained with Eoin MacNeill were for the I.R.B., a far more compact and a more militantly separat-

---

[18]This pledge affirmed the traditional separatist doctrine that England's difficulty was Ireland's opportunity. See P. S. O'Hegarty, *The Victory of Sinn Fein* (Dublin, 1924), p. 18.

[19]The I.R.B. itself included only about 2,000 members in early 1914. See Diarmuid Lynch, *The I.R.B. and the 1916 Rising*, edited by F. O. Donoghue (Cork, 1957), p. 24.

ist group to manipulate. MacNeill, of course, had no knowledge of the I.R.B. plan; neither had he any intention of staging an insurrection. In early 1916, the Irish Volunteers numbered no more than 16,000 and the Citizen Army could claim only about 200 men.[20] Moreover, many of the Irish Volunteers, particularly those outside of Dublin, had no guns at all and their batallions were not nearly as strong in the field as they were on paper. The odds which confronted them were considerable. In addition to the 6,000 effective British troops in Ireland at this time, the authorities also had the services of the 9,500 members of the armed Royal Irish Constabulary, and more than 1,000 members of the unarmed Dublin Metropolitan Police.[21]

MacNeill was not categorically opposed to an armed uprising. Indeed, he believed that if the Volunteers were threatened with suppression or disarmament, or if the British sought to apply conscription to Ireland, there would be no alternative but to fight. In such an event, however, he did not anticipate a conventional war with pitched battles fought over strategic Dublin strongholds, but rather the kind of country-wide guerrilla warfare which later typified the 1919–1921 Irish War for Independence.[22]

Meanwhile, MacNeill and his associates devised a strategy intended to hone the Irish Volunteers into a highly organized and tightly disciplined force. Their hope was that these Volunteers would serve as a pressure group after the war, rather than being thrown into a hopeless struggle against British might during the war. But that objective was complicated by the fact that twelve of the original thirty-member Irish Volunteer Provisional Committee were also members of the I.R.B., and three of the eighteen non-I.R.B. members joined

[20]There were actually 211 men, women and boys who took part in the 1916 Easter Rising. See Donal Nevin, "The Irish Citizen Army," in O. Dudley Edwards and Fergus Pyle, eds., *1916: The Easter Rising* (London, 1968), p. 130.

[21]See notes in F. X. Martin, ed., "Eoin MacNeill on the 1916 Rising," *Irish Historical Studies,* 12 (March, 1961), pp. 242–244.

[22]For one of the more authoritative analyses of Volunteer strategy, see B. Hobson, *Ireland Yesterday and Tomorrow* (Tralee, 1968), pp. 69–71.

that secret brotherhood a short time afterwards.[23] While they did not enjoy the national prominence of Eoin MacNeill or exercise any real political influence, the I.R.B. members did share a unity of purpose which gave them a degree of strength out of all proportion to their numbers. MacNeill was aware of the I.R.B. presence, if not its magnitude, in the rank and file of the Irish Volunteers, and he frequently suspected that the brotherhood was attempting to gain control of the Volunteer organization. Yet MacNeill felt that he needed the dedicated and talented I.R.B. leaders, as they did him, and he further thought that he would be able to guide the Irish Volunteer movement on a middle course between the Redmondites and the physical force men. MacNeill's folly was that he underestimated the conspiratorial effectiveness of the I.R.B.[24]

Before the end of 1914, a headquarters staff had been formed to coordinate the military preparations of the Irish Volunteers. MacNeill was Chief of Staff, Bulmer Hobson was Quartermaster and The O'Rahilly was Director of Arms. Hobson, of course, was in the I.R.B., and The O'Rahilly, who disliked that secret society, was not. Still, The O'Rahilly agreed with the physical force separatists who favored a rising while England was engaged in war, but only if it were a planned insurrection with a reasonable chance of success. To ensure that end, The O'Rahilly subsequently joined in an undertaking to procure German aid for the Irish Volunteers.[25]

There was not, however, any consensus among the physical force separatists, and several prominent figures among them did not share The O'Rahilly's concern for ensuring beforehand that an armed rebellion have some prospect for

---

[23]The three were Patrick Pearse, Thomas MacDonagh and Joseph Plunkett.

[24]The I.R.B. also underestimated MacNeill's resolve, as the events of Holy Week 1916 would show, and that mutual misjudgment was a fundamental weakness in their unspoken alliance. See F. X. Martin, "MacNeill and the Foundation of the Irish Volunteers," in F. X. Martin and F. J. Byrne, eds., *The Scholar Revolutionary* (Shannon, 1973), pp. 135–136.

[25]Marcus Bourke, *The O'Rahilly* (Tralee, 1967), p. 100.

success. The socialist, James Connolly, wrote in a February 5, 1916 editorial for the *Worker's Republic:* "Without the slightest trace of irreverence but in all due humility and awe, we recognize that of us, as of mankind before Calvary, it may truly be said 'without the shedding of Blood there is no Redemption.' "[26] This allusion to the necessity for a blood sacrifice in order to awaken the Irish nation to the urgency of its plight was, by this date, a familiar theme in the writings of quite a different kind of Irish separatist, the poet and playwright Patrick Pearse.

POETS AND REVOLUTIONARIES

Patrick Pearse, Thomas MacDonagh and Joseph Plunkett, as members of the Irish Volunteer headquarters staff, served respectively as Director of Military Organization, Director of Training, and Director of Military Operations.[27] All three were poets, Gaelic enthusiasts, and romantic revolutionaries; and all were members of the I.R.B. These men, all deeply religious Catholics, preached a messianic doctrine combined with a doctrine of sacrifice. Their romantic nationalism was strongly influenced by mysticism but, although they expressed themselves in mystical terms, theirs was not a religion of meekness. It was an apocalyptic religion, a religion of retribution. Pearse, for example, wrote, "Ireland will not find Christ's peace until she has taken Christ's sword."[28] William Butler Yeats was wrong when, in his poem entitled "September, 1913," he declared,

---

[26]C. D. Greaves, *The Life and Times of James Connolly* (London, 1961) pp. 318–319.

[27]For further background on the staff and Volunteers, see F. X. Martin, ed., *The Irish Volunteers, 1913–1915* (Dublin, 1963), pp. 194–195.

[28]For the text of this ode to violence, see "Peace and the Gael" in P. H. Pearse, *Collected Works: Political Writings and Speeches* (Dublin, 1924). Pearse failed in his attempt to create a synthesis between the Celtic hero Cuchulainn and Christ, between strength and compassion. Lee, *The Modernisation of Irish Society*, p. 148.

"Romantic Ireland's dead and gone.
It's with O'Leary in the grave."

Romantic Ireland was still very much alive and these three, Pearse, MacDonagh and Plunkett, who were soon to enter the hallowed pantheon of nationalist martyrs, were the very embodiment of its messianic zeal.

PATRICK PEARSE

Pearse, the son of an English monument sculptor, was born in Dublin in 1879. Upon graduating from the old Royal University, he studied law for a time and was called to the bar, but his interests took him instead to the Gaelic League whose weekly paper he began editing in 1903. He was an enthusiastic supporter of the literary revival, and in 1908 he founded his bilingual school, St. Edna's, for the purpose of imbuing the younger generation with a love for their history, language and literature. Like the Gaelic League itself, Pearse's earlier apolitical views were altered by the ideas and events which were then reshaping Irish life. By 1913, at the time of Larkin's fight with the Dublin employers, the Ulster crisis, and the home rule debate, Pearse was convinced that the root of all of his country's ills lay in foreign domination. Thereafter, he was to be found in the vanguard of militant separatists demanding an end to British imperialism in Ireland.[29] Proclaimed Pearse, "There are many things more horrible than bloodshed; and slavery is one of them."

THOMAS MacDONAGH

Thomas MacDonagh, the son of a school teacher in county Tipperary, was born the same year as Pearse. MacDonagh

[29]Angered by the British Government's equivocation over the home rule bill, Pearse, as early as 1912, had declared, "Let the foreigner understand that if we are cheated now there will be red war in Ireland." Pearse, *Collected Works: Political Writings and Speeches*, p. 230.

attended University College, Dublin, where he eventually taught as an assistant lecturer in English. He was also deeply involved in the Gaelic revival and assisted Pearse with the creation of his bilingual school in 1908. Like Pearse, Mac-Donagh was a poet and playwright with no particular political philosophy, and he too turned towards physical force after the police brutality against Larkin's union members during their 1913 strike. An interest in military tactics took MacDonagh first into the Volunteers, where he helped Bulmer Hobson plan the gun landing at Howth, and later into the I.R.B. hierarchy. In 1915, when the body of Jeremiah O'Donovan Rossa was sent from America by the Clan-na-Gael for burial in Ireland, MacDonagh organized the Volunteer parade which followed the old Fenian to Glasnevin cemetery. Before his execution by a British firing squad after the Rising of 1916, MacDonagh, like Pearse, would describe his fate as a welcome sacrifice: "It is a great and glorious thing to die for Ireland. . . . When my son, Don, was born I thought that to him and not to me would this be given. God has been kinder to me than I hoped."[30]

JOSEPH PLUNKETT

Joseph Plunkett, the youngest of these three poets, was born in Dublin in 1887 to a prominent Irish family. His father, a papal Count, was the Director of the National Museum and, in spite of a keen regard for Arthur Griffith's Sinn Fein doctrines, was generally apolitical until the 1916 Rising. Joseph was in fragile health and for that reason the youth spent much of his childhood in the warm climate of the Mediterranean, avoiding the dampness of his homeland and seeking the sunshine he needed. A romantic nationalist from an early age, Joseph Plunkett loved poetry and soldiering. He met

---

[30]Donagh MacDonagh, "Plunkett and MacDonagh," in F. X. Martin, ed., *Leaders and Men of the Easter Rising: Dublin 1916* (New York, 1967), pp. 171–176.

MacDonagh for the first time in 1910 when the latter was asked to tutor him for the matriculation examination in Irish for the National University of Ireland. In the years that followed, Plunkett, who found his inspiration in the works of St. John of the Cross and St. Catherine of Siena, became an enthusiastic organizer of revolution. Plunkett edited the November 1914 issue of *The Irish Review* which contained the "Manifesto to the Irish Volunteers," and the more provocative "Twenty Plain Facts for Irishmen." The British Government deemed these statements to be seditious and subsequently seized this number of the *The Irish Review* under the Defense of the Realm Act, thereby hastening the demise of this financially troubled but distinctive publication.[31] By the end of 1914, Pearse, MacDonagh and Plunkett were devising methods for street-fighting in Dublin and, in 1915, plans were formulated for the anticipated insurrection to which all these men were committed, and for which all were prepared to die.

THE I.R.B. PLANS A MILITARY VICTORY

Even though a few of the romantic nationalists in the I.R.B. may have thought that a blood sacrifice would awaken Ireland from its apathy and inspire a reaction which would drive the British from the country, they nonetheless supported their more pragmatic I.R.B colleagues who preferred to plan a military victory. On the same day in July 1914 that Erskine Childers had sailed his *Asgard* with its shipment of arms for the landing at Howth, Roger Casement had left for America in order to confer with John Devoy about the Clan-na-Gael's

---

[31]Within the three and one-half years of its existence, *The Irish Review* published every writer connected with militant separatism except Eoin MacNeill, far to the right, and Sean O'Casey, equally far to the left. Ibid., pp. 166–169.

assistance in procuring more weapons.[32] Devoy, the Fenian patriarch, was impressed with Casement's sincerity but was dubious about his competence to serve the cause in such a critically important task.[33] Ironically, Devoy's misgivings concerning Casement had been partly allayed by the earlier assurances of a mutual friend, Bulmer Hobson, and a letter from Eoin MacNeill which introduced Casement as the accredited representative of the arms-subcommittee of the Irish Volunteers. Hobson, although still in the I.R.B., had left its Supreme Council, and he agreed essentially with Mac-Neill's views. Both men wished to arm the Irish Volunteers for the purpose of serving as a pressure group to assure home rule after the war, or to act as a guerrilla force during the war should the British attempt to disarm Irish civilians or to conscript them into military service. But Devoy's Clan-na-Gael supported the I.R.B. in its plan for an armed insurrection while England was still at war, and it was Hobson who later would reveal the I.R.B.'s imminent designs to MacNeill in an effort to stop them. A further irony was that Casement would, in April 1916, hazard his life in an attempt to stop the insurrection which he had come to believe was doomed to failure.[34]

In July 1914, however, Casement was enthusiastically soliciting money for weapons from Irish-American organiza-

---

[32]Besides Devoy, Casement also met with such prominent Clan members as New York State Supreme Court Justice Daniel Cohalan and a naturalized Irish-American from Philadelphia, Joseph McGarrity, who had made his fortune in the liquor trade.

[33]John Devoy would later write, in a letter to Lawrence de Lacey dated July 20, 1916, "We knew he [Casement] would meddle in his honest but visionary way to such an extent as to spoil things, but we did not dream that he would ruin everything as he has done." Documents Relative to the Sinn Fein Movement, Cmd. 1108 of 1921, (H.M.Stationary Office, London), p. 19.

[34]There is an ever growing body of literature on the life of the enigmatic Casement. For some of these studies extending over the past forty-five years see: Denis Gwynn, *The Life and Death of Roger Casement* (London, 1931); William J. Maloney, *The Forged Casement Diaries* (Dublin, 1936); Geoffrey de G. Parmiter, *Roger Casement* (London, 1936); Rene MacColl, *Roger Casement* (London, 1965); H. Montgomery Hyde, *The Trial of Sir Roger Casement* (London, 1960; and, most recently, B. L. Reid, *The Lives of Roger Casement*, (New Haven, 1976).

tions with the help of the Clan-na-Gael. Through Devoy's arrangements, Casement met with the German Ambassador at Washington, Count von Bernstorff, and made plans to visit Germany. Because of the outbreak of war between Britain and Germany, certain precautions were necessary in making such a journey across seas controlled by the English Navy. Casement finally sailed for Europe on October 15, 1914, aboard the Norwegian ship *Oskar II,* under the name of James Landy and armed with the passport of the real Landy, together with other credentials provided by von Bernstorff. The German Ambassador advised his Government of Casement's threefold purpose for going to Berlin: to recruit an Irish brigade from Irish prisoners of war in Germany, to secure general German support for a declaration of Irish independence, and, more specifically, to arrange for arms to be shipped to Ireland. But as one biographer wrote: "What the luckless Casement did not know, either then or later, was that nearly all the messages passing between von Bernstorff and the Wilhelmstrasse in Berlin, were being intercepted and read by the British, a fact which lent an added touch of futility to his efforts over the next eighteen months."[35]

BRITISH CODE-BREAKING

Precisely how the British managed to decipher the coded messages to and from Berlin with great accuracy and regularity, which the Germans felt confident was not possible, is at once one of the more bizarre and intriguing developments of the war. England had declared war against Germany on August 4, 1914, and before the sun rose the next morning an English cable ship, the *Telconia,* moved through a North Sea mist in what was the Royal Navy's first offensive action, and one which would prove more lethal than any single naval

---

[35]MacColl, *Roger Casement,* p. 110.

engagement for the duration of hostilities. The *Telconia's* mission was to cut the German transatlantic cables at a point some miles off Emden, where the Dutch coast joins the German. Having successfully accomplished that objective, the British sealed off Germany from direct cable communication with the overseas world. Thereafter, the burden of that nation's communications fell on Nauen, the powerful German wireless station outside Berlin. Nothing can prevent an enemy from picking wireless messages out of the free air, and nothing did. In England, the Director of Naval Intelligence, operating from the now famous facility known as Room 40, coordinated the work of studying intercepts in code which began pouring in from a wide variety of listening posts. More than a few on the staff at Room 40 were amateur cryptographers whose only qualifications were either a flair for mathematical patterns or a gift for puzzle solving, and a competence in the German language. The product of their collective talent and dedication was remarkable, but the most decisive breakthrough in the effort to crack German codes and ciphers came not in Room 40, but rather in the icy waters of the Gulf of Finland.[36]

In the night fog of August 20, 1914, the German light cruiser *Magdeburg* had run aground off the island of Odensholm in the Gulf of Finland. With two Russian cruisers bearing down upon her, the German vessel's captain ordered his signalman to take the ship's code book into a dinghy and to throw the book, which was in a lead container to insure sinking, overboard into deep water. But the *Magdeburg* came under heavy Russian fire and the body of the dead signalman, still clasping the code book in his arms, was recovered by Russian seamen rescuing German survivors.[37] The

[36]Barbara Tuchman, *The Zimmermann Telegram* (New York, 1958), pp. 10–12.

[37]Ibid., pp. 14–15. According to another account, the Russians discovered the body of the German signalman when it washed ashore a few days later. In all other important details, however, these two sources are in agreement. See Admiral Sir William James, *The Code Breakers of Room 40* (New York, 1956), pp. 29–30.

Russian Admiralty at St. Petersburg, exhibiting rare generosity to an ally, concluded that the code book could best be used by the British Admiralty, and sent it by fast cruiser to London where it arrived on October 13. British Naval Intelligence found that the code book contained, in addition to the work columns on which the naval code was based, the key to the cipher system according to which the code was varied from time to time. That disclosure compromised nearly all of Berlin's telegraph communications from that date forward, and had the most serious consequences not only for Germany herself, but also for the Irish separatists who sought collaborative action with that country.[38]

CASEMENT'S GERMAN MISSION

Roger Casement's mission to Germany was, partly because of this unsuspected British advantage and partly because of his own character traits and peculiarities, virtually a total disaster. After eluding detection when the British warship H.M.S. *Hibernia* stopped, searched, and briefly detained the *Oskar II,* Casement, upon landing at Christiania, Norway, narrowly escaped being kidnapped by agents of Mansfeldt de Cardonnell Findlay, the British Minister to that country.[39] Arriving in Berlin on October 31, 1914, Casement immediately began negotiations with German Under-Secretary of State Arthur Zimmermann and later with Chancellor Theobald von Bethmann-Hollweg, for permission to recruit an Irish Brigade from the Irish prisoners of war in German camps. The brigade was to be formed solely to fight for Ireland under the

---

[38]For a better appreciation of how specific was the information which Berlin communicated to its Embassy in Washington, and vice versa, regarding German plans to assist an Irish insurrection, see Documents Relative to the Sinn Fein Movement, Cmd. 1108 of 1921, pp. 1–14.

[39]A Norwegian seaman, Adler Christensen, who was travelling as Casement's servant, was purportedly offered £5,000 by Findlay to assist in the kidnapping. For further details, see Desmond Ryan, *The Rising* (Dublin, 1966), pp. 32–34.

Irish flag, and it would be paid only from Irish sources.[40] In December 1914, the German Government issued a declaration which embraced all of Casement's goals, but represented a dubious triumph due to the considerable qualifications which Berlin attached to its statement. The Germans agreed to permit the formation of an Irish brigade, but the shipment of any substantial amounts of arms and ammunition to the Irish Volunteers, or the provision of any other form of military assistance would have to await the improbable event of a German victory over the British Navy. Much attention was therefore given by Berlin to the creation of an Irish Brigade which would provide an excellent propaganda weapon for discouraging the recruitment of Irishmen for the British Army. In the weeks and months that followed, however, the German Government, the Clan-na-Gael, and the I.R.B. leaders in Ireland were, all for different reasons, sharply critical of Casement's mismanaging his mission, and of his raising a brigade which ultimately numbered only fifty men.[41]

EFFORTS TO PROCURE GERMAN ARMS

Meanwhile, in Ireland, the militant separatists grew restless. Joseph Plunkett was sent to Germany, in April 1915, on an assignment for the I.R.B. Supreme Council. Plunkett met with Chancellor von Bethmann-Hollweg and discussed the possibility of Germany's simply landing a quantity of arms in Ireland sometime in the spring of 1916. While in Berlin, Plunkett also visited Casement who was despondent over the

---

[40]Roger McHugh, "Casement and German Help," in F. X. Martin, ed., *Leaders and Men of the Easter Rising*, p. 180.

[41]For an account of the inhospitable treatment accorded these uniformed members of the Irish brigade by German soldiers, who found the Irish nearly as objectionable as the French and brawled with them in various beer gardens, see MacColl, *Roger Casement*, pp. 145–146; see also Ryan, *The Rising*, pp. 34–35.

poor response to his recruitment effort for the Irish Brigade. Plunkett tried to help but, having little success, he returned to Ireland and next travelled to New York in order to inform John Devoy of his discussions in Germany. In Dublin, the I.R.B. established a Military Council in 1915 which was to be responsible for the planning and execution of an insurrection in early 1916. Its members included Eamonn Ceannt, Patrick Pearse, Joseph Plunkett, Sean MacDermott, and Tom Clarke. James Connolly and Thomas MacDonagh joined later, and all seven of these men were to be the signatories of the Proclamation of Independence.[42]

Acting upon the advice of comrades from county Kerry, the Military Council determined that Fenit pier was the most suitable site for landing German arms in Ireland, and Tom Clarke promptly notified John Devoy to this effect. Additionally, Robert Monteith, an Irish Volunteer organizer and a veteran of the British Army, travelled secretly to Germany at the direction of Tom Clarke for the purpose of helping Roger Casement with the Irish Brigade. Monteith found Casement more discouraged than ever over the failure of the German Army to reach the Calais coast and resigned to abandoning the idea of an Irish Brigade in the belief that Germany was in no position to offer meaningful assistance to the separatists in Ireland. Casement did, however, obtain permission from the German War Office for Monteith to resume recruitment for the Irish Brigade, and to train its members.[43] Plunkett had felt during his visit to Germany that Sir Roger

[42]Eamonn Ceannt has remained the least known of these seven conspirators. Born in Galway in 1881, he spent most of his life in Dublin where he worked as a civil servant. His extreme nationalism had developed along a familiar path, taking him from the Gaelic League and Sinn Fein to the Volunteers, which he helped found, and ultimately into the I.R.B. See Florence O'Donoghue, "Ceannt, Devoy, O'Rahilly and the Military Plan," in F. X. Martin, ed., *Leaders and Men of the Easter Rising*, pp. 195–196.

[43]Roger McHugh, "Casement and German Help," in F. X. Martin, ed., *Leaders and Men of the Easter Rising*, p. 181. For a personal account of Monteith's experiences in Germany, and for testimony of his esteem for Roger Casement, see Robert Monteith, *Casement's Last Adventure* (Dublin, 1953), pp. 91–141.

had impeded recruitment by insisting upon a demonstrable patriotic motive among the men whom he enlisted for the Irish Brigade. Indeed, Plunkett shocked Casement by his somewhat cynical remark that the I.R.B. would get the men if it had to kidnap them.[44] After Monteith's arrival in Germany, Casement attempted to convince the German Foreign Office to use his Irish Brigade, now numbering fifty-two men, to aid Turkish forces fighting the British in the Middle East. The motive behind Casement's suggestion remains unknown and, in any case, the Germans by this time greeted Casement and his ideas with suspicion and hostility.[45] Casement's isolation was nearly complete. The I.R.B. was now conducting its negotiations with Germany through John Devoy and the German Ambassador in Washington. Casement was still trusted by the Irish, but he was thought to be a defeatist. Accordingly, he was not kept fully informed of the secret deliberations between the I.R.B. and Berlin which preceded the April 1916 insurrection in Ireland.

PLANS FOR THE RISING

The I.R.B. Military Council was so cautious in its preparations that when it did agree, at the end of 1915, upon Easter 1916 as the date for the rising, that information was withheld even from members of the I.R.B. Supreme Council. Tom Clarke, Sean MacDermott, and Denis McCullough constituted the brotherhood's three-man executive body, and McCullough, although he was the president, was not informed of the decision. Perhaps the reason for McCullough's being kept in ignorance of the date was that he lived in Belfast, and thus his opportunity for communication with his fellow members of the I.R.B. Supreme Council was restricted. Otherwise, Council members were kept apprised on a need-to-know basis

---

[44]Ryan, *The Rising,* pp. 39–40.
[45]MacColl, *Roger Casement,* pp. 149–150.

which preserved their conspiracy from the traditional betrayal, but only at the cost of creating much confusion among the rank and file of the I.R.B. in the country at large.[46]

What concerned the I.R.B. Military Council most in January, 1916, was not their prospective adversaries, the British troops and the Royal Irish Constabulary stationed throughout Ireland, but rather the volatile Citizen Army under the command of James Connolly. The editorials in his *Worker's Republic* had for some weeks been an open incitement to immediate insurrection. Then, on January 19, Connolly disappeared; neither his family nor his closest friends had any news of him until, on January 22, he reappeared as suddenly and mysteriously as he had vanished. He had spent the intervening time in consultation with members of the I.R.B. Military Council who told him of their plans for an Easter revolt and persuaded him to act with them. The circumstances surrounding Connolly's disappearance, and the question of whether it was indeed voluntary or more a case of being kidnapped by the I.R.B., have not yet been fully explained because Connolly never confided the reasons for his absence either to friends or family.[47] What is certain, however, is that Connolly joined the I.R.B. Military Council during this period and thereafter was privy to all of its plans and preparations.

Irish Volunteer Chief of Staff Eoin MacNeill also had been alarmed by the strident tone of the *Worker's Republic,* and by the growing bellicosity of the Citizen Army. It was for this

---

[46]For more of the particulars regarding the complex and often confusing roles played by the principal I.R.B. leaders, see Maureen Wall, "The Background to the Rising: from 1914 to the Issue of the Countermanding Order on Easter Sunday, 1916," in K. B. Nowlan, ed., *The Making of 1916* (Dublin, 1969), pp. 157–189.

[47]Ryan, *The Rising,* pp. 47–48. A recent biography contends that the meeting between Connolly and the I.R.B. Military Council took place a week or more before January 19. See Samuel Levenson, *James Connolly: A Biography* (London, 1973), p. 282; another biography claims that it was Connolly who induced the Military Council to commit itself to unconditional insurrection. See Greaves, *Connolly,* pp. 390–392. Both studies reject the allegation that Connolly was kidnapped.

reason that MacNeill met with Connolly and Patrick Pearse sometime in mid-January, 1916. MacNeill bluntly warned Connolly that the latter would be badly mistaken if he precipitated an insurrection in the belief that the 16,000 man Irish Volunteer force would enter such a conflict to prevent the destruction of the 200 man Citizen Army.[48] MacNeill thought that an indispensable condition of a rising was a reasonably calculated prospect for success, and that any other action would be militarily foolish and morally criminal. MacNeill was a separatist by sentiment and conviction, but he was convinced that Britain would withdraw every available soldier from the western front to prevent the establishment of an Irish Republic. Short of a British military defeat in the war, MacNeill believed Ireland would have to achieve its independence in stages. The meeting ended inconclusively, with Connolly departing and Pearse remaining behind. Pearse assured MacNeill that he would persuade Connolly to adopt a more reasonable view. What Pearse did not tell MacNeill was that the I.R.B. Military Council had already agreed on a specified date for the insurrection, and that both he and Connolly were using MacNeill as a screen for their preparations. In the end, however, it would be MacNeill who, by a single stroke, would do more to contain and curb the rising of 1916 than all the power of Britain.[49]

THE GERMAN ARMS PROPOSAL

Meanwhile, plans proceeded for procuring German assistance for a rising in Ireland. Upon receiving I.R.B. confirmation in early February that the insurrection was planned for Easter Sunday, April 23, John Devoy sent a cable to Berlin,

---

[48]Connolly provoked MacNeill into this remark by contending that the Citizen Army would fight in Dublin whether or not the Irish Volunteers did. F. X. Martin, ed., "Eoin MacNeill on the 1916 Rising," *Irish Historical Studies*, 12, p. 246.

[49]Ryan, *The Rising*, pp. 62–63.

by way of the German Embassy in Washington, asking rather vaguely for arms to be delivered "between Good Friday and Easter Sunday." He further stated, "We expect German help immediately after beginning action."[50] This was followed by a letter from Devoy which specified the need for 100,000 rifles, for artillery, and for German officers and artillery men.

Roger Casement was recuperating from an illness at a Munich hospital in early March when Robert Monteith brought him news of Devoy's cable. Both men then made inquiries of the German General Staff in Berlin and next of the German Admiralty, where they learned of the arrangements which Berlin had proposed to Devoy. A German steamer, the *Aud,* was to transport 20,000 rifles, 10 machine guns, 5 million rounds of ammunition, and the fifty odd members of the Irish Brigade to the west coast of Ireland. The *Aud* was to be met off Innistooskert in Tralee Bay between Friday and Sunday, April 20–23, by a pilot boat, showing two green lights as an identifying signal, which would lead the arms ship into a designated pier. On March 12, 1916, a wireless code message in German was sent from the German Embassy in Washington to Berlin which read: "Irish agree to proposition. Necessary steps have been taken."[51]

Casement was frantic. He had envisioned a large, well-equipped Irish Brigade, supported by a German expeditionary force of perhaps 50,000 men, assisting the Irish Volunteers in an insurrection against British forces in Ireland. The Germans, however, had ignored Casement. Furthermore, the Germans had made no pretense about their inability to provide anything more than a small quantity of arms when the I.R.B. approached Berlin without ever informing Casement. Indeed, Devoy had even requested Berlin to keep Casement in Germany since his presence in Ireland would merely cause confusion.[52] Unaware of Devoy's

[50]Documents Relative to the Sinn Fein Movement, Cmd. 1108 of 1921, p. 9.
[51]Ibid., p. 10. For a first hand account of these Berlin meetings, see Monteith, *Casement's Last Adventure,* pp. 134–138.
[52]John Devoy, *Recollections of an Irish Rebel* (New York, 1929), p. 472.

communication, Casement first sought to block the use of the Irish Brigade for what he deemed a madcap venture, and next attempted to get a message through to Dublin strongly urging that no rising should take place under the circumstances. He succeeded in keeping the brigade in Germany but, before he could issue any warning to Dublin, the arms ship sailed from the port of Lübeck on April 9 for its destination off the Kerry coast. Casement then prevailed upon the German Admiralty to provide a submarine to take himself, Monteith and Daniel Bailey, a member of the Irish Brigade, to the west of Ireland for the ostensible reason of assisting in the arms landing and distribution. What Casement really intended was to arrive in Ireland before the *Aud* landed, and to warn the Irish leaders that the paucity of German aid doomed their insurrection to failure. He was determined to stop or to postpone the rising at Easter, but he was prepared to die in it if his arguments failed to persuade his Irish comrades.[53] The Admiralty consented to the request for a submarine, but secretly instructed its commander not to allow Casement ashore until the arms cargo from the *Aud* had been safely delivered.

What next ensued helped seal the fate of what was at best an improbable undertaking. On April 18, John Devoy, acting on a message received from the Military Council of the I.R.B. in Dublin, requested the German Embassy in Washington to send Berlin an urgent message stating that the arms should be landed precisely on the evening of Easter Sunday in order to minimize the risk of discovery by British coastal patrols. It would appear that Pearse and the Military Council assumed incorrectly that the *Aud* was equipped with a wireless and, acting on the assumption that their message would reach the ship, they arranged to have a pilot boat at Innistooskert available on Easter night only.[54] Collaboration be-

---

[53]Monteith was in favor of participating in the rising whenever it took place. McHugh, "Casement and German Help," in F. X. Martin, ed., *Leaders and Men of the Easter Rising*, p. 182.

[54]Cork, Kerry and Limerick brigades were also alerted by Pearse to provide security for the landing and distribution of arms on Easter, April 23.

tween Berlin and the I.R.B. Military Council had always been difficult because of the necessity of communicating with each other via the German Embassy in Washington, or by agents travelling as passengers on ships which still sailed between Germany and neutral America. When the I.R.B. unilaterally changed the date for the arms landing, the absence of a better system of communication with the Germans led to a disastrous consequence.

FAILURE OF THE ARMS SCHEME

Having broken the German code, British naval intelligence was able to interpret the messages which were monitored between Washington and Berlin.[55] And, as if this were not damaging enough, the New York office of a German agent, Wolf von Igel, was raided by the American secret service on April 18. Almost the first thing the agents found was the transcript of the message just received from Dublin, and radioed to Berlin, respecting the I.R.B. request not to land the arms in Kerry until the night of Easter Sunday, April 23. The Irish leaders had evidently concluded that it would be too dangerous to have the landing precede a rising by even a few days and, accordingly, had decided to synchronize their effort as much as possible. The Americans immediately shared this captured information with the British who by this time were better informed than the German captain of the *Aud.* He was already at sea, and without radio contact.

On the late afternoon of Thursday, April 20, German Captain Karl Spindler brought the *Aud,* disguised as a Norwegian freighter, to its appointed rendezvous in Tralee Bay. Spindler sighted the submarine which carried Casement and

---

[55]The British knew, for example, that the code word which the Germans would send to Ireland if the arms ship left on schedule was FINN; and that the code word BRAN would be used if the ship was detained. See Documents Relative to the Sinn Fein Movement, Cmd. 1108 of 1921, p. 11. "As soon as the password was signalled, the necessary steps were taken on the Irish coast." James, *The Code Breakers of Room 40,* p. 111.

his two comrades, but he made no contact with it and watched for a signal from the Irish pilot boat which was to guide his ship to the landing. After vainly waiting for almost twenty-four hours in dangerous prominence off the Irish coast, Spindler made for the open seas. He was, however, intercepted by British warships on Good Friday evening and ordered into Queenstown Harbour. As his ship was being led into that British naval facility on the following morning, Captain Spindler lowered the Norwegian flag and struck the German colors. He then maneuvered the *Aud* across the narrow channel, ordered his crew to abandon ship, and scuttled her. Whatever slender chance the Irish insurgents may have had of mounting an insurrection large enough to have even the faintest hope of success disappeared with the arms which went down on the *Aud*.[56]

On the early morning of the same day, Good Friday, Casement, Monteith, and Bailey were put into a dinghy by the German submarine commander who then headed for safer waters. Casement, who was in failing health, almost drowned when the dinghy capsized and exhaustion compelled him to wait in the ruins of an old fort while his companions went off in the hope of making contact with the Volunteers. That afternoon, Casement was discovered by two members of the Royal Irish Constabulary. He was arrested and taken to Tralee where a used railway ticket, for the trip from Berlin to Wilhelmshaven, was found in his pocket. He spent that night in the Tralee jail from which he could have been rescued by the Volunteers if the local commander, Austin Stack, had not been under strict instructions not to take any prema-

---

[56]There is some question as to how useful the weapons would have been to the Irish in any event. The machine guns were of the Maxim type, bored to take the German mauser bullet, and the rifles were of Russian manufacture, having been captured at the Battle of Tannenburg. Requirements for a dual ammunition supply would have created complications in any military action. See Monteith, *Casement's Last Adventure*, p. 138; and James, *The Code Breakers of Room 40*, p. 111. For the personal account of the captain of the *Aud*, see Karl Spindler, *The Mystery of the Casement Ship* (Tralee, 1965).

ture action until the rising broke out in Dublin.[57] The following day, Roger Casement was taken in great secrecy by
British authorities to Dublin, and thence to London, where
in due course he stood trial for treason.

Another bizarre sequence of events in Irish separatist activity was unfolding in Dublin during this same week. On
April 19, a document was acquired by several respectable
Irish newspapers. The document purported to outline British
military plans for the suppression of the Irish Volunteers and
the arrest of various unreliable parties. Exactly who transmit-
ted the document to the press was unknown, but it was
alleged to have been prepared by British officials headquar-
tered at Dublin Castle and, after a brief attempt to prevent
its publication, government authorities issued a disclaimer
which characterized the "Castle Document" as a complete
fabrication.[58] Whether or not the document was forged by
the I.R.B., as has been argued but never proven, the net
result was to prompt Eoin MacNeill into action. He rapidly
called the headquarters staff together and sent out a general
order to the Irish Volunteers urging that they prepare themselves to resist suppression.[59]

CONFLICT OVER THE PLANNED RISING

On the day following the publication of the "Castle Document," Thursday, April 20, Bulmer Hobson discovered by
chance that the I.R.B. was planning to launch an insurrection
that Sunday. Hobson immediately informed MacNeill who
went directly to Patrick Pearse and confronted him with the

---

[57]Kee, *The Green Flag,* pp. 562–563.
[58]The document also designated Sinn Fein, the Gaelic League, and the
Redmondite National Volunteers as targets for suppression.
[59]For a full account of the "Castle Document" episode, see F. X. Martin,
ed., "Eoin MacNeill on the 1916 Rising," *Irish Historical Studies,* 12 pp.
247–258.

story. Pearse admitted to the outraged MacNeill that the I.R.B. had made plans for a rising without consulting him. MacNeill replied that he would not allow the I.R.B. to sacrifice the lives of his half-armed Volunteers and that as Chief of Staff he would do everything possible to stop the insurrection short of telephoning the British authorities at Dublin Castle.[60]

Before MacNeill could issue orders countermanding those given by Pearse, another development changed the situation once again. News of Roger Casement's arrest and detention had reached I.R.B. headquarters in Dublin, and Patrick Pearse, Thomas MacDonagh and Sean MacDermott went as a delegation to MacNeill's house to ask that he do nothing since his commands would be defied by some, cause confusion for others, and would not in any case prevent the rising. For MacNeill, the most persuasive argument seems to have been the revelation, entirely new to him, that a German ship with arms was in or near Irish waters. This was not a deception, for the I.R.B. had not yet learned of the fate of the *Aud*. MacNeill therefore agreed not to interfere and to let the arrangements for the following Sunday stand.

On Saturday evening, however, MacNeill was visited by The O'Rahilly and a Volunteer officer who presented the Chief of Staff with two startling disclosures. One was that the "Castle Document" was almost certainly a forgery, which meant that the authorities had not decided to suppress the Irish Volunteers and that MacNeill's warning therefore had been unnecessary. But more shocking to MacNeill was the news of the sinking of the *Aud*. Again the Volunteer Chief confronted Pearse and told him that countermanding orders were to be sent afterall. The conspirators recognized that MacNeill, in trying to prevent the rising, was acting consistently and courageously according to the principles he had publicly and repeatedly enunciated. For his part, MacNeill,

---

[60]Ryan, *The Rising*, pp. 90–92.

though deeply injured by the many deceptions, steadfastly defended the honor of his former comrades at his subsequent court-martial, as well as in later life.[61]

Messages countermanding the rising were sent to all parts of the country in the early hours of Easter morning. Insofar as the insurrection had been planned for that evening, there was sufficient time to reach most, if not all, of the Volunteer corps. MacNeill, true to his word that he would do everything possible to prevent the rising, published an order in the *Sunday Independent* prohibiting all Volunteer movements for that day.

Without the German arms and the aid of the Irish Volunteers throughout the country, there was no longer any military justification for proceeding with the rising. But to men like Pearse, Clarke, Plunkett, Ceannt, and Connolly, the odds were not nearly so important as the blood-sacrifice which they now perceived as the sole means of regenerating Irish nationalism.[62] In order to prevent any further interference by MacNeill, Pearse sent him a message declaring that the Dublin parades for Sunday had been countermanded according to MacNeill's instructions. And indeed that was so, for the I.R.B. Military Council had secretly changed the time of its uprising from Sunday evening to the noon hour of the following day.[63] The I.R.B. plan was to seize certain specific

---

[61]F. S. L. Lyons, *Ireland Since the Famine* (New York, 1971), pp. 355–356.

[62]Even The O'Rahilly, who had spent part of the weekend contacting different Volunteer units throughout Ireland to ensure that they would not support the intended Easter Sunday uprising, responded to the news of an insurrection on the following day by joining forces with what he regarded as a hopeless and mindless enterprise. William Butler Yeats explained such behavior later with the lines:

> Because I helped to wind the clock
> I came to hear it strike.

Levinson, *James Connolly*, p. 287. The O'Rahilly's actual remark was: "If the men I have trained to fight are going into action, I must be with them" Bourke, *The O'Rahilly*, p. 120.

[63]Lyons, *Ireland Since the Famine*, p. 357; see also Ryan, *The Rising*, pp. 95–98.

strongholds in the city of Dublin, the number of which was necessarily restricted by the size of the force which the conspirators could reasonably expect to muster. The revolutionaries hoped to hold these posts for as long as possible so that their example might inspire a country-wide uprising, or perhaps qualify the survivors for some international recognition as belligerents at the peace conference following the World War. They had few illusions, however, and Pearse, Connolly, and the other leaders were prepared to die for their belief that the blood of patriots would bring to bloom the rose tree of Irish freedom.[64] Accordingly, as the streets of downtown Dublin assumed a festive air on the morning of Easter Monday, a bank holiday, a small band of revolutionary separatists paraded boldly to their mission of destiny.

---

[64]William Butler Yeats would later write,

> There's nothing but our own red blood
> Can make a right Rose Tree.

William Butler Yeats, "The Rose Tree," *Collected Poems* (New York, 1944), pp. 210–211. Connolly cheerily told a comrade, "We are going out to be slaughtered." To him, the important thing now was to act. Any rising was better than none. Levenson, *James Connolly*, p. 297.

Chapter 6

The Easter Rising: Rebellion And Reprisal (1916)

BRITAIN'S FAILURE TO ANTICIPATE THE IRISH INSURRECTION

If the Irish revolutionary leaders had been successful in their arms smuggling venture and in their attempt to effect a national rising, there is little doubt that the 1916 Easter week insurrection would have presented a serious problem to the London government at a very critical time in the war. The British failure to maintain a more closely coordinated surveillance of Irish revolutionary potential is therefore somewhat perplexing. As early as September 1914, wireless communications between German Ambassador Count von Bernstorff in Washington and the Foreign Office in Berlin included specific references to the projected plans of militant Irish separatists. On September 27, von Bernstorff sent a coded message to Berlin which began: "I am telegraphing because written reports are too unsafe." He then proceeded to inform his superiors of Casement's proposal to form an Irish brigade from Irish prisoners of war.[1] It was not until several weeks later, after the receipt of the German code book from the Russian Admiralty, that the British were able to decipher these communications. But by the time Casement arrived in Berlin the only important thing relating to his mission which London did not know was "the exact manner and date of Casement's attempt to return to Ireland."[2]

During the next eighteen months, Irish separatists in both Dublin and America conspired with the German government in planning an insurrection in Ireland. Their collaboration was closely followed by British intelligence whose code breakers monitored wireless messages and whose mail censors routinely read and recorded communications sent by letter.[3] Yet, when a rising did occur in April 1916, both civil and military authorities in Ireland appeared to have been caught off guard for lack of specific information about the plans of the Irish insurgents. Where had British intelligence gone wrong?

Incredible as it seems today, there was no direct communication between the British Admiralty, which gathered a substantial part of the intelligence on the prospective Irish insurrection, and the civil administration responsible for the governance of Ireland. The British authorities at Dublin Castle had placed informers within the Irish Volunteer movement but their reports, which often conflicted, left officials more skeptical than apprehensive over the likelihood of an impending rising. Government authorities did not realize that their undercover sources knew no more than they themselves did about the specific arrangements for the insurrection since all final plans were kept in strictest confidence by

---

[1] Documents Relative to the Sinn Fein Movement, Cmd. 1108 of 1921 (H. M. Stationary Office, London), p. 3.

[2] Admiral Sir William James, *The Code Breakers of Room 40* (New York, 1956), pp. 43–44.

[3] Documents Relative to the Sinn Fein Movement, Cmd. 1108 of 1921, pp. 4–13.

the I.R.B. Military Council, and in that group there were no informers.[4]

British initiative in dealing with the situation in Ireland was further hampered by the essentially triangular division of the civil administration's executive branch, and by the differing perceptions which civilian and military leaders had of the danger posed by Irish separatists. As the Chief Secretary for Ireland, Augustine Birrell was the British official principally responsible for the administration of the country. When Birrell was given this political appointment in 1908, it was the practice for the Chief Secretary to conduct most of his work at the Irish Office in London. The daily administrative work at Dublin Castle was therefore left to the permanent Under-Secretary, a civil service officer. Birrell spent increasingly less time in Ireland after the outbreak of World War I, believing that he could best meet the demands of the Cabinet, of which he was a member, from his post in London where he had the dual advantage of direct communication with Dublin Castle and easy access to the Irish Parliamentary Party leaders at Westminster.[5] It is also true that Birrell never enjoyed the journey to and from Dublin on the Irish Sea, and he liked it still less when hazard was added to discomfort by the wartime activities of German submarines.

Because of Birrell's lengthy absences from Ireland, Under-Secretary Sir Matthew Nathan was effectively the man in charge of the government in that country. Nathan, who had taken office in October 1914, was a capable and conscientious administrator who believed that it would be his task to aid in the lawful transfer of power to a home rule government upon the conclusion of the war. Just as Birrell was in frequent contact with Irish Parliamentary Party Chairman John Redmond in London, Nathan often met with John Dillon who

---

[4]F. S. L. Lyons, *Ireland Since the Famine* (New York, 1971), pp. 363–364.

[5]After 1913, Birrell had a personal reason for not travelling to Ireland as often as he might otherwise have done. His wife Eleanor was chronically incapacitated with a brain tumor. Leon O Broin, *The Chief Secretary* (London, 1969), p. 136.

spent much of his time in Dublin. Nathan essentially agreed with Dillon's view that the arrest of Irish Volunteer leaders would only enhance the prestige of the militant separatists, but he acted erratically in applying the law. Political extremism in Ireland was decidedly a growing force in 1916, and the government only exacerbated the problem by its failure to meet that challenge with a decisive policy. Radical newspaper editors were dealt with firmly on occasion, when some were jailed and others deported, but just as frequently the police merely seized or destroyed the printing facilities, leaving the publishers free to begin newspapers under different mastheads, which they invariably did. Moreover, Volunteer units drilled openly and paraded with greater regularity than ever during the early months of 1916, brandishing their ill-assorted arsenal of weapons in open defiance of the government and its wartime Defense of the Realm Act. But Nathan wrote Birrell as the year 1916 began that things were "fairly quiet" in Ireland. Rather curiously, neither man appeared terribly troubled by their shared feeling that the Royal Irish Constabulary, a force that had been traditionally regarded as the eyes and ears of the government in areas outside Dublin, was "lethargic and not much good for detective purposes."[6]

The third member of the British administrative triumvirate in Ireland was the newly appointed Viceroy, Lord Wimborne, who had succeeded Lord Aberdeen in 1916. The Viceroy, or Lord Lieutenant, was the symbol of the crown in Ireland and served as the personal representative of the king at affairs of state. As such, he was restricted by statute from political involvement in the government. That restraint had not prevented Lord Aberdeen from certain utterances and activities which embarrassed the Irish Office and expedited his resignation from the Lord Lieutenancy. Birrell instructed Dublin Castle to see that the new Viceroy served in a purely "ornamental" fashion. There is a touch of irony in this admo-

---

[6]These were Birrell's words, and Nathan depicted the detective work of the Dublin Metropolitan Police as being no better. Leon O Broin, *Dublin Castle and the 1916 Rising* (New York, 1971), pp. 62–63.

nition since it was Lord Wimborne who, at the last moment, very nearly prevented the insurrection from taking place.[7]

On March 22, 1916, General Lord French, commander of the Home Forces in Britain, received word from the military intelligence division that an insurrection was planned for April 22 in Ireland and that arrangements had been made to land German arms at some coastal area near Limerick prior to that date. French promptly told Birrell that "disloyal organizations" should be suppressed and that the military garrisons in Ireland should be strengthened at once. Birrell asked Nathan for Dublin Castle's opinion on these recommendations and, on April 10, Nathan replied: "Though the Irish Volunteer element has been active of late, I do not believe that its leaders mean insurrection or that the Volunteers have sufficient arms if the leaders do mean it."[8] Accordingly, no urgency was placed upon strengthening the garrisons and that proposed undertaking was still under consideration when the rising occurred one month later.

On April 17, General L. B. Friend, commander of the British Army in Ireland, relayed a message to Dublin Castle from the commanding officer of the Queenstown defenses in county Cork. The latter reported he had received information regarding an imminent arms landing in that region of the country, together with dates and details which generally corroborated the earlier report given to French. The Dublin police were placed on alert and the Royal Irish Constabulary took similar precautions in the southern and south-western counties, but both Nathan and the police commissioner remained skeptical of reports which they regarded as little more than unfounded rumors. The Under-Secretary appeared more reassured than alarmed when, on Saturday, April 22, he learned of the sinking of the *Aud* and the arrest of Roger Casement. Nathan interpreted these developments

---

[7] O Broin, *The Chief Secretary,* pp. 124–134.
[8] O Broin, *Dublin Castle,* pp. 72–73.

to mean that an insurrection had indeed been planned, but that it had failed before it could begin. He wrote Birrell that evening to say that the Irish Volunteers were to hold parades about the country on the following day (Easter Sunday) but, he added, "I see no indication of a 'rising'."[9] Nathan and his staff had mistakenly assumed that Casement was the central figure in the conspiracy and that his capture, together with the sinking of the *Aud,* precluded any immediate threat from Irish insurgents. The next day's publication in the *Sunday Independent* of Eoin MacNeill's notice countermanding the Irish Volunteer parades left the civil authorities confirmed in their belief that the danger was over.[10] The military command in Ireland was perhaps not as optimistic, but General Friend did judge the situation to be sufficiently controlled as to permit him to go on leave.

Early Easter Sunday morning, Nathan received word that Daniel Bailey, one of the two men who had accompanied Casement to Ireland, had been captured in Tralee; the other, Robert Monteith, was still missing. Bailey had made a full confession, admitting that he had come to Ireland in a German submarine and that arms and ammunition were to be landed from a ship in support of an Irish insurrection. When Nathan visited with the Lord Lieutenant before noon that same day, the latter implored him to arrest the known leaders of the Irish Volunteers who were still at liberty to plan new conspiracies. With some misgivings, Nathan agreed to send a cipher telegram to the Chief Secretary inquiring if the Volunteer leaders could be arrested and interned in England. Cautious civil servant that he was, Nathan asked Birrell: "Can this be proceded with subject to the concurrence of the Law Officers, Military Authorities and Home Office?"[11]

---

[9]Ibid., pp. 81–82.
[10]Maureen Wall, "The Plans and the Countermand: the Country and Dublin," in K. B. Nowlan, ed., *The Making of 1916* (Dublin, 1969), p. 221.
[11]O Broin, *Dublin Castle,* p. 84.

THE EASTER RISING BEGINS

Meanwhile, the news had arrived at Dublin Castle that "Sinn Feiners" had forcibly seized 250 pounds of gelignite and had taken it to Liberty Hall, the headquarters of James Connolly's Citizen Army. The Lord Lieutenant responded by urging the Under-Secretary to arrest the known ringleaders of militant separatist organizations without awaiting authorization from Birrell. Lord Wimborne wanted sixty to one-hundred of them locked up that very night, and he offered to sign the warrants himself and to assume full responsibility. Nathan agreed to meet with Wimborne again that evening, together with the Chief Commissioner of the Dublin police, the ranking intelligence officer at Dublin Castle, and two officers from the staff of General Friend who was away in England. At that meeting, it was agreed that Bailey's testimony and other evidence linking the Volunteers to the German enemy justified preventive arrests in anticipation of British Home Secretary Sir H. Samuel's concurrence. But the police and military men persuaded the Lord Lieutenant that Easter Monday would be an inauspicious day to launch an attack on Liberty Hall, thought to be the headquarters of the conspiracy, since the city would be teeming with holiday crowds and Volunteers from the countryside.[12] Nathan met with members of his staff the next morning at Dublin Castle in order to plan the precautionary measures which would be required before and during the actual arrests. As they deliberated, rifle fire sounded beneath the Under-Secretary's office window. A policeman lay dead at the front gate of the courtyard below; sixteen armed Citizen Army men moved toward designated positions in order to occupy defensible positions around the sprawling Dublin Castle complex. The real rising had begun.

---

[12]Desmond Ryan, who was a participant in the Easter Monday insurrection, writes that the streets of Dublin were indeed filled that day with "holiday makers." Desmond Ryan, *The Rising* (Dublin, 1966), p. 115. See also O Broin, *The Chief Secretary*, p. 173.

If the rising took the British by surprise, the majority of people in Ireland were no less astonished.[13] Crowds of bewildered and uncomprehending civilians watched detachments of armed men force the evacuation of various buildings in Dublin and begin preparations to withstand a military attack. Some revolutionaries wore uniforms of their own design, but most either displayed various insignias or exhibited no special designation whatever. Their force never included more than 1600 men, 200 or so were from the Citizen Army and perhaps 1360 were drawn from the Irish Volunteers.[14] The insurgents seized previously selected strongholds which they hoped to hold for as long as possible. Even their defensive strategy was faulty, however, for they failed to establish a base of operations at the city's center, College Green, by seizing either the Bank of Ireland or Trinity College. The General Post Office on Sackville Street, which served as headquarters for Patrick Pearse in his dual role as head of the provisional government of the republic of Ireland and commander-in-chief of the armed insurgents, was a solid building and was well adapted to endure a lengthy siege. But it was also poorly located for maintaining communications with the detachments holding the Four Courts, the College of Surgeons in St. Stephen's Green, and the several other rebel strongholds throughout the city.[15]

---

[13]Eoin MacNeill and other Irish Volunteer leaders were as surprised by the events of Easter Monday as were John Redmond and his colleagues in the Irish Parliamentary Party.

[14]There were women who participated in the rising as well. Countess Markievicz was one of two women commissioned in the Citizen Army; nine women participated in the attack on Dublin Castle, and thirty-four of them were in the armed contingent which seized the General Post Office. All told, some seventy-seven women were arrested after the rising. Brian Farrell, "Markievicz and the Women of the Revolution," in F. X. Martin, ed., *Leaders and Men of the Easter Rising: Dublin 1916* (New York, 1967), pp. 234–235.

[15]For an excellent account of the military tactics and logistics of the insurrection, see G. A. Hayes-McCoy, "A Military History of the 1916 Rising," in Nowlan, ed., *The Making of 1916*, pp. 255–304.

THE EASTER RISING

On Easter Monday, April 24, 1916, the British Army had only 111 officers and 2,316 other ranks on active duty in Dublin.[16] Its total force in Ireland consisted of approximately 3,000 cavalry, 17,000 infantry and 1,000 artillery troops. Within forty-eight hours of the rising, the Irish insurgents were outnumbered twenty to one, and additional British reinforcements continued to pour into the city. On Wednesday, Liberty Hall was blasted by artillery from the grounds of Trinity College, and by shells from the British gunboat *Helga* which had moved up the Liffey River from Dublin harbor to a strategic position opposite the Customs House. By this time, British troops had occupied Trinity College and also the Shelbourne Hotel overlooking St. Stephen's Green. This meant that the insurgents fighting in the northern and southern strongholds of the city had been effectively separated; the isolation and suppression of these forces was now only a matter of time. Outside of Dublin most of the regional Volunteer leaders were confused by the turn of events and frustrated by their inadequate supply of arms which, except in a few rare and localized instances, prevented the organization from taking action in the countryside.[17]

Accounts of the fighting which convulsed Dublin during Easter week 1916 have been told many times, often by the participants themselves or by eyewitnesses to the occurrence.[18] The character of the 1916 armed rebellion is espe-

[16]J. Bowyer Bell, *The Secret Army* (New York, 1971), p. 10. General Sir John Maxwell set the figure for all ranks at 2,427. *On the Rebellion in Ireland*, Cmd. 8311 of 1916, (H. M. Stationary Office, London), p. 160.

[17]There were local successes of varying size and duration in Wexford, Enniscorthy and Ferns. Liam Mellows led a Volunteer force from Galway into action but a lack of weapons forced them into an early retreat. Only Thomas Ashe, with a guerrilla column of less than fifty men, managed to win pitched battles in the countryside north of Dublin and to remain at large until Pearse's order to surrender.

[18]The best account by a participant is Ryan, *The Rising;* there are other excellent accounts by both participants and eyewitnesses in Roger McHugh, ed., *Dublin 1916* (New York, 1966); see also James Stephens, *Insurrection in Dublin* (London, 1916).

cially noteworthy, for it differed markedly from the guerrilla warfare which Irish Republicans would wage a few years later in the Irish war for independence. At noon on Easter Monday, 1916, in a proclamation read to a perplexed audience gathered in front of the General Post Office, Patrick Pearse formally announced the establishment of a provisional government of the Irish Republic.[19] The Irish Volunteers, the Citizen Army and the other combatants who joined Pearse's force became the new army of the Irish Republic and, although they lacked standard uniforms, they fought pitched battles in accord with the prevailing conventions of war. The British decision to treat the survivors of Pearse's army as traitors rather than as prisoners of war was legally defensible but tactically foolish. In their next militant challenge, Irish separatists would make no pretense of fighting by the rules and would instead adopt the methods which are now familiar to this century's many wars of national liberation.[20]

By Thursday evening the shelling by British artillery was intense; the words "Irish Republic" on the green flag above the General Post Office were scorched to a deep brown by flames which now consumed the top part of that building.[21] On the main floor Pearse and his men continued fighting for another day until, on Friday evening, the G.P.O. became untenable due to the smoke and flames. Against the roar of British cannon, described by one Irish insurgent as "deafening," the small force attempted its escape.[22] The O'Rahilly was killed when he led a vain attack against one of the British barricades, and the remainder of Pearse's detachment sought the refuge of nearby houses since the cordon of

---

[19]See appendix A for text.

[20]For further comment on the degree to which Ireland may be viewed as the precursor to more recent wars of national liberation, see Thomas E. Hachey, "Terrorism, Guerrilla Warfare and the Legacy of Partition: Ireland as a Case Study for Third World Nations," in Ray Johnston, ed., *The Politics of Division, Partition and Unification* (New York, 1976).

[21]Max Caufield, *The Easter Rebellion* (London, 1964), p. 332.

[22]Diarmuid Lynch, *The I.R.B. and the 1916 Rising*, edited by F. O'Donoghue (Cork, 1957), p. 175.

enemy troops had sealed all exits in the area. Connolly had been wounded twice earlier in the week and most of Pearse's other comrades were weak, exhausted and under considerable emotional strain. At noon on Saturday April 29, Pearse sent Elizabeth O'Farrell, one of the three women who had stayed with his force until the end, in search of the British military commander, Brigadier-General W. H. M. Lowe. She carried a white flag and this message of surrender: "The Commandant General of the Irish Republican Army wishes to treat with the Commandant General of the British forces in Ireland."[23]

After several exchanges between the two sides, during which O'Farrell carried messages to and fro, Pearse and Connolly agreed to sign a ceasefire order on the British terms of unconditional surrender. At 3:30 that afternoon Pearse, wearing his Volunteer uniform with its Boer War style slouch hat, ceremonially surrendered his sword to General Lowe on the steps of the gutted post office.[24] Under a British escort, Elizabeth O'Farrell carried Pearse's surrender order to the various isolated Volunteer strongholds throughout that day and part of the next. The Irish insurgents at each of these locations yielded reluctantly to the order. The last to capitulate was the force at Boland's Bakery which was under the command of Eamon de Valera, a young officer who would later play a dominant role in his nation's history.[25]

Meanwhile, on Thursday of Easter week, the London Government had dispatched Major-General Sir John Maxwell to Ireland and had entrusted him with absolute power over all military and civilian authorities for such time as would be necessary to reestablish law and order. There had been isolated instances of atrocities on both sides. A Volunteer, for example, had shot and killed a civilian who was attempting to extricate his cart from a barricade which the Irish insur-

---

[23]For Elizabeth O'Farrell's account of the surrender, see McHugh, ed., *Dublin 1916*, pp. 206–219.
[24]Robert Kee, *The Green Flag* (London, 1972), p. 569.
[25]Other future Irish leaders who surrendered with Patrick Pearse included Michael Collins, Desmond Fitzgerald and James Ryan.

gents had erected in St. Stephen's Green.²⁶ A mentally deranged officer in the British Army had arrested three journalists on the streets of Dublin during the insurrection and, without any trial or hearing, had ordered their execution before a make-shift firing squad. One of these victims was Francis Sheehy-Skeffington, an eccentric but widely admired advocate of humanitarian causes. He was also a temperance leader, a defender of women's rights, a socialist and, above all else, a pacifist.²⁷ At the time of his arrest he was in the embattled areas of the city helping the wounded and restraining his fellow-citizens from looting. And a fair share of looting, vandalism and arson took place in parts of Dublin since the police had been withdrawn from the onset of the fighting. Criminal elements were quick to take full advantage of that absence. But some of the plundering was done by the poor whose wretched existence was made truly desperate due to the increasing scarcity of food and the wholesale destruction of their dwellings. Martial law had been proclaimed in Dublin on Easter Monday, and had been extended to the rest of the country on Tuesday. The full implications of that ruling did not become apparent to the population, however, until General Maxwell undertook to discharge his duty after the insurgents had surrendered.²⁸

THE AFTERMATH OF THE EASTER RISING

The cost of the six day rising had been heavy, both in terms of the loss of human life and in the damage to property. A

²⁶Stephens, *Insurrection in Dublin,* p. 18.

²⁷For an instructive essay on Sheehy-Skeffington, written by his son, see Owen Sheehy-Skeffington, "Francis Sheehy-Skeffington," in O. Dudley Edwards and Fergus Pyle, eds., *1916: The Easter Rising* (London, 1968), pp. 135–148.

²⁸Lyons, *Ireland Since the Famine,* pp. 372–374. General Lord French, Commander of the Home Forces, gave General Maxwell a free hand in putting down the rebellion and in punishing those who had participated in it. Gerald French, *Life of Field Marshall Sir John French* (London, 1931), p. 341.

British military and police casualty list released on May 11 stated that approximately 120 of their number had been killed, with 383 listed as wounded. The number of Irish Volunteers reported as killed in action was 52, and the complete Irish casualty list, including civilians, was announced later as 450 dead and 2,614 wounded. Sackville Street, once one of Europe's most beautiful streets, lay in ruins and throughout central Dublin the burnt-out shells of once grand buildings dotted the landscape. All told, the estimated cost of destruction to the city was placed at £2,500,000.[29]

It was against this collective outrage that General Maxwell began to seek retribution following the surrender of the Irish insurgents in Dublin. Large scale arrests were made throughout the country, and several thousand persons were taken into custody. A total of 169 men and one woman, Countess Markievicz, were convicted by general court martial and no less than ninety death sentences were declared. Nearly 1800 men and five women were deported to England and interned there for periods generally extending from a few weeks to several months and more.[30] General Maxwell intended to crush revolutionary nationalism in the egg, and he initially enjoyed the support of a majority of the people and of the press in Ireland. Many among the Dublin poor were hungry and unemployed after the rebellion, and the middle-class was angry at the destruction of its shops and businesses. Given the temper of the time, it is easy to understand how General Maxwell might have misinterpreted public sentiment when he decided to act upon the death sentences which had been passed by the courts.[31]

There were also British and Irish political casualties in the wake of the Dublin insurrection. Wimborne, Birrell and Nathan were all compelled to resign, and only Wimborne was

---

[29]For the statistics on the cost to life and property, see Edgar Holt, *Protest in Arms: The Irish Troubles, 1916–1923* (London, 1960), pp. 116–117.

[30]One estimate of the total number of those arrested is approximately 3,500, and those deported to England as 1,706. See Bell, *The Secret Army*, p. 12.

[31]For a commentary on the Irish press reaction to the rising, see Edwards and Pyle, eds., *1916: The Easter Rising*, pp. 255–271.

later reinstated. The Irish Parliamentary Party did not know it then, but the executions which followed the Easter week insurrection had doomed constitutional nationalism to an early demise. John Redmond expressed a feeling of "detestation and horror" over the fighting in Dublin, and felt that Ireland was still loyal since only 1500 men had joined the insurrection while 150,000 Irishmen were then "wearing the king's uniform in the British Army."[32]

John Dillon, the only Irish Parliamentary Party leader who had actually witnessed the insurrection in Dublin, was in a better position than his chief to assess the mood of the people in Ireland. Dillon wrote Redmond on April 30: "You should urge strongly on the Government the *extreme* unwisdom of any wholesale shooting of prisoners. The wisest course is to execute *no one* for the present." Otherwise, Dillon predicted, the effect on public opinion might be "disastrous in the extreme."[33] Redmond conveyed this advice to Prime Minister Asquith who in turn asked General Lord French to caution Maxwell that wholesale executions could result in a negative reaction both in Britain and in Ireland. But French also told General Maxwell that the government would not interfere with his freedom of action.[34] It is, therefore, not surprising that Maxwell, a soldier rather than a statesman, should have acted as he did.[35] He began a series of courtmartials on May 3, and fourteen Irish separatists were condemned to death and executed during the next nine days. As the General later explained, the great loss of life and destruction of property caused by the rising, compounded by Ger-

---

[32]Denis Gwynn, *The Life of John Redmond* (London, 1932), pp. 474; 491. Only a few weeks earlier, Redmond had received a letter with the king's thanks for the gift of a book entitled *Irish at the Front* which contained a preface by the Irish Parliamentary Party chairman. See Clive Wigram for H.R.H., Buckingham Palace, to John Redmond, April 3, 1916. *Redmond Mss.* 15, 188. National Library of Ireland.

[33]Gwynn, *The Life of John Redmond,* p. 475.

[34]French, *Life of Field Marshall Sir John French,* pp. 340–341.

[35]Maxwell was a professional soldier who had served without unusual distinction in the Sudan and South Africa, and who seems to have had no particular qualifications for dealing with the delicate political problems which confronted him. Holt, *Protest in Arms,* p. 118.

man intrigue on the part of its leaders, required the most severe sentences in order to deter others from imperiling the future safety of the realm.[36]

It is true that the insurrection had involved a treasonable conspiracy, as well as the deaths of many British soldiers. The penalty for such an offense almost certainly would have been capital punishment in virtually any of the nations then at war in 1916. Maxwell's blunder was not in authorizing the executions, but rather in his dilatory handling of the courts-martial. Beginning on May 3, and lasting until May 12, Irish insurgents who were sentenced to death were shot by a firing squad in a yard at Kilmainham jail. Each day new names were added to the list of the dead; these included Pearse, MacDonagh, Clarke, MacDermott and Ceannt. Joseph Plunkett was executed in spite of the fact that he was already dying of a tubercular condition; James Connolly, gravely wounded, needed to be tied to a chair in order to remain erect before being shot. Public opinion in Ireland began to change notably. When these same men had been led off to jail following their surrender, people had cursed and jeered them. The executions, however, made the British appear vindictive and cruel, while the imprisonment of hundreds without trial seemed arbitrary. To a very real extent, General Maxwell helped Pearse fulfill his dream of a "blood sacrifice" which would awaken Ireland from her apathy. Within a few weeks the "dirty traitors" of Easter week would become gallant martyrs and national heroes. Their pictures would adorn Irish homes and their speeches and poems would become an enduring inspiration to many. In a verse composed shortly after the rising, Yeats wrote "a terrible beauty is born." That terrible beauty would soon take the form of a virulent renewal of militant separatism in Ireland.[37]

---

[36]O Broin, *Dublin Castle*, p. 126.

[37]P. S. O'Hegarty, a member of the I.R.B. and a participant in the insurrection, admits that republicanism in Ireland might have been destroyed if the Government had demonstrated clemency instead of vengeance. P. S. O'Hegarty, *The Victory of Sinn Fein* (Dublin, 1924), pp. 3–4.

Throughout the days in which the executions were conducted there were numerous appeals made to the London Government on behalf of the Irish prisoners by Irish Party leaders, English liberals, and Roman Catholic bishops in the United Kingdom. On May 5, 1916, the British Ambassador to Washington, Sir Cecil Spring Rice, telegraphed the London Foreign Office that Cardinal Gibbons of Baltimore urged the British to consider leniency toward the Irish prisoners. Gibbons, the Ambassador said, felt all respectable Irishmen condemned the revolt but there was a danger of manufacturing martyrs with senseless executions.[38] Spring Rice sent another message on May 10 stating that the executions were creating considerable discussion in the United States.[39] What influence, if any, American opinion had upon the London Government's decision to halt the executions is uncertain. But seventy-five of the ninety prisoners initially sentenced to death did have their sentences commuted to various terms of penal servitude. Two of the more eminent among these were Countess Markievicz who, much to her chagrin, was spared because of her sex; and Eamon de Valera, whom, it has been said, the British spared because they thought him to be an American citizen. There is no evidence to support this assumption, however, and the likelihood is that de Valera was shown the same clemency accorded to seventy-four others who were under the sentence of death but had not signed the proclamation of the Provisional Government.[40]

The United States State Department did make inquiries with the British respecting an American citizen, Jeremiah (Diarmuid) Lynch, who had been arrested for his participa-

---

[38]Spring Rice to Foreign Secretary, 5 May 1916, *FO* 371/2851. One foreign office member reacted: "It would require a vast amount of 'manufacturing' to turn Casement into a Martyr." *FO* Minute, 5 May 1916, Ibid.

[39]Spring Rice to Foreign Secretary, 10 May 1916, *FO* 371/2797. The Ambassador had also written a few days previously that the *New York Times* and several other leading American newspapers, all of which had condemned the rising, regarded the executions as incredibly stupid. Spring Rice to Foreign Secretary, 4 May 1916, *FO* 115/2073.

[40]Alan Ward, *Ireland and Anglo-American Relations, 1899–1921* (Toronto, 1969), pp. 117–118.

tion in the rising.[41] However, no official representations were made on behalf of de Valera. United States and world opinion doubtlessly were a concern to the British, but the London Government's decision to suspend the executions was prompted primarily by internal considerations.[42]

THE TRIAL OF ROGER CASEMENT

Perhaps by May 12, after the execution of 14 men in Dublin and one in Cork,[43] it was already too late for any British policy of restraint to check the rising spirit of Anglophobia in Ireland. Yet, the situation was aggravated still further by Roger Casement's trial in London, during which friends in England, Ireland and America vainly attempted to intercede on his behalf up to the very day of his execution on August 3 at Pentonville prison. One thing which made the Casement trial a particularly bitter event in this acrimonious period of Anglo-Irish affairs was the fact that the prosecutor, Sir Frederick Smith, was a man who had himself organized armed resistance to the crown only two years before in Ulster.[44] In the United States, Casement's sister, Agnes Newman, made a futile appeal on April 27 to Acting Secretary of State Frank Polk who told her that the State Department had no legal ground for intervention in British courts save in cases involving American citizens. On the following day, Gertrude Bannister, Casement's cousin in London, appealed to Foreign

---

[41]Page to Foreign Secretary, 19 May 1916, *FO* 372/907. American Ambassador Walter Hines Page made the inquiry at the direction of the United States State Department.

[42]For evidence that the London Government was concerned with political reaction in the United Kingdom, and not with that in the United States or elsewhere, see *FO* Minute, 11 May 1916, *FO* 371/2797.

[43]Thomas Kent, a Cork Volunteer who had killed a policeman two days following the insurrection, was executed by a firing squad in Cork on May 9.

[44]For Casement's trial, see H. Montgomery Hyde, *The Trial of Sir Roger Casement* (London, 1960).

Secretary Sir Edward Grey for clemency.[45] The London Government received communications counseling leniency for the defendant from a number of prominent Americans and from a few prominent Englishmen, including the British Ambassador to the United States.[46] Prime Minister Asquith and his Cabinet were unmoved, however, even after the United States Senate passed a resolution on July 29, by a vote of 46 to 19, with 30 abstentions, calling for "clemency in the treatment of Irish political prisoners." The British responded by saying that they were not favorably impressed by the action of the Senate on behalf of the Irish prisoners since, if humanity was its motive, that body had never shown a similar concern over German atrocities in Belgium or over Turkish massacres in Armenia. American opinion probably was a factor in the Cabinet's deliberations, but the conclusion it reached on August 2 was that clemency simply could not be granted in Sir Roger's case.[47]

Irish Americans were represented at the trial by Philadelphia attorney M. F. Doyle, who was retained by Casement's sister and paid $5,000 by John Devoy and the Clan na Gael.[48] Doyle wanted the defendant to plead the truth, that he had gone to Ireland to prevent a rising; to plead not guilty to treason; and to demand to be held as a prisoner of war.[49]

---

[45]Bannister to Grey, 28 April 1916, *FO* 800/196. She also wrote to Under-Secretary Lord Cecil who replied that it would be impossible to interfere in any way with the trial "even if I were disposed to do so." Cecil to Bannister, 4 May 1916. Ibid.

[46]Ambassador Spring Rice warned London repeatedly of the adverse effect which Casement's execution would have upon American opinion, and Irish-American electors in particular. The Foreign Office, however, concluded: "We could expect nothing but hostility from the Irish vote in any case." *FO* Minute, 31 May 1916, *FO* 371/2797.

[47]Ward, *Ireland and Anglo-American Relations*, p. 120.

[48]British Ambassador Spring Rice, in a ciphered telegram to the London Foreign Office, made an unsubstantiated claim that Irish American leaders favored Casement's execution because it would contribute further to anti-British sentiment. Spring Rice to Foreign Secretary, 30 July 1916, *FO* 371/2797.

[49]For Doyle's secret negotiations with the British respecting possible pleas, see *FO* 371/2798.

Casement refused to state that his return to Ireland had been for the purpose of preventing a rising, for he believed that doing so would undermine whatever benefit had accrued to Ireland from it. His chief counsel, A. M. Sullivan, second Sargeant of the Irish Bar, therefore prepared a defense based on a challenge to the prosecution's interpretation of the Treason Act of 1351. The statute, known as 25 Edward III, Cap. 2, was sufficiently ambiguous as to make it appear that a man could not be tried for treason if his offense had been committed outside the realm. Sullivan could have rendered a far more effective defense for his client had he acted upon an initial impulse to compare the treasonable utterances of the Unionist leaders before the war with those of Casement after it.[50] But as Casement's biographer Brian Inglis has shown, Sullivan was anxious not to offend Attorney General Sir Frederick Smith who "would not be pleased to be reminded of what he said, before the war."[51] Ultimately, however, it was not so much Sullivan's apparent intimidation as it was his client's sexual indiscretions which proved most damaging to the defense in this trial.

Sir Roger Casement's diaries for 1903, 1910, and 1911 had been found in a trunk and taken from his former lodgings in London by government authorities, apparently late in 1914. Most of the material in them relates pedestrian and inconsequential occurrences. There are, however, occasional entries which portray the writer as a compulsive and obsessive homosexual.[52] Some members of the London Government were hopeful that it might be possible to avoid another execution and its attendant negative impact upon world opinion, by having Casement declared insane. Prime Minister

---

[50]George Dangerfield, *The Damnable Question* (Boston, 1976), p. 243.

[51]Brian Inglis, *Roger Casement* (London, 1973), p. 342.

[52]References to homosexual activities represent perhaps no more than five per cent of the diaries' contents. See Peter Singleton-Gates and Maurice Girodias, eds., *The Black Diaries* (New York, 1959). British Home Secretary Sir William Joynson-Hicks threatened, in 1925, to prosecute author Peter Singleton-Gates under the Official Secrets Act if he attempted to publish this book.

Asquith's Cabinet was split between ministers advocating execution and those favoring Casement's confinement to an asylum for the purpose of denying Irish nationalism another martyr. On July 5 the Cabinet submitted copies of Casement's diaries for psychological analysis. Opposition to Casement's execution by Cabinet members became more difficult when the psychologist reported that the defendant, though abnormal, was certainly not certifiably insane.[53]

Some of Casement's defenders have insisted that the compromising passages in the diaries were the forged interpolations of Captain, later Admiral, Reginald Hall, chief of British naval intelligence. It is true that Hall very probably was one of the London Government officials who, during the trial, circulated photographic reproductions of diary excerpts among selected members of the House of Commons, the diplomatic corps, and the press in an effort to destroy or neutralize sympathy for Casement.[54] The authenticity of the diaries, however, has since been established to the satisfaction of several competent and objective investigators.[55]

Casement's homosexuality was irrelevant to the charge of high treason for which he was hanged. It was a measure of the hatred and bitterness which pervaded Anglo-Irish affairs after the rising that such smear tactics were so extensively employed by ministers of the British Government. British Ambassador Spring Rice wrote a prominent member of the Irish-American community, Bourke Cockrane, on May 14, 1916, "It seems that Casement has for years been abnormal sexually."[56] In a subsequent communication to Foreign Secretary Grey, which the latter reproduced for the confidential use of the British Cabinet, Spring Rice reported that "The

---

[53]Ward, *Ireland and Anglo-American Relations,* pp. 114–121; see also Roy Jenkins, *Asquith* (New York, 1966), pp. 403–404.

[54]James, *The Code Breakers of Room 40,* pp. 113–114.

[55]In addition to biographers H. Montgomery Hyde and Rene MacColl, the diaries have been indentified as Casement's by the distinguished handwriting expert Dr. Wilson Harrison. See Rene MacColl, *Roger Casement* (London, 1965), p. 7.

[56]Spring Rice to Cockrane, 14 May 1916, *FO* 115/2073.

agitation in Congress is rather checked by the dread that some publication will be made exposing the private character of Casement, which makes statesmen somewhat wary of making impassionate encomiums which may afterwards be made to assume a somewhat ridiculous aspect."[57] Such diverse people as the Archbishop of Canterbury and the Chairman of the Irish Parliamentary Party were influenced in their attitudes toward Casement as a result of disclosures from the diaries.[58] Neither of these men, however, favored the death sentence which had been pronounced against Casement. But the war was going badly for England and clemency for the Irish "traitors" was not a politically attractive cause. As the Home Secretary told his wife, it "would be bitterly resented by the great mass of the people in Great Britain and by the whole of the army."[59] Indeed, the degree of resentment felt in England was reflected in the treatment accorded the executed prisoners even after death. General Sir John Maxwell denied Pearse's body the right of burial in consecrated ground; instead it was placed in quick-lime. Roger Casement's remains were similarly treated, and the British Government refused to permit Casement's reburial in Ireland for another fifty years.

---

[57]Spring Rice to Foreign Secretary, 4 August 1916, *FO* 371/2798. The Ambassador, acting upon instructions from London, also informed Apostolic Delegate Monsignor Bonzano in Washington that "His Majesty's Government were in possession of evidence which would make it extremely undesirable that priests of the Catholic Church should publicly ascribe to Casement the character of a Christian martyr, whose life should be held up as a model to the faithful." Spring Rice to Foreign Secretary, 15 August 1916, Ibid.

[58]Denis Gwynn, *The Life and Death of Roger Casement* (London, 1931), pp. 16–17.

[59]Inglis, *Roger Casement,* p. 366.

Chapter 7

Reaction to the Rising: The Growth of Sinn Fein (1916–1918)

Realizing that Ireland could not be governed indefinitely under martial law, Prime Minister Herbert Asquith undertook a fact-finding visit to that country from May 12 to May 19, 1916. In that short time he visited with Nationalists in Dublin, Unionists in Belfast, republican prisoners at Richmond Barracks, and British military authorities at Dublin Castle.[1] Upon his return to London, Asquith informed the House of Commons that the old machinery of government in Ireland had ceased to function and announced that the time had come for a new departure. Because he believed that the swift implementation of a home rule settlement might yet afford his ministry a viable Irish policy, Asquith asked his fellow party and cabinet member David Lloyd George to initiate discussions concerning a home rule agreement with Irish Nationalist and Unionist leaders.

As a result of the coalition ministry which Asquith had

---

[1]Roy Jenkins, *Asquith* (New York, 1966), pp. 397–398.

formed in 1915, Ulster Unionists exercised a far stronger control over the government in 1916 than they had enjoyed before World War I. In order to accomodate this new political reality, Lloyd George persuaded John Redmond to restrict the application of the 1914 Government of Ireland Act to the twenty-six southern counties only, excluding for the moment the six northeastern counties in Ulster. Lloyd George next converted Sir Edward Carson to this view with such remarks as "The Irish-American vote will go over to the German side, they [the Germans] will break our blockade and force an ignominious peace on us, unless something is done, even provisionally, to satisfy America."[2] Ulster Nationalists loudly condemned Lloyd George's partition scheme, but finally accepted it after Redmond threatened to resign from the leadership of the Irish Parliamentary Party. Carson experienced similar resistance from Southern Unionists who accused their leader of abandoning them. For his part, Lloyd George had achieved even this modest agreement only through deception; his strategy had been to promise Redmond that the exclusion of the six counties was temporary, while simultaneously assuring Carson that it was permanent.[3]

Redmond's ablest colleague, John Dillon, supported his chief in the negotiations with Lloyd George only from a sense of party loyalty. Dillon's skepticism proved well founded when the ambiguities in Lloyd George's "Headings of Agreement" on Ireland were attacked in Parliament. Lord Lansdowne, a Conservative Cabinet minister, publicly denounced the partition formula as a surrender to force despite the fact that Redmond had already agreed to maximum safeguards for Britain's military and naval interests in Ireland.[4]

[2]William O'Brien, *The Irish Revolution and How It Came About* (London, 1923), p. 273

[3]Edgar Holt, *Protest in Arms: The Irish Troubles, 1916–1923* (London, 1960), pp. 116–117.

[4]Some Irish Parliamentary Party members, like T. P. O'Connor, believed it would be necessary for an Irish government to maintain a British military presence in Ireland even after home rule. It was the only way, O'Connor

John Redmond felt compelled to withdraw his earlier endorsement of the proposed compromise after Lansdowne's speech, and Lloyd George responded that the settlement had been wrecked by extremists on both sides. Asquith's ministry at least could appear to the United States as having attempted to solve the Irish problem, but the failure to reach an agreement dealt a serious blow to John Redmond and to the cause of constitutional nationalism in Ireland.[5]

PRIME MINISTER LLOYD GEORGE CREATES A COALITION GOVERNMENT

In July 1916, Minister of Munitions David Lloyd George assumed the post of Secretary of State for War. Thereafter, Conservatives who were discontented with Asquith's wartime leadership actively supported Lloyd George's determined bid to gain control of the British war effort.[6] How the dynamic Lloyd George displaced the more serene and less flamboyant Asquith as Prime Minister on December 7, 1916, was of less importance to the cause of Irish separatism than was the new coalition ministry which was next created. Sir Edward Carson, who had been succeeded by F. E. Smith as Attorney General in Asquith's coalition on November 3, 1915, returned to the Cabinet as the First Lord of the Admiralty. Walter Long, a staunch Ulster Unionist supporter, became Colonial Secretary. Lord Curzon, Lord Milner, and

---

reasoned, to reassure Unionists who were fearful that the Nationalists could not or would not keep extremists in check. T. P. O'Connor to John Dillon, 28 June 1916. *Redmond MSS.*, National Library of Ireland, Ms. 15,215.

[5]For the best account of this entire episode, see F. S. L. Lyons, *John Dillon: A Biography* (London, 1968), pp. 387–403.

[6]For Lloyd George's own account of the events which led to his assumption of the premiership, see David Lloyd George, *War Memoirs*, Vol. 1 (London, 1938), chapter 35. Lord Beaverbrook is credited with having planned much of the strategy which led to Lloyd George's displacement of Asquith. For Beaverbrook's informed view, see Lord Beaverbrook, *Politicians and the War, 1914–1916* (London, 1960), pp. 362–545.

Andrew Bonar Law, all of whom had urged Ulster to defy both king and constitution in 1914, were appointed to the War Cabinet.

IRISH ALIENATION FROM BRITAIN INCREASES

T. P. O'Connor, the Irish Parliamentary Party member from Liverpool, thought it would be propitious for the new Prime Minister to announce the release of Irish political prisoners on the occasion of his first speech to the House of Commons as head of government. O'Connor wrote Lloyd George on December 11, 1916:

> Thursday is your debut, your premiere, and that is the occasion to do something striking. No announcement at a later date, however satisfactory, could have the same effect. Given on Thursday, the announcement stamps it as the beginning of a new era between the Government and Ireland, as a message of peace. The main defect of so many reforms carried out in Ireland has been lack of promptitude and lack of graciousness; I am afraid if you defer the announcement this new message will suffer from the same things.[7]

Lloyd George responded the next week with a goodwill gesture in which he announced the release of 560 of those prisoners who had been interned without trial and had not been sentenced by court-martial.[8] It was, however, too late for gestures. The national mood in Ireland had become in-

---

[7]In this same letter, O'Connor complimented Lloyd George on "the dramatic originality and courage of your [Cabinet] appointments." T. P. O'Connor to the Prime Minister, 11 December 1916. *Lloyd George MSS.,* F/42/2/1, Beaverbrook Library.

[8]The British Government was not prepared, however, to publish the particulars of the Courts Martial. John Dillon had been told by Asquith that these proceedings would be published, but Bonar Law wrote the latter saying that the Cabinet had decided not to in view of "the present state of Ireland." A. Bonar Law to Herbert Asquith, 28 February 1917, *Bonar Law MSS.,* 84/6/53, Beaverbrook Library.

creasingly restive and notably more hostile toward Britain from the time when the Irish prisoners had left home at Easter to their return at Christmas.[9] Roger Casement's trial, the failure of Lloyd George's home rule negotiations, and the persistent rumors that conscription would soon be applied to Ireland all contributed to the growing alienation of the Irish people from the British government. Martial law had been somewhat relaxed as a result of the appointment of H. E. Duke as Chief Secretary for Ireland, but the country remained under the control of the immensely unpopular Major General Sir John Maxwell until his recall in November, 1916.

Meanwhile, the I.R.B., the secret society which had been responsible for the planning and execution of the Easter rebellion, was actively seeking to exploit public disenchantment with the British parliamentary system. This advanced nationalist organization had not been destroyed but only forced underground in the period following the insurrection. In the internment camps in England the I.R.B. men succeeded in politically radicalizing Irish Volunteers who had previously embraced the moderate views of their chief, Eoin MacNeill, and who had participated in the Easter rebellion only because they had been trained to follow orders.[10] Upon their return to Ireland, these I.R.B. recruits joined forces with those in the organization who had escaped arrest and were already planning the next armed rebellion against Britain. What the I.R.B. required, however, was a more broadly based national organization through which it could exploit

---

[9]Michael Collins was surprised by the tepid reception given him in his community upon his return. Margery Forester, *Michael Collins: The Lost Leader* (London, 1971), p. 61. Many people who were angry at Britain were not certain of exactly where their sentiments lay. The prisoners released a short time later under an amnesty, however, were given a tumultuous welcome. Sympathy in Ireland had swung behind the men who had been jeered and taunted at the time of their arrests.

[10]At internment camps like Frongoch in Wales new men were recruited for the I.R.B. Old tactics and strategies were discussed, lengthy seminars on Republican philosophy were held, and morale was sustained by raising havoc with the carefully regulated prison system. J. Bowyer Bell, *The Secret Army* (New York, 1971), p. 14.

the political discontent in the country, and channel it toward the militant separatist goal of an Irish republic. For many advanced nationalists, Sinn Fein appeared best suited to fulfill that purpose.

SINN FEIN

Sinn Fein was at this time still committed to the same tactics which that organization had advocated since 1906: passive resistance, nonattendance at Westminster, and self-reliance in every aspect of the country's existence. But its public image was something different. It is noteworthy, for example, that Prime Minister Asquith, after having met with Irish political prisoners during his week long inquiry in Ireland, referred to them as "Sinn Feiners."[11] Indeed, many people in both Ireland and Britain believed that the rising had been the work of Arthur Griffith's separatist following, a conviction which was strengthened by frequent press references to the "Sinn Fein Rebellion."[12] This was perhaps a reasonable assumption since the real architects of the insurrection were members of a secret organization known only to a small group of people, whereas Sinn Fein had been a highly vocal and visible separatist movement for more than a decade. There were Sinn Feiners who participated in the rising, but they did so as Volunteers, or as Citizen Army men, and not as members of Griffith's organization.[13]

Arthur Griffith had declined to join the Supreme Council of the I.R.B. in 1914, fearing that his free expression of opinion in national affairs would be hampered as a result of such membership. He was as astonished as was Irish Volunteer Commander-in-Chief Eoin MacNeill when he learned of the

[11]Jenkins, *Asquith,* p. 398.
[12]Irish newspapers, no less than those in Britain and America, referred repeatedly to the Easter week insurrection as the "Sinn Fein Rebellion".
[13]F. S. L. Lyons, *Ireland Since the Famine* (New York, 1971), p. 380.

intended rising on Saturday, April 22. Griffith hoped that MacNeill's countermanding order would prevent an outbreak, but once it occurred he promptly offered to join the insurgents in what he perceived as a heroic but misguided struggle. The leaders at the embattled General Post Office replied that Griffith should not join them since the propaganda value of his future newspaper work would be more valuable to Ireland. The wisdom of that decision was soon evident. Although Griffith endured arrest and imprisonment, both of which were quickly becoming credentials for political respectability in Ireland, he was released before the end of the year. He then resumed publishing *Nationality*, the voice of Sinn Fein, with a campaign demanding Ireland's right to put her case before a Peace Conference when the war was over.[14]

Sinn Fein's development into a formidable political force in Ireland began in early 1917 when the death of J. J. O'Kelly, Irish Parliamentary Party M.P. for North Roscommon, required the holding of a by-election in that constituency. The advanced nationalists decided to challenge the Irish party nominee and chose as their candidate Count Plunkett (George Noble), the Papal count who was the father of the executed Joseph Plunkett and of two other sons then in English prisons. Plunkett had been dismissed by the government from his position as Director of the National Museum in Dublin and deported to England because his son had been one of the seven signatories of the proclamation issued by the Irish insurgents at the outset of Easter week.[15] Although Plunkett ran as an Independent, Arthur Griffith's Sinn Fein organization was extremely active in his support. Plunkett's identification with advanced separatism doubtlessly ac-

---

[14]Ibid., See also Sean O Luing, "Arthur Griffith and Sinn Fein," in F. X. Martin, ed., *Leaders and Men of the Easter Rising: Dublin 1916* (New York, 1967), pp. 62–63. The I.R.B. had such respect for Griffith that its leadership promised to keep him informed of "all developments" even after he had declined to join them.

[15]Plunkett was also expelled from the Royal Dublin Society because of his sons' activities.

counted for his decisive victory which, when announced on February 5, showed him to have received nearly three times as many votes as had the Irish party's nominee.[16] Plunkett then announced that he did not intend to take his seat in the "foreign parliament" at Westminster.

The ominous implications of this political challenge for constitutional nationalism were not lost upon the leadership of the Irish party. That party had dominated virtually every Irish constituency outside East Ulster for nearly forty years.[17] Both Redmond and Dillon made concerted efforts on behalf of their candidates in Sinn Fein contested by-elections which were held in May, July, and August, but Sinn Fein won all three. Even more notable was the East Clare by-election held that autumn. The Sinn Fein candidate was Eamon de Valera, the senior surviving commandant of the Easter rebellion. De Valera's death sentence had been commuted earlier to twenty-years imprisonment. On June 15, 1917, he and the other 117 remaining Irish prisoners arrested after the insurrection had been freed in accordance with a general amnesty which Prime Minister Lloyd George had granted as a goodwill gesture. Perhaps the Irish Parliamentary Party did not expect to win the East Clare election, with so much of the electorate now sympathetic to the rebellion leaders, but de Valera's landslide victory could only have dismayed constitutional Nationalists.[18] When the Sinn Fein victors followed

---

[16]Denis Gwynn, *The Life of John Redmond* (London, 1932), p. 539.

[17]Prior to 1917, Sinn Fein had been primarily an urban movement. Plunkett was selected as the Sinn Fein candidate for rural North Roscommon mainly because he was the father of an executed rebel leader, and he made no pretense at campaigning on local issues. His impressive victory was both a repudiation of the Parliamentary Party and a vote for the 1916 rising. See Joseph Lee, *The Modernisation of Irish Society, 1848–1918* (Dublin, 1973), pp. 157–158.

[18]De Valera campaigned on a platform which went far beyond the home rule act on the statute book. He told East Clare constituents that he was committed to the principle of liberty and complete independence for Ireland. P. S. O'Hegarty, *The Victory of Sinn Fein* (Dublin, 1924), p. 32. The result of the polling was 5,010 votes for de Valera and 2,035 votes for the Irish party candidate, Patrick Lynch, who came from one of the most established families in county Clare. The Earl of Longford and Thomas P. O'Neill, *Eamon de Valera* (Boston, 1971), pp. 64–65.

Plunkett's example and refused to take their seats at Westminster, the credibility of the Irish Parliamentary Party as the voice of nationalist Ireland was seriously compromised both at home and in the House of Commons.

THE IRISH CONVENTION

During the spring of 1917, Prime Minister Lloyd George came under increased pressure to reach an Irish settlement. He was urged to accomplish that goal by members of his government who were concerned about the effect of the Irish problem on the war effort, by political leaders from several of the Dominions, and by the President of the United States.[19] When America joined the Allied war effort in April 1917, President Woodrow Wilson pledged his country's support for the right of "self-determination" for all people. Wilson received many demands from Irish-American groups that this pledge be extended to Ireland, and the President responded by asking Lloyd George to demonstrate London's good faith by attempting to reconcile Irish nationalist demands.[20] The British Prime Minister tried once more to win John Redmond's agreement to the plan for immediate home rule for twenty-six counties, with northeastern Ulster excluded for some indefinite period. Redmond refused but suggested convening a conference of Irishmen, drawn from all segments of society, who would seek to resolve the various

[19]A. J. P. Taylor argues that Lloyd George's aim at this time "was more to satisfy American and Dominion opinion than to find a solution." A. J. P. Taylor, *English History, 1914–1945* (Oxford, 1965), p. 83. For President Wilson's influence upon the Prime Minister regarding the Irish question in this critical period for Anglo-American relations see Francis Carroll, "American Opinion on the Irish Question, 1910–1923" (Ph.D. dissertation, Trinity College, Dublin, 1969), pp. 185–251.

[20]For a further analysis of America's involvement in Anglo-Irish affairs prior to the United States entry into the war see Alan Ward, *Ireland and Anglo-American Relations, 1899–1921* (Toronto, 1969), pp. 126–140; another account, which is partisan to the Irish and hostile to President Wilson, is Charles Tansill, *America and the Fight for Irish Freedom, 1866–1922* (New York, 1957).

impediments to self-government for their country. Lloyd George welcomed the idea and promised to pay the administrative costs for the gathering. The Irish Convention, as it came to be known, met in Dublin and held its first session on July 25, 1917, and its last on April 5, 1918.[21]

Sir Horace Plunkett agreed to serve as chairman for the Irish Convention and ninety-five delegates were appointed by such widely disparate constituencies as the Irish Parliamentary Party, Ulster Unionists, Southern Unionists, the Catholic Church, the Presbyterian Church, the Church of Ireland, Chambers of Commerce, and others. Even Sinn Fein was offered five seats, but it declined to participate in the Convention. After eight months of sessions, the Convention came to a futile end. Two of the reasons for its failure were the boycott by Sinn Fein and the continued determination of Ulster Unionists to resist home rule in any form. Perhaps the most notable result of the Convention was the creation of a permanent schism between the Southern Unionists, led by Lord Midleton, who believed that a restricted form of home rule was the most feasible policy for all Ireland, and the Ulster Unionists, who consistently voted against every motion for an Irish parliament.[22] John Redmond, his health failing, labored hard to form an alliance with the Southern Unionists by promising concessions which ultimately served only to alienate him from some of his Irish party colleagues.[23] Redmond died at the age of 61 on March 6, 1918, in the knowledge that the cause to which he had devoted his life, self-government for all of Ireland within the British Empire, had ended in failure.

---

[21]The definitive study on the convention is R. B. McDowell, *The Irish Convention, 1917–1918* (London, 1970).

[22]For Midleton's own account of the Ulster Unionist-Southern Unionist schism at this time, see The Earl of Midleton, *Ireland-Dupe or Heroine* (London, 1932), pp. 110–121; see also by the same author, *Records and Reactions, 1856–1939* (London, 1939), pp. 237–238.

[23]Redmond even considered limiting the power of an Irish parliament to levy its own customs duties, a proposition which was opposed by members of his own party and also by several convention delegates representing the Catholic hierarchy in Ireland.

While the Irish Convention was in progress, Sinn Fein continued to hold meetings, conduct membership drives and, owing to the government's ill-considered policies, grow in size and prosperity. Dublin Castle conducted a campaign of selective harrassment against Sinn Fein; some of the organization's meetings were banned, its uniforms were prohibited, and a number of its leaders were arrested. One of those apprehended was Thomas Ashe who was charged with attempting to incite the civilian population against the government and sentenced to a year's hard labor.[24] In Mountjoy jail Ashe went on a hunger strike and died a month later. His death was partly a consequence of the harsh treatment and forcible feedings to which he had been subjected.[25] The resurgence of the Easter week spirit in Ireland was evident at Ashe's funeral on September 30, 1917. Government regulations against para-military dress and the bearing of arms were flagrantly disregarded when Thomas Ashe was buried at Glasnevin cemetery by uniformed Irish Volunteers who fired three volleys over his grave.[26]

In September, 1917, Sinn Fein was plagued by opposing groups within its ranks which shared only their opposition to British rule in Ireland. The relationship of the I.R.B. to the Irish Volunteers, and of both groups to Sinn Fein, was not at all clear. The resulting confusion was a legitimate concern of all advanced nationalists. Arthur Griffith was still an advocate of nonviolence. He opposed those who demanded an independent republic and who would espouse forcible means if they should be required. Sinn Fein's tenth annual convention (Ard-Fheis) in October 1917 became the scene of a pro-

---

[24]Thomas Ashe had been among the prisoners released under the terms of Lloyd George's amnesty in June, 1917. Shortly thereafter, he was elected President of the Supreme Council of the I.R.B. Sean O Luing, *I Die in A Good Cause: A Study of Thomas Ashe* (Dublin, 1970), p. 124.

[25]Holt, *Protest in Arms*, p. 145.

[26]The funeral was conducted under the auspices of the Irish Volunteers but it was Ashe's I.R.B. comrade, Michael Collins, who gave the brief eulogy at the burial. P. Beaslai, *Michael Collins and the Making of a New Ireland*, Vol. 1 (London, 1926), p. 166.

tracted and sometimes bitter struggle between republican and nonrepublican delegates. Eamon de Valera produced a compromise agreement which in fact constituted a victory for the republicans. His resolution read: "Sinn Fein aims at securing the international recognition of Ireland as an independent Irish Republic. Having achieved that status the Irish people may by referendum freely choose their own form of government." On October 25, the Sinn Fein delegates endorsed the compromise formula and unanimously elected Eamon de Valera president.[27] Arthur Griffith, the organization's original founder, had graciously stepped aside. Griffith believed that de Valera could provide Sinn Fein with the unity needed to defeat the Irish Parliamentary Party and to implement the political objectives affirmed in the convention's resolution.[28]

Although effective unity among the advanced nationalists was still absent, and total harmony would never be achieved, a major step in that direction was taken when Sinn Fein President de Valera was elected president of the Volunteers. Most of militant separatism's political and military forces in Ireland were thereby joined under a common leadership.[29] The I.R.B. maintained its separate and secret existence and succeeded in infiltrating the executive bodies of Sinn Fein and the Irish Volunteers. Never again, however, did the I.R.B. assume the importance it had in 1916. But one I.R.B. member, Michael Collins, enabled the organization to serve a useful intelligence function during the guerrilla war waged by Irish nationalists between 1919 and 1921.[30]

---

[27]The Sinn Fein convention also adopted a new constitution at this October 25, 1917 assembly. For the text, see Dorothy Macardle, *The Irish Republic* (New York, 1965), p. 915.

[28]Among the militant separatists, there was little doubt that the fight for Irish independence would require physical force. One contemporary Volunteer wrote: "The men had little use for anyone who was not of the physical force belief. Gaelic Leaguers and members of Sinn Fein Clubs who did not belong to the Volunteers were sneered at." Ernie O'Malley, *Army Without Banners* (Boston, 1937), p. 56.

[29]Calton Younger, *A State of Disunion* (London, 1972), pp. 47–48.

[30]The I.R.B. doubtlessly played a crucial role in 1916, but thereafter, as the fight for Irish independence became more open and widespread, the importance of the organization was considerably diminished. Nonetheless,

MICHAEL COLLINS

Born in county Cork in 1890, Michael Collins emigrated to England at the age of 16. During his years in London, Collins became interested in Irish nationalism, first through the Gaelic Athletic Association and the Gaelic League and then, in 1909, through the local chapter of the I.R.B. He returned to Ireland in January 1916 and worked for a Dublin accounting firm. Collins participated in the Easter rebellion and, after the rising, was one of the leading political organizers in the prison camp at Frongoch. The strategy which had preceded the 1916 insurrection, Collins felt, revealed a lack of essential organization.[31] Volunteer President Eamon de Valera agreed with this opinion and, because of his esteem for the man who held it, he appointed Collins Director of Organization for the Irish Volunteers.

EAMON DE VALERA

Eamon de Valera's background differed markedly from Collins'. Born in New York in October 1882, de Valera was the son of a Spanish father and an Irish mother. After his father's death in 1884, de Valera was sent to Ireland where he was raised by his mother's family in county Limerick, attended Blackrock College, and ultimately received a degree in mathematics from the old Royal University. He was drawn to Irish nationalism first through the Gaelic League and later

---

between the years 1919 and 1921 the I.R.B. functioned almost as a government within a government. The I.R.B. participated in, but maintained a separate existence from, the self-proclaimed Irish republican government and army. Indeed, the I.R.B. was a complicating factor in the Irish Free State Army as late as 1924. Lyons, *Ireland Since the Famine*, p. 438.

[31]For an account of Michael Collins' early career, see Rex Taylor, *Michael Collins* (London, 1965), pp. 11–86; Desmond Ryan, *Remembering Sion* (London, 1934), pp. 229–238; and Younger, *A State of Disunion*, pp. 101–108.

through Eoin MacNeill's Irish Volunteers. Reluctantly, de Valera joined the I.R.B. prior to the Easter rebellion. He refused to rejoin later because the Catholic Church opposed such secret societies, and because he believed that the inefficient Easter week strategy had been largely due to the confusion caused by secret and open organizations seeking to work in tandem. That view did not, however, create any difficulty in de Valera's relationship with Michael Collins. Each had a profound respect for the other's abilities and patriotism; when they did disagree, either in 1917 or later, it was rarely over any matter involving the I.R.B.[32]

THE CONSCRIPTION CRISIS

A new crisis in Anglo-Irish relations was precipitated when the British Army suffered a severe manpower shortage due to the March 1918, German offensive in France. Unionist members of the British Cabinet insisted that conscription be extended to Ireland because morale problems would be created in Britain if a recommended bill raising the conscription age from 50 to 55 in all parts of the United Kingdom except Ireland were adopted.[33] Prime Minister Lloyd George and Conservative leader Bonar Law both doubted the wisdom of applying conscription to Ireland. Chief Secretary for Ireland Henry Duke warned that drafting Irishmen would be equivalent to recruiting Germans, and would also be counter-productive since British troop strength in Ireland would have to be increased in order to enforce conscrip-

[32]Even de Valera's break with Collins over the 1921 Anglo-Irish Treaty, although not satisfactorily explained to this day, had nothing to do with the latter's involvement in the I.R.B. For de Valera's early career, see Mary Bromage, *De Valera and the March of a Nation* (London, 1956), pp. 15–82; Longford and O'Neill, *Eamon de Valera* pp. 1–75; Younger, *A State of Disunion*, pp. 223–232.

[33]Minister for National Services Sir Auckland Geddes estimated the number of new conscripts required by the British Army to be 150,000. War Cabinet meeting 372 (13), 25 March 1918, *CAB.* 23/5.

tion.[34] The pressure upon the Prime Minister was so acute that, despite these warnings, he introduced a Military Service Bill in the House of Commons on April 10, 1918, which extended conscription to Ireland. The Bill empowered the government to apply conscription "whenever the necessity arose," and was coupled with a pledge to introduce home rule before conscription took effect. The promised home rule, however, was based upon the partition principle.[35] John Dillon, chairman of the Irish party since the death of Redmond, withdrew his following from Westminster and returned to Dublin where he joined forces with Sinn Fein. The British Government was thus able to accomplish for Irish separatism what the Irish had never managed—an alliance between constitutional and revolutionary nationalism.

Opposition to conscription was, except for northeastern Ulster, practically universal in Ireland. The Irish Catholic bishops immediately and unanimously condemned the government's action and declared that "conscription forced in this way on Ireland is an oppressive and inhuman law which the Irish have a right to resist by every means that are consonant with the laws of God."[36] Local groups from all over Ireland denounced conscription as "unjust," "tyrannous," and "insane."[37]

On April 18, a conference was held at the Mansion House of the Lord Mayor of Dublin at which all sections of nationalist opinion were represented. Delegates included John Dillon and Joseph Devlin for the Irish Parliamentary Party, Eamon de Valera and Arthur Griffith for Sinn Fein, Tim

---

[34]War Cabinet meetings 374 (12) and 375 (2), 27 March 1918, *CAB.* 23/5.

[35]Prime Minister Lloyd George was advised by Lord Cecil that conscription should not be contingent upon home rule and, in any event, Ulster's interests had to be protected. Lord Robert Cecil, Minister of Blockade, to Lloyd George, 7 April 1918, G. T. paper 4166, *CAB.* 24/47. For an excellent analysis of the Cabinet deliberations on the conscription issued, see Calton Younger, *Ireland's Civil War* (London, 1970), pp. 62–82.

[36]For a thorough discussion of the Catholic hierarchy's response to conscription see David W. Miller, *Church, State and Nation in Ireland, 1898–1921* (Dublin, 1973), pp. 401–407.

[37]Robert Kee, *The Green Flag* (London, 1972), p. 619.

Healy and William O'Brien for the dissident element in the old home rule party, and three representatives for the labour organizations. This assembly ratified a pledge to be taken at the church door of every parish on the following Sunday, April 21, which read: "Denying the right of the British government to enforce compulsory service in this country, we pledge ourselves solemnly to one another to resist conscription by the most effective means at our disposal."[38] Irish unity was, however, short-lived. Less than two weeks later, Arthur Griffith became the Sinn Fein candidate in a by-election for the East Cavan seat traditionally held by the Irish Parliamentary Party. Griffith declared that there could be no meaningful alliance between Sinn Fein and the Irish party until the latter accepted the Sinn Fein program of total independence for Ireland and representation at the post-war Peace Conference. Dillon dismissed this as a lunatic policy, and the Irish anticonscription coalition was at an end.[39]

On May 11, 1918, Edward Shortt succeeded Henry Duke as Chief Secretary for Ireland, and Field Marshall Lord French was sent to Dublin to replace Lord Wimborne as Lord Lieutenant.[40] French's appointment represented a significant change in the character of the office, for the Lord Lieutenant had heretofore been a figurehead. It was, however, precisely because the British were anticipating resistance to conscription that French was sent to Dublin.[41] Within a week of his arrival French took drastic measures to prevent a recurrence of the 1916 insurrection. On the night

---

[38]William O'Brien, M.P. for Cork, who attended this conference, has attributed authorship of the pledge to Eamon de Valera. O'Brien, *The Irish Revolution and How It Came About,* pp. 361–362.

[39]Lyons, *John Dillon,* p. 435.

[40]Lord Wimborne was not so troubled by his dismissal as he was by the succession of a military man to the Lord Lieutenantcy, and he warned Prime Minister Lloyd George of the potential consequences of such a selection. Wimborne to Lloyd George, 28 April and 9 May 1918, *Lloyd George MSS.,* F48/6/5/7,8.

[41]French promised to reestablish the authority of the government in Ireland. French to Lloyd George, 5 May 1918, *Lloyd George MSS.,* F/48/6/10.

of May 17, seventy-three of the leading Sinn Fein political activists, including Griffith and de Valera, were arrested and deported to English jails. The reason for this action was given in a proclamation by French: "It has come to our knowledge that certain subjects of his Majesty the King, domiciled in Ireland, have conspired to enter into, and have entered into, treasonable communication with the German enemy."[42] Such was the infamous "German plot," which few people outside Unionist and some government circles actually believed.[43] There is reason to think that some Sinn Fein leaders deliberately allowed themselves to be arrested in the hope that it would help them win the East Cavan by-election. If that was their expectation, it proved sound. Griffith won by an impressive margin in that constituency's June polling.

British repression in Ireland intensified in the weeks that followed. On July 3, the Irish Volunteers, Sinn Fein, and even the Gaelic League were declared illegal and their meetings prohibited.[44] The Volunteers, under the direction of Michael Collins who had escaped arrest, proceeded to establish an efficient intelligence and communications network which would prove extremely useful in the Anglo-Irish war of 1919–1921 (See Chapter 10). Meanwhile, the organizational genius of Harry Boland succeeded in bringing Sinn Fein, at the very time when it was proclaimed illegal in Ireland, to its largest membership ever. It has been estimated that the total num-

[42]Chief Secretary for Ireland Edward Shortt admitted to the Prime Minister that Dublin Castle did not have the evidence to prove the charge of complicity with enemy agents against those who had been arrested. Shortt to Lloyd George, 20 May 1918, *Lloyd George MSS.*, F45/6/3.

[43]Joseph Dowling, a veteran of Casement's ill-fated Irish Brigade, was apprehended by British authorities on April 12, 1918, after he had been landed in Galway by a German submarine. The Sinn Fein leaders knew nothing of Dowling, although they later learned that Berlin had sent him on its own initiative in the hope of re-establishing communications with the Irish Volunteers. Macardle, *The Irish Republic*, pp. 253–254.

[44]On June 15 thirteen counties were declared "proclaimed districts" under the Criminal Law and Procedure Act of 1887. People arrested in these counties could be taken elsewhere for trial. Three days later, several districts were declared "Special Military Areas" which meant that meetings, fairs and public assemblies were disallowed.

ber of Sinn Fein members grew during 1918 from approximately 66,000 to over 112,000.[45]

Fortunately for both Britain and Ireland, London never imposed conscription on the Irish, but that decision was conditioned more by the German retreat in France during late June than by any sensitivity to Sinn Fein opposition.[46] By October, the German armies had been pushed back to their own frontiers and Berlin had indicated its willingness to sue for an armistice. The war ended on November 11, 1918 without the need for the conscription which Parliament had already authorized the government to apply to Ireland. It remained to be seen whether the militant separatism of Sinn Fein would remain popular when the threat of compulsory military service no longer existed, or whether the Irish constitutional Nationalists would lead the country to a peaceful and lasting association within the British Empire through home rule. That answer would not be long in coming.

---

[45] Holt, *Protests in Arms,* p. 165.

[46] Colonial Secretary Walter Long wrote the Prime Minister on May 7: "If we are to fight the Roman Catholic Church and the Sinn Fein, we shall choose our battle ground and not let them dictate to us what it shall be." Long urged the Prime Minister not to let conscription be that battle ground. Long to Lloyd George, 7 May 1918, Lloyd George *MSS.,* F32/5/31.

Chapter 8

Dail Eireann and the Irish Separatist Appeal to the Peace Conference (1919)

Two weeks after the Armistice on November 25, 1918, the British Parliament was dissolved in order to permit the first national election in eight years. Polling was scheduled for December 14, and a mixed mood of excitement, anticipation and apprehension pervaded the British Isles. The Irish Parliamentary Party prepared for the forthcoming election in the grave knowledge that its very existence was at stake. Sinn Fein had announced its intention to contest every constituency in Ireland, and no one could really predict the true strength of the republican movement throughout the country. In Britian, however, Prime Minister Lloyd George was principally concerned with the postwar perpetuation of his coalition government, the re-election of his political allies, and the resolution of national and global problems of considerable magnitude. As Winston Churchill later recalled, the preoccupations of the government at the time of the Armistice included demobilizing the Army, reconstructing a peacetime industry and economy, the Peace Conference with its projected treaty, and the vast confusion which afflicted so much of European and world affairs. Irish nationalist activities simply were not among the immediate concerns of British statesmen in the heady and hectic weeks following the war and, despite Sinn Fein's solemn declaration for an Irish republic, London's response was temporarily characterized by benign neglect. As Churchill noted, "So much was going on all over the world and our own affairs pressed upon us so importunately, that the significance of these [Sinn Fein] demonstrations was hardly noticed."[1]

THE ELECTION OF 1918

What was in fact taking place in Ireland should have compelled the interest of the London Government, for Irish revolutionary fervor was about to ignite a war of national liberation. Sinn Fein issued its election manifesto which, even after government censoring, constituted a clear warning from the new militant separatist leadership of that organization of its intention to secure the establishment of an Irish Republic. The Sinn Fein manifesto also pledged: to withdraw Irish representation from Westminster and to deny the right of the British Government to legislate for Ireland; to create a constituent assembly of the Irish M.P.'s returned in the national election; to appeal to the Peace Conference for the establishment of Ireland as an independent nation.[2]

---

[1]Winston S. Churchill, *The World Crisis*, Vol. 5 (New York, 1957), p. 296. By early January, Lloyd George was already at the Peace Conference in Paris "where he was thinking more about Allied support for the White Russians against the Bolsheviks than about . . . the Sinn Feiners." Edgar Holt, *Protest in Arms: The Irish Troubles, 1916–1923* (London, 1960), p. 169.

[2]For the full text of the original manifesto and of the edited version which the British censors authorized for distribution, see appendices 6 and 7 in Dorothy Macardle, *The Irish Republic* (New York, 1965), pp. 919–922.

Sinn Fein labored under some real disabilities in the three week campaign which followed. Its publications were suppressed, most of its leaders were in jail, and the organization's election directors were routinely detained or arrested by the authorities. Moreover, the Irish Parliamentary Party attempted to win public favor by having popular Nationalist M.P.'s like Arthur Lynch and Stephen Gwynn appear in uniform to give election speeches before large audiences. Sinn Fein responded by organizing a systematic and efficient counter-campaign with the purpose of reducing such meetings to chaos in order to prevent the speakers from being heard.[3] Sinn Fein and the Nationalist parties cooperated only in the six northeastern constituencies in order to avert the risk of losing Ulster seats to Unionists on a split vote. In eight of those electoral districts having a small Nationalist majority the Sinn Fein and Nationalist leaderships agreed to contest four seats each. Prior to the dissolution of Parliament, the Nationalists held 68 seats, the Unionists 18, Sinn Fein 7, and William O'Brien's splinter group of nationalists, together with a handful of Independents, had 10. Few people could have anticipated the dimensions of Sinn Fein's electoral triumph. Of a total of 105 seats allotted to the Irish in the British Parliment, 73 were won by Sinn Fein; the Unionists returned 26 and the Irish Parliamentary Party was reduced to six seats.[4]

While there could be little doubt that constitutional nationalism had been rendered a sizable vote of no confidence from the electorate, Sinn Fein was not entirely justified in claiming a mandate from the Irish people to establish a republic. Many soldiers on leave or otherwise separated from their units had not received their absentee ballots even during the two week grace period following the election which

---

[3] Robert Kee, *The Green Flag* (London, 1972), p. 623.

[4] "Owing to the fact that individual candidates (e.g. Mr. de Valera) were returned for more than one seat, the seventy-three constituencies won by Sinn Fein were represented by sixty-nine members. Because of redistribution, the total number of Irish seats in this election was 105, not 103 as previously." F. S. L. Lyons, *Ireland Since the Famine* (New York, 1971), p. 396.

was intended to accomodate late voting by these men. It is reasonable to assume that many of the Irish soldiers' votes would have been cast for the Irish Parliamentary Party candidates rather than for Sinn Fein since the latter was often thought of as "pro-German" by the fighting forces.[5] Also noteworthy was the fact that almost one-third of the Irish electorate did not vote, and of those who did, only 47 percent chose Sinn Fein candidates.[6] Indeed, many of the votes which Sinn Fein did receive were not so much an endorsement of the Sinn Fein program as they were a backlash against prevailing British policies. To an undetermined number of people, the republic was more a symbol than a political system.[7] A Sinn Fein leader declared after the election, "The people have voted for Sinn Fein. What we have to do now is to explain to them what Sinn Fein is."[8]

THE ESTABLISHMENT OF DAIL EIREANN

True to their pledge, the Sinn Fein victors refused to take their seats at Westminster and gathered instead at the Dublin Mansion House on January 7, 1919. There they made arrangements to convene Dail Eireann (Assembly of Ireland)

---

[5]Another variable in this election was the recent legislation which had expanded the franchise. Included among the new voters were all women in the United Kingdom over the age of thirty. The Irish electorate in December 1918, totaled 1,931,588 compared with 698,098 on the old register. Of the new electorate, 800,000 were estimated to be women. See the reference to the analyses by the *Irish Independent*, December 5, 1918 in Kee, *The Green Flag*, p. 624.

[6]Since Sinn Fein candidates ran unopposed in 26 constituencies, nearly one-fourth of the total Irish electorate was won by them before the polling even began; the Nationalist party was revealed to be in a hopeless state of decline when it was unable to offer any kind of challenge for these twenty-six seats. For a further discussion of the implications of the voting patterns in this election, see W. Alison Phillips, *The Revolution in Ireland* (London, 1923), pp. 152–153.

[7]Donald Akenson, *The United States and Ireland* (Cambridge, Mass., 1973), p. 51.

[8]P. S. O'Hegarty, *The Victory of Sinn Fein* (Dublin, 1924), p. 32.

as an independent constituent assembly of the Irish nation. Invitations were extended to the Unionist and Nationalist candidates elected in the December polling. Although few acceptances were expected, the invitations were consistent with Sinn Fein's presumption that it was duly mandated to prepare a political program on behalf of all of Ireland. Both Unionist and Irish Parliamentary Party M.P.'s ignored the call.[9] When the first session of the Dail Eireann met on January 21, only twenty-seven Sinn Fein representatives attended; thirty-four of the elected candidates were in prison and eight more were otherwise unable to participate at the initial meeting.

Proceedings at that first assembly on January 21, 1919 were conducted in both Irish and English. The members in attendance ratified a provisional constitution which provided for a President, chosen by the Dail, who would head a cabinet of four ministers. The cabinet appointments were to be nominated by the President and then confirmed by the Dail. A declaration of independence was also unanimously approved, but Sinn Fein saw its purpose to be more a reaffirmation of principle for foreign consumption than a new tenet in Irish political life. Dail members felt that since the Irish Republican Army, on behalf of the Irish people, had proclaimed the Irish Republic in 1916, the declaration was really a reiteration of the previous proclamation and not a new departure.[10] The Dail concluded its meeting with the ratification of a document called the Democratic Programme. The declaration stated that "all right to private property must be subordinated to the public right and welfare" and affirmed "the right of every citizen to an adequate share of the produce of the Nation's labour." It further promised that the first duty of the Government of the Republic

---

[9]Unionist Sir Robert Woods was the only one who bothered to send a refusal.

[10]The January 21, 1919 declaration of independence demanded the evacuation of British troops and administrators from Ireland. *Dail Eireann: Minutes of Proceedings,* 21 January 1919, pp. 15–16.

would be to ensure that no child would suffer from lack of food or clothing, and that "all shall be provided with the means and facilities requisite for their proper education and training as Citizens of a Free and Gaelic Ireland."[11] Precisely how these goals were to be achieved in the aftermath of the country's liberation was, not surprisingly, left undefined. Finally the Dail appointed Eamon de Valera, Arthur Griffith, and Count Plunkett as its delegates to the Peace Conference in Paris. The fact that de Valera and Griffith were at that time in English prisons made their selection tactically effective for propaganda purposes.

On the following day the Dail reassembled at the Dublin Mansion House and went into executive session during which members of the Irish, British, and world press were denied admittance.[12] Sean O'Kelly was appointed envoy to the Peace Conference and was sent to Paris to obtain admission to the Conference for the delegates appointed by the Dail. Cathal Brugha was named President of the Ministry *pro tem.* It was generally accepted that the acutal presidency of the government would be entrusted to Eamon de Valera, the head of both the Sinn Fein and the Irish Volunteers, upon his release from jail. Ministry positions were filled next: Eoin MacNeill (Finance Minister), Michael Collins (Home Affairs), Count Plunkett (Foreign Affairs) and Richard Mulcahy (National Defense).[13] When de Valera was permitted to join the Dail and to assume its presidency in April 1919, the Cabinet

---

[11]Ibid., pp. 22–23. The Dail, during this two hour assembly, also issued a "message to the Free Nations of the World" which asked for recognition and support for the Irish Republic by all free nations of the world. Ibid., p. 20.

[12]The *Manchester Guardian,* The *Daily News,* The *Daily Mail,* the *Freeman's Journal,* the *Irish Independent,* the *Irish Times* and several American newspapers were among those covering the first session of the Dail Eireann.

[13]One indication of how some I.R.B. men still harbored bitter memories of Eoin MacNeill's countermanding order on Easter Sunday 1916 was evident from the dissenting vote cast against his appointment by the East Kerry Representative Piaras Beaslai. *Dail Eireann: Minutes of Proceedings,* 22 January 1919, p. 26.

was reorganized and expanded.[14] Meanwhile the militantly separatist Cathal Brugha presided over the first sessions of the Dail and that body's uncompromising endorsement of an Irish Republic was due in part to him and to similarly doctrinaire delegates. Perhaps a more flexible, if not more moderate, Sinn Fein declaration would have emerged had Eamon de Valera or Arthur Griffith been at liberty to participate in the Dail from the outset.[15]

THE SINN FEIN IDEALS

Disagreement between Dail members over the Democratic Programme revealed the difference between professed principles and actual practice in Sinn Fein. The rising of 1916 had resulted in the death of Connolly and other socially militant leaders and, with the entry of mainly middle- and lower middle-class members into Sinn Fein during 1917 and 1918, the organization became politically more conservative. The social aspirations of the first Irish Republic were accepted in the form of the Democratic Programme by Dail Eireann on January 21, 1919 partly to accomodate Thomas Johnson, Cathal O'Shannon, William O'Brien and other class conscious workers' organizers in the labour movement;[16] and partly

---

[14]Arthur Griffith (Home Affairs), Cathal Brugha (Defense), Count Plunkett (Foreign Affairs), Countess Markievicz (Labour), Eoin MacNeill (Industries), Michael Collins (Finance), William Cosgrave (Local Government). *Dail Eireann: Minutes of Proceedings*, 2 April 1919, p. 36.

[15]De Valera, who would later speak obliquely of an "external association" in which an independent Ireland would remain within the British Commonwealth, soon found himself in what one contemporary characterized as "the straight-jacket of the Republic." P. S. O'Hegarty, *A History of Ireland Under the Union, 1801–1922* (London, 1952), p. 729. Arthur Griffith, of course, had never perceived a republic to be the ultimate objective of the organization which he founded.

[16]This William O'Brien, the trade unionist, is not to be confused with William O'Brien, M.P., the leader of the All-for-Ireland League and the old home rule party.

because the Programme was a revised version of a testament by the revered Patrick Pearse. An early draft of the document, for which Thomas Johnson was primarily responsible, was objected to by Michael Collins and then revised by Sean O'Kelly. Every statement reflecting communist or syndicalist ideas was rejected, but the final version was still sufficiently radical to proclaim that "all right to private property must be subordinated to the public right and welfare." It is fair to conclude, however, that the Dail might not have approved the Democratic Programme had there been any immediate prospect of putting it into effect. But there was not, and the fact remains that the majority of Sinn Fein was primarily concerned with achieving the national independence of a formerly dependent colony.[17]

Unlike the provisional revolutionary governments of national liberation movements in more recent years, Sinn Fein did not view the struggle with its imperialist enemy in ideological terms. The Irish republicans did not seek the establishment of a regime whose political philosophy was either hostile to or profoundly different from that of Great Britain. Neither was their movement a conflict between classes, as in the instance of latter-day peasant and/or proletarian movements. Sinn Fein included members from virtually every social and economic sector in Irish society, although its leadership contained a rather high proportion from the ranks of the educated, lower middle-class. To the extent that Sinn Fein sought the establishment of a constitutional democracy independent of British control, its revolutionary aims were more akin to those of the American patriots of 1776 than to the socialist goals of many Third World revolutionaires in this century. It is equally true, however, that Sinn Fein, like later national liberation fronts, included a diverse group of nation-

---

[17]Patrick Lynch, "The Social Revolution that Never Was," in Desmond Williams, ed., *The Irish Struggle, 1916–1926* (Toronto, 1966), pp. 45–48. An I.R.B. colleague of Michael Collins' later asserted: "The Irish Nationalist tradition has always been national rather than proletarian, and it takes quite a quantity of innoculation for the jargon of which the modern world is so enamoured to take root here." O'Hegarty, *A History of Ireland Under the Union,* p. 727.

alists whose common determination to end colonial rule superceded their conflicting preferences for the form of the
future Irish nation.[18]

LONDON'S REACTION TO DAIL ACTIVITIES

Republican pretensions and the solemn deliberations of Dail
Eireann were, however, regarded by British officialdom in
January 1919 as little more than an elaborate charade. Prime
Minister Lloyd George left the Irish problem largely to the
care of his new Chief Secretary for Ireland, Sir Ian Macpherson, and to Lord French who continued to serve as Viceroy.
The London Government was undecided about whether or
not Dail Eireann should be suppressed at the outset. London
ultimately concluded that the situation in Ireland, however
ominous in appearance, was nonetheless controllable. The
new House of Commons which assembled on February 4 was
an overwhelmingly Conservative body, and the Irish benches, for the first time since the union of Britain and Ireland
in 1801, were almost empty. Winston Churchill, who was
Secretary of State for War in the new government, very
probably reflected the majority view in Commons when he
rejoiced in the Sinn Fein boycott of Westminster. Churchill
feared that Sinn Fein, "an untamed, untutored band of hat-
ers, carrying into English public life a malignity unknown for
generations," might align itself with the Labour party and,
worse yet, convert the United Kingdom into a socialist
state.[19]

---

[18]Cathal Brugha and Austen Stack were representative of the uncompromising republican separatists, as were perhaps Michael Collins and the I.R.B.
in 1919. Eamon de Valera typified another shade of Sinn Fein opinion which
was committed to the principle of Irish independence from Britain but
nonetheless favored a continuing relationship between the two countries in
some sort of external association. Still others in Sinn Fein would have been
content in 1919 with full dominion status in spite of their professed allegiance to the Irish Republic.

[19]Churchill, *The World Crisis*, p. 297.

Churchill's apprehensions appear, in retrospect, to have had little foundation. In any event, the Irish nationalist threat to British rule was not located at Westminster. London's attention might more profitably have been focused upon Ireland where, having asserted itself as a sovereign government, the Dail Eireann was undertaking to displace the "alien" authorities. Two events of January 21, 1919 served as a serious warning of what lay ahead for Ireland. On that date, the first blood was shed in the Irish War for Independence as the 3rd Tipperary Brigade, acting solely upon its own authority, ambushed an explosives convoy at Soloheadbeg, killing two policemen in the process.[20] That same day, the Dail held its first meeting in Dublin and appointed its representatives to the Peace Conference at Paris. It was the latter initiative which British policy-makers perceived as a potentially divisive and dangerous development for His Majesty's Government.

Would the Peace Conference provide a forum where the Irish could appeal their claim for self-determination over the head of the British Government? This was a question which was of particular concern to the London Foreign Office. A Foreign Office paper, entitled *A Memorandum prepared for the consideration of the British Government in connection with the forthcoming Peace Settlement,* was prepared in the autumn of 1918. In it the problems likely to confront His Majesty's Government were considered. The document warned that there would probably be attempts to include in the Treaty provisions supporting the rights of national minorities to self-determination and entitling such minorities to present their cases to the Peace Conference. On both of these points the memorandum counseled that as much discretionary power as possible should be left in the hands of the

---

[20]The purpose of the attack was to procure explosives for the manufacture of home-made grenades. For an account by a participant in the ambush, see Dan Breen, *My Fight for Irish Freedom* (Tralee, 1964), pp. 38–58. It marked the first occasion in the two years and eight months since the Easter rising that a policeman or soldier had been killed in Ireland.

Allied Powers. It further declared that it would be clearly inadvisable to make even the smallest concession in the direction of admitting . . . "the claim of the American negroes, or the Southern Irish, or the Flemings or Catalans, to appeal to an Inter-State Conference over the head of their own Government."[21]

SINN FEIN AND ANGLO-AMERICAN RELATIONS

Another part of that same memorandum argued that states which allowed propaganda subversive to the governments of their neighbors should be denied membership in the League of Nations. Although that statement was doubtlessly directed against the Communists, there were those in the London Foreign Office who felt that Washington was deserving of censure for its failure to rebuke the activities of pro-Sinn Fein organizations in America. British Foreign Office officials were incensed, for example, when President Wilson, after delivering a speech on the League of Nations in New York, reportedly told a delegation of Irish-American Sinn Fein supporters that, although he could make no formal commitment, he was in thorough accord with their aspirations for Ireland.[22] One Foreign Office member thought that if the president did not retract the statement, he should be told upon his arrival in Paris that his indiscretion was unusual for a head of state.[23] The president, however, had been misquoted and neither then nor later did he champion Ireland's cause at Britain's expense. His insistence on the principle of self-determination for all peoples should have predisposed him to sympathize with the Sinn Fein claim to Irish indepen-

---

[21]For the complete text of the memorandum, see A. Zimmern, *The League of Nations and the Rule of Law*, 1918–35 (London, 1936), pp. 197–209.

[22]Lord Reading to the Foreign Secretary, 5 March 1919, *FO*371/4248.

[23]See Foreign Office minutes on the above telegram No. 455, 6 March 1919, Ibid.

dence except that President Wilson, like Prime Minister Lloyd George, thought of this principle only in terms of the regions controlled by the defeated Central Powers. But as the leader of the Democratic Party, which commanded the allegiance of the vast majority of Irish-Americans, Wilson could scarcely afford to be openly hostile to the Irish demands. Furthermore, Wilson repeatedly impressed upon Lloyd George the need for some kind of Irish settlement agreeable to American opinion. He did not, however, presume to suggest the conditions for such an accord and publicly adopted a noncommittal position while he was in essential agreement with Prime Minister Lloyd George that the Irish question was indeed an internal matter in British politics.[24]

By resisting the temptation either to qualify or to reject the principle of self-determination in reference to Ireland, the British shrewdly avoided alienating the American President. Washington and London held opposing views on a number of subjects under consideration at the Peace Conference, and no purpose would have been served if England had made self-determination yet another source of difference. Moreover, that principle was recognized by Britain as a sensible device in seeking a solution to the complex problems of central and southeastern Europe. Resolutions favoring self-determination for Ireland advanced by United States senators and congressmen, state legislators, and a wide variety of American organizations were endured, not always gracefully, by a London Government which claimed to perceive no contradiction in supporting independence for Poland or Czechoslovakia, but not for Ireland. This tactic succeeded in averting a serious rupture in Anglo-American relations and ultimately placed upon Woodrow Wilson the

---

[24]The son of a Presbyterian minister of Scottish descent, Wilson may not have been sympathetic to Catholics and Nationalists for reasons of heritage. One author has stated that Wilson's "inherited mistrust of the Southern Irish caused him to look askance at their pretensions." Nicholas Mansergh, *The Irish Question, 1840–1921* (London, 1968), pp. 277–278.

onus of refusing a hearing to the Irish delegates to the Peace Conference. The president eventually would tell the Irish deputation that the Committee of Four, consisting of the United States, Britain, France and Italy, had decided that no small nation should appear before it without the unanimous consent of the whole Committee.[25]

IRELAND PETITIONS THE PEACE CONFERENCE

On February 22, 1919, Irish Envoy Sean T. O'Kelly addressed a letter to the President of the Peace Conference, Premier Georges Clemenceau of France, in which the claim of the Government of the Irish Republic was formally registered. It requested the Conference to receive the Irish delegates appointed by the Dail Eireann in order that they might secure from the represented nations recognition of Ireland's indisputable right to independence. The letter further asked for the Conference's endorsement of Ireland's claim to membership in the League of Nations.[26] It was only as a constituent member that Ireland claimed admission to the League, as O'Kelly indicated in a subsequent letter to Premier Clemenceau. This was an important qualification since Article X of the Draft Covenant of the League committed the contracting nations to respect the existing territorial integrity and political independence of all member states of the League. Were Ireland to be internationally registered as an appendage of the British Crown, Article X might have been interpreted in such a way as to perpetuate her subjection. But with Ireland recognized as an independent republic, such an article would be the protector and guarantor of her integrity. British influence at the Conference militated pow-

[25]Ibid., p. 281.

[26]For the full text of this communication, see Sean T. O'Kelly to the Quai d'Orsay, 22 February 1919, *FO*371/5475.

erfully against any hearing of Ireland's claim, however, and O'Kelly's letter elicited no reply from Clemenceau. France had been traditionally friendly to Ireland and very probably favored Ireland's demand for complete independence, but that preference was conditioned by France's resolution to do nothing which would weaken England, her wartime ally.[27]

IRISH-AMERICAN ACTIVITIES

Irish-American activities were beyond the control of the British Government and at times they even threatened to counter the official policies of the Wilson Administration. A number of Hibernian groups in the United States had been vocally anti-British and pro-German during World War I and, even after America's entry into that conflict, had remained staunchly Anglophobic. Perhaps the most powerful and influential of these organizations was the Friends of Irish Freedom. It had been founded in New York City in March 1916, primarily to assist any movement which sought the establishment of an independent Ireland. The Clan-na-Gael, the American counterpart of the Irish Republican Brotherhood, exercised a degree of control within the Friends of Irish Freedom similar to that which the I.R.B. enjoyed within Sinn Fein. Clan leaders like New York Supreme Court Justice Daniel Cohalan and Fenian veteran John Devoy were the real leaders and spokesmen of the F.O.I.F. (Friends of Irish Freedom) even though less controversial Irish-Americans often served as national presidents of that organization.[28] On December 10, 1918, the F.O.I.F. and other Irish societies sponsored a huge meeting at New York's Madison Square Garden for the purpose of rallying American and world opin-

---

[27]Mansergh, *The Irish Question,* pp. 278–282.
[28]James McGurrin, *Bourke Cockran: A Free Lance in American Politics* (New York, 1948), pp. 236–237.

ion on behalf of Ireland's right to a hearing at the Peace Conference. The gathering of many thousands was addressed by William Cardinal O'Connell of Boston, Judge Cohalan, John Devoy, and New York Governor Charles Whitman. A resolution endorsing Irish self-determination was sent via wireless from the meeting to the president who was then enroute to the Conference abroad the U.S.S. *George Washington.*[29]

While the British Government might have felt reasonably assured that such appeals, or even the petitions which were sent from all over the United States and from places as distant as Argentina and Australia,[30] would not produce any fundamental change in the president's thinking on Ireland, Congressional action on the Irish question was viewed more warily in London. On December 12, 1918, hearings were held by the House Committee on Foreign Affairs on a resolution introduced by Illinois Congressman Thomas Gallagher which requested the American delegation to the Peace Conference to present the right of Ireland "to freedom, independence, and self-determination." In the third session of the 65th Congress there were eight such resolutions introduced with reference to self-determination for Ireland, and Congressional committees heard countless hours of testimony from native Irishmen and Irish-Americans alike.[31] California Senator James Phelan introduced a similar resolution which so alarmed President Wilson that he sent instructions from Paris, through Secretary of State Robert Lansing, directing the State Department "to use the utmost pressure to see that

---

[29]*New York Times,* December 11, 1918. The full text of Judge Daniel Cohalan's address, together with a number of anti-British pamphlets which the F.O.I.F. distributed and sold at this Madison Square Garden meeting, is located in the *Cohalan MSS.,* American Irish Historical Society, New York.

[30]Alan Ward, *Ireland and Anglo-American Relations, 1899–1921* (Toronto, 1969), p. 167.

[31]For representative testimony given to the Congressional committee which held hearings on the Gallagher resolution, see U. S. Congress, House, Committee on Foreign Affairs, *The Irish Question: Hearings before the Committee on Foreign Affairs on H. J. Res. 357,* 12 and 13 December 1918, 65 Cong., 3 Session, House Document 1832, Washington, D.C., 1919.

the matter is not acted on at this Congress."[32] The Phelan resolution was accordingly kept in committee but sentiment in the House of Representatives was too strong to be checked. An amended resolution was passed in that chamber on March 4, 1919, by the overwhelming margin of 216 ayes to 45 nays which read:

> Resolved by the House of Representatives (the Senate concurring), that it is the earnest hope of the Congress of the United States of America that the Peace Conference, now sitting in Paris, in passing upon the rights of various peoples, will favorably consider the claims of Ireland to the right of self-determination.[33]

The British Embassy in Washington sent the London Foreign Office a copy of the resolution which provoked one official in that ministry to respond angrily, "I should like to see the House of Commons passing a resolution in favour of self-determination for Hayti and Nicaragua."[34]

PATRICK McCARTAN'S DIPLOMATIC EFFORTS

Britain was equally unhappy with the diplomatic offensive launched on behalf of the Irish Republic by Ulster Nationalist and I.R.B. editor Dr. Patrick McCartan who, it seemed, was acting independently of both the Sinn Fein leadership in Dublin and the Irish-American leadership in the United States.[35] McCartan sent a communication to American Secretary of State Robert Lansing, and to the heads of all foreign

---

[32]Lansing to Polk, 15 February 1919, *State Department,* 841d.00/16.
[33]*U.S. Congressional Record,* 65 Cong., 3 Session, 1919, vol. 57, pp. 5027–5057.
[34]This writer apparently thought that the United States presumed to exercise prerogatives in Central America and in the Carribean similar to those of Britain in Ireland. See accompanying Foreign Office minutes for Barclay to the Foreign Secretary, 7 February 1919, *FO* 371/4248.
[35]Foreign Office minute, 8 January 1919, *FO* 371/4248.

missions accredited to the United States, on January 3, 1919. It began:

> I have the honour to inform you that, exercising their inherent right of Self-Determination, the sovereign people of Ireland, on December 28, 1918, by more than a two-thirds majority, severed all political relations with Great Britain.

The document further stated that the Republic of Ireland denied the right of any foreign government to enter into negotiations with the British government on any matter concerning the Irish people.[36] Acting in his capacity as "Envoy of the Provisional Government of Ireland," McCartan actually anticipated the Dail Eireann's formal declaration of independence by nearly three weeks. Irish reaction to McCartan's announcement ranged from surprise among some Sinn Feiners in Dublin to anger among some Irish-Americans who thought his behavior to be both precipitous and presumptuous.[37] McCartan's action reflected the absence of co-ordination between Sinn Fein supporters on both sides of the Atlantic which would later complicate Irish efforts to harmonize the activities of all parties seeking self-determination for Ireland. There is evidence to suggest that the British Government, which was doubtlessly the least pleased by the announcement, unsuccessfully attempted to have McCartan expelled from the country by the United States State Department.[38]

[36]McCartan to Lansing, 3 January 1919, *State Department*, 841d.00/17. The British Embassy in Washington was not sent a copy but obtained one from the Belgian Embassy. Barclay to the Foreign Secretary, 7 January 1919, *FO* 371/4248.

[37]See, for example, the comment in John Devoy's newspaper the *Gaelic American*, January 11, 1919. The Dail Eireann did not officially appoint McCartan as its envoy to Washington until April, 1919.

[38]When the British Consul General to New York later asked the London Foreign Office to protest the establishment of an Irish Consulate in New York, one British official thought such an effort would be futile since the State Department had ignored London's earlier request to suppress McCartan's mission in Washington. Consul General to the Foreign Secretary, 31 October 1919, *FO* 115/2515.

THE SINN FEIN PRISONERS

The Peace Conference formally opened on January 12, 1919, and representatives of the twenty participating nations were confronted with an awesome amount of business. Meanwhile, the British Government sought to decide the fate of the Sinn Fein prisoners who were still interned in England. At a Cabinet meeting in London on February 4, 1919, Chief Secretary for Ireland Ian Macpherson announced that Lord French, the Viceroy or Lord Lieutenant of Ireland, had recommended the immediate release of the men imprisoned in England since discipline among them had completely deteriorated, and there were rumors of a hunger strike being undertaken by all twenty-eight of the prisoners in question. Secretary of State for War Winston Churchill objected that the Government would appear weak if it relented simply because of an inability to keep discipline in its jails. Churchill reminded his colleagues that the Government had not shrunk from the prospect of forced feeding a few years before when the prisoners were suffragettes. Other members of the Cabinet agreed with Churchill's view that the subject was too important to resolve without further information. Macpherson was instructed to ask Lord French for a more complete statement on the reasoning behind his recommendation.[39]

After advising Lord French of the Cabinet's request, Macpherson conducted a personal inspection of prisons in both Ireland and England, and subsequently prepared a written report on his findings for Prime Minister Lloyd George. When the British Cabinet next discussed the status of the Sinn Fein prisoners on March 4, 1919, it had before it Chief Secretary Macpherson's report and a memorandum from Lord French. Macpherson noted that there were two groups

---

[39]War Cabinet meeting 526 (3), 4 February 1919, *CAB.* 23/9. Andrew Bonar Law presided at this meeting since the Prime Minister was attending the Peace Conference in France.

of Irish prisoners: those who had been convicted in a court of law under the Defense of the Realm Act and were imprisoned in Ireland; and those who had been arrested and deported without trial and were held in England. The Chief Secretary described the Irish prisons containing the former group as abominable enough to warrant condemnation by any sanitary authority. English prisons were depicted as being so unhealthy that conditions had already caused an epidemic requiring the transfer of many prisoners from jails to hospitals. Scores of prisoners, Macpherson noted, had been handcuffed for several weeks and the Medical Commissioner had reported their showing signs of marked anemia. Aside from humanitarian considerations, the Chief Secretary thought the situation demanded action for political reasons. The Chief Secretary concluded his report by recalling, "When Thomas Ashe died on our hands in prison he did more to stimulate Sinn Feinism and disorder in Ireland than anything I know."[40]

The Cabinet next considered Lord French's memorandum. Responding to Churchill's earlier admonition that the Government's release of the prisoners would be an act of weakness, the Viceroy declared that this might be so if the imprisonment were effecting any good results, and if it could be prolonged. But the Government could hardly lose credit, argued French, by reasonably conceding at that time what it would be compelled to yield later after public clamor and turbulence in Ireland. It was the Viceroy's considered judgment, based upon what he characterized as reliable information from all quarters of Irish society, that the radical elements in Sinn Fein had discredited themselves in the public eye by their absurd posturing in the Dail Eireann. Lord French remarked,

> The Irish people can stand anything except derision and when the leaders of an Irish movement make themselves into a laughing stock before all the world their leadership is doomed.

---

[40]G.T. 6906, Irish Office to the Prime Minister, 27 February 1919, *CAB.* 24/76.

The Viceroy's memorandum ended on a similar note, insisting that the release of the prisoners would in fact strengthen the emerging moderate faction in Sinn Fein.[41] There was some discussion of the memorandum in the Cabinet, during which the Chief Secretary of Ireland urged his colleagues to accept Lord French's recommendation since the political prisoners were an embarrassment to the Government. This was particularly true of those who had been elected as members of Parliament since they could claim privilege if they indicated an intention to take their seats at Westminster. Prime Minister Lloyd George, who had taken a recess from the Peace Conference and who presided at this Cabinet meeting, was well aware of the importance of denying Sinn Fein any additional political martyrs so long as the Irish question remained a source of international controversy. Accordingly, the Cabinet authorized the Chief Secretary on March 4, 1919 to release the Sinn Fein prisoners in England.[42]

DE VALERA RETURNS TO IRELAND

Two months before, on February 3, Michael Collins and Harry Boland had helped Eamon de Valera escape from Lincoln jail. De Valera, who had been in hiding since that time, first in Manchester and later in Ireland, was at liberty to travel freely following the Cabinet decision respecting Irish prisoners. The Dail Eireann's executive body decided that he should be given an official reception. In a statement issued on March 22, 1919, the Sinn Fein government announced that "President" de Valera would arrive in Dublin on March 26, and would be received at the gates of the City by the Lord Mayor of Dublin who would escort him to the Mansion House. De Valera was also expected to address the Irish people after being given the keys to the City by the

[41]G.T. 6912, Memorandum by Lord French, 7 February 1919, *CAB.* 24/76.
[42]War Cabinet meeting 541 (4), 4 March 1919, *CAB.* 23/9.

Lord Mayor. Such an honor had previously been reserved for royalty, and the enthusiastic response from bands and organizations seeking to participate in the demonstration caused some alarm at Dublin Castle and at the Irish Office in London. On the same day in which the Dail Eireann executive made its announcement, the Chief Secretary for Ireland telegraphed Bonar Law, who chaired the Cabinet while the Prime Minister was attending sessions of the Peace Conference, and asked for permission to prohibit the reception for de Valera which the Irish Office deemed as "the first overt act in defiance of His Majesty's Government in Ireland."[43]

When the Cabinet next met two days later, on March, 24, Bonar Law advised its members that the Chief Secretary's request enjoyed the support of Lord French, who very probably had been surprised by the immoderate conduct of Sinn Fein in the wake of the prisoner release. There was little discussion and no dissent as the Cabinet swiftly approved the proposal to prohibit Dail Eireann's reception plans for de Valera.[44]

In retrospect, it may seem curious that the Chief Secretary, with the Viceroy concurring, should have characterized the intended reception as the first overt act in defiance of His Majesty's Government in Ireland. By March 1919, the Dail Eireann had announced itself to the world as the government of an independent Irish Republic, had established executive, legislative and judicial branches which were already functioning to some degree, had petitioned the nations gathered at the Peace Conference for recognition, and had begun to act upon its sworn pledge to fight British rule in Ireland by every means possible. All of this was done quite overtly and was indisputably in defiance of His Majesty's Government. There were, however, any number of reasons for British authorities to attribute as little significance as possible to Sinn Fein activities in early 1919. Among these were London's determination to ignore the pretensions of Dail Eireann since any acknowledgment might lend it greater

---

[43]Macpherson to Bonar Law, 22 March 1919, *CAB.* 24/77.
[44]War Cabinet meeting 550 (5), 24 March 1919, *CAB.* 23/9.

credence in Ireland and, more importantly, outside Ireland. The campaign for Irish self-determination in the United States, in the dominions of the Empire, and amongst the nations gathered at the Peace Conference troubled the British Government far more than any of the political or military actions on behalf of that cause within Ireland itself.

THE VERSAILLES PEACE CONFERENCE

Twenty nations were represented on January 12, 1919, at the formal opening of the Peace Conference at the Palace of Versailles outside Paris. A Council of Ten, which was shortly succeeded by the Council of Four, attempted to provide an ordered approach to the immense amount of business confronting the Conference. Most of the period to February 15, when Wilson returned briefly to the United States, was spent in writing the Covenant of the League of Nations and there was little opportunity, even if the Council had been favorably disposed, to consider Ireland's claim to self-determination. Sean T. O'Kelly addressed a letter to President Wilson on February 8, explaining his mission and extending the official invitation of the Corporation of Dublin (Dublin city government) to visit Ireland and to receive in person the freedom of the city.[45] When Wilson replied, two months later, he made no comment regarding O'Kelly's mission and merely expressed regret that his engagements made a visit to Ireland impossible. It was an intensely frustrating and disappointing experience for the Envoy of the Irish Republic. His repeated announcement that President de Valera would come to Paris in a matter of hours if Ireland were only granted a hearing was greeted with indifference by most delegates to the Peace Conference. A correspondent for the

[45]The Dublin Corporation had conferred that honor upon President Wilson *in absentia* on January 3, 1919.

London *Daily Mail* reported to his British readers how O'Kelly was enjoying little success in his contacts with the Conference diplomats at Paris who neither understood nor cared about the Provisional Government of the Irish Republic.[46] It was increasingly apparent to the supporters of Irish freedom that London's opposition to bringing Ireland's case before the Peace Conference would be overcome only if pressure from within the United States compelled President Wilson to champion the Irish cause.

THE IRISH RACE CONVENTION

Mass meetings of Irish-Americans in December and January were merely a prelude to the Irish Race Convention which met in Philadelphia on February 22 and 23, 1919. More than five thousand people attended, including some thirty bishops and archbishops, and the keynote address was delivered by the eighty-five year old dean of the American Catholic hierarchy, James Cardinal Gibbons of Baltimore. A resolution was passed calling upon the Peace Conference to apply to Ireland the great doctrine of national self-determination and to recognize the right of the people of Ireland to select for themselves, without interference, the form of government under which they chose to live.[47] Other and more radical resolutions declared that a state of war existed between England and Ireland, and that no League of Nations would be supported which did not recognize Ireland's right to self-determination. An Irish Victory Fund was launched during this Irish Race Convention and the sum of one million dollars was pledged and ultimately collected. Lastly, the Convention appointed an American Commission for Irish Indepen-

---

[46]Correspondent Andre Viollis reported that he had interviewed the Irish Envoy in "the rather banal environment of a Paris hotel bedroom." *Daily Mail* (London), February 27, 1919.

[47]Charles Tansill, *America and the Fight for Irish Freedom, 1866–1922* (New York, 1957), p. 300.

dence which was instructed to journey to Paris for the specific purpose of presenting Ireland's case before the Peace Conference and securing permission from Britain for the three delegated Dail Eireann members to serve as Ireland's representatives. The American Commission was chaired by Frank P. Walsh. A lawyer and a native of St. Louis, Walsh had been active in Irish and labor organizations, and had served as a Wilson appointee on the Federal Industrial Commission. Also named to the Commission were Edward F. Dunne, a former Mayor of Chicago and past Governor of Illinois who had retained a keen interest in Ireland since his college days at the University of Dublin, and Michael J. Ryan, a prominent Philadelphian, who had been active both in state politics and in Irish organizations like the Clan-na-Gael.

Indeed, it was the militant influence of the Clan-na-Gael which dominated the proceedings of the Irish Race Convention at Philadelphia and sought to apply immediate pressure upon President Wilson. The President had returned to Washington in February to settle some neglected but urgent official responsibilities and was scheduled to return to the Peace Conference in approximately two weeks. Upon the adjournment of the Philadelphia Irish Race Convention, a committee of twenty-four prominent Irish-Americans travelled to Washington on February 25 for the purpose of consulting with the president. They were denied an interview at the White House, ostensibly because of scheduling difficulties, but Mr. Wilson did agree to a brief reception with the committee following a speech he was to deliver in New York City a few days later. It was then that the president, upon being asked to present the Convention's resolution on Irish self-determination at the Peace Conference, declared that he should not be called upon to make such a public and potentially volatile statement. Frank Walsh next inquired if Mr. Wilson would at least use his influence to ensure that the delegates selected by the people of Ireland were represented at the Conference. Again the president demurred, and his interview with the Committee ended on an inconclusive note and in a less than cordial atmosphere.[48]

BRITAIN AND IRISH-AMERICAN ACTIVITIES

London was kept thoroughly informed of the pressures which Irish-Americans were attempting to exert upon Wilson. From the British Embassy in Washington, Lord Reading sent a telegram to Prime Minister Lloyd George which read in part:

> Situation is undoubtedly being made difficult for the President but I am convinced that he will not commit himself to bringing matter before the Peace Conference.[49]

The British Ambassador further advised his Government that it would be unwise to deny visas to the members of the American Commission for Irish Independence if the United States Government should give them passports for travel to Paris. This advice prevailed despite recommendations to the contrary made by some Foreign Office personnel to the Prime Minister.[50] In a lengthier dispatch which analyzed the Philadelphia Irish Race Convention in particular and, more generally, the Irish issue in America, Ambassador Reading stated that the American Catholic hierarchy should be numbered among the growing number of prominent United States organizations that supported the Sinn Fein cause. He

---

[48] *New York Times*, March 5, 1919. President Wilson had refused to meet with the committee unless Judge Cohalan excused himself from that group. Cohalan's supporters later claimed that Wilson's animosity toward Cohalan was not due, as was often contended, to the latter's pro-German stance prior to America's entry into World War I. Rather, it was due, some alleged, to the fact that Cohalan had supported Champ Clark over Woodrow Wilson for the democratic presidential nomination at the party's 1912 Baltimore convention. Unsigned article, "Daniel Florence Cohalan," *The Recorder: Bulletin of the American Irish Historical Society* 10 (December, 1947), p. 3.

[49] Reading to the Prime Minister, 2 March 1919, *FO* 371/4248.

[50] Foreign Office minute, 3 March 1919, *FO* 371/4248.

further noted that while undue importance need not be given to the numerous resolutions on Ireland passed by state legislatures, since some were motivated more by a desire to appease the local Irish vote than out of any sense of conviction, it would be wrong to underestimate the damage which the campaign for Irish representation at the Peace Conference might ultimately render to Anglo-American relations.[51]

THE AMERICAN COMMISSION FOR IRISH INDEPENDENCE

Upon their arrival in Paris on April 11, 1919, the three members of the American Commission for Irish Independence began a concerted effort to place the Irish question squarely before the Peace Conference. Frank Walsh visited with presidential advisor Colonel House on April 15, and asked House to speak to President Wilson and to Prime Minister Lloyd George on behalf of the three delegates appointed by Dail Eireann who were still seeking to represent their claim for Irish self-determination at the Conference. Although Walsh communicated the same message in a subsequent meeting with the president, and when all three members of the Commission met with House on April 18, it was to no avail. Colonel House then tried unsuccessfully to obtain an interview for the three Americans with the British Prime Minister. In an April 25 letter to a friend, House confided that he had had several talks with Lloyd George concerning the Irish question, and expressed the belief that the Prime Minister was earnestly trying to effect some solution since the subject had become as much of a political issue in America as it was in England.[52] House did succeed, moreover, in persuading Lloyd George to authorize passports to Ireland for the Irish-

[51]Reading to the Foreign Secretary, 5 March 1919, *FO* 371/4248.
[52]House to Sir Horace Plunkett, 25 April 1919, *Plunkett MSS.*, Plunkett Foundation for Co-operative Studies, London. Plunkett was also a friend to President and Mrs. Woodrow Wilson with whom he frequently corre-

American delegation. They arrived in Dublin on May 3, and almost immediately became the subject of widespread controversy.

According to John W. Davis, the American Ambassador to London, Michael Ryan made a number of speeches in which he virtually encouraged his Irish audiences to rise in armed rebellion against British rule.[53] Walsh and Dunne were reported to be less extreme in their public addresses, but the American Commission nonetheless provoked a bitter reaction in London. Under the heading "Friend or Enemy?", the unionist *Morning Post* rebuked President Wilson as the party most responsible for facilitating the American Commission's journey to Ireland.[54] One member of the House of Commons demanded to know if the Prime Minister intended to see the Irish-American delegation upon its return to Paris, and if the Government was aware of the consequences which it courted by permitting revolutionary propagandists to visit Ireland in such volatile circumstances. Bonar Law replied for the Government that Mr. Lloyd George had no intention of receiving the American Commission at any time but that he found some advantage in permitting unrestricted travel to Ireland in order to illustrate to the world that His Majesty's Government was the victim rather than the perpetrator of violence in that country.[55] In the House of Lords, Viscount Midleton observed that the Prime Minister's decision was not only unwise, but was also improper. He recalled that the Lord Lieutenant of Ireland, Lord French, had been granted the prerogatives of a Cabinet member, and a member of the Cabinet had a right to be consulted on the business of his department before action was undertaken by anyone. Fur-

---

sponded. In most of his letters, Plunkett offered the president advice on the troublesome Irish question. See for example Plunkett to Wilson, 2 March 1919, *Plunkett MSS.*

[53]Davis to the Secretary of State, 28 May 1919, *State Department,* 841d.00/57.

[54]*Morning Post* (London), May 6, 1919.

[55]*Parl. Debates,* Commons, 5th Series, 14 May 1919, Vol. 115, col. 1581.

thermore, complained Midleton, the Irish-Americans had been given a spontaneous tour of Mountjoy prison while a delegation from the House of Lords had been denied such a visit sometime earlier because proper preparatory arrangements had not been made.[56]

From the outset of their sojourn in Ireland, the American Commission delegates angered the London Foreign Office by their open collaboration with Sinn Fein.[57] They received, for example, passports for Ireland from Irish Envoy Sean T. O'Kelly in Paris, in addition to those authorized by the British Government. At a special session of the Dail Eireann held on May 9, President de Valera welcomed the Americans in the name of the Republic and expressed regret that the delegates would not remain long enough to investigate fully the frightful situation then prevailing in Ireland.[58] The brevity of their stay, however, did not prevent the American delegates from preparing a report on the conditions in Ireland which, upon their return to Paris on May 12, they sought to bring before the Peace Conference.

Following a few renewed but unsuccessful attempts at persuading the United States representatives that the Dail Eireann delegates should be granted a hearing, the American Commission sent copies of their report on alleged British atrocities and violations of human rights in Ireland to both Prime Minister Lloyd George and President Wilson. The situation was made all the more awkward and embarrassing for both the British and the American officials at Paris when on the next day, June 7, the news arrived from Washington that the United States Senate had passed a resolution requesting the American Peace Commission to endeavor to secure a hearing for the Dail Eireann delegates and expressing its sympathy with Irish aspirations for self-government. The language of the Senate resolution was considerably more forceful than the House of Representatives resolution of

---

[56] *Parl. Debates*, Lords, 5th Series, 22 May 1919, Vol. 34, cols. 795–814.
[57] Foreign Office minute, 8 May 1919, *FO* 371/4248.
[58] *Dail Eireann: Minutes of Proceedings*, 9 May 1919, pp. 82–85.

March 4, and was further endorsed by the dramatic margin of sixty to one.[59]

According to Stephen Bonsal, a veteran foreign news correspondent for the New York *Herald* who sat behind the president at the Peace Conference and afforded him instant translations of all French speeches, Mr. Wilson's first inclination was to tell the Irish "to go to hell."[60] Political considerations, however, required him to be more cautious, and the president chose instead to reject requests for a hearing on self-determination for Ireland on the grounds that the appeal of any small nation could only be heard if the Council of Four was unanimously agreed. Moreover, he accused the members of the American Commission of having undermined, by their scandalous improprieties in Ireland, his private negotiations with Lloyd George for allowing the Dail Eireann delegates to present their case before the Conference.[61] Although there is no evidence to support Wilson's claim that he was engaged in such an effort, there can be little doubt that the Irish-American delegates' activities in Ireland had indeed alienated the British Prime Minister. On May 14, Bonar Law told the House of Commons that the Prime Minister was willing to receive American citizens at Paris, but not "American citizens who go to Ireland and not only take part in politics, but in a rebellious movement."[62]

Upon their return to Paris, the delegates of the American Commission for Irish Independence further weakened their own effort by engaging in the sort of fratricidal strife which would continue to haunt the international movement for Irish independence. Michael Ryan concluded that the views

---

[59] *U. S. Congressional Record*, 66 Cong., 1 Session, 1919, Vol. 58, p. 733. Thirty-five Senators chose not to vote at all, while Senator John Sharp Williams of Mississippi was the only member to cast a negative vote on the resolution.

[60] Stephen Bonsal, *Unfinished Business* (London, 1944), pp. 138–139.

[61] Ward, *Ireland and Anglo-American Relations*, p. 183.

[62] *Parl. Debates*, Commons, 5th Series, 14 May 1919, Vol. 115, cols. 1581–1582. Bonar Law further remarked that it had been the Prime Minister's hope that the delegates of the American Commission would help United States public opinion to better understand the British position on Ireland.

of his colleagues, Walsh and Dunne, regarding conditions in Ireland were too extreme, and he departed for the United States without signing their report to the Peace Conference. The final, but not unexpected, blow to Irish hopes for any hearing on their claim for self-determination at the Peace Conference was dealt by French Premier Georges Clemenceau, the President of the Conference. He ruled that any intervention in the affairs of Allied states would exceed the responsibility of the Conference which had as its duty the task of instituting "better conditions of peace in parts of the territories which joined in the war against us."[63]

THE IRISH QUESTION GROWS MORE OMINOUS

Lloyd George had succeeded in countering all efforts to plead Ireland's cause by going beyond Britain and before an international tribunal, but it was still a limited victory. By the summer of 1919, British civil administration in Ireland had deteriorated in nearly every part of the country, and incidents between Crown forces and guerrilla insurgents were steadily increasing. Hibernian groups in America and in the self-governing dominions of the Empire were intensifying their agitation on behalf of Irish freedom to a degree which was both embarrassing and troubling to the London Government. Even in England itself there was, if not common agreement on its solution, general recognition by Liberals and Conservatives alike that the Irish problem was a critical issue requiring immediate attention. The Liberal *Manchester Guardian* expressed the hope that the Government's refusal to permit the Irish a hearing at the Peace Conference did not mean that the Irish question would be neglected since its equitable resolution directly effected England's

---

[63]Clemenceau to Secretary of State Lansing, undated, *State Department*, 841d.00/52.

standing among the nations of the world.[64] The *Times* of London, the leading Conservative newspaper, observed that the attempt to suppress Sinn Fein in Ireland by police and military action had proven a total failure.[65] As Englishmen debated the possible remedies to the Irish question, the Dail Eireann was shifting its attention from Paris to the United States in an undertaking which would make Irish separatism a disruptive, and potentially dangerous, element in the course of Anglo-American relations.

---

[64]*Manchester Guardian,* April 4, 1919.
[65]The *Times* (London), August 18, 1919.

Chapter 9

Irish Separatism and American Politics: The British Response (1919–1921)

Britain had won a round, but not the match, in its bout with Irish separatism. Ireland's failure to gain a hearing at the Peace Conference prompted advanced nationalists to appeal the Irish cause before a still broader international forum, the court of world opinion. The United States, because of its twenty million or more citizens of Irish extraction, became the special target not only for Irish nationalist activities but also for a British countercampaign of notable dimensions. Dail Eireann members Liam Mellows, Harry Boland, and Diarmuid Lynch were already in America by the spring of 1919, together with Patrick McCartan who was the envoy of the government of the Irish Republic.[1] These nationalists, in collaboration with Irish-American organizations which actively supported them, intensified the campaign to win both

[1] Dorothy Macardle, *The Irish Republic* (New York, 1965), p. 310.

public and official support in the United States for the Dail. Historians are not agreed over the impact which American opinion had in the formulation of Britain's Irish policy at this time, but most would concede that it exercised some influence.[2] Indeed, the British Foreign Office documents which were opened to public inspection for the first time in 1967 certainly support this view.

BRITAIN AND IRISH SEPARATIST PROPAGANDA

Economic and political considerations were the compelling factors behind the rapid dismantling of England's comprehensive propaganda network in the United States following World War I; but it was not undertaken without some misgiving. The British Embassy in Washington advised the London Foreign Office on January 1, 1919, that while a reduction in the propaganda machinery was perhaps necessary, there still existed a need for combating the anti-British propaganda of militant Irish separatists.[3] The Embassy also thought that an effective response to such attempts at cultivating Anglophobia might be accomplished through a series of unofficial lecture tours quietly sponsored by the government and featuring speakers already popular with American audiences. Author Sir Arthur Conan Doyle and former British Ambassador to Washington Lord Bryce were suggested because of their popularity with Americans.[4] Although neither of them

---

[2] Oliver MacDonagh feels that the influence of Irish-Americans upon British policy in Ireland has been greatly exaggerated. Oliver MacDonagh, *Ireland* (Englewood Cliffs, N.J., 1968), pp. 128–129; Nicholas Mansergh holds almost the opposite view. Nicholas Mansergh, *The Irish Question, 1840–1921* (London, 1968), p. 282; Francis Carroll, who researched the recently opened British Foreign Office and Cabinet papers, takes the middle ground and argues that American, or Irish-American opinion had a qualified influence upon British policy in Ireland. Francis Carroll, "American Opinion on the Irish Question, 1910–1923" (Ph.D. dissertation, Trinity College, Dublin, 1969), pp. 310–373.

[3] Eric Drummond to Philip Kerr, 1 January 1919, *FO* 800/329.

[4] Geddes to Curzon, 14 January 1919, *FO* 800/329.

ever participated in such an effort, the London Government did engage a number of speakers whose lectures in the United States were thinly disguised propaganda efforts that extended intermittently throughout the two-year war for Irish independence.[5]

Irish separatist propaganda pervaded nearly every quarter of American society and the London Government was often required to meet the challenge on local, state and national levels. British consulates in over a dozen cities throughout the United States were under instructions to keep the British Embassy in Washington informed on all noteworthy Hibernian activities in each of their respective localities.[6] The Embassy then communicated all such reports to the Foreign Office which made the policy decisions respecting tactics and deciding upon appropriate responses; these ranged from a protest to the State Department over the impropriety of a U.S. district attorney's expression of public sympathy with Sinn Fein[7] to the confidential authorization for the Chicago consulate to pay informers for useful information on the plans of Irish organizations.[8] Aside from an occasional note of dismay in the Foreign Office minutes, which were only for internal use, London officials offered no response to the formal resolutions passed by several state legislatures calling for the recognition of Ireland's right to self-determination.[9]

Nearly all of the diplomatic and private correspondence regarding the influence of Irish separatists in America which reached the London Foreign Office during 1919 was pessi-

[5]For numerous references to the speakers who lectured on the Irish question in America for the London Government, see the Embassy and consular files, *FO* 115 class for 1919–1921.

[6]For a representative sampling of such consular reports, see *FO* 115/2513.

[7]Consulate-General, San Francisco, to the British Embassy, Washington, 3 February 1921, *FO* 115/2671.

[8]British Embassy to the Consulate-General, Chicago, 27 April 1921, *FO* 115/2673.

[9]For examples of such state resolutions, see copies of same from the Rhode Island, Massachusetts, New Hampshire and Nevada legislatures in *State Department*, 841d.00/25.

mistic. One British diplomat wrote from New York that the harm being done to Anglo-American relations by the Irish situation was impossible to exaggerate.[10] Horace Plunkett wrote from Washington to say: "In forty years of experience in America I consider that the anti-British sentiment has never been so responsive to Irish propagandism."[11] Throughout this period and even later, the Foreign Office reaction was almost always tempered by restraint. London was in fact horrified by United States Secretary of State Bainbridge Colby's remark to British Ambassador Sir Auckland Geddes that it was a great pity His Majesty's Government did not make clear to Americans the close similarity, if not identity, between Bolshevism and Sinn Fein.[12] The Foreign Office lost little time in reminding Ambassador Geddes that Mr. Colby was perhaps unaware that such an analogy would be quite unfair, as well as unwise, since Sinn Fein leaders were making efforts to control Bolshevik elements in the Irish republican movement and had on more than one occasion protected land owners who were not Sinn Feiners from "spoilation at the hands of cruder theorists than the Sinn Feiners themselves."[13]

The prudent caution which generally typified the London Government's efforts in combating Sinn Fein propaganda in America did not limit the British in this struggle to a purely passive role. Literature which discussed the Irish problem in a vein sympathetic to the English view was widely distributed in America by British officials, and visits to Irish jails were arranged for American journalists to disprove Irish

---

[10]William Wiseman to Ian Malcolm, 3 July 1919, *Wiseman MSS.*, British Museum.

[11]Plunkett to the Foreign Office, 16 March 1919, *FO* 115/2514.

[12]Geddes to Curzon, 6 June 1920, *FO* 371/4550.

[13]Foreign Office to the British Embassy, Washington, 8 June 1920, *FO* 371/4550. It is noteworthy that the British Government published a number of captured Sinn Fein documents in 1921 which contained drafts for a proposed treaty between the Soviet Union and the Republic of Ireland, as well as other evidence of official communication between these two parties. See *Intercourse Between Bolshevism and Sinn Fein*, Cmd. 1326 of 1921, (H. M. Stationary Office, London), pp. 1–5.

charges of English mistreatment of political prisoners.[14] One
of the things which troubled London most was the seemingly
disproportionate attention given by the American press to
British military or police reprisals in Ireland as opposed to
the comparatively scant coverage accorded atrocities committed by the Irish Republican Army.[15] On December 15,
1920, the *Washington Times* carried a news story on the
burning of Cork City by the paramilitary force known in
Ireland as the Black and Tans. The latter were described by
Washington Times correspondent Dennis O'Connell as a
unit composed largely of "ex-convicts and criminals who
were given the option of service in Ireland or terms in English penal institutions." This story caused at least one Foreign Office official to lose his composure. He recommended
that the London Government punish such irresponsibility by
denying that reporter and his newspaper access to the information on Ireland routinely accorded members of the press
by the Irish Office.[16] In much the same way, the Foreign
Office informed the London correspondent of the Philadelphia *Public Ledger* that publication of Sinn Fein appeals for
an American boycott of British products would invite reprisals by English firms which advertised in that newspaper.[17]

Another concern to the London Government was the
effort by Irish separatists to enlist the support of the Irish-

[14]British Embassy to the Foreign Office, 29 June 1919, *FO* 371/4249.

[15]Consulate General, New York, to the Foreign Office, 22 October 1920,
FO 395/351. See also Foreign Office minutes, 23 October 1920, *FO*
395/351. Ambassador Geddes warned Foreign Secretary Curzon at about
this same time that the success of anti-English propaganda in the United
States made "an effective rebuttal a matter of extreme urgency." Geddes to
Curzon, 11 December 1920, *FO* 115/2601.

[16]Foreign Office minute, 18 December 1920, *FO* 395/352.

[17]British Embassy to the Foreign Office, 5 July 1921, *FO* 371/5633. A
more cooperative Frederick Dixon, editor of the *Christian Science Monitor*,
published materials on the Irish problem provided him by British officials.
On one occasion, the paper was instrumental in exposing an Irish plot to
destroy British insurance companies in America with bankruptcy rumors.
Consulate-General, New York, to the Foreign Office, 25 April 1921, *FO*
115/2673.

dominated American Catholic hierarchy for their cause. The British were well aware of the influence which the Church exerted upon the Irish community, and Foreign Office records reveal the extent to which England went to explain its policies in Ireland and to cultivate important American Catholic churchmen during the war against Germany.[18] Britain's victory in the war provided her with the opportunity of keeping the support of prominent Catholic prelates in the United States who might otherwise have endorsed the demand for Irish independence. When London ordered the postwar expulsion of German Catholic missionaries from Palestine, India and other parts of the empire, James Cardinal Gibbons of Baltimore sent word to the Foreign Office that he was hopeful American clergymen might replace them.[19] Gibbons had never identified with Irish nationlists who demanded an Irish republic, but he had lent his considerable prestige to the cause of self-determination for Ireland.[20] The Cardinal's request provided London with a trump card and it was used to good advantage. A national conference of American bishops was to meet in Washington during October 1920, and Irish separatists were lobbying to have that body pass a resolution in favor of Irish independence. Prior to the conference, however, Monsignor Francis Kelly journeyed to London for the purpose of negotiating the replacement of German Catholic missionaries in British territories with members of American Catholic religious orders.[21] The British told Kelly that one condition of such an agreement would be that the American Catholic hierarchy abstain from any public endorsement of the Sinn Fein movement in Ireland. It was in compliance with that condition that Monsig-

[18]See, for example, Geoffrey Butler to the Foreign Office, 18 January 1918, *FO* 395/215.
[19]British Embassy to the Foreign Office, 4 March 1919, *FO* 371/4248.
[20]Charles Tansill, *America and the Fight for Irish Freedom, 1866–1922* (New York, 1957), pp. 298–301.
[21]Foreign Office minute, 11 November 1920, *FO* 395/351.

nor Kelly lobbied successfully among the bishops and prevented the adoption of a resolution on Ireland by the conference.[22]

DE VALERA'S AMERICAN TOUR

Perhaps the single most notable intrusion of Irish separatism into American politics was the visit of Sinn Fein President Eamon de Valera to the United States which extended from June 1919 to December 1920. De Valera had decided in early 1919, when hope was dwindling that the Peace Conference would respond to the appeal of nationalist Ireland, that he would personally take his country's cause to the American people at the earliest opportunity. The Sinn Fein President had three main objectives in visiting America: to secure United States recognition for the Irish Republic; to float the Dail Eireann External Loan; and to give Ireland's national claim the widest possible publicity. So eager was de Valera to undertake his mission that, after his escape from Lincoln prison in February 1919, he only agreed to return first to Ireland for a Dail meeting after much prodding by Michael Collins.

The shifting reactions of the British Government toward the Sinn Fein President provide a measure of the increasing anxiety with which London viewed de Valera's sojourn in the United States. In September 1919, three months after his arrival in America, de Valera was declared an alien by the Home Office on the grounds of his American birth. That ministry further announced that he would be denied a visa for re-entry into Ireland and that he would be deported if he

---

[22]Monsignor Kelly and the London Government communicated with one another after his return to the United States through Robert Wilberforce, the Director of the British Library of Information in New York. See, for example, Wilberforce to the Foreign Office, 28 October 1920, *FO* 395/351.

returned clandestinely to that country.[23] By December 1920, however, Foreign Secretary Lord Curzon was instructing British Ambassador Geddes to urge the American Government's expulsion of de Valera from the United States.[24]

The British were not the only ones who were disturbed by President Eamon de Valera's visit to the United States. A number of Irish-Americans and many Americans generally were eventually alienated by his involvement in American politics, and particularly by his misguided decision to attend the Democratic and Republican national conventions in 1920. Following his unceremonious arrival as a stowaway aboard the S. S. *Lapland* in New York on June 11, 1919, de Valera immediately conferred with Dail colleagues Liam Mellows and Harry Boland, as well as with the leaders of the Clan-na-Gael.[25] Fenian John Devoy and New York Supreme Court Justice Daniel Cohalan immersed themselves in elaborate arrangements, scheduling a press conference for the Irish President on June 23, with a cross-country speaking tour to follow. Accordingly, after addressing huge rallies in both New York and Boston, de Valera began a national tour on July 17. He was enthusiastically received by large gatherings organized by local Irish-American groups at which he was accorded numerous honors traditionally reserved for heads of states.[26]

[23]Foreign Office minute, 26 September 1919, *FO* 371/4249. The Home Office, in denying him a visa, took no notice of the fact that de Valera, after his escape from prison in England, had travelled in disguise to Ireland, and then to England where he left by ship as a stowaway for America.

[24]Curzon to Geddes, 5 December 1920, *FO* 115/2601. The British Government apparently had decided that de Valera was a British subject afterall and sought his extradition. For his part, the Sinn Fein President never claimed American nationality. When he was asked about his citizenship during an interview in the United States, de Valera replied: "When I became a soldier of the Irish Republic I became a citizen of that Republic." Macardle, *The Irish Republic,* p. 310.

[25]Mary Bromage, *De Valera and the March of a Nation* (London, 1956), pp. 90–92.

[26]Perhaps the most detailed account of de Valera's stay in the United States is Katherine O'Doherty, *Assignment America: De Valera's Mission to the United States* (New York, 1957).

DISSENSION AMONG IRISHMEN

From the start, however, de Valera was handicapped by his ignorance of American politics and his unwillingness to share authority with Clan-na-Gael leaders in matters which involved Irish-Americans. The Irish president, for example, had little patience with Cohalan's campaign against the League of Nations and perceived it as the Judge's personal vendetta against President Wilson. De Valera regarded such internal dissensions as distractions from the one important issue of Irish independence. On at least one occasion he accused Clan-na-Gael leaders of hating England more than they loved Ireland. For their part, Cohalan and Devoy were equally stubborn men who had long dominated Irish-American affairs and had no intention of abdicating that role to anyone, not even to president de Valera.[27]

In time, each of the parties realized that a profound difference in policy lay behind their personal rivalries and dissensions. For Devoy, and more especially for Cohalan, the paramount consideration of the future was Anglo-American trade rivalry and the conflict that would inevitably result. Cohalan welcomed the prospect of such a struggle, and viewed the League of Nations as an insidious British plot to inhibit America's freedom of action. President de Valera, however, had no objection to the League if Ireland was a member, and even anticipated an era of peaceful relations between England and Ireland.[28] On February 5, 1920, in an interview for the *Westminster Gazette*, de Valera suggested that an independent Ireland would be willing to provide Britain with guarantees against foreign attacks originating in the Irish republic, just as Cuba did with the United States under the terms of the Platt Amendment. The Irish president then asked rhetorically,

---

[27]Differences between de Valera and the Clan were particularly acute in matters relating to fund-raising. See Patrick McCartan, *With De Valera in America* (New York, 1932), pp. 137–143.

[28]F. S. L. Lyons, *Ireland Since the Famine* (New York, 1971), p. 420.

Why doesn't Britain do with Ireland as the United States did with Cuba? Why doesn't Britain declare a Monroe Doctrine for her neighbouring island? The people of Ireland, so far from objecting, would cooperate with their whole soul.[29]

To his opponents, these remarks seemed to suggest that the president was beginning to compromise his demand for a republic, and the schism between them widened still further.

For a time the Foreign Office could afford to observe, with more amusement than concern, how the fratricidal strife among rival Irish groups prevented them from taking any united action.[30] Since other circumstances apart from the Irish question had already strained relations between Washington and London in 1920, the British Foreign Office was understandably anxious that Irish republicans not cause further friction. Accordingly, His Majesty's diplomatic corps in the United States kept a close watch over Irish separatist activities. In April 1920, however, the British Consulate-General in New York reported to London that a *detente* had been reached between the feuding de Valera and Cohalan factions. The peace was not expected to last, for there was still disagreement over the control and disbursement of the funds collected from the sale of bond-certificates. But temporary unity had brought the Irish together long enough to seek a Senate resolution calling for the abrogation of all commercial treaties between Great Britain and the United States. The Irish argued that such action was not unprecedented. Some years earlier, American Jews had prodded the Senate into passing a resolution against Russia because of that country's anti-Semitic policies.[31] The potential threat of this Irish manuever was not lost upon the Foreign Office where one

---

[29]O'Doherty, *Assignment America*, pp. 131–132.
[30]An examination of the Foreign Office minutes, dispatches, and telegrams concerning the Irish question for the period between June of 1919 and March of 1920 clearly illustrates this fact. See *FO* 371 class.
[31]Consulate General, New York, to the Foreign Secretary, 6 April 1920, *FO* 371/4550.

member concluded, "This might lead to an awkward position if cleverly pushed."[32]

SINN FEIN PROPAGANDA

As Irish separatist propaganda in America intensified in the weeks immediately preceding that country's political conventions, the Foreign Office received heavy pressure to respond in kind. Charles des Graz, Director of the British Library of Information in New York City, warned the London Government that Sinn Fein allegations of British misrule in Ireland would increase during the heated American political campaigns. Des Graz implored the Foreign Office to waste no time in responding to what he deemed to be crude attempts to turn United States public opinion against Britain.[33] A substantial number of similar petitions were sent to His Majesty's Government from unofficial sources in America. One not atypical letter, from a sympathetic Philadelphian, suggested that support for the Irish home rule movement in the United States was probably stimulated by American hope that some Irish-Americans would return home to Ireland and there exercise their proven abilities for misgovernment.[34]

Despite such petitions, the evidence seemed to indicate that Sinn Fein propaganda was effective. Certainly, Sinn Fein succeeded in influencing the United States Congress. On March 18, Senator Peter Gerry of Rhode Island had added his own reservation to the fourteen already tied to the Treaty of Versailles by its most implacable enemy, Senator

---

[32]Foreign Office minute, 20 April 1920, *FO* 371/4550.

[33]British Library of Information to the Foreign Office, 29 March 1920, *FO* 395/352.

[34]This was an open letter to the British Government published in the London *Morning Post* on April 21, 1920. One recorded comment at the Foreign Office read: "Excellent as from an American pen." Foreign Office minute, 23 April 1920, *FO* 395/349.

Henry Cabot Lodge of Massachusetts. The Gerry reservation, which expressed sympathy with the Irish demand for political self-determination,[35] was ultimately defeated when the Senate later rejected the whole Treaty. Nonetheless, Irish pressure upon the legislators prevailed and, in May 1920, a congressional resolution expressing concern over conditions in Ireland and sympathy with the political aspirations of its people was passed.[36] Bewildered and exasperated, British Embassy officials in Washington reported to London: "After discussing ... Washingtonian principles of abstention from European entanglements, the Senate ... indulged in a five day orgy of criticism of the doings ... of Great Britain in Ireland."[37] The temper at the Foreign Office, however, continued to be largely tolerant since the congressional resolutions were dismissed as the inevitable charades of an election year.[38]

The British Parliament however, was less philosophic than the Foreign Office. Some M.P.'s lent their voices to the growing chorus protesting the Government's inaction. On May 6, 1920, one member of the House of Commons demanded to know whether the Government contemplated any representations to the President of the United States on the subject of Irish bond certificates which were being sold in America to support revolution in Ireland.[39] Another inquired if any steps were being taken to destroy the malicious Sinn Fein propaganda campaign which affected the whole structure of Anglo-American relations.[40] Andrew Bonar Law replied negatively to both questions, offering the Government's rationale that any such impulsive action on Britain's part could only harm relations with the United States.[41]

---

[35] *U. S. Congressional Record*, 66 Cong., 2 Session, 1920, Vol. 59, p. 4522.
[36] *New York Times*, May 29, 1920.
[37] British Embassy to the Foreign Office, 1 April 1920, *FO* 371/4550.
[38] Foreign Office minute, 11 June 1920, *FO* 371/4550.
[39] *Parl. Debates*, Commons, 5th Series, 6 May 1920, Vol. 128, col. 2215. Irish activists in America were condemned in the upper chamber of the British legislature on this same date. See *Parl. Debates*, Lords, 5th Series, 6 May 1920, Vol. 40, col. 193–195.
[40] *Parl. Debates*, Commons, 5th Series, 6 May 1920, Vol. 128, col. 2215.
[41] Ibid.

The debate in Parliament continued for more than two weeks thereafter, and the subject of American attitudes became as much an issue as was the Irish question itself. Some members insisted that the Government need not be concerned with American views of a British domestic problem.[42] Others considered it only realistic to acknowledge that American opinion was a significant factor in British policy-making.[43] The latter contention was more closely in accord with the Foreign Office which simultaneously valued United States goodwill and deplored the impropriety of America's intrusion into England's internal affairs. Moreover, the Foreign Office recognized the wisdom of a recommendation submitted by Sir Arthur Willert when he left London to attend the national political conventions in America. Willert, the London *Times* correspondent in Washington, D.C., strongly advised Under-Secretary of State Cecil Harmsworth to avoid any "official" British propaganda in the United States until after the presidential election.[44]

BRITAIN'S STANCE TOWARD SINN FEIN

It is unlikely that the London Government would have deemed such overt activity to be necessary, since the acrimonious quarrel between Cohalan and de Valera had already weakened the Sinn Fein cause in America.[45] Moreover, by May of 1920 the Foreign Office had concluded that propagandizing in the United States could often be conducted through friendly American press correspondents assigned to London.[46] This is not to suggest, of course, that British offi-

---

[42]Ibid., 18 May 1920, Vol. 129, cols. 1272–1308.
[43]Ibid., col. 1339.
[44]Foreign Office minute, 14 May 1920, *FO* 395/349.
[45]This was not simply the opinion at the Foreign Office, for editorials in Irish-American newspapers such as the *Gaelic American* admitted to it openly.
[46]Foreign Office minute, 25 May 1920, *FO* 395/349.

cials never contemplated more aggressive action to promote their own ends or to counter Irish propaganda. William Randolph Hearst so provoked British ire through his abusive press campaign that one Foreign Office member seriously considered the possibilities of denying that publisher his Canadian paper supply.[47] Oil magnate E. L. Doheny incurred London's wrath when he subscribed ten thousand dollars to Irish Republican bond certificates. Advised by the British Embassy in Washington that Doheny would soon be negotiating with the Admiralty for fuel contracts in England, the Foreign Office promptly alerted that ministry to the oilman's politics.[48]

Aside from a few such impulsive reactions, London generally made a deliberate effort to appear indifferent to Sinn Fein activities in America. Discontented with so passive a strategy, Britain's Ambassador to Washington, Sir Auckland Geddes, deluged Whitehall with plans for countering Irish propaganda in the United States.[49] When eighty-eight members of the House of Representatives sent Prime Minister Lloyd George a telegram protesting the reportedly arbitrary imprisonment of Irishmen, Ambassador Geddes felt that the occasion presented an unrivaled opportunity to publicize the British point of view. Geddes strongly urged the Prime Min-

---

[47]There is no doubt that the Hearst publications caused great agitation at the Foreign Office. See Foreign Office minute, 26 March 1920, *FO* 395/349. When the Foreign Office learned from its Consulate-General in New York that the Hearst publications were dependent upon Canadian suppliers for approximately 250,000 tons of paper per year, there was speculation as to whether the Canadian paper could be allotted to the non-Hearst press in the United States. A Foreign Office minute attached to the following dispatch read: "I do not imagine however that any official action in such a matter could be taken by the Canadian Government, but perhaps unofficial steps could be taken." Consulate-General, New York, to the Foreign Office, 24 June 1920, *FO* 371/4550.

[48]British Embassy to the Foreign Office, 27 March 1920, *FO* 371/4550. The Foreign Office directed that a copy be sent to the Admiralty.

[49]Ambassador Geddes frequently offered unsolicited advice to the Foreign Office on a wide number of subjects and London more often than not responded with something less than enthusiasm. A typical example was the Ambassador's attempt to have his Government brand Sinn Fein a Bolshevik organization. Geddes to Curzon, 6 June 1920, *FO* 371/4550.

ister to reply publicly to the telegram by offering all possible assurances and explaining the complexities of the issue.[50] Although Lloyd George ultimately rejected that particular suggestion, he wavered for a time between a sarcastic reply and no reply at all. To the great relief of the Foreign Office, he chose the latter option.[51]

Perhaps the Republican and Democratic Conventions of 1920 did more than anything else to reveal the limitations of the Sinn Fein advocates in American politics. While the British Foreign Office continued to avoid any act or posture which might offend American sensibilities, the Irish reached their height of conspicuousness and pretentiousness during the time of the political conventions.[52] A united effort by Irish leaders to secure a plank in one or both party platforms favoring United States recognition of the Republic of Ireland ended in the usual bickering and recriminations between rival Irish groups.

THE REPUBLICAN CONVENTION

The National Council of the Friends of Irish Freedom charged a committee, led by Judge Cohalan, to seek a resolution on Ireland at the Republican Convention in Chicago. Only reluctantly did the Judge agree to Eamon de Valera's demand that the resolution favor nothing less than recognition of the Irish Republic.[53] Believing that Senator Hiram Johnson was the candidate who would best serve Irish interests, Cohalan worked actively in support of Johnson's bid for the Republican presidential nomination. De Valera objected

[50]Geddes to Curzon, 5 May 1920, *FO* 371/4550.

[51]Lloyd George communicated his decision to the Foreign Office through his private secretary, Philip Kerr. Foreign Office minute, 18 May 1920, *FO* 371/4550.

[52]Patrick McCartan tells of the pressure tactics and the circus tricks by which the Irish made their presence felt at the Republican Convention in Chicago. See McCartan, *With de Valera in America,* pp. 190–191.

[53]Nelson M. Blake, "The United States and the Irish Revolution, 1914– 1922" (Ph.D. dissertation, Clark University, 1936), p. 362.

to promoting individual candidates instead of a party platform plank demanding recognition for an Irish republic, and he accused Judge Cohalan of sacrificing the Sinn Fein cause for personal ambitions. The Irish president arrived in Chicago on the eve of the convention amidst much fanfare and proceeded to set up headquarters independent of The Friends of Irish Freedom. The delegates to the convention were then treated to the spectacle of a fratricidal struggle between de Valera and Cohalan supporters.[54]

On the afternoon of June 9, the subcommittee on resolutions was asked to vote on President de Valera's proposed plank seeking recognition for the Republic of Ireland. Judge Cohalan had submitted a separate resolution which sought to have the convention go on record simply as favoring the right of the Irish people to determine their own form of government. Cohalan had tried without success to impress upon the Irish president the realities of American politics and the necessity for exercising restraint in seeking the convention's endorsement. De Valera's resolution was soundly defeated by a vote of eleven to one while Cohalan's milder plank passed by a margin of seven to six.[55] Even though the accepted resolution went far beyond most expectations of home rule advocates, de Valera believed that anything short of the recognition of a republic constituted a repudiation of Irish claims.[56] He therefore publicly disavowed the Cohalan resolution, prompting one subcommittee member to withdraw his endorsement in disgust. That withdrawal left a tie vote on the resolution, and the Republican platform was completed without any Irish plank. De Valera, with his distrust of Cohalan and his ignorance of American politics, was chiefly responsible for this negative result.[57]

---

[54] *New York Times,* June 8, 1920.

[55] The first vote on the Cohalan plank was six to six requiring the committee chairman to cast a vote in order to break the tie.

[56] Blake, "The United States and the Irish Revolution," p. 364.

[57] Alden Jamison, "Irish Americans, The Irish Question and American Diplomacy, 1895–1921" (Ph.D. dissertation, Harvard University, 1942), Vol. 2, p. 790. A pro-Cohalan interpretation of the events at Chicago was given

British Ambassador Sir Auckland Geddes wrote Foreign Secretary Lord Curzon about the proceedings at Chicago, and noted that the lack of enthusiasm for an Irish plank among the convention delegates was especially significant. He suggested that the entire affair illustrated

> the immense influence Irishmen can exert on American politicians if they proceed wisely; and how ready American politicans are to withdraw themselves from that influence if they can find some colourable pretext for doing so."[58]

Geddes also commented on the renewed schism in the Irish leadership, a fact which became common knowledge once de Valera and Cohalan publicly exchanged verbal assaults after the political conventions.[59]

London took a keen interest in the Irish controversy and, quite by chance, gained a rather instructive insight into Irish separatist activities at the Chicago convention. The source of this new information was a packet of letters which British authorities seized from seaman William Barry who was acting as a courier between Sinn Fein leaders in Ireland and those in America.[60] By far the lengthiest communication in the packet was a letter from Sean Nunan, de Valera's lieutenant at the convention, to Arthur Griffith, Acting President of the Dail, dated June 21, 1920. Nunan informed Griffith that Eamon de Valera personally requested that an account of the events which occurred before, during, and in the few days following the Republican Convention in Chicago be sent to the Dail Cabinet in Dublin. Not surprisingly, the bent of the letter was to contrast Cohalan's treachery with de Valera's

in the *Gaelic American,* June 26, 1920 and in the *Newsletter of the Friends of Irish Freedom,* No. 51, June 19, 1920. De Valera's own statement on the subject appeared in the *New York World,* June 20, 1920 and his stand was strongly defended by the *Irish World,* June 26, 1920, as well as by the *Sinn Feiner,* June 26, 1920.

[58]Geddes to Curzon, 16 June 1920, *FO* 371/4550.
[59]*Gaelic American,* June 19, 1920; *Irish World,* June 26, 1920.
[60]*New York Times,* July 7, 1920.

noble efforts. Nunan accurately recounted how Cohalan had attempted to win de Valera's support for Hiram Johnson's candidacy with the argument that if Johnson became president he would do the right thing for Ireland. Nunan assured Griffith that de Valera was not beguiled by a strategy so reminiscent of the old tale of "trust Asquith."[61]

Foreign Office officials were already reviewing their own strategy even before the Chicago convention came to a close. A Foreign Office minute of June 14 read in part:

> Though it is too early to speak with anything like confidence, we can probably congratulate ourselves on having successfully passed the first stage in the difficult period in the beginning of this year and November next, so far as the reaction of the Irish question on American politics—and therefore on Anglo-American relations—is concerned . . . What has happened confirms the wisdom of our policy in refraining consistently from anything like direct propaganda methods which could easily have been misinterpreted as attempts to influence American electoral opinion and would probably have produced an unfavorable reaction. There has, of course, been a great deal of propaganda done both from here and in the United States, but it has been done almost exclusively through American channels.[62]

THE DEMOCRATIC CONVENTION

Satisfied with the outcome of events at the Republican Convention, British policy-makers next turned their attention to the Democratic Party and to its upcoming political gathering at San Francisco. On June 19, 1920, the *Times* of London carried a statement by President Woodrow Wilson condemning the Republican party platform as "the apotheosis of reaction" while exhorting his own party not to evade the

---

[61]Foreign Office to the British Embassy, 24 December 1920, *FO* 115/2601. Other letters carried by William Barry included one from Peter MacSwiney to his brother Terence MacSwiney, Lord Mayor of Cork, and another from James O'Mara to Arthur Griffith. They all expressed an anti-Cohalan sentiment.

[62]Foreign Office minute, 14 June 1920, *FO* 395/349.

issue of the Treaty or the League.[63] In analyzing the presidential remarks, the Foreign Office felt certain that the more Wilson succeeded in forcing the Democratic party to make the League of Nations the essential plank in their platform, the more difficult it would be for the Democratic party to work with the Irish. Irish-Americans had, after all, taken the lead in denouncing the League of Nations as a British plot to entrap the United States in European entanglements. This divergence in views was expected to deny the Democratic party the solid support which it traditionally received from the Irish vote.[64] It proved to be a reasonably fair assumption.[65]

On June 27 the Foreign Office was jarred by a telegram from Ambassador Geddes containing an urgent appeal which went completely contrary to the British Government's policy of remaining outwardly detached from the political scene in the United States. Geddes often made such requests, and there were those in the London Government who considered him a greater threat than the Irish to the harmony of Anglo-American relations.[66] On this occasion the Ambassador reported that some of Britain's strongest supporters in the Southern states had been offended by Prime Minister Lloyd George's public remarks comparing his efforts in Ireland to President Lincoln's exertions on behalf of the Union. The Ambassador petitioned the Prime Minister to release a statement of appreciation for Southern friendship to the American press while the Democratic Convention was underway in San Francisco. Geddes said it could be of "extraordinary value in determining the course of events

---

[63]The *Times* (London), June 19, 1920.

[64]Foreign Office minute, 19 June 1920, *FO* 395/349.

[65]Blake, "The United States and the Irish Revolution," p. 391.

[66]On one occasion when Irish groups rallied for the passage of the Mason Bill, a proposal to provide a United States legation to the Republic of Ireland, Geddes felt compelled to speak out against the bill in a public address. The Foreign Office was not told of his plans until it was too late to stop him. Geddes to Curzon, 24 May 1920, *FO* 371/4550.

there."[67] No one at the Foreign Office doubted that such a step would be extraordinary, but they all agreed that the result would be far different from what the Ambassador anticipated. A clerk in the American Department of the Foreign Office expressed the view that the recommendation courted disaster and concluded bluntly, "I shall not be surprised if Sir A. Geddes gets himself or the Prime Minister into a mess before long—I hope it will be Sir A. Geddes."[68]

London hoped that the Republican party's total omission of an Irish plank from its platform would allow the Democrats to do as they pleased with the issue, especially as the Irish were again divided and fighting among themselves. Indeed, on June 25 a spokesman for the Friends of Irish Freedom announced that organization's decision to refrain from any official activity at the Democratic Convention. The Cohalan-Devoy forces obviously had concluded that President Wilson's opposition to any plank calling for recognition of an Irish republic would very probably prove decisive.[69] They also felt that de Valera was not disposed to moderate his demand for outright recognition despite the fact that the Irish-American political bosses, upon whom he was depending for support, were plainly preoccupied with local and national affairs.[70] Judge Cohalan and his supporters were conspicuously absent from San Francisco. Although they publicly urged support for de Valera at the Democratic Convention, they privately hoped to see the onus of defeat fall

[67]Geddes to Curzon, 25 June 1920, *FO* 115/2599. Although dated the 25th it was not acknowledged at the Foreign Office until the 27th.

[68]Foreign Office minute, 28 June 1920, *FO* 371/4550. When the Prime Minister did speak of the Irish question in America during an address to Parliament the next day, he made no mention of the South. Instead, he confidently predicted that the people of the United States would never support the Irish claim to a republic. *Parl. Debates,* Commons, 5th Series, 28 June 1920, Vol. 131, col. 170.

[69]Tansill, *America and the Fight for Irish Freedom,* p. 380.

[70]Rocco M. Paone, "The Presidential Election of 1920" (Ph.D. dissertation, Georgetown University, 1950), pp. 270–271.

squarely upon all their enemies in the Irish separatist movement.[71]

Reports reaching the Foreign Office regarding Irish activities at the Democratic Convention were reassuring to London. On June 29, Britain's Consul-General in San Francisco
sent word that de Valera's reception in that city had been
extremely poor despite an intense ten-day publicity campaign by Irish organizations prior to his visit. A staff member
from the Consulate who witnessed the official welcoming
ceremonies testified that only a "motley crowd" of a few
hundred "rougher class" Irish, a Hibernian band, and six East
Indian Sikhs wearing Irish insignia were on hand. The presence of every prominent city official, including the mayor,
was notably lacking at the affair.[72] Newspaper accounts
which described the crowds welcoming de Valera as large
and enthusiastic were declared to be patently false.[73]

Just as at the Republican Convention a few weeks before,
Eamon de Valera, on June 29, argued before the Democratic
Resolution Committee on behalf of a plank supporting the
recognition of Irish independence by the United States. The
Committee not only ruled against the Sinn Fein President's
proposal by a vote of 31 to 17, but it also rejected a milder
plank favored by the Wilson Administration which asked that
the Irish question be referred to the League of Nations.[74]
Instead, the Committee adopted a bland resolution which
stated: "Within the limitation of international comity and
usage, this convention repeats the several previous expres-

[71]John Devoy to Judge Cohalan, 28 June 1920, *Cohalan MSS.*, American
Irish Historical Society, New York.

[72]Consulate-General, San Francisco, to the British Embassy, Washington,
29 June 1920, *FO* 115/2599. This report was subsequently forwarded to
London.

[73]Ibid. This also disputes Dorothy Macardle's contention that de Valera
was accorded every token of popular support at San Francisco. See Macardle, *The Irish Republic*, p. 371.

[74]Blake, "The United States and the Irish Revolution," p. 367. The Irish
were not fooled by this obvious attempt on Wilson's part to win support for
his cherished League.

sions of the sympathy of the Democratic party of the United States for the aspirations of Ireland for self-government."[75]

After two setbacks in almost as many weeks, de Valera decided upon a less ambitious objective and, with the help of Frank P. Walsh and other close advisors, he prepared another proposition for the consideration of the full convention. The new plank differed little from the resolution advanced by Cohalan at Chicago. De Valera dropped the demand for formal recognition of the Republic; the new appeal asked only for the continuance of America's long established policy of granting recognition to any nation which established a government by free vote of the people. Seven members of the Resolutions Committee were finally prevailed upon to present this milder plank to the convention as a minority report.[76]

On July 7 the convention was required to choose between the innocuous Resolutions Committee plank and de Valera's substantially modified plank. One historian described the scene this way:

> The conditions were not favorable for the Irish; the delegates were tired from a long sitting and Edward L. Doheny, the oil magnate who had been selected to present the minority proposal, was a sorry contrast to the titans of debate, [William Jennings] Bryan and [Bourke] Cockran, who had been jousting on the prohibition issue. Doheny in the confusion of his maiden speech confided that he had come to San Francisco as a "candidate-at-large," and, when the Convention made evident its amusement, the poor man forgot part of his oration.[77]

When the roll call was taken, the Irish made a rather impressive showing, but the minority plank was defeated by a vote of 665 1/2 to 402 1/2.[78] Having endured countless hours

---

[75] *New York Times*, July 3, 1920.
[76] Tansill, *America and the Fight for Irish Freedom*, pp. 381–382.
[77] Blake, "The United States and the Irish Revolution," p. 368.
[78] *Gaelic American*, July 10, 1920; an account sympathetic to de Valera's role at San Francisco appeared in the *Sinn Feiner*, No. 3, July 10, 1920.

of empty oratory, a good deal of which was aimed at the Irish vote, the Democratic delegates ultimately did little more than express sympathy with Irish aspirations.

THE IRISH EFFORT FAILS

The presidential campaign did not begin in earnest until after Labor Day, but the Irish effort to win American recognition for the Sinn Fein Republic was already lost. Neither the Irish nor the British entertained any illusions about that fact.[79] The split between de Valera and Cohalan became permanent when the Irish president unsuccessfully attempted to seize control of the Friends of Irish Freedom and then established a rival Irish-American organization of his own. In their frustration with both party platforms, Irish spokesmen throughout America condemned the Wilson Administration, the Democratic party, the Republican party, and some even accused other Irishmen of being British spies.[80] By contrast, the London Foreign Office refused to be drawn into the American political arena by the Irish issue. Even when Democratic presidential candidate James Cox stated that the Irish people had a right to be independent if they so desired, the Foreign Office declined any official comment and left it to the Republicans to dispute Mr. Cox.[81] But in the final analysis, the Irish question was not a major issue in the campaign of 1920. It might have been an important

---

[79]A sense of complete and utter defeat was manifest in the tone of the *Irish World*, July 10, 1920. Among the *Cohalan MSS.* there are a good number of letters, apart from those published in the Tansill book, by prominent Irish-Americans expressing the same view. *Times* correspondent Sir Arthur Willert and British Library of Information Director Charles des Graz were equally confident that the Sinn Fein quest for independence was a dead issue in America. Willert to W. Tyrrell, Foreign Office, 16 July 1920, *FO* 395/351; des Graz to Curzon, Foreign Office, 6 July 1920, *FO* 395/350.

[80]For charges and counter-charges, see the *Irish World*, July 10, 1920; and the *Gaelic American*, August 7, 1920.

[81]Foreign Office minute, 4 October 1920, *FO* 395/451.

factor if a united Irish effort had succeeded in securing strong planks on behalf of Irish independence at the Republican and Democratic Conventions, or if the British Foreign Office had succumbed to the temptation of openly combating Sinn Fein's propaganda and activities in America.

DE VALERA GAINS CONTROL

Eamon de Valera doubtlessly was responsible in part for the disharmony which hampered the Irish separatist effort during his eighteen months in America, but he had every reason to be dissatisfied with those who organized the Irish-American financial contributions to the Irish cause. By the end of 1920 the Irish Victory Fund had produced nearly a million dollars, about three-quarters of which had been retained in the United States for use in the campaign against the League of Nations.[82] De Valera therefore undertook to destroy the power of Cohalan and the Friends of Irish Freedom. In January 1920, the Irish president launched his own bond-certificate drive. Irish bond-certificates were sold with the promise that they would be exchanged for Irish Republican bonds soon after international recognition of an Irish republic. The Victory Fund closed down, and money poured into de Valera's bond-drive. Five and a half million dollars were subscribed, far outstripping even the sizeable funds raised in previous Irish-American campaigns, and four million dollars were actually spent in Ireland.[83] Indeed, without this money it would have been difficult, if not impossible, to sustain the war in Ireland.[84]

---

[82]Tansill, *America and the Fight for Irish Freedom*, p. 347.

[83]Alan Ward, "America and the Irish Problem, 1899–1921," *Irish Historical Studies*, 16 (March, 1968), p. 87.

[84]Despite these funds, American Consul in Dublin F. T. F. Dumont told Secretary of State Charles E. Hughes that one of the factors which prompted the Irish to accept a truce in July, 1921, was the insufficiency of their financial resources. Dumont to Hughes, 9 June 1921, *State Department*, 841d.00/381.

After achieving control of fund-raising in America, de Valera next sought to establish a huge popular movement of his own through which the needed monies might be procured. In November 1920, the Irish president founded the American Association for the Recognition of the Irish Republic; that organization soon displaced the Friends as the leading Irish separatist movement in America.[85] The American Commission on Conditions in Ireland which, in 1921, widely publicized a somewhat distorted account of the suffering inflicted by the hostilities in Ireland,[86] and the American Committee for Relief in Ireland which, beginning in 1921, raised five million dollars for Irish relief, were controlled by Americans loyal to Eamon de Valera. Moreover, these activities attracted the attention and support of many Americans who were not of Irish extraction.[87]

DE VALERA RETURNS TO IRELAND

In December 1920, de Valera left America as a stowaway aboard the S. S. *Celtic* from New York to Liverpool. Once again he eluded British authorities, and arrived secretly at his home in Ireland on Christmas Day.[88] His return probably had been prompted by the arrest of Acting-President Arthur Griffith the previous month and, as he told the Dail on January 25, 1921, by the length and severity of the Anglo-Irish war. He admitted being disconcerted by the bitterness and harshness of the struggle, and wondered if the Irish Republi-

---

[85]De Valera founded the organization in Washington, D.C., on November 16, 1920. Edward L. Doheny of Los Angeles became its first president. O'Doherty, *Assignment America*, p. 194.

[86]See The American Commission on Conditions in Ireland, *Evidence on Conditions in Ireland* (Washington, 1921).

[87]Ward, "America and the Irish Problem" *Irish Historical Studies*, 16, p. 88.

[88]In early 1921, the British took elaborate precautions to ensure that the Irish President was not arrested, since by that time the London Government was anxious to begin negotiations for a truce.

can Army had the resources to push an aggressive warfare to a climax. The Irish president even alarmed some members of the Dail when he suggested that it might be necessary to diminish Irish attacks against the enemy in order to ease the burden of the people.[89] Most members of the Dail did not, of course, know that the British Government had already sent out peace feelers in December, 1920, by dispatching a spokesman to negotiate confidentially with Irish leaders in Dublin.[90]

President de Valera could report to his comrades in the Dail Cabinet that he had succeeded in achieving two of his three objectives in America. He had indeed given Ireland's claim the widest possible publicity, and his fund-raising had exceeded all expectations. The singularly notable failure of his mission was his inability to secure formal recognition of the Irish Republic by the United States Government. Perhaps it had never been a feasible goal and, in any event, the prospects for such recognition were even more remote in 1921.[91] Many Irish-Americans, traditionally Democratic voters, had cast their ballots for Republican candidate Warren G. Harding in the 1920 presidential election. Once in power, however, the victorious Republicans ignored their Irish supporters, knowing that the latter had voted Republican in 1920 more in opposition to the League of Nations than in support of the party's candidate. To the British, President Warren G. Harding was reassuringly congenial and, in May 1921, he even expressed his regret to the British Ambassador

[89]Lyons, *Ireland Since the Famine*, p. 421. For the text of President de Valera's remarks on this occasion, see *Dail Eireann: Minutes of Proceedings*, 25 January 1921, pp. 240–241. De Valera characterized the Anglo-Irish war as a struggle between might and right. Ireland had the power of moral resistance. The question was how long the people could sustain their resistance.

[90]The Roman Catholic Archbishop of Perth, Australia, Dr. Patrick Clune, volunteered to hold preliminary discussions with Sinn Fein on behalf of the British. Clune met first with Michael Collins, and next with Arthur Griffith and Eoin MacNeill, at Mountjoy jail, where they were incarcerated since their arrest following Bloody Sunday in November 1920.

[91]In later life, de Valera conceded that, had he been in President Wilson's place, he would not have granted recognition to the Irish Republic.

over the difficulties which the Irish problem had created for Anglo-American relations.[92] United States and world opinion would still be courted by the British and Irish alike, but it was becoming abundantly clear that the real resolution of their differences would be ultimately determined by the fortunes of the tragic war then raging in Ireland.

---

[92]Foreign Office minute, 11 May 1921, *FO* 115/2673.

Chapter 10

War for Independence and the Partition Compromise (1919–1922)

Ireland endured hostilities between British crown forces and Irish separatist guerrilla units for two and a half years in what some would later call the War for Irish Independence, while others would refer to it as the Anglo-Irish war. By any name, it was a tragic conflict in which atrocities were perpetrated in the name of freedom, and reprisals were executed in the enforcement of law and order.[1] The fighting fell essentially into three separate phases. In the first of these, which extended through the year 1919 and into the early months of 1920, the struggle was characterized by isolated incidents which in time escalated in size and frequency. The second

---

[1] One euphemism for the conflict employed both by contemporaries and others since that time is "The Troubles." For two Irish Republican Army accounts, see Tom Barry, *Guerrilla Days in Ireland* (Cork, 1949), and Dan Breen, *My Fight for Irish Freedom* (Tralee, 1964). For accounts by British Army officers, see Brigadier General F. P. Crozier, *Ireland for Ever* (London, 1932), General Sir Nevil Macready, *Annals of an Active Life*, Vol. 2 (London, 1942).

phase, lasting from March through December of 1920, witnessed a more intensive Irish insurgency. This was answered in kind by determined British counter-measures, and the violence on both sides reached an appalling climax in the last two months of the year. The final phase of the conflict was conducted between January and July 1921, while peace negotiators were pursuing a truce which was finally obtained in July. It was, however, this concluding chapter of the war which saw Irish separatists systematically exploit the tactics of ambush and assault in classic guerrilla fashion. The British were planning a response of massive retaliation, possibly including the scorched earth and concentration camp policies of the Boer War, when the announcement of peace ended the necessity for further strategies.[2]

THE ROYAL IRISH CONSTABULARY

Most of the early phase of the conflict was in fact a contest between the Irish Volunteers, soon to be known as the Irish Republican Army or the I.R.A., and the Royal Irish Constabulary, the armed national police force known as the R.I.C. There is reason to believe that in the beginning some Dail ministers attempted to minimize the bloodshed as much as possible. On at least one occasion in 1919, Arthur Griffith intervened successfully with Michael Collins to prevent violence planned by the I.R.A. in Cork.[3] Indeed, the Dail's preliminary campaign against the R.I.C. was not calculated to terrorize the members of that organization. Rather, it was

---

[2]F. S. L. Lyons, *Ireland Since the Famine* (New York, 1971), p. 410. Lord French wanted to place the Irish conflict on a war basis as had been done in the Boer War when the rebels were seized and put into concentration camps. Prime Minister Lloyd George declined on the grounds that "you do not declare war against rebels." Note of conversation, 30 April 1920, *CAB* 23/21.

[3]P. S. O'Hegarty, *The Victory of Sinn Fein* (Dublin, 1924), pp. 46–48. The I.R.A. leadership itself took steps to restrain the Tipperary Brigade from acting upon its intention, announced in early 1919, to kill anyone associated with the British military or civilian authorities in that county after a specified date. Dorothy Macardle, *The Irish Republic* (New York, 1965), p. 290.

meant to impress those hated fellow Irish with the degree of contempt in which they were held by separatists and their supporters. At the April 10, 1919 meeting of the Dail, President Eamon de Valera declared that the R.I.C. was no ordinary civil force and was not to be compared to the police in a democratic society. The R.I.C., insisted the Sinn Fein President, was a military organization, armed with rifles and bayonets, which brutally enforced English rule against its own countrymen. De Valera urged that R.I.C. members be ostracized by the people of Ireland in order that they "be shown and made feel how base are the functions they perform and how vile is the position they occupy."[4] In many parts of the country people responded to the president's appeal not only by shunning the R.I.C., but also by refusing to sell it food or to engage in any transactions whatever with its members.[5] That policy demoralized the R.I.C. far more than did the murder of a few of its number. When many R.I.C. members resigned, and no new replacements could be recruited from the Irish population, the London Government took the fateful step of hiring World War I veterans from England to supplement the depleted ranks of the R.I.C.

In its struggle with the I.R.A., the Royal Irish Constabulary enjoyed the advantages of superior weaponry, excellent communication facilities, and the support of the substantial garrison of British Army regulars quartered in Ireland. But the R.I.C. also labored under real disabilities. Its members were often housed in isolated barracks amidst a hostile population. Moreover, the organization suffered from chronic morale problems due to the expected implementation of home rule.[6] That prospect diminished any attraction for a career in

---

[4]*Dail Eireann: Minutes of Proceedings,* 10 April 1919, pp. 67–68.

[5]The boycott extended even to a donkey carrying turf for the police. J. Bowyer Bell, *The Secret Army* (New York, 1971), p. 20.

[6]Other morale problems were created by the incredibly austere regulations which governed the lives of the members of the R.I.C. For an instructive essay, see Richard Hawkins, "Dublin Castle and the Royal Irish Constabulary," in Desmond Williams, ed., *The Irish Struggle, 1916–1926* (Toronto, 1966), pp. 167–181; see also G. C. Duggan, "The Royal Irish Constabulary," in O. Dudley Edwards and Fergus Pyle, eds., *1916: The Easter Rising* (London, 1968), pp. 91–99.

the R.I.C. since the force could only anticipate the worst at the hands of a native government, and could also expect to lose all claim upon the British Government. By March of 1920, R.I.C. strength was less than 9,700 compared with a pre-World War I total of 12,000;[7] and this decline occurred when its duties and responsibilities were more difficult than ever before. It was in March 1920, that the new recruits from Britain began to arrive. Because of a shortage of the green cloth (so dark it appeared black) used for R.I.C. uniforms, the new members of the force at first wore khaki shirts and trousers with the dark R.I.C. caps. This combination inspired a derisive Irish separatist name for these men—the Black and Tans—borrowed from the name of famous hounds from county Limerick.[8] An essentially native, colonial police force was thus transformed into an organization which included mercenaries who knew little and cared less about the nature of the Irish problem.

I.R.A. GUERRILLA TACTICS

If there was no clear British military strategy during this first stage of the Anglo-Irish war, neither was there an I.R.A. master plan. The objective of the Irish Republican Army was to attack the enemy wherever he appeared vulnerable, to seize weapons and ammunition whenever possible, and to disrupt the machinery of administration so as to render the country ungovernable by the British. Since uniforms, insignia, and general observance of the conventions of war had not spared the leaders of the 1916 Rising from execution for treason, guerrilla tactics were deemed the only alternative even by Sinn Fein moderates who regretted such a necessity. And guerrilla war it was, with no front lines and, on the Irish

---

[7]For further reference to R.I.C. strength, see R. B. McDowell, *The Irish Administration* (London, 1964), pp. 135–145.

[8]Edgar Holt, *Protest in Arms: The Irish Troubles, 1916–1923* (London, 1960), p. 171.

side, no uniforms or standardized weapons. Ambushes in the countryside by the "flying columns," executions in the towns and cities by special "squads," kidnapping and holding of hostages, arson, sabotage and hunger strikes by Irish prisoners, were but some of the tactics employed by the I.R.A. Against such methods the British reacted with nightly curfews in Dublin and Cork, the substitution of martial law for civilian rule in several counties, tanks and armored cars on city streets as a show of force, and raids upon the homes of suspected gunmen by the R.I.C. and British soldiers. Throughout it all, life went on much the same as before the conflict. Shops were open, trains ran, and race meetings were attended by the usual crowds and spirited fanfare which normally accompanied those festive occasions. The majority of the people, if not sympathetic supporters of the I.R.A., at least gave no comfort to the R.I.C and their English comrades. For a variety of reasons, including inclination, fear of I.R.A. "justice," compassion for Irish boys under pursuit, and distaste for the often brutal R.I.C. reprisals, the Irish population helped in obstructing the operations of the British and in aiding those of the Irish Republican Army.[9]

Few wars of national liberation have ever been launched with such meager resources as those possessed by the I.R.A. in 1919. There were virtually no funds for running the government ministries or for purchasing the armaments needed to fight English soldiers. Weapons and ammunition, always in short supply in the I.R.A. were smuggled into Ireland aboard steamers from Liverpool and Glasgow. Some arms from Hibernian groups in the United States were later secretly shipped to Queenstown and other Irish ports.[10] Crude gre-

---

[9]Charles L. Mowat, *Britain Between the Wars* (London, 1968), pp. 66–67.

[10]The British made a considerable effort to help the United States Justice Department identify and prosecute Americans involved in arms smuggling to Ireland. When an employee of the Auto Ordnance Company of New York, manufacturer of Thompson machine guns, was implicated in the illicit traffic, the occasion proved embarrassing to Washington and London alike. Owner John P. Thompson's son, it was discovered, was married to the daughter of George Harvey, United States Ambassador to Great Britain. British Embassy to the Foreign Office, 21 September 1921, *FO* 371/5656.

nades and mortars were manufactured in the cellars of bicycle shops, while a few automatic weapons were acquired through ambushes and assaults against R.I.C. barracks in the countryside. One British general surmised that 100,000 men were available to the I.R.A.[11] The real total, however, was closer to 15,000. Of this number, Michael Collins estimated the effective fighting force as never exceeding 5,000; even that figure was reduced to 3,000 by the time of the truce in 1921. Against this force the British could summon 50,000 troops and 15,000 police by 1920, and the total number of British soldiers may have reached 80,000 before the fighting ceased.[12]

In their struggle to survive against overwhelming British military might, the Irish republicans proved remarkably resourceful. Guerrilla warfare often provided the I.R.A. with the element of surprise, but that advantage was most telling only when augmented with hard and reliable intelligence. Michael Collins' success as Director of Intelligence was due in part to friends in the Dublin Metropolitan Police force, and to a few of the detectives in Dublin Castle's G squad who telephoned to alert him when a raid was imminent. His counter-intelligence contacts extended to agents in the post office, the railways, the customs service, and even into government offices in London. The nerve center of Collins' spy network was, for a time, located in a crude makeshift office on Crow Street, within two hundred yards of the British authorities at Dublin Castle. Classified files, personal dossiers ranging from

[11]Major General Henry Tudor, who was appointed police adviser to the R.I.C. in 1920, made this estimate. D. G. Boyce, *Englishmen and Irish Troubles* (London, 1972), pp. 49–50. Lord French, the Viceroy, concurred, and Chief Secretary for Ireland Ian Macpherson assumed the I.R.A. strength in 1921 to be 200,000. Giovanni Costigan, *A History of Modern Ireland* (New York, 1970), p. 342.

[12]British and Irish sources differ as to the actual number of men under arms in His Majesty's service. General Macready put the total British forces in Ireland in 1920, military and police, at about 40,000. Macready, *Annals of an Active Life*, Vol. 2, p. 533. John Murphy places the figure somewhat higher. John Murphy, *Ireland in the Twentieth Century* (Dublin, 1975), p. 22; for figures on I.R.A. strength, see Lyons, *Ireland Since the Famine* p. 415, see also George Dangerfield, *The Damnable Question* (Boston, 1976) p. 323.

those of military officers to Government leaders, and documents stolen from British police, military, and civilian administrative headquarters were among the materials kept at Crow Street. It was also at this facility that Liam Tobin, a specialist at deciphering codes, conducted much of his work.[13]

One thing which hindered the otherwise efficient I.R.A. operation was the fact that Minister of Defense Cathal Brugha and Minister of Finance Michael Collins often functioned more as rivals than as colleagues. Brugha particularly resented the way in which Collins, in his capacity as Director of Intelligence, was deeply involved in military strategy. Equally divisive was the uneasiness, if not distrust, which existed between those leaders of the I.R.A. who were members of the Irish Republican Brotherhood and those who were not. As a former member of the I.R.B., Brugha knew that the secret, oath-bound organization regarded its Supreme Council as the legitimate government of the Republic of Ireland. In an effort to eliminate such conflicting loyalties and to harmonize the I.R.A. military campaign, Cathal Brugha, in August 1919, won the Dail's approval of a resolution imposing the same oath of allegiance upon the members of that assembly and the rank and file of the I.R.A. Each deputy and each Volunteer was required to swear to "support and defend the Irish Republic and the Government of the Irish Republic, which is Dail Eireann, against all enemies, foreign and domestic . . . without any mental reservation or purpose of evasion, so help me, God."[14]

Throughout the spring of 1919 the I.R.A. spent the greater part of its energies in procuring the arms and explosives which were desperately needed before that rapidly growing

---

[13]Rex Taylor, *Michael Collins* (London, 1965), pp. 99–100.
[14]*Dail Eireann: Minutes of Proceedings*, 20 August 1919, p. 151. Michael Collins objected to the I.R.A. taking the Dail oath but agreed on the condition that a separate I.R.A. executive should remain in being as an advisory body to the minister of defense. Macardle, *The Irish Republic*, p. 305. Even then, some brigade officers were not sworn until the middle of 1920. Ernie O'Malley, *Army Without Banners* (Boston, 1937), p. 145.

organization could attempt military action of any significance. On March 20, Volunteers of the Dublin Brigade
seized arms and ammunition from a British arsenal near Col-
linstown and, in April, another group staged a similar raid on
a police barrack in county Cork. British authorities at Dublin
Castle, acting with the authorization of the London Government, responded to the insurgents by suspending civil administration in several counties and placing them under
military control as was permitted by the Defense of the
Realm Act. Tanks and armored cars began patrolling some of
the towns and roads in the south and western parts of the
country where the fighting would always be most intense,
while the guerrilla units maintained a low profile in the
mountainous terrain which offered them some sanctuary.[15]

THE DAIL GOVERNMENT

On April 1, 1919, Dail Eireann met in private session and
began to effect its declared intention of taking over the administration of Ireland from British authorities. After Eamon
de Valera became president, he appointed a new cabinet of
eight ministers and named Lawrence Ginnell, a former Nationalist M.P., Director of Propaganda. The significance of
the expanded cabinet lay in the fact that it was principally
these eight people who would inherit the burden of imple-
menting the Sinn Fein program after de Valera left for
America in June 1919.[16]

Although Britain did not officially suppress the Dail until

---

[15]It was during this period that ambushes, followed by reprisals, began to
form the pattern of warfare which would typify so much of the Anglo-Irish
conflict.

[16]Each of the ministers was to receive an annual salary not to exceed
£500, and the Dail fixed the President's annual salary at £1,000. *Dail Eireann: Minutes of Proceedings*, 2 April 1919, pp. 36–37. The Dail ministry
of propaganda was efficiently organized and, by August of 1919, had pamphlets on the Sinn Fein program available for both foreign and domestic
consumption. See *Ducibella Barton MSS.*, (8786) National Library, Dublin;
see also *Gavan Duffy MSS.*, (15,439) National Library, Dublin.

September, the proportion of its members who were fugitives from the police compelled it to go underground; the Dail was able to conduct only thirteen sessions during the next three years. Taken collectively, these sessions involved twenty-one meetings of which fourteen were held in 1919, three in 1920, and four in 1921.[17] It was therefore left to the cabinet ministers, acting without the check of the larger parliamentary body, to provide an alternative government for Ireland. Operating under the most primitive conditions and from secret locations which were changed frequently and abruptly, some of the ministers performed their tasks with true distinction. Finance Minister Michael Collins succeeded in raising a Dail Eireann national loan of £357,802.[18] Labour Minister Countess Markievicz managed the settling of industrial disputes. Minister of Agriculture Robert Barton was similarly successful in establishing a Land Bank which advanced loans to farmers for land purchases. A land commission was also formed to administer a plan of land acquisition and distribution which was intended to serve as a model for more extensive reforms after independence had been achieved. Local Government Minister William Cosgrave, together with his capable assistant minister Kevin O'Higgins, established valuable contacts with county, city, town, and village officials throughout the country. In the local elections the following year, 1920, Sinn Fein won a sweeping victory as it dominated 28 out of 33 County Councils, 182 out of 206 Rural District Councils, and 138 of the 154 Poor Law Boards. Moreover, out of 127 corporations and town councils Sinn Fein controlled 72 completely, and shared its authority with different nationalists groups in 26 others.[19]

Dail Eireann, or the ministry which functioned on behalf

---

[17]J. L. McCracken, *Representative Government in Ireland* (London, 1958), pp. 23–24.

[18]Taylor, *Michael Collins*, pp. 245–246.

[19]Lyons, *Ireland Since the Famine*, p. 405. Cosgrave and O'Higgins succeeded in taking over some of the routine work performed by the official headquarters of Irish local government through the cooperation of friendly postal officials who sent them mail addressed to the Custom House in Dublin. Holt, *Protest in Arms*, pp. 177–178.

of that constitutent assembly, also sought to substitute its own legal system for the one which then prevailed under Dublin Castle officialdom. Justice was administered through Sinn Fein parish courts, district courts, and a supreme court sitting in Dublin and composed of not less than three Dail appointed judges. At first these courts handled only civil matters, but criminal proceedings were later conducted, and in many areas of Ireland the United Kingdom judicial system was supplanted, often leaving official courtrooms empty. The conduct of these Irish revolutionary courts underscored the fact that the Sinn Fein war against Britain was a nationalist struggle, not an ideological one. There were no radical departures from the British judicial system and proceedings were determined by British legal and governmental practice, except where the law had been amended by the Dail Eireann. Since these tribunals were declared illegal by the Dublin Castle administration, many of them were driven underground. There were, however, perhaps as many as 900 parish courts and over 70 district courts in operation when an armistice concluded the hostilities two years later.[20] It is also noteworthy that the Dail Eireann provisional government expected the national liberation forces to be subject to the law as were the citizenry, a standard of justice not always attained but, as in the instance of some of the more recent guerrilla movements, calculated to win the respect of the native population. On one occasion, for example, a member of the Dail asked if Sinn Fein courts might not ensure that damage caused to private homes by Volunteers be paid for by the Volunteers through the advance of Dail funds.[21]

THE DAIL AND THE I.R.A.

From May to December 1919, the British Government in Ireland appeared to be in partial retreat, as it closed down

---

[20]Lyons, *Ireland Since the Famine*, p. 406.
[21]*Dail Eireann: Minutes of Proceedings*, 29 June 1920, p. 178.

the smaller police barracks in the remoter parts of the south and west. Eighteen British policemen were killed during this period, and the death toll accelerated rapidly as the war intensified. But neither then nor later would Britain acknowledge that the conflict was anything more than a domestic or civil disturbance. Similarly, the Dail Eireann never formally declared war against Britain, although the Volunteer or I.R.A. magazine, *An-t-Oglach*, issued a statement on January 31, 1919, which was tantamount to a declaration.[22]

That bold step, seemingly at odds with the Dail's more cautious approach, was not surprising since the relationship between the Sinn Fein government and the I.R.A. remained vague and ill-defined throughout the war. The Volunteers were in many ways independent of the Dail and Cabinet and, occasionally, of their own headquarters staff who were not always informed of initiatives planned by local commanders. In a message addressed to the "Irish abroad" at the April 10, 1919 meeting of the Dail, President de Valera affirmed: "The Minister of National Defense is, of course, in close association with the voluntary military forces which are the foundation of the National Army."[23] Not until March 1921, however, only a few months before the truce ending the Anglo-Irish hostilities, did the Dail accept its President's recommendation and assume public responsibility for I.R.A. military actions.[24]

In the autumn of 1919 the British authorities made a concerted effort to save a rapidly deteriorating situation in Ireland. Sinn Fein, the Gaelic League, and the Volunteers were now officially suppressed in 27 counties; but I.R.A. attacks against crown forces continued unabated. On the night of November 17, the Cork No. 3 Brigade slipped aboard a British naval sloop in Bantry Bay and seized the contents of its

---

[22]The paper declared that Volunteers, in the execution of their military duties, were entitled legally and morally to kill soldiers and policemen if it was necessary to do so in overcoming their resistance. The state of war which the paper said then existed in Ireland was cited as the justification for such action.

[23]*Dail Eireann: Minutes of Proceedings*, 10 April 1919, p. 47.

[24]Timothy Patrick Coogan, *The I.R.A.* (London, 1970), p. 25.

armory while the officers were on shore. Even more daring was the I.R.A. attempt to assassinate the Viceroy, Lord French, as he was returning from his country house to Viceregal Lodge on December 19. The plan misfired, and the only casualty was an I.R.A. man; but it was an ominous sign of the growing temerity of the separatist forces.[25]

LLOYD GEORGE'S PARTITION COMPROMISE

Since the beginning of 1919, London had been attempting to provide a constitutional solution to the most critical problem in any Irish settlement: a political arrangement which would allow the Catholic and Protestant communities of Ireland hegemony in their respective spheres while proceeding toward an ultimate fulfillment of their common destiny. By the end of 1919, Prime Minister Lloyd George had begun toying with the idea of combining a form of Irish self-government with partition of the country. He devised a plan for the creation of two parliaments in Ireland, an idea which differed from any previous British proposal, and was certainly not in accord with the demands advanced by either the nationalist or Unionist camps. Under this formula, each parliament would have very limited powers with the understanding that both would subsequently amalgamate into a single parliament and government for the whole of Ireland.[26] The conservative provisions of the plan provided for an eventual national parliament in Dublin with powers substantially less than those which had been accorded Ireland in the home rule bill and placed in the statute book in 1914. The proposals were scarcely calculated to appeal to Sinn Fein nationalists

---

[25]Holt, *Protest in Arms*, pp. 190–192.

[26]Lloyd George felt that his plan would have to be placed into operation in both the North and the South if the Council of Ireland was to achieve its purpose. Cabinet conclusions, 29 December 1920, *CAB*. 23/23.

whose representatives in the Dail had overwhelmingly decided upon the establishment of an independent Irish republic and whose partisan forces were already conducting a guerrilla war against the British authorities for that cause. Unionist reaction in Ulster, however, was cautiously receptive.[27]

In February 1920, Lloyd George introduced a bill which generally embraced the proposals which he had presented to the House of Commons for consideration the previous December. The British strategy in seeking to enact the bill was probably twofold: to shelve temporarily an awkward legislative problem; and to persuade the United States that London had some Irish policy besides calculated violence. As such, the bill was a palliative and a subterfuge because the British Government was aware that a modified form of home rule would satisfy neither republicans nor the majority of the Irish population.[28] And London was equally convinced that, for reasons of national security, total independence for Ireland would have to be resisted by whatever means necessary. Once again the British resorted to a carrot and stick approach to the Irish problem as the government simultaneously intensified the military effort against Sinn Fein while attempting to mediate differences with that foe through a variety of third parties.[29]

Nationalists viewed with contempt the formal proceedings

[27]Ulster Protestants accepted the Prime Minister's plan, however reluctantly, because they perceived it "as at least safeguarding what they regarded as the legitimate primacy of their interests." Robert Kee, *The Green Flag* (London, 1972), p. 665.

[28]Moreover, Southern Unionists felt betrayed because the Prime Minister, contrary to his February 25, 1918, promise to Irish Convention Chairman Sir Horace Plunkett, had given guarantees only to Unionists in six counties. Lord Midleton to Lloyd George, 13 March 1920, *Lothian MSS.*, GD40/17/79, Scottish Record Office, Edinburgh.

[29]Lloyd George's private secretary, Philip Kerr, wrote Chief Secretary for Ireland Sir Hamar Greenwood of the need to keep the English people aware of the real situation in Ireland since the London Government might undertake "very strong action in the near future." Kerr to Greenwood, 3 May 1920, *Lothian MSS.*

at Westminster pertaining to the Irish bill proposed by Prime Minister Lloyd George. Ulster Unionists were suspicious of the suggested Council of Ireland which was to be representative of both the Northern and Southern parliaments. The Council was intended to provide a measure of unity from which stronger bonds might be forged. Although the Council's authority was restricted to railways, fisheries, contagious diseases, and only those additional powers which the two parliaments agreed to confer upon it, the Unionists were as hostile as the nationalists to this arrangement. Northern Protestants were particularly dismayed by the part of the proposal which accorded counties Donegal, Monaghan, and Cavan to the southern parliament since these areas, together with the counties of Armagh, Antrim, Down, Derry, Fermanagh, and Tyrone, were all a part of the historic province of Ulster. The Ulster Unionist Council met in Belfast on March 4, 1920, and reluctantly consented to the planned division. Ulster leader Sir Edward Carson bitterly observed that Northern Ireland had little choice since nationalists would outnumber Unionists if all of Ulster were to be administered by a Northern parliament. With six counties, a Unionist and Protestant majority in parliament could be assured even though a large nationalist minority was unavoidable. It was also reasoned that the economy and resources of the six-county region were sufficiently varied to render it economically capable of subsisting as a separate political entity. Amidst much soul-searching and deep misgivings, therefore, Ulster Unionists made a pragmatic decision to desert their fellow Unionists in Donegal, Cavan, and Monaghan as they had earlier parted company with the Unionists of southern Ireland.[30]

---

[30]For a contemporary account of this anguished decision reached by the Ulster Unionist Council in March 1920, see Ronald McNeill (Lord Cushendun), *Ulster's Stand for Union* (London, 1922), p. 279; see also Ian Colvin, *The Life of Lord Carson*, Vol. 3 (London, 1936), pp. 377–383.

REACTION TO THE PARTITION PLAN

Reaction in Ireland to Lloyd George's partition plan was characterized by heightening tensions and increased violence in Ulster and in the rest of the country. The I.R.A. operated less effectively in Ulster than in the other three provinces since the nationalist population was a minority in the northeastern sector of that region.[31] Indeed, guerrilla warfare would have been impossible to conduct successfully anywhere in Ireland in the absence of a sympathetic population willing to provide food and shelter to small and mobile "flying columns." Nonetheless, I.R.A. gunmen mounted attacks against the police in Ulster and, occasionally, against Protestant workmen who were militantly hostile toward all nationalists. Riots which left twenty persons dead broke out in Londonderry between Catholic and Protestant groups in May and June of 1920. During July and August, civil disorders spread to Belfast where 4,000 people were left homeless and destitute. Orange clubs were revived in response to Sinn Fein, and armed Ulster Volunteers engaged in illegal drills without interference from the Government. Another reaction to the separatists was the organization of the Protestant Workman's Union which terrorized Roman Catholics in the Belfast shipyards. Catholics from isolated villages had begun to pour into Belfast where their co-religionists at relief centers attempted to serve the needs of these refugees and the victims of mounting civil strife within the city. It was against this background that the London Government, contrary to the recommendation of its military commander in Ireland, General Macready, agreed to authorize the formation of a special constabulary of loyal citizens in Ulster for the purpose of preserving order. Organized and paid for by the British,

---

[31]In Ulster, the British enjoyed the asset of substantial native support which they lacked elsewhere. Florence O'Donoghue, *No Other Law* (Dublin, 1954), p. 247.

these groups became the infamous B specials whose behavior was frequently indistinguishable from the fanatical terrorists of the I.R.A. except that the former possessed a legitimacy which the latter lacked.[32]

THE PERIOD OF MILITARY DECISION

It was in Dublin, however, and in the south and west of Ireland that the very worst outrages of the conflict between British Crown forces and Irish separatists took place. The second phase of the Anglo-Irish war, which extended from March to December 1920, was really the period of military decision. The six months that followed, from January through June 1921, were devoted more to political than to military strategy although some of the most desperate fighting occurred during this period. Since the detailed narrative of these armed hostilities has often been recounted, it will suffice here to highlight some of the incidents which comprised the most tragic chapter in Ireland's history since the horrible famine of the 1840s.

The Black and Tans, shortly after their March 1920, arrival in Ireland, were augmented by the Auxillary Division of the R.I.C. Referred to by the Irish as the "Auxis," these troops were recruited in England from ex-officers of the British Army and wore distinctive dark-blue uniforms. The "Auxis," an elite mercenary force, included both courageous and honorable men, as well as sadists and neofascist types. When elements of the latter group responded to I.R.A. atrocities with indiscriminate outrages of their own, the commandant of the Auxis, Brigadier General F. P. Crozier, experienced difficulty in restraining them. This lack of control and the tendency of the new tough-minded Chief Secretary for Ire-

[32]Macready, *Annals of an Active Life*, Vol. 2, pp. 487–489; Hugh Martin, *Ireland in Insurrection* (London, 1921), pp. 167–176.

land, Sir Hamar Greenwood, to overlook Auxi "excesses," ultimately resulted in Crozier's resignation.[33]

On the eve of Easter Sunday, April 4, 1920, the I.R.A. raided income tax offices in Dublin and throughout the country, burning all records and neutralizing the government's tax gathering machinery. Also destroyed were 315 vacated R.I.C. barracks, thereby denying the British the use of these outposts for any counter-offensive. Two days later some 100 Sinn Fein prisoners in Mountjoy jail undertook a hunger strike to compel the authorities either to treat them as prisoners of war or to release them. When the British Government declared that it would not be intimidated by such tactics, the Irish Labour Party scheduled a general strike in support of the Mountjoy prisoners for April 13. Even the Catholic hierarchy, which had been vocal in its condemnation of Sinn Fein violence, issued a public statement to draw attention to the imminence of an "appalling tragedy."[34] After ten days the Government released the prisoners unconditionally to avoid the total breakdown of civilian life which the general strike threatened.

Throughout the summer and autumn of 1920, the "Black and Tans" and "Auxis" countered with reprisals which were almost always unauthorized. British officers could no longer stroll safely from their headquarters in Dublin Castle to their clubs in Stephens Green. In the countryside, Irish natives came to dread the police vans which would descend upon a town in the dead of night and turn out the occupants of houses suspected of harboring Sinn Fein partisans. In many instances property was destroyed whether or not any incriminating evidence was discovered in order to provide an object lesson to those who might collaborate with the

---

[33] When Crozier resigned in February 1921, he published a narrative of the events which prompted his decision in the May 24, 1921 issue of the London *Daily News*. See also Brigadier General F. P. Crozier, *Impressions and Recollections* (London, 1930), p. 279.

[34] Holt, *Protest in Arms*, pp. 205–207.

separatists.[35] Because of its inferior numbers and inadequate weapons, the I.R.A. could not hope to best the British in an open fight. It could and did keep the country in a state of chaos, and provoked the British into open and violent retaliation. It was a war which the separatists could not win in any military sense, but the avoidance of defeat was a triumph in itself. Meanwhile, the propaganda battle which Sinn Fein was conducting both in America and in the Dominions pursued the intangible goals which could not be won by force of arms. Every government outrage or reprisal was given the widest possible publicity, often with some embellishment.[36]

London's announcement of the Restoration of Order Act in August, 1920, constituted a virtual acknowledgement that Ireland had become ungovernable. The Act extended the powers of the military by providing for courts martial in treason and felony cases.[37] This measure proved inadequate, however, and on December 10, 1920, martial law was declared in four southern counties; it was subsequently extended to four additional counties in the following month.

Another crisis occurred when Terence MacSwiney, the Lord Mayor of Cork and commander of an I.R.A. brigade, was arrested in August 1920, and sent to Brixton jail in England. His decision to conduct a hunger strike confronted the

---

[35]Black and Tans were also accused of shooting prisoners on the pretext that they were "attempting to escape." H. W. Nevinson, *Last Changes, Last Chances* (London, 1929), p. 183; for further accounts of this paramilitary force, see Richard Bennett, *The Black and Tans* (London, 1966).

[36]One indication of the success which Sinn Fein propagandists enjoyed in the United States during 1920 is the many instances in which the British Ambassador in Washington advised the London Foreign Office of the blatant Sinn Fein distortions in the American press. There are also Foreign Office minutes expressing similar concern over press notices in Canada and Australia. See *FO* 371, *FO* 115, and *FO* 395 classes for 1920. See also reports by Ambassador Geddes of 24 and 26 November 1920, *Bonar Law MSS.*, 104/5/21, Beaverbrook Library.

[37]This act was taken in spite of the fact that Sir Warren Fisher, in submitting his findings following an investigation of the Dublin Castle administration in May 1920, urged the British Government to appoint a strong Under-Secretary in order to remove the military from the civilian administration of Ireland. Bonar Law to Lloyd George (Fisher's confidential report on Dublin Castle enclosed), 13 May 1920, *Lloyd George MSS.*, F/31/1/32, Beaverbrook Library.

authorities with a dilemma. The British were anxious to prevent his death, but they were even more determined to establish the principle that Irish prisoners would not gain release through hunger-strikes.[38] MacSwiney's death on October 25, after a fast of seventy-four days, shocked public opinion in England as it did elsewhere, and further intensified the pressure on the London Government to effect some resolution to the Irish problem.[39]

On "Bloody Sunday," November 21, 1920, a climax in the conflict was reached. At dawn, an I.R.A. squad operating under direct orders from Michael Collins launched a simultaneous raid on hotels and private residences scattered throughout Dublin; a dozen men were killed. The victims, Collins claimed, were British Army intelligence agents who had been sent to Dublin in an undercover effort to discover and destroy the Sinn Fein and I.R.A. headquarters. Collins' intelligence network included detectives on the force at Dublin Castle who allegedly provided him with the identities of the British Army agents.[40] In what was perhaps a fit of retaliation, Black and Tans invaded a Gaelic football match at Dublin's Croke Park that same afternoon and fired indiscriminately on the players and the crowd. Twelve people died and sixty were wounded.[41] The events of that day dem-

---

[38]Chief Secretary for Ireland Edward Shortt favored MacSwiney's release, as did King George V. In a communication to the King's private secretary, Lord Stamfordham, Bonar Law explained the government's view by saying that a majority of the Cabinet was concerned with the negative effect which MacSwiney's release would have upon the widows and dependents of policemen and soldiers who had been murdered in Ireland by the I.R.A. Law to Stamfordham, 26 August 1920, *Bonar Law MSS.*, 101/4/83.

[39]"The death of MacSwiney, on 25 October 1920, caused a sense of shame in England, and Londoners lined the route in respectful silence as the coffin passed through the streets on its way to Holyhead [for burial in Cork]." Boyce, *Englishmen and Irish Troubles*, p. 89.

[40]For a detailed description of these events, compiled from the testimony of eyewitness accounts and contemporary newspapers, see James Gleeson, *Bloody Sunday* (London, 1962).

[41]There is evidence which suggests that the R.I.C. and the Auxilliaries who raided Croke Park had actually planned that move several days before. See Margery Forester, *Michael Collins: The Lost Leader* (London, 1971), p. 172. The police were, in any case, in an angry mood after the murders earlier that day.

onstrated once again that the I.R.A. and the police were equally capable of barbaric behavior.

A new wave of atrocity and reprisal took place a few weeks later when an I.R.A. brigade under the command of Tom Barry ambushed two trucks transporting Auxis. Only one man survived, and he had been left for dead.[42] Another ambush followed on December 11, in which one Auxi was killed. Then, on the night of December 11, the Auxilliaries took their revenge. Charging into the streets of Cork, they destroyed shops and houses, and then set fire to the city. Vast areas were gutted as firemen stood by helplessly, their hoses cut by the rampaging Auxis. When first questioned in the House of Commons, Chief Secretary for Ireland Sir Hamar Greenwood denied that British forces had been involved, and insisted that Cork had been burned by its own citizens. But a subsequent military inquiry was so damaging that the Cabinet decided to suppress the findings since they would have been "disastrous to the government's whole policy in Ireland."[43]

In 1921 the fighting became even more intense, and the incidents of violence continued to increase despite the imposition of martial law in eight counties. The most sensational and destructive I.R.A. exploit of 1921 was the attack on the Dublin Customs House on May 25. Some 120 men occupied the building, ordered the staff to vacate the premises, and then set it afire. Auxis who were summoned to the scene killed six, wounded 12, and captured 70 of the insurgents. The building was destroyed, however, and with it many irreplaceable government records. It was a senseless loss, especially since British and Irish negotiators were already in secret communication with one another and a truce was less than two months away. Meanwhile, the London Government was also attempting to implement the two parliaments

---

[42]For an I.R.A. account of this engagement, see Barry, *Guerrilla Days in Ireland*, pp. 38–49.
[43]Calton Younger, *Ireland's Civil War* (London, 1970), p. 129.

of Ireland formula which Prime Minister Lloyd George had earlier proposed.

THE GOVERNMENT OF IRELAND ACT

In the absence of other alternatives, the partition plan which had been the subject of debate and deliberations at Westminster for almost a year became British law after it received royal assent on December 22, 1920. Few were enthusiastic over the passage of the Government of Ireland Act, and it came into being almost by default since the strongest argument the Government had made on its behalf was that "something" had to be done in Ireland. The law was in fact ignored by Southern Ireland and never became effective for the twenty-six counties since it was superceded by the Treaty of 1921. But Northern Ireland's separate existence began with this Act, and the region became a distinct political entity within the United Kingdom, a status which the Treaty of 1921 recognized and accepted.

British Unionists who wished to guarantee protection against domination by a Dublin parliament to Protestants of Northern Ireland had proven the staunchest advocates of The Government of Ireland Act. A number of British Conservatives, together with some Liberals, supported the Act in the belief that it was necessary to prevent civil war between Catholics and Protestants in Ireland. But the Act ignored the reality of the Irish nationalist opposition which regarded partition as anathema and rejected modified versions of home rule as unacceptable. Neither did the Act satisfy any desire for self-government in Northern Ireland, for it was not a settlement desired by Ulster Protestants. They had resisted home rule for all of Ireland and had never sought it for themselves. What they desired most was to maintain the union of Britain and Ireland which had served the interests of the Protestant Ascendancy in Ireland so well for 120 years.

Failing that, Ulster Unionists were reluctantly resigned to allowing most of the country to take the direction it liked as long as their own region remained a constituent part of the United Kingdom. Hence, no element of any political persuasion in Ireland wanted or welcomed the partition of the country into two separate entities. Its implementation was an expedient imposed on the nation by a British Government which was the object of increasing pressure from within England and from America and the Dominions to end the bloodshed in Ireland. London sought nothing more than the immediate objective of holding two groups of Irishmen from each other's throats and providing them with an opportunity for living peaceably apart, since they seemed unable to live peaceably together.[44]

ATROCITIES AND ANTI-WAR SENTIMENT

Elections for the parliaments of Northern and Southern Ireland were set for May 24, 1921, and the preceding months were marked by what was perhaps the most desperate fighting of the Anglo-Irish war. Exasperated British officials were helpless to prevent the violence on both sides as murders, kidnappings, the execution of hostages, ambushes, raids, and incendiarism continued to serve as effective weapons for the I.R.A. in keeping their vastly more powerful adversary off balance. Both the London Government and its military command in Ireland were frustrated and embarrassed by the apparent inability of a major world power to win a decisive military victory over the comparatively miniscule but tenacious guerrilla forces of Sinn Fein. The English maintained the fiction that they were involved in a police action to quash a rebellion in Ireland. To have conceded even a state of general belligerency would have compro-

---

[44]J. C. Beckett, "Northern Ireland" *Journal of Contemporary History*, 6 (1971), No. 1, p. 124.

mised the international case, because the British insisted that Ireland was an internal problem and asked the cooperation of foreign governments in preventing arms shipments by I.R.A. sympathizers abroad. Moreover, London was hoping to fight a limited campaign against Sinn Fein without jeopardizing the prospects for a future peace with the Irish people if one could be negotiated without humiliation or dishonor.[45]

Mounting casualties, both civilian and military, atrocity stories, the worsening of unsolved social problems, and unemployment throughout England combined to produce considerable antiwar sentiment in Britain. Disillusion grew after World War I and gripped the collective consciousness of the population, particularly the working classes. English war veterans did not find the golden age forecast by President Woodrow Wilson in the speech he had delivered at Manchester, England in December 1918; nor was there any evidence of "the world fit for heroes" that Prime Minister Lloyd George had promised. People were tired of violence and its waste, especially since the Irish war seemed to many a senseless and immoral struggle. Prominent Anglican clergymen, including the Archbishop of Canterbury, the Asquith wing of the Liberal Party, and the Labour Party joined in condemning the Government's prosecution of the war in Ireland. A growing chorus of denunciations was heard from the pulpit, the Opposition benches in the House of Commons, and the editorial pages of the left-wing press. All argued that the terror tactics of the I.R.A. did not justify reprisals which seemed little different from genocide. They demanded an end to the war and a settlement which would accord a negotiated form of home rule and allow the Irish people to govern themselves.[46]

---

[45]Prime Minister Lloyd George wrote the Chief Secretary for Ireland of his concern that none of the police involved in the burning of Cork had been punished. The Prime Minister reminded the Chief Secretary that the latter was responsible for curbing R.I.C. lawlessness. Lloyd George to Greenwood, 25 February 1921, *Lloyd George MSS.*, F/19/3/4.

[46]For an excellent analysis of British opinion on the Irish question during this period, see Boyce, *Englishmen and Irish Troubles*, pp. 83–141.

THE ELECTION OF 1921

In the May 24 balloting, Sinn Fein treated the election, held under British auspices, as a new election of the Dail. Sinn Fein won all but four of the 128 seats in uncontested elections held in the South. Once again the republican Sinn Feiners refused to participate in any but their own assembly. The four members elected by Trinity College, Dublin, together with the senators nominated by the Lord Lieutenant, the official representative of the British Crown, met as the Parliament of Southern Ireland on June 28. Following a brief address from the throne of the Lord Chief Justice, the membership adjourned the charade and the Southern Parliament never emerged again.

Predictably, election patterns were different in the North where Unionists elected forty members, the Nationalists and Sinn Fein twelve, including Eamon de Valera, Michael Collins, and Arthur Griffith who were also elected for southern constituencies. Sir James Craig was elected prime minister of the new government of Northern Ireland and King George V arrived in Belfast to open the parliament on June 22. The king took advantage of the opportunity to express the acute concern of the British Monarchy over the affairs in Ireland. In remarks published in part by the English and Irish press, George V declared to the assembled parliament of Northern Ireland:

> I speak from a full heart when I pray that my coming to Ireland today may prove to be the first step towards an end of strife amongst her peoples, whatever their race or creed. In that hope I appeal to all Irishmen to pause, to stretch out the hand of forbearance and conciliation, to forgive and forget and to join in making for the land which they love a new era of peace, contentment and goodwill.[47]

---

[47]For the full text of the king's address, see Harold Nicolson, *King George V* (London, 1967), pp. 459–460.

George V's appeal doubtlessly contributed to the spirit which ultimately permitted both sides to enter into negotiations. But the passions generated by the war made the road to peace long and difficult. I.R.A. gunmen and Ulster patriots kept hatreds aflame in the North while in Dublin the Dail decided to boycott all trade between Southern Ireland and Ulster. Many Ulstermen who were hitherto indifferent to partition were converted by such policies into supporters of Unionism. The southern Irish were treating the Ulstermen as foreigners, and the consequence was that spiritual partition supplemented the political.[48]

A TRUCE IS ATTAINED

Prime Minister Lloyd George took the initiative following the King's speech at Belfast, and invited Eamon de Valera to join in a tripartite conference between the British Government and representatives of northern and southern Ireland. Absent from his proposal were the terms Sinn Fein had previously found unacceptable, such as the surrender of arms or the barring of certain individuals from the conference table. After consulting with his chief ministers, de Valera replied that he would agree to negotiations on two conditions: an actual truce would have to be declared before the President of the Dail Eireann travelled to London; and Northern Ireland Prime Minister Sir James Craig was to be excluded from discussions.[49] Lloyd George agreed and the long-awaited truce came at noon on July 11, 1921. Eamon de Valera ar-

---

[48]Mowat, *Britain Between the Wars*, p. 81.

[49]Sir James Craig and Eamon de Valera met separately with Lloyd George at No. 10 Downing Street. Although some have suggested it was Eamon de Valera's idea that he meet alone with Lloyd George at their initial session, the decision was in fact the British Prime Minister's. See de Valera to Lloyd George, 13 July 1921, and Lloyd George to de Valera, 13 July 1921, *Lloyd George MSS.*, F/14/6/9 and F/14/6/10.

rived in London on the following day, accompanied by four members of his Cabinet.[50] The subsequent Anglo-Irish deliberations were conducted at the prime minister's residence at No. 10 Downing Street.[51]

Although the truce seemed to come quite suddenly, there had been frequent unofficial contacts between the opposing sides. Lord Derby, General J. C. Smuts of South Africa, and Archbishop Patrick Clune of Perth, Australia were but a few of the mediators who held secret talks on behalf of the British Government with Sinn Fein representatives. There were also circumstances which inclined both parties toward a truce, if not a negotiated settlement. The British Government found itself besieged by appeals from its own citizenry, and many others in America, Europe, and from all parts of the empire called for a cessation of hostilities in Ireland.[52] Conservatives like Robert Cecil changed their position and joined critics of the war while others like Winston Churchill, Lord Birkenhead, and Austen Chamberlain warned Lloyd George that he would never gain national support for his Irish policies until he granted that country the widest possible measure of self-government. Even General Sir Henry Wilson, Chief of the Imperial General Staff and hawkish supporter of the war against Sinn Fein, told the prime minister quite bluntly that the choice was "to go all out or to get out."[53]

---

[50]Both the agreement to a truce and the concession of direct negotiations were obtained from the British prime minister by Southern Unionist leader Lord Midleton. The Earl of Midleton, *Records and Reactions, 1856–1939* (London, 1939), pp. 258–259.

[51]For an instructive account of these meetings, see The Earl of Longford and Thomas P. O'Neill, *Eamon de Valera* (Boston, 1971), pp. 132–138.

[52]Lloyd George's sensitivity to these pressures is evident from a letter which he wrote King George saying that he was "absolutely confident that we shall have public opinion overwhelmingly on our side throughout the Empire and even in the United States when our proposals are published." Lloyd George to George V, 21 July 1921, *Lloyd George MSS.*, F/29/4/60.

[53]Wilson recognized the need for the government to have public support before undertaking strong, coercive measures in Ireland; but he also thought the British Cabinet to be altogether too indecisive and fully expected that the British Army in Ireland "shall be kicked out." Sir C. E. Calwell, *Field-Marshall Sir Henry Wilson: His Life and Diaries*, Vol. 2 (London, 1927), p. 246; 295–296.

For its part, the I.R.A. was facing critical shortages of men and materials. Its arsenals had never contained anything more than machine-guns, rifles, and home-made bombs, and with the depletion of these the I.R.A. was scarcely able to engage in anything more than harassment. As Michael Collins would later admit, at the time of the truce Irish resistance could not have lasted more than a few more weeks.[54] The people of the towns and countryside upon whose support, or at least indifference, the guerrillas depended, were growing increasingly weary of the long and costly war of attrition. Their physical and psychological endurance had reached the breaking point. People were becoming more anxious for an end to the violence and a return to normalcy than they were about possible political solutions. Like the British, Sinn Fein thought the moment propitious for an armistice since the conditions required to continue the war effort were growing decidedly worse.[55]

PEACE NEGOTIATIONS

Initial conversations between Lloyd George and de Valera were unproductive. Lloyd George repeatedly stressed the restrictions under which he labored as Prime Minister of the United Kingdom; de Valera responded by lecturing him on the history of English exploitation in Ireland. Lloyd George did offer Ireland virtual dominion status, which was more than any previous British Government had ever proposed, but he also attached some rather vital qualifications. England would continue to maintain certain air and naval facilities in Ireland, besides reserving the right to recruit volunteers

---

[54]Collins actually told Sir Hamar Greenwood that at the time of the truce "you had us dead beat. We could not have lasted another three weeks." Lord Beaverbrook, *The Decline and Fall of Lloyd George* (New York, 1963), p. 84.

[55]For perceptive analyses of the situation by contemporaries, see P. S. O'Hegarty, *The Victory of Sinn Fein*, pp. 52–58, and C. J. C. Street, *Ireland in 1921* (London, 1922), pp. 145–155.

from that country for the British armed forces. A contribution to the British war debt would be stipulated; and the Irish government in the south would be expected to recognize the legitimacy of the Northern Ireland Parliament.[56] De Valera judged these terms to be unacceptable but agreed to return to Dublin and submit them for the Dail's consideration. That body's recently elected membership renounced the limited dominion status proferred by London, collectively took an oath to bear allegiance to the Irish Republic, and authorized de Valera as President of that Republic to form a new Cabinet with which to administer the country.[57]

Neither side wished a total breakdown of negotiations, however, and de Valera made a conciliatory gesture when he announced that he was not "a doctrinaire Republican." He also declared that he would support a treaty which permitted Ireland to enter a free association with the British Commonwealth of nations. Lloyd George pursued the opportunity for an agreement and, after a lengthy exchange of letters which were published by newspapers in both countries, the British prime minister offered to join de Valera in another conference. The purpose of the new meeting would be to ascertain how the association of Ireland with the British Empire could best be reconciled with Irish national aspirations. For reasons which neither de Valera nor his biographers have ever satisfactorily explained, the President of the Irish Republic excluded himself from the delegation which went to London to negotiate a treaty. Some have contended that de Valera did not wish to risk his political reputation by direct association with what he must have known would be a less than favor-

---

[56]In reporting on his July 14 meeting with de Valera to the King, Lloyd George emphasized that he had not allowed an Irish Republic or a separate Irish nation outside the British Empire to be discussed. Lloyd George to George V, 14 July 1921, *Lloyd George MSS.*, F/29/4/57.

[57]King George V, who had been urging moderation in his government's policy toward Ireland, was annoyed by this development. He wrote Lloyd George saying he thought the Dail Eireann position to be extravagant, and added that the Prime Minister was the person who "could best deal with these impossible, impracticable people." King George V to Lloyd George, 27 August 1921, *Lloyd George MSS.*, F/29/4/69.

able agreement. Others have defended the decision claiming, as did de Valera himself, that the Irish president remained in Dublin to insure that extreme republican colleagues like Cathal Brugha and Austen Stack did not torpedo any British proposal short of an outright republic. De Valera also felt his remaining in Ireland was the best guarantee for insuring that an Anglo-Irish treaty would be given careful consideration in Dublin before it was accepted.[58]

Arthur Griffith, Michael Collins, E. J. Duggan, George Gavan Duffy, and Robert Barton comprised the Irish delegation. Their counterparts at meetings held at the prime minister's residence in Downing Street were Lloyd George, Austen Chamberlain, Lord Birkenhead, and Winston Churchill, all men who were experienced in the skills and nuances of politics and diplomacy. Two questions dominated the conference sessions which extended from October 11 to December 6, 1921: would Ireland remain within the empire as a dominion, or be in "external association" with it as a republic; and would Ulster be included. The Irish delegates were never unanimously agreed on the first question, but they conceded everything—first the republic, then external association—for the sake of winning the second question, a united Ireland, unpartitioned.[59]

THE QUESTION OF DOMINION STATUS

In the course of the deliberations, the British consented to allow the Irish to design an oath which would stress primary allegiance to an Irish dominion or Free State rather than to the crown. But de Valera was pressured by the same extreme

---

[58]De Valera's official biography offers these last two explanations, and others, to explain the Irish president's decision to remain in Dublin. They are credible, if not entirely convincing, reasons. Longford and O'Neill, *Eamon de Valera*, p. 146.

[59]Mowat, *Britain Between the Wars*, pp. 89–91.

republicans he had allegedly remained in Dublin to control, and the Irish president sent word to his delegates in London that neither the oath nor dominion status could be considered. Michael Collins and Arthur Griffith, however, were induced to accept dominion status in return for Lloyd George's promise that Ulster's boundaries would be so contracted by a Royal Boundary Commission that it would be forced to join Southern Ireland in order to survive. There was an element of deceit on both sides in this bargain. The prime minister could not predict the consequences should his or any other British Government provoke Ulster by any radical reshaping of its boundaries. Lloyd George knew this, but he seldom seemed troubled by any sense of obligation to deliver on promises. Michael Collins agreed to dominion status for Ireland so that the British would consent to end partition and to abandon Ulster. He too was insincere. Collins had no intention of forever renouncing the claim to a republic. Dominion status and membership in the community of nations known as the British Commonwealth were not desirable in themselves. But Collins saw it as a stepping stone, a new posture from which Ireland could and would strike out again for the cherished Republic. As he later told the Dail when urging that assembly to accept dominion status, it was "not the ultimate freedom that all nations desire and develop to, but the freedom to achieve it."[60]

THE TREATY OF 1921

Lloyd George knew that the Irish delegates had promised the Dail Cabinet they would sign no treaty before submitting it to the Dail. He also knew that the compromises and concessions made by Collins and particularly by Griffith would not be supported by the fanatical republicans in Ireland. Accord-

---

[60] *Dail Eireann, Official Report: Debate on the Treaty Between Great Britain and Ireland Signed in London on 6 December 1921*, p. 32.

ingly, on the afternoon of December 5, the prime minister brought the protracted negotiations to a sudden halt with the declaration of an ultimatum. Holding two sealed envelopes, one in each hand, he addressed the Irish delegates saying:

> Here are the alternative letters which I have prepared, one enclosing Articles of Agreement reached by His Majesty's Government and yourselves, and the other saying that Sinn Fein representatives refuse to come within the Empire. If I send this letter it is war, and war within three days. Which letter am I to send? Whichever letter you choose travels by special train to Holyhead and by destroyer to Belfast ... we must know your answer by ten p.m. tonight. You can have until then, but no longer, to decide whether you will give peace or war to your country.[61]

The Irish delegates were told that each of their signatures would be necessary if orders to resume hostilities were not to be sent to the British military command in Ireland.[62] Lloyd George may have been bluffing, but the Irish could not afford to gamble on that assumption, and no one knew that better than Michael Collins. Peace had eroded the tight I.R.A. organization, and its intelligence system had become far less effective during the idle months of the armistice. Collins and other leaders who had previously been unfamiliar to authorities were now widely recognized. The majority of the Irish population was content with the peace and could not be depended upon by the I.R.A. for future assistance if the war was resumed. By contrast, the British forces had been given a respite by the truce. They had not abandoned their entrenched positions at the time of the cease-fire, and they had plenty of reserves to draw upon. The likely outcome

---

[61]Lord Longford, *Peace by Ordeal* (London, 1967), pp. 239–240. First published in 1935, this work remains the best account of the treaty deliberations.

[62]Viceroy Lord Fitzalan had written the prime minister some months earlier to say that the Irish would make demands but that they were in no position to take the field again, "no matter what they ask for or what is refused them." Fitzalan to Lloyd George, 18 August 1921, *Lloyd George MSS.*, F/17/2/8.

of a renewed Anglo-Irish war was painfully apparent to reasonable men like Collins and Griffith. At 2:30 a.m. on December 6, 1921, the Irish delegates affixed their signatures to the agreement which ended 120 years of British rule in all but six counties of Ireland.[63]

REACTION TO THE TREATY

De Valera rejected the treaty and also led the opposition when it was subsequently debated in the Dail. While it is generally believed that a majority of the population in Southern Ireland favored the treaty because it wanted peace, impassioned speeches for and against the treaty by scores of representatives in the Dail revealed a substantial division among the Irish separatist leadership.[64] When the tally was finally taken, the treaty was ratified by a margin of sixty-four votes to fifty-seven.[65] De Valera promptly resigned as president of the Dail, and Arthur Griffith was elected to succeed him. Some I.R.A. commanders refused to accept the verdict of their government. With the support and encouragement of de Valera and other irreconcilable republican politicians, they plunged the country into a bloody civil war which lasted until May, 1923. It was left to the Provisional Government of the Irish Free State to suppress such internal insurrection since the British Parliament, which transferred official powers to the Free State in March 1922, evacuated all of its forces from Southern Ireland by December of that year.[66] Civil

[63]For the background to this last and crucial conference between the Irish and British representatives, see Taylor, *Michael Collins*, pp. 247–252. For the text of the Articles of Agreement as signed on December 6, 1921, see Appendix 2.

[64]*Dail Eireann. Official Report: Debate on the Treaty Between Great Britain and Ireland Signed in London on 6 December 1921*, pp. 5–410.

[65]For the actual roll call, see Ibid., pp. 410–411.

[66]Colonial Secretary Winston Churchill wrote the Provisional Government of the Irish Free State, via Alfred Cope at Dublin Castle, to say that the British held the Free State government responsible for keeping the I.R.A. irregulars in check, and for maintaining the peace in Ireland. Churchill to Cope, 24 August 1922, *Lloyd George MSS.*, F/10/3/37.

wars are nearly always more vicious than those fought against an alien people, and in this respect the violent internecine struggle between Irishmen was no exception. Rebels who had once fought the state were now themselves the state, and they battled their former comrades with more viciousness and brutality than anything witnessed by the Anglo-Irish war. The Irish Free State executed 77 rebels, as compared to 24 military executions by the British in 1920–21, and 11,000 men were in internment camps by the end of the civil war. Free State casualties included Arthur Griffith, who died of a heart attack under the strain of leadership in those difficult days,[67] and Michael Collins, who was assassinated in his native county Cork by gunmen from the I.R.A. force he once controlled. Memories of this fratricidal conflict have left scars upon the Irish community which survive to the present day.

THE IRISH FREE STATE

On December 6, 1922, the establishment of a Free State Government was proclaimed and the Provisional Government came to an end. In accordance with the provisions of the Anglo-Irish treaty, Northern Ireland was allowed to vote on its own future and, in a decision announced on December 7, it promptly exercised its option not to join the Free State. Discussions between representatives of Northern and Southern Ireland on the boundary question proved completely fruitless; the new British prime minister, Andrew Bonar Law, a longtime Unionist and Ulster ally, opposed any redistricting scheme which threatened the existence of Northern Ireland. Several years of unsuccessful bargaining for the an-

---

[67]The British Government, in conveying its condolences to Mrs. Griffith, was very concerned "to steer clear of anything which could be turned by de Valera into a statement that Griffith was more acceptable to England than to Ireland." Cope to Smith, 12 August 1922, *Lloyd George MSS.*, F/10/3/34.

nexation of Ulster's Roman Catholic areas finally led Irish
Free State representatives, in an agreement signed in London in 1925, to recognize the boundary of Northern Ireland.[68] In return the English Government relieved the Irish
Free State of its obligation to contribute to the British War
debt, a concession which scarcely compensated for the perpetuated partition. There was much reason for disappointment, for none of Ireland's dreams had been fulfilled:

> Not the Gaelic League's Irish speaking nation, nor Yeats's liter-
> ary-conscious people, nor the republic of the I.R.A., nor the
> worker's republic of Connolly, nor Griffith's economically self-
> sufficient dual monarchy, nor Redmond's home rule within an
> empire which the Irish had helped to build, nor Carson's United
> Kingdom.[69]

Ireland's struggle against English rule, from the days of the
Fenians and before, assumed four separate and distinct
forms: pressure through a parliamentary party within the
British political system; passive resistance and civil disobedience; the gradual displacement of the existing British government in Ireland by a native parliament; and armed
insurrection.[70] The last two of these, almost exclusively, prevailed in the period from 1916 through 1922. With the establishment of the Free State, the majority of Irish separatists
felt that their objective had been fulfilled. Some were content with having attained the dominion status accorded by
the Treaty; others felt that their efforts were vindicated in
achieving the potential for full independence inherent in the
strategy anticipated by Michael Collins. Still, a minority of
unregenerate separatists remained opposed to any form of
association with Britain and never acquiesced to even a temporary partition of their country. Since the larger number of

---

[68]For an authoritative account on the Boundary Commission see Denis
Gwynn, *The History of Partition, 1912-1925* (Dublin, 1950), pp. 222-236.
[69]Donal McCartney, "From Parnell to Pearse," in T. W. Moody and F. X.
Martin, eds., *The Course of Irish History* (Cork, 1967), p. 312.
[70]Oliver MacDonagh, *Ireland* (Englewood Cliffs, N.J., 1968), p. 75.

these irreconcilables lived in Northern Ireland, that troubled territory was fated to endure continued conflict in the years following the Anglo-Irish settlement of 1922.[71]

Irish separatism did not end in 1922. Rather it evolved both in scope and in character. Nationalist Ireland overwhelmingly, even if unenthusiastically, accepted the border which divided six counties of Ulster from the rest of the country; and the reality of dominion self-government for the twenty-six other counties. Those who continued to struggle for an unpartitioned republic fought in what became an essentially regional, no longer a national, movement. Similarly, the contemporary I.R.A. in Ireland has ceased to be a monolithic organization. Today's factionalized I.R.A. reflects the ideological divisions generic to contemporary political life. There is little trace, for example, of the romantic nationalism which drew its inspiration from the ideals of the French Revolution in the Marxist branch of the present-day I.R.A. known as "the officials." Irish separatism may have survived 1922, but it is—in the words of Yeats—all changed, changed utterly.

---

[71]For a useful treatment of Northern Ireland since the partition of 1920, see Liam de Paor, *Divided Ulster* (Baltimore, 1970), pp. 101–205.

Epilogue

IRELAND SINCE PARTITION: THE SOUTH

Ireland, except for the larger part of Ulster, was finally free of direct English control after nearly 800 years. But there was little reason or opportunity to celebrate during the civil war which convulsed the country from June, 1922, until May, 1923. The conflict left over 600 killed, 3,000 wounded, and more than £30 million worth of property destroyed. Out of a population of 2,750,000 in the Free State, about 130,000 were unemployed in 1923. There were also 12,000 anti-treaty sympathizers, including de Valera, in jails or in internment camps. William T. Cosgrave and Kevin O'Higgins, president and vice-president of the Executive Council of the Dail, provided the strong leadership which the Free State so desperately needed after the deaths of Griffith and Collins. When the Irish Army mutiny of 1924 resulted from the Government's attempt to demobilize its troops following the civil war, political control over the military and the very survival of the state were imperiled. In these circumstances, the Free State Government was at a decided disadvantage in contesting the decisions of the Boundary Commission. Cosgrave's acceptance of the tripartite agreement signed in London, on December 3, 1925, in which Britain, the Irish Free State and Northern Ireland agreed to allow the boundary of the 1920 partition to stand unchanged, was inspired by the recogni-

---

This epilogue draws upon a chapter from an earlier publication. For the initial text, together with accompanying footnotes, see Thomas E. Hachey, "The Partition of Ireland and the Ulster Dilemma" in Thomas E. Hachey, ed., *The Problem of Partition: Peril to World Peace.* (Chicago, 1972), pp. 31–43.

tion that Northern Ireland was an accomplished fact which the Free State could scarcely alter. The South's internal turmoil made a resolution of the boundary problem appear all the more attractive to Dublin.

Cosgrave and O'Higgins were no more reconciled to either limited dominion status or to the partition of their country than were de Valera and his supporters. The former, however, believed as Michael Collins had that while the treaty had not provided Ireland with the freedom which all nations desire, it had given it "the freedom to achieve it." In 1923 the Irish Free State entered the League of Nations, and in the following year appointed its own minister to Washington, a step which no other dominion had yet attempted. The Irish Free State struck a blow for the principle that dominions were the full equals of Great Britain in the international community by its bid for election to the League of Nations Council in 1926. Furthermore, Cosgrave's representatives assumed leadership roles in the Imperial Conferences of 1926 and 1930, and their views found expression in the British Parliament's Statute of Westminster in 1931 which empowered any dominion to repeal unilaterally United Kingdom legislation hitherto binding in its territory.

After Eamon de Valera's release from prison in 1924, he broke his ties with both the Irish Republican Army and with the more militant anti-treaty republicans. Neither group wished to seek change through constitutional means, especially since entering the Dail would require taking the hated Oath of Allegiance to the British Crown. De Valera resigned from Sinn Fein in 1926 after failing to reach any agreement on this issue and founded the Fianna Fail (Warriors of Ireland) party. In the general election of June 1927, Fianna Fail won forty-four seats in the Dail—only three fewer than the party in power. Cosgrave followed with an electoral amendment bill designed to vacate the seats of deputies who failed to take the Oath, a parliamentary tactic which forced de Valera and his deputies to capitulate and accept the Oath. The bill had important consequences for Irish democracy in that it compelled the second party in the state to accept a fully responsible role in the parliamentary system and made the change of administration possible in the future. Once the stability of democratic procedures was firmly established within the Irish Free State, its leaders were able to turn their attention to the quest for greater independence and to an end to partition.

When the Fianna Fail party succeeded in winning seventy seats in the general election of March 1932, Eamon de Valera assumed the premiership and formed his first government with the support of the Labour party in the Dail. The triumph of the anti-treaty Fianna Fail party and de Valera's return from the political wilderness did not reflect any popular endorsement of a republic or the end of partition. De Valera had come to power by calling for larger and more comprehensive unemployment benefits, protection for Irish industry, and repudiation of the debts owed Britain. He naturally felt no compunction to preserve a treaty he had never supported, and he continued the work Cosgrave had begun with the campaign to achieve greater independence for dominion governments. De Valera introduced changes that were intended to make Ireland a republic without a formal declaration. He proceeded to remove from the Free State Constitution the Oath of Allegiance to the Crown, the right of appeals to the British Privy Council from Irish judicial decisions, and British citizenship for Irish citizens. London protested that these unilateral repeals were illegal since they violated the treaty which was ratified by both governments in 1922. Unmoved, de Valera replied that he regarded the treaty to be illegal and continued his assault by deleting all reference to the King from the Irish constitution.

In May 1937, de Valera introduced a new constitution to replace the one which had been imposed upon Ireland sixteen years earlier. It declared the right of the "Irish nation" to choose its own form of government and its relations with other nations. The new constitution also claimed as "national territory" the whole of Ireland but acknowledged that "pending the reintegration of the national territory" the laws of its parliament would apply only to the area of the Irish Free State, an implicit admission that the partition of Ireland was a fact which the Dublin Government remained unable to change. De Valera's proposals were nonetheless sufficiently radical to make the twenty-six counties of the South a republic in everything but name. The new state would be called Eire (Gaelic for Ireland) and would be headed by a president elected by popular vote. Actual power would be exercised by a prime minister and his cabinet, together with a parliament consisting of the Dail and a Senate. In a plebiscite held on July 1, the Irish people approved the new constitution, but not by any significant margin. Uncompromising republicans rejected it because it did not establish the "Republic of Ireland," while other Irishmen seemed unconvinced that any change was necessary. Despite this opposition, the new constitution superceded the Irish Free State on December 29, 1937, and both the British Government and the Dominions declared their acceptance of the country's new name without admitting to any fundamental change in the nature of its government.

Encouraged by his success, de Valera next led a delegation to London in January 1938, where he met with a British deputation headed by Prime Minister Neville Chamberlain. When Northern Ireland Prime Minister Lord Craigavon (the former Sir James Craig) learned that de Valera was making a strong bid for the termination of partition, or at least for the British government's benevolent neutrality in the matter, the Ulster leader called for an election on November 9 on the issue of "no surrender." Unionists in Northern Ireland responded with a strong vote which increased Craigavon's already secure majority in the Stormont (Northern Ireland) Parliament. Craigavon's intention, of course, was to forewarn London, and the message was duly received. The British refused to yield on the partition question but instead sought to appease de Valera with other concessions. In place of land annuities and other payments due her, Britain agreed to accept a single, lump sum of £10 million and simultaneously renounced other claims amounting to more than £100 million. Another agreement provided for freedom of trade, subject to specific quotas and preferential duties. Much to the displeasure of Winston Churchill, then a member of Parliament, Prime Minister Chamberlain also consented to abandon certain naval facilities in Irish ports guaranteed Britain by the Anglo-Irish Treaty of 1921. Churchill rejected Chamberlain's reasoning that the removal of this affront to Irish sovereignty would improve relations, and he correctly predicted that the concession would prove costly since Ireland would remain neutral if England became involved in any future European war.

Ending partition remained de Valera's major unfinished task. He was opposed to the formal declaration of an Irish Republic precisely because he feared such a step might only serve to perpetuate the division. When the Second World War began, de Valera resolutely committed his country to neutrality, and in taking that action he enjoyed the support of the vast majority of his countrymen. As long as Ireland remained divided by a partition which Britain supported, de Valera had no intention of joining Britain in a campaign for democratic freedom and self-determination for other nations. Ireland's neutrality was partly responsible for the country's increased unemployment and rising emigration, but the people endured these and other hardships willingly. Appeals from both Prime Minister Churchill and President Franklin Roosevelt had no effect upon the Irish determination to remain out of the war although the Irish people gave their moral support to the Allied cause. Irish neutrality was, moreover, frequently one-sided. British airmen who parachuted from disabled planes into Ireland were returned safely to England. German airmen were interned in Ireland for the remainder of the war. 50,000 Irish recruits voluntarily served in the British armed forces. Germany accepted Ireland's partisan neutrality since the Irish at least denied the use of their ports to the British Navy.

Ireland's first postwar general election was held in 1948 and, after sixteen consecutive years in power, Fianna Fail was defeated. De Valera's party remained the largest party in the Dail, but a coalition of opposition parties combined to form a governing majority. There was no evident consensus in the national vote other than a general desire for change for its own sake. John A. Costello of the Fine Gael (Tribe of Gaels) party became the new taoiseach (prime minister). One of the more bizarre developments in modern Irish history followed in 1948 when Fine Gael, the old pro-treaty party which had fought the republican anti-treaty forces in 1922, passed the Republic of Ireland Bill in the Dail over the opposition of de Valera and other life-long republicans. Costello recommended the formal establishment of an Irish Republic as a means of removing the ambiguities in the constitutional position and of taking "the gun out of politics" in the twenty-six counties. The latter reference was to the nefarious activities of the illegal I.R.A. which operated on both sides of the border. The British Government responded with the Ireland Act of 1949 and fortunately left the new Republic all of the advantages of the old relationship. The Irish would continue to be invested with the same rights and obligations as citizens of the United Kingdom. But the same act also guaranteed Ulster Unionists that Northern Ireland should never leave the United Kingdom unless she did so voluntarily and on her own initiative.

Welfare services, industrialization, and I.R.A. violence constituted some of the major political issues during the 1950s. Southern Irish politicians continued to urge an end to partition, but debate on the subject incited fewer passions each year. Eamon de Valera again became head of government from 1951 to 1954, and his tenure was followed by another Fine Gael administration under John Costello from 1954 to 1957; de Valera was returned as taoiseach for the last time in 1957. Two years later he was elected president of the Irish Republic, and Sean Lemass succeeded him both as taoiseach and as leader of the Fianna Fail party.

The 1960s seemed to herald the beginning of a new era of greater harmony and understanding in Ireland. Tensions between North and South were visably reduced, and in 1964 the Northern Ireland Government recognized the all-Ireland Irish Congress of Trade Unions as a negotiating body. The Anglo-Irish free trade agreement of the following year removed economic barriers which had hampered trade between the Republic and the Six Counties. The agreement was highlighted by a dramatic meeting between Sean Lemass, the taoiseach of the Irish Republic, and Captain Terence O'Neill, Prime Minister of Northern Ireland, which held out the promise of closer and more constructive relations between the two parts of Ireland. Eamon de Valera was re-elected president of the Republic of Ireland in June 1966, and optimists speculated that the unification of the nation might be achieved during his term of office. But that was before the Civil Rights Association in Ulster (a nonpolitical, nondenominational organization which principally reflected the aspirations and frustrations of Northern Ireland's Catholic middle-class) marched in August 1968 as part of a demonstration protesting poor housing in Dungannon. The movement spread and ugly confrontations ensued, leading to the battlegrounds of Londonderry and Belfast where British troops attempted to restrain both Catholic and Protestant militants from engaging in civil war.

Sectarian violence in Northern Ireland produced a reaction in the Republic of Ireland where many among the Catholic majority expressed concern for their co-religionists in Ulster. That concern was translated into political pressure which prompted the Dublin ministry to endorse positions which impeded, rather than assisted, better Anglo-Irish understanding. In 1969, for example, the Government of the Irish Republic declared that it would not stand idly by while the northern Catholic minority came under attack. The declaration was not so much a warning to London as it was a policy statement intended for domestic consumption. Dublin officials recognized that they lacked the resources to alter the situation in the North even if British troops should be withdrawn from that area. Attempts by the Irish Republic to have United Nations peace-keeping forces brought into Northern Ireland, and representations made by Dublin to the European Commission on Human Rights concerning the conduct of British soldiers in Ulster were not without some political inspiration; nor were they calculated to improve relations between the Republic and the United Kingdom. Dublin did arrest and try a number of its citizens, including a government cabinet minister, accused of complicity in arms-smuggling across the border dividing the Republic from Northern Ireland. Indiscriminate and callous bombings and killings by the I.R.A. so shocked public opinion in the South that the Dublin government, by late 1972, adopted strong measures to restrain the I.R.A. from launching attacks against Northern Ireland from operational bases located along the border in the Republic.

In early 1973, a British-sponsored plebiscite was held in Ulster on the issue of whether the Six Counties should remain a part of Britain or join the Irish Republic. The result was predictable as the Protestant majority, aided by the large number of Ulster Catholics who boycotted the vote, produced an overwhelming mandate for maintaining ties with Britain. Shortly thereafter, an election was also held in the Irish Republic, where the result was not at all predictable. Prime Minister Jack Lynch and his Fianna Fail party, which had controlled the Dublin Government for thirty-five of the previous forty-one years, was narrowly defeated by a new coalition of the conservative Fine Gael party and the socialist Labour party. Most informed observers attributed the victory of Ireland's new prime minister, Liam Cosgrave, to issues other than the Ulster problem. Significantly, the people of the Republic appeared more concerned with taxes, housing, pensions, and living costs than they were with schemes for Ireland's unification, or the I.R.A. The political parties in

Ireland are generally agreed in their opposition to I.R.A. violence, North and South. Both Fianna Fail and Fine Gael have declared that London should recognize Northern Ireland as a part of Ireland, rather than as a British province; but most party leaders in the Irish Republic, whatever their political affiliation, believe that the unity of Ireland cannot be coerced.

Ireland's most prominent separatist, president Eamon de Valera, died in 1973. His death ended a political career which had spanned more than five decades, during which time the partition of Ireland remained unchanged. His successor, president Erskine Hamilton Childers, a Protestant, was a man of pronouncedly moderate views and his tenure of office, which lasted until his death in November 1974, complemented the new era of improved Anglo-Irish relations advanced by Prime Minister Liam Cosgrave. That new spirit, perhaps best expressed by the Sunningdale conference of December 1973, survived the repeated failures of power-sharing formulas in Northern Ireland, as well as subsequent disappointments. With no peace in sight at the approach of 1977, and with the violence in Ulster entering its ninth consecutive year, government officials in both the Dublin and London governments continue to strive for a solution to the Ulster question. The urgency of that effort was dramatically underscored by the July 21, 1976, assassination in Dublin of British Ambassador Christopher Ewart-Biggs and the August bombing of a Dublin courthouse. Despite denials of responsibility by both the normally non-violent "Official" branch of the I.R.A. and by the terrorist "Provisional" faction, the Government of the Irish Republic promptly declared a state of emergency. The Dail further introduced two bills which increased the powers of the police in combating I.R.A. activities and provided more severe penalties for membership in the I.R.A. and other subversive organizations.

IRELAND SINCE PARTITION: THE NORTH

Three counties in the historic province of Ulster were surrendered by the Unionists in the Government of Ireland Act, 1920, because their inclusion would have given the region a Catholic nationalist majority. The six remaining counties comprised slightly less than one-fifth of the island but contained about one-third of the island's inhabitants. London never intended to include only those counties with Unionist majorities. Tyrone and Fermanagh were made a part of the new state of Northern Ireland despite their nationalist majorities for two reasons: it was hoped that an area large enough to make the North economically and politically viable would pacify the Protestant Unionists; and that the security provided by the latter's two-to-one majority over the Catholic nationalists would produce a tolerant northern government which would seek to conciliate and integrate the minority. But it did not. The mood of Ulster Unionists was reflected by Sir James Craig, the first Prime Minister of Northern Ireland, who announced that the Six Counties would be a Protestant nation for a Protestant people.

Northern Ireland's inception as a separate state within the United Kingdom in 1920 was accompanied by the most serious outbreak of sectarian violence since the religious riots in Belfast during 1886. Northern Ireland greeted the news of the Anglo-Irish treaty with sullenness in 1921, and responded to the continued civil strife in Ulster by passing the Civil Authorities (Special Powers) Act in 1922 which, after several renewals, was made permanent in 1933. By its terms, the Northern Ireland Minister for Home Affairs and the police were given sweeping powers of search, arrest and imprisonment without trial. Through this and similar means order was restored in the North, and Protestant Unionist rule perpetuated among the 1,250,000 population, about one-third of whom were Catholic and largely nationalist. The subsequent gerrymandering of constituencies and the large number of Class B special police (11,514 of them supplemented 2,867 regular police in 1936) severely checked nationalist ambitions.

A resurgence of sectarian strife followed the persistent depression and unemployment which gripped Northern Ireland in the 1930s. The two great Ulster industries, linen and ship building, were in decline and agriculture suffered locally and in Britain from the industrial depression. An attack on an Orange demonstration in 1931 set off a wave of reprisals culminating in 1935 with widespread rioting in Belfast which claimed a number of lives. The incidents of violence continued intermittently into the 1940s and justified, in Unionist eyes, the retention of the Special Powers Act.

Events in the rest of Ireland during this period also helped to sustain old antagonisms in the North. The Irish Free State's dismantling of the 1921 Anglo-Irish treaty after 1932, and the new Irish constitution of 1937, gave encouragement to Ulster's nationalists and correspondingly renewed Unionist determination to remain within the United Kingdom and the Empire. Relations between northern and southern Ireland began to improve only after the dimunition of I.R.A. violence which plagued the border regions during the period between 1956 and 1962. But the apparent lessening of tensions was deceptive, and the grievances of the Catholic minority were again manifest in the civil rights movement which began in the late 1960s.

Fear and suspicion kept alive old hatreds between Northern Ireland's Catholics and Protestants. Despite the poverty and unemployment which they shared with Catholics, Ulster Protestant workers and farmers followed the political leadership of the ultra-right Unionist party. And the leadership of that party used no-popery to control Six County politics and to avoid seriously confronting that region's severe social and economic problems, a burden which was eased by the generosity of the British welfare state. Northern Irish politicians exploited the bigotry of the Protestant masses whose religious zeal was expressed in racist rhetoric. Catholics were frequently characterized as an inferior species: lazy, superstitious, improvident, treacherous, and irresponsible. Northern Irish Unionists accepted as an article of faith the necessity of excluding Catholics from positions of power in order that they not destroy the existence of the Six Counties. There is, of course, justification for some of their political apprehensions. Most Ulster Catholics are nationalists, and they have traditionally regarded the partition of their country as an unholy bargain struck between Orangemen and British politicians.

Catholic ghetto life in the Six Counties has produced a nationalism and cultural alienation much more intense than that in Southern Ireland. Catholics attend parochial schools which emphasize Irish history, culture and language; they play Gaelic football; and their Sunday night socials frequently include traditional folk-type dances. Protestants attend schools emphasizing British history and culture; they play soccer and rugby; and they dance to the rock music popular in Britain. The result has been the growth of two entirely alien and antagonistic cultural groups existing side by side in a State where life is made all the more precarious by economic depression and growing unemployment.

Although Irish Protestant alarmists interpreted the civil rights movements of the late 1960s as another subversive attempt by Catholics to seek Ulster's annexation by the Republic, the agitators were actually more unionist than the Unionists in that they sought British standards of administration. Some Catholic moderates, inspired by the civil rights movement in America, came to appreciate the potential for a better life in a Northern Ireland supported by the British welfare state. A few Unionist politicians also re-evaluated the situation and noted that the increasing Catholic population would someday mean a Catholic majority. Apartheid and oppression did not strike them as either attractive or viable permanent policies. Catholic moderates were joined by Protestant liberals in the Northern Ireland Civil Rights Association, a coalition organized in 1967 which included socialists, republicans, and university students. They asked the Government to provide jobs, housing, better education, and greater suffrage for the Catholic minority; and marched and demonstrated to rally support for their cause.

Northern Ireland Prime Minister Terence O'Neill, partly at the urging of British Prime Minister Harold Wilson, made a few modest concessions which brought an immediate response from the fanatics of the Orange Lodges. Ian Paisley, the arch-enemy of popery, and William Craig, the leader of the backlash Protestant Vanguard, led the counter-attack. Caught between civil rights agitation and Orange fanaticism, O'Neill resigned. His successor, James Chichester-Clark, also promised changes but moved too slowly for Catholics and much too quickly for militant Orangemen. He too resigned and was succeeded by yet another moderate, Brian Faulkner. By this time, the days of moderation had passed. Orange extremists, the timidity of politicians, and the impatience of Catholic radicals—socialist and republican—combined to destroy the spirit and influence of the 1967 civil rights movement. But they also destroyed the parliament at Stormont as Brian Faulkner's Northern Ireland Government was displaced in March 1972, by the extension of British rule over Ulster after civil disorders threatened to plunge the Six Counties into a state of anarchy.

In February 1973, Protestant Vanguard leader William Craig outlined a plan for a Dominion of Ulster, with power-sharing "in a majority framework," should Northern Ireland be excluded from the United Kingdom. Although Craig's proposal was not given serious attention by Protestant moderates, it illustrated the resolute determination of militant Unionists "to go it alone" rather than ever submit to the jurisdiction of the Irish Republic.

The British Government published a White Paper, *Constitutional Proposals for Northern Ireland* (Cmd. 5259), on March 20, 1973, one year following the suspension of the Stormont parliament. As had been expected, that legislature was not to be restored. Rather, the White Paper called for the creation of a Northern Ireland Assembly, elected by proportional representation, and a nominated Executive. If the plan succeeded, powers would be gradually devolved upon the Assembly, but control of the police, elections, legal appointments and some taxation would remain in the hands of the London Government. British troops were to stay in Ulster as long as they were required, and the police force was to be strengthened. New anti-terrorist legislation was intended to replace the Special Powers Act, and a "Charter of Human Rights" was to be provided. These and other provisions were embodied in the Northern Ireland Constitutional Bill which was subsequently passed at Westminster. Extremist groups among the Unionists denounced the legislation as a "sell-out" to the Irish Republic, and the I.R.A. rejected it as a British attempt to continue control of the North.

Elections were nonetheless held on June 28, and the Northern Ireland Assembly conducted its first meeting at Stormont on July 31. Brian Faulkner and a following of moderate Unionists who accepted the broad principles of the new constitution attempted to make common cause with the minority Social Democratic and Labour Party (SDLP). Ian Paisley's Democratic Union Party (DUP) and the Vanguard United Progressive Party (VUPP) formed a loyalist coalition in opposition to Faulkner and tried repeatedly to overthrow him in meetings of the Unionist Council. It was an inauspicious beginning for the fledgling Assembly.

These political events took place after a year of unrest and violence. Horrifying murders and bombings were executed by both the I.R.A. and a new secret organization called the "Ulster Freedom Fighters." By summer, 1973, the Army claimed to have killed or apprehended most of the leaders of the Provisional I.R.A., the more militant wing of that splintered organization. In the North and in the Republic, many I.R.A. officers were in custody. Many Protestant extremists were also in detention, and an increasing number of people were being brought to trial for the outrages committed in the last two years. The I.R.A., under pressure in Belfast, switched its bombing campaign to the border areas. Letter bombs also caused injuries in Ulster, the United Kingdom, and abroad.

On December 6, 1973, Brian Faulkner, the Chief Executive of the newly formed Northern Ireland Executive, met with British Prime Minister Edward Heath and Irish Republic Prime Minister Liam Cosgrave at Sunningdale in Berkshire. This tripartite conference was significant in a number of ways. Britain formally recognized that an Ulster settlement was very much a legitimate interest of the Dublin Government; the Government of the Irish Republic openly conceded that the status of Northern Ireland could not be changed until the majority wished it; and the Executive of Northern Ireland consented to the establishment of a Council of Ireland, one function of which would be to promote cooperation between North and South on police matters. Following the Sunningdale Conference, on December 31, the new Executive in Ulster was sworn in at formal ceremonies. After 21 months of London's direct rule, the Six Counties once again had an administration of their own.

On January 1, 1974, Brian Faulkner officially became the head of the new Northern Ireland Executive, a coalition of nine Protestants and six Roman Catholic ministers. During its brief five month existence, the new Executive functioned more smoothly than had been anticipated, as Catholic and Protestant department heads worked amicably with one another and with the civil service. The Executive coalition ultimately failed, however, since many Unionist politicians refused to take part in any power-sharing Executive. Direct rule from London was reimposed after the militant Ulster Workers' Council called for an all-out strike against both the Executive and the Sunningdale agreement for an All-Ireland Council.

The collapse of the Executive was greeted with relief by Ulster Protestants. They had interpreted the policy of Sunningdale as a step toward coercing Ulster into an Irish

Republic. Among Catholics, there was deep disappointment at the end of the power-sharing experiment and an increased pressure on the I.R.A. to end violence and negotiate with the British Government. Most Catholics believed that if the I.R.A. campaign continued, the Unionist position would further strengthen and any gains made since 1969 would be thrown away.

With the advent of 1977, the likelihood of peace in Northern Ireland remains dim despite the loss of more than a thousand lives since the first civil rights demonstrations in 1968. Moreover, the continuance of partition is almost a certainty for the indefinite future; and that probability may represent a greater loss for all Irishmen than is commonly recognized. Ultimate unity between North and South, Catholic and Protestant, could promote greater liberty in Ireland. If the myths perpetuating religious and racial bigotry were discarded, a common effort could be made to solve the problems of poverty, unemployment, low agricultural production and emigration in all of Ireland. Unity of North and South would help Catholics and Protestants emancipate each other; Protestants from their fears and bigotry, Catholics from their parochialism. Indeed, the influx of a large Protestant minority would diminish the unwholesome influence of the Catholic Church on the Dublin Government, leading to a desirable separation of organized religion from the functions of the state. It would also expedite the demise of the Irish Republic's traditional role in enforcing the dictates of Catholic morality, particularly with respect to legislation in the areas of divorce, abortion, birth control, and censorship.

On a more practical level, however, the conflicts between Catholics and Protestants, nationalists and Unionists, must first be reconciled in Ulster before any meaningful discussion of unification can be contemplated. In an era when Irishmen in both the United Kingdom and in the Irish Republic belong to the same European Economic Community, there exists some prospect that the need to promote shared interests may someday diminish the importance of traditional differences. Perhaps the uncompromising separatist and the unyielding Unionist may yet learn that a common humanity is more important than religious creeds, and that their neighbor's civil liberties are the safeguards of their own freedoms.

Appendix 1

Poblacht na h-Eireann
The Provisional Government
of the
Irish Republic
To the People Of Ireland.

IRISHMEN AND IRISHWOMEN: In the name of God and of the dead generations from which she receives her old tradition of nationhood, Ireland, through us, summons her children to her flag and strikes for her freedom.

Having organized her manhood through her secret revolutionary organisation, the Irish Republican Brotherhood, and through her open military organisations, the Irish Volunteers and the Irish Citizen Army, having patiently perfected her discipline, having resolutely waited for the right moment to reveal itself, she now seizes that moment, and supported by her exiled children in America and by gallant allies in Europe, but relying in the first on her own strength, she strikes in full confidence of victory.

We declare the right of the people of Ireland to the ownership of Ireland and to the unfettered control of Irish destinies, to be sovereign and indefeasible. The long usurpation of that right by a foreign people and government has not extinguished the right, nor can it ever be extinguished except by the destruction of the Irish people. In every generation the Irish people have asserted their right to national freedom and sovereignty; six times during the past three hundred years they have asserted it in arms. Standing on that fundamental right and again asserting it in arms in the face of the world, we hereby proclaim the Irish Republic as a Sovereign Independent State, and we pledge our lives and the lives of our comrades in arms to the cause of its freedom, of its welfare and of its exaltation among the nations.

The Irish Republic is entitled to, and hereby claims, the allegiance of every Irishman and Irishwoman. The Republic guarantees religious and civil liberty, equal rights and equal opportunities to all its citizens, and declares its resolve to pursue the happiness and prosperity of the whole nation and of all its parts, cherishing all the children of the nation equally, and oblivious of the differences carefully fostered by an alien Government, which have divided a minority from the majority in the past.

Until our arms have brought the opportune moment for the establishment of a permanent National Government, representative of the whole people of Ireland and elected by the suffrages of all her men and women, the Provisional Government hereby constituted, will administer the civil and military affairs of the Republic in trust for the people.

We place the cause of the Irish Republic under the protection of the Most High God, Whose blessing we invoke upon our arms, and we pray that no one who serves that cause will dishonour it by cowardice, inhumanity, or rapine. In this supreme hour the Irish nation must, by its valour and discipline, and by the readiness of its children to sacrifice themselves for the common good, prove itself worthy of the august destiny to which it is called.

Signed on behalf of the Provisional Government:

THOMAS J. CLARKE,
SEAN Mac DIARMADA,   THOMAS MacDONAGH,
P.H. PEARSE,   EAMONN CEANNT,
JAMES CONNOLLY,   JOSEPH PLUNKETT.

Appendix 2

Articles of An Agreement for a Treaty Between Great Britain and Ireland As Signed on December 6, 1921

1. Ireland shall have the same constitutional status in the Community of Nations known as the British Empire as the Dominion of Canada, the Commonwealth of Australia, the Dominion of New Zealand, and the Union of South Africa, with a Parliament having powers to make laws for the peace, order and good government of Ireland and an Executive responsible to that Parliament, and shall be styled and known as the Irish Free State.

2. Subject to the provisions hereinafter set out the position of the Irish Free State in relation to the Imperial Parliament and Government and otherwise shall be that of the Dominion of Canada, and the law, practice and constitutional usage governing the relationship of the Crown or the representative of the Crown and of the Imperial Parliament to the Dominion of Canada shall govern their relationship to the Irish Free State.

3. The representative of the Crown in Ireland shall be ap-

pointed in like manner as the Governor-General of Canada, and in accordance with the practice observed in the making of such appointments.

4. The oath to be taken by Members of the Parliament of the Irish Free State shall be in the following form:

> I . . . do solemnly swear true faith and allegiance to the Constitution of the Irish Free State as by law established and that I will be faithful to H. M. King George V, his heirs and successors by law, in virtue of the common citizenship of Ireland with Great Britain and her adherence to and membership of the group of nations forming the British Commonwealth of Nations.

5. The Irish Free State shall assume liability for the service of the Public Debt of the United Kingdom as existing at the date hereof and towards the payment of war pensions as existing at that date in such proportion as may be fair and equitable, having regard to any just claims on the part of Ireland by way of set off or counterclaim, the amount of such sums being determined in default of agreement by the arbitration of one or more independent persons being citizens of the British Empire.

6. Until an arrangement has been made between the British and Irish Governments whereby the Irish Free State undertakes her own coastal defence, the defence by sea of Great Britain and Ireland shall be undertaken by His Majesty's Imperial Forces. But this shall not prevent the construction or maintenance by the Government of the Irish Free State of such vessels as are necessary for the protection of the Revenue or the Fisheries.

The foregoing provisions of this article shall be reviewed at a Conference of Representatives of the British and Irish Governments to be held at the expiration of five years from the date hereof with a view to the undertaking by Ireland of a share in her own coastal defence.

7. The Government of the Irish Free State shall afford to His Majesty's Imperial Forces:

(*a*) In time of peace such harbour and other facilities as are indicated in the Annex hereto, or such other facilities as may from time to time be agreed between the British Government and the Government of the Irish Free State; and

(*b*) In time of war or of strained relations with a Foreign Power such harbour and other facilities as the British Government may require for the purposes of such defence as aforesaid.

8. With a view to securing the observance of the principle of international limitation of armaments, if the Government of the Irish Free State establishes and maintains a military defence force, the establishments thereof shall not exceed in size such proportion of the military establishments maintained in Great Britain as that which the population of Ireland bears to the population of Great Britain.

9. The ports of Great Britain and the Irish Free State shall be freely open to the ships of the other country on payment of the customary port and other dues.

10. The Government of the Irish Free State agrees to pay fair compensation on terms not less favourable than those accorded by the Act of 1920 to judges, officials, members of Police Forces, and other Public Servants, who are discharged by it or who retire in consequence of the change of Government effected in pursuance hereof.

Provided that this agreement shall not apply to members of the Auxiliary Police Force or to persons recruited in Great Britain for the Royal Irish Constabulary during the two years next preceding the date hereof. The British Government will assume responsibility for such compensation or pensions as may be payable to any of these excepted persons.

11. Until the expiration of one month from the passing of the Act of Parliament for the ratification of this instrument, the

powers of the Parliament and the Government of the Irish Free State shall not be exercisable as respects Northern Ireland, and the provisions of the Government of Ireland Act, 1920, shall, so far as they relate to Northern Ireland, remain of full force and effect, and no election shall be held for the return of members to serve in the Parliament of the Irish Free State for constituencies in Northern Ireland, unless a resolution is passed by both Houses of the Parliament of Northern Ireland in favour of the holding of such elections before the end of the said month.

12. If, before the expiration of the said month, an address is presented to His Majesty by both Houses of the Parliament of Northern Ireland to that effect, the powers of the Parliament and the Government of the Irish Free State shall no longer extend to Northern Ireland, and the provisions of the Government of Ireland Act, 1920 (including those relating to the Council of Ireland), shall, so far as they relate to Northern Ireland, continue to be of full force and effect, and this instrument shall have effect subject to the necessary modifications.

Provided that if such an address is so presented a Commission consisting of three persons, one to be appointed by the Government of the Irish Free State, one to be appointed by the Government of Northern Ireland, and one who shall be Chairman, to be appointed by the British Government shall determine, in accordance with the wishes of the inhabitants, so far as may be compatible with economic and geographic conditions, the boundaries between Northern Ireland and the rest of Ireland, and for the purposes of the Government of Ireland Act, 1920, and of this instrument, the boundary of Northern Ireland shall be such as may be determined by such Commission.

13. For the purpose of the last foregoing article, the powers of the Parliament of Southern Ireland under the Government of Ireland Act, 1920, to elect members of the Council of Ireland, shall, after the Parliament of the Irish Free State is constituted, be exercised by that Parliament.

14. After the expiration of the said month, if no such address

as is mentioned in Article 12 hereof is presented, the Parliament and Government of Northern Ireland shall continue to exercise as respects Northern Ireland the powers conferred on them by the Government of Ireland Act, 1920, but the Parliament and Government of the Irish Free State shall in Northern Ireland have in relation to matters in respect of which the Parliament of Northern Ireland has not power to make laws under that Act (including matters which under the said Act are within the jurisdiction of the Council of Ireland) the same powers as in the rest of Ireland subject to such other provisions as may be agreed in manner hereinafter appearing.

15. At any time after the date hereof the Government of Northern Ireland and the provisional Government of Southern Ireland hereinafter constituted may meet for the purpose of discussing the provisions subject to which the last foregoing Article is to operate in the event of no such address as is therein mentioned being presented, and those provisions may include:

> (*a*) safeguards with regard to patronage in Northern Ireland,
> (*b*) safeguards with regard to the collection of revenue in Northern Ireland,
> (*c*) safeguards with regard to import and export duties affecting the trade or industry of Northern Ireland,
> (*d*) safeguards for minorities in Northern Ireland,
> (*e*) the settlement of the financial relations between Northern Ireland and the Irish Free State,
> (*f*) the establishment and powers of a local militia in Northern Ireland and the relation of the Defence Forces of the Irish Free State and of Northern Ireland respectively;

and if at any such meeting provisions are agreed to, the same shall have effect as if they were included amongst the provisions subject to which the powers of the Parliament and

Government of the Irish Free State are to be exercisable in Northern Ireland under Article 14 hereof.

16. Neither the Parliament of the Irish Free State nor the Parliament of Northern Ireland shall make any law so as either directly or indirectly to endow any religion or prohibit or restrict the free exercise thereof or give any preference or impose any disability on account of religious belief or religious status or affect prejudicially the right of any child to attend a school receiving public money without attending the religious instruction at the school or make any discrimination as respects state aid between schools under the management of different religious denominations or divert from any religious denomination or any educational institution any of its property except for public utility purposes and on payment of compensation.

17. By way of provisional arrangement for the administration of Southern Ireland during the interval which must elapse between the date hereof and the constitution of a Parliament and Government of the Irish Free State in accordance therewith, steps shall be taken forthwith for summoning a meeting of members of Parliament elected for constituencies in Southern Ireland since the passing of the Government of Ireland Act, 1920, and for constituting a provisional Government, and the British Government shall take the steps necessary to transfer to such provisional Government the powers and machinery requisite for the discharge of its duties, provided that every member of such provisional Government shall have signified in writing his or her acceptance of this instrument. But this arrangement shall not continue in force beyond the expiration of twelve months from the date hereof.

18. This instrument shall be submitted forthwith by His Majesty's Government for the approval of Parliament and by the Irish signatories to a meeting summoned for the purpose of the members elected to sit in the House of Commons of Southern Ireland, and, if approved, shall be ratified by the necessary legislation.

BIBLIOGRAPHY

1. Manuscript Sources

A. Official Papers

Public Record Office, London—Foreign Office and Cabinet Records

National Archives, Washington, D.C.—Department of State Records

B. Private Papers

Scottish Record Office, Edinburgh—Lord Lothian, mss.

National Library of Ireland, Dublin—Ducibella Barton, mss.; Gavan Duffy, mss.; John Redmond, mss.;

British Museum, London—William Wiseman, mss.

Plunkett Foundation for Co-operative Studies, London—Horace Plunkett, mss.

Beaverbrook Library, London—David Lloyd George, mss.; Andrew Bonar Law, mss.

American Irish Historical Society, New York—Daniel F. Cohalan, mss.

2. Printed Sources

A. Great Britain

The Parliamentary Debates (official report), 3rd and 5th series, House of Commons.

The Parliamentary Debates (official report), 3rd series, House of Lords.

Cmd. 1108 of 1921; *Documents Relative to the Sinn Fein Movement*

Cmd. 1326 of 1921; *Intercourse Between Bolshevism and Sinn Fein*

B. Ireland

Dail Eireann. Minutes of Proceedings of the First Parliament of the Republic of Ireland, 1919–21: Official Record, Dublin, 1921.

Dail Eireann. Official Report: Debate on the Treaty Between Great Britain and Ireland Signed in London on 6 December 1921, Dublin, 1922.

C. United States

Congressional Record, 65 Congress, 3 Session, 1919, vol. 57.
Congressional Record, 66 Congress, 1 Session, 1919, vol. 58.
Congressional Record, 66 Congress, 2 Session, 1920, vol. 59.

3. Newspapers

Manchester Guardian, the Times, Daily Mail, Morning Post, Irish Independent, New York Times, New York World, Sinn Feiner, Irish World, Gaelic American, Newsletter of the Friends of Irish Freedom

4. Diaries, Letters, Memoirs, Biographies, Histories, and Articles

Akenson, Donald. *The United States and Ireland.* Cambridge, Mass., 1973.

Armour, W. S. *Armour of Balleymoney.* London, 1934.

Barry, Tom. *Guerrilla Days in Ireland.* Cork, 1949.

Beaslai, P. *Michael Collins and the Making of a New Ireland.* London, 1926, 2 vols.

Beaverbrook, Lord. *The Decline and Fall of Lloyd George.* New York, 1963.

Beaverbrook, Lord. *Politicians and the War, 1914–1916.* London, 1960.

Beckett, J. C. "Gladstone, Queen Victoria and the Disestablishment of the Irish Church, 1868–9," *Irish Historical Studies,* 13, March, 1962.

Beckett, J. C. "Northern Ireland," *Journal of Contemporary History,* 6, 1971, No. 1.

Beckett, J. C. *The Making of Modern Ireland, 1603–1923.* London, 1969.

Bell, J. Bowyer. *The Secret Army.* New York, 1971.

Bennett, Richard. *The Black and Tans.* London, 1966.

Blake, Robert. *The Unknown Prime Minister.* London, 1955.

Bonsal, Stephen. *Unfinished Business.* London, 1944.

Bourke, Marcus. *The O'Rahilly.* Tralee, 1967.

Boyce, D. G. "British conservative opinion, the Ulster question, and the partition of Ireland, 1912–21," *Irish Historical Studies*, 17, March, 1970.

Boyce, D. G. *Englishmen and Irish Troubles.* London, 1972.

Boyle, John W. "Ireland and the First International," *The Journal of British Studies*, 2, May, 1972.

Breen, Dan. *My Fight for Irish Freedom.* Tralee, 1964.

Bromage, Mary. *De Valera and the March of a Nation.* London, 1956.

Brown, Thomas N. *Irish-American Nationalism, 1870–1890.* Philadelphia, 1966.

Buckland, P. J. "The Southern Irish Unionists and British Politics, 1906–14," *Irish Historical Studies*, 15, March, 1967.

Buckland, Patrick. *Irish Unionism: One. The Anglo-Irish and the New Ireland, 1885–1922.* Dublin, 1972.

Butler, David and Jennie Freeman, eds. *British Political Facts, 1900–1967.* New York, 1968.

Calwell, Sir C. E. *Field-Marshall Sir Henry Wilson: His Life and Diaries.* London, 1927, 2 vols.

Caufield, Max. *The Easter Rebellion.* London, 1964.

Churchill, Winston S. *The World Crisis.* New York, 1957, 6 vols.

Clarkson, J. D. *Labour and Nationalism in Ireland.* New York, 1925.

Colum, Padraic. *Ourselves Alone.* New York, 1959.

Colvin, Ian. *The Life of Lord Carson.* London, 1934, 3 vols.

Connolly, James. *Labour in Irish History.* Dublin, 1956.

Coogan, Timothy Patrick. *The I.R.A.* London, 1970.

Corish, P. J. *A History of Irish Catholicism: Political Problems, 1860–78.* Dublin, 1967.

Costigan, Giovanni. *A History of Modern Ireland.* New York, 1970.

Cronne, H. A., T. W. Moody and D. B. Quinn, eds. *Essays in British and Irish History in Honour of James Eddie Todd.* London, 1949.

Crozier, Brigadier General F. P. *Impressions and Recollections.* London, 1930.

Crozier, Brigadier General F. P. *Ireland for Ever.* London, 1932.

Curtis, L. P. Jr. *Coercion and Conciliation in Ireland, 1880–1892: A Study in Conservative Unionism.* Princeton, 1963.

Dangerfield, George. *The Strange Death of Liberal England.* New York, 1961.

Dangerfield, George. *The Damnable Question.* Boston, 1976.

D'Arcy, William. *The Fenian Movement in the United States, 1858–1868.* Washington, 1947.

De Paor, Liam. *Divided Ulster.* Baltimore, 1970.

Devoy, John. *Recollections of an Irish Rebel.* New York, 1929.

Digby, Margaret. *Horace Plunkett.* Oxford, 1949.

Duffy, Charles Gavan. *The League of North and South.* London, 1886.

Dunleavy, Garath W. *Douglas Hyde.* Lewisburg, Pa., 1974.

Dunleavy, Janet Egleson. *George Moore: The Artist's Vision, the Storyteller's Art.* Lewisburg, Pa., 1973.

Edwards, O. Dudley and Fergus Pyle, eds. *1916: The Easter Rising.* London, 1968.

Ervine, St. John. *Craigavon, Ulsterman.* London, 1949.

Fergusson, James. *The Curragh Incident.* London, 1964.

Figgis, Darrell. *Recollections of the Irish War.* London, 1927.

Fogarty, L., ed. *James Fintan Lalor.* Dublin, 1947.

Foot, M. R. D. and H. C. G. Matthew, eds. *The Gladstone Diaries.* Oxford, 1974, 3 vols.

Forester, Margery. *Michael Collins: The Lost Leader.* London, 1971.

French, Gerald. *Life of Field Marshall Sir John French.* London, 1931.

Gallagher, Frank. *The Indivisible Island.* London, 1957.

Gleeson, James. *Bloody Sunday.* London, 1962.

Greaves, C. D. *The Life and Times of James Connolly.* London, 1961.

Green, A. S. *Irish Nationality.* London, 1912.

Gwynn, Denis. *The Life of John Redmond.* London, 1932.

Gwynn, Denis. *The Life and Death of Roger Casement.* London, 1931.

Gwynn, Denis. *The History of Partition, 1912–1925.* Dublin, 1950.

Gwynn, Denis. *Young Ireland and 1848.* Cork, 1949.

Hachey, Thomas, ed. *The Problem of Partition: Peril to World Peace.* Chicago, 1972.

Hammond, J. L. *Gladstone and the Irish Nation.* London, 1964.

Hendrick, Burton. *The Life and Letters of Walter H. Page.* New York, 1922, 3 vols.

Henry, R. M. *The Evolution of Sinn Fein.* Dublin, 1920.

Hobson, B. *Ireland Yesterday and Tomorrow.* Tralee, 1968.

Holt, Edgar. *Protest in Arms: The Irish Troubles, 1916–1923.* London, 1960.

Horgan, John J. *Parnell to Pearse.* Dublin, 1949.

Hurst, Michael. *Parnell and Irish Nationalism.* London, 1968.

Hyde, H. M. *Carson.* London, 1953.

Hyde, H. Montgomery. *The Trial of Sir Roger Casement.* London, 1960.

Inglis, Brian. *Roger Casement.* London, 1973.

Jaffres, A. N. *W. B. Yeats: Man and Poet.* London, 1949.

James, Admiral Sir William. *The Code Breakers of Room 40.* New York, 1956.

Jenkins, Roy. *Asquith.* New York, 1966.

Johnston, Ray, ed. *The Politics of Division, Partition and Unification.* New York, 1976.

Joyce, James. *Finnegans Wake.* New York, 1959.

Kee, Robert. *The Green Flag.* London, 1972.

Larkin, Emmet. *James Larkin: Irish Labour Leader, 1876–1947.* London, 1968.

Larkin, Emmet. *The Roman Catholic Church and the Creation of the Modern Irish State.* Philadelphia, 1975.

Lee, Joseph. *The Modernisation of Irish Society, 1848–1918.* Dublin, 1973.

Levenson, Samuel. *James Connolly: A Biography.* London, 1973.

Lloyd George, David. *War Memoirs.* London, 1938, 2 vols.

Longford, The Earl of and Thomas P. O'Neill. *Eamon de Valera.* Boston, 1971.

Longford, Lord. *Peace by Ordeal.* London, 1967.

Lynch, Diarmuid. *The I.R.B. and the 1916 Rising,* ed. by F. O. Donoghue. Cork. 1957.

Lyons, F. S. L. *Ireland Since the Famine.* New York, 1971.

Lyons, F. S. L. *John Dillon: A Biography.* London, 1968.

McCaffrey, Lawrence J. *The Irish Question, 1800–1922.* Lexington, Kentucky, 1968.

McCaffrey, Lawrence J. *The Irish Diaspora in America.* Bloomington, Indiana, 1976.

McCaffrey, Lawrence J. *Irish Federalism in the 1870's: A Study in Conservative Nationalism.* Philadelphia, 1962.

Macardle, Dorothy. *The Irish Republic.* New York, 1965.

McCartan, Patrick. *With De Valera in America.* New York, 1932.

McCartney, Donal. "The Church and Fenianism," *University Review* 4. Winter, 1967.

MacColl, Rene. *Roger Casement.* London, 1965.

McCracken, J. L. *Representative Government in Ireland.* London, 1958.

McCready, H. W. "Home Rule and the Liberal Party," *Irish Historical Studies,* 13, September, 1963.

MacDonagh, Oliver. *Ireland.* Englewood Cliffs, N. J., 1968.

McDowell, R. B. *The Irish Administration.* London, 1964.

McDowell, R. B. *The Irish Convention, 1917–1918.* London, 1970.

McDowell, R. B. *Alice Stopford Green: A Passionate Historian.* Dublin, 1967.

MacGiolla Choille, Brendan, ed. *Intelligence Notes, 1913–16.* Dublin, 1966.

McGurrin, James. *Bourke Cockran: A Free Lance in American Politics.* New York, 1948.

McHugh, Roger, ed. *Dublin 1916.* New York, 1966.

McNeill, Ronald (Lord Cushendun). *Ulster's Stand for Union.* London, 1922.

Macready, General Sir Nevil. *Annals of an Active Life.* London, 1942, 2 vols.

Maloney, William J. *The Forged Casement Diaries.* Dublin, 1936.

Mansergh, Nicholas. *The Irish Question, 1840–1921.* London, 1968.

Mansergh, Nicholas. *Ireland in the Age of Reform and Revolution.* London, 1940.

Marreco, Anne. *The Rebel Countess.* London, 1967.

Martin, F. X., ed. "Eoin MacNeill on the 1916 Rising," *Irish Historical Studies,* 12, March, 1961.

Martin, F. X., ed. *The Irish Volunteers, 1913–1915.* Dublin, 1963.

Martin, F. X., ed. *Leaders and Men of the Easter Rising: Dublin, 1916.* New York, 1967.

Martin, F. X. and F. J. Byrne, eds. *The Scholar Revolutionary.* Shannon, 1973.

Martin, F. X., ed. *The Howth Gun-Running, 1914.* Dublin, 1964.

Martin, Hugh. *Ireland in Insurrection.* London, 1921.

Mason, Ellsworth and Richard Ellman, eds. *The Critical Writings of James Joyce.* New York, 1959.

Midleton, The Earl of. *Records and Reactions, 1856–1939.* London, 1939.

Midleton, The Earl of. *Ireland—Dupe or Heroine.* London, 1932.

Miller, David W. *Church, State and Nation in Ireland, 1898–1921.* Dublin, 1973.

Mitchell, Arthur. *Labour in Irish Politics.* Dublin, 1974.

Monteith, Robert. *Casement's Last Adventure.* Dublin, 1953.

Moody, T. W., ed. *The Fenian Movement.* Cork, 1968.

Moody, T. W. and F. X. Martin, eds. *The Course of Irish History.* Cork, 1967.

Moore, George. *Hail and Farewell.* London, 1937.

Mowat, Charles L. *Britain Between the Wars.* London, 1968.

Murphy, John. *Ireland in the Twentieth Century.* Dublin, 1975.

Nevinson, H. W. *Last Changes, Last Chances.* London, 1929.

Nicolson, Harold. *King George V.* London, 1967.

Norman, Edward. *The Catholic Church in Ireland in the Age of Rebellion, 1859–1873.* London, 1965.

Norman, Edward. *A History of Modern Ireland.* Coral Gables, Florida, 1971.

Nowlan, K. B., ed. *The Making of 1916.* Dublin, 1969.

O'Brien, Conor Cruise. *States of Ireland.* New York, 1973.

O'Brien, Conor Cruise. *Parnell and His Party.* Oxford, 1957.

O'Brien, Conor Cruise, ed. *The Shaping of Modern Ireland.* London, 1960.

O'Brien, Francis William, ed. *Divided Ireland.* Rockford, Illinois, 1971.

O'Brien, R. Barry. *The Life of Charles Stewart Parnell.* London, 1898, 2 vols.

O'Brien, William. *The Irish Revolution and How It Came About.* London, 1923.

O'Brien, William. *Forth the Banners Go,* ed. by Edward Mac-Lysaght. Dublin, 1969.

O'Brien, W. and D. Ryan, eds. *Devoy's Post Bag.* Dublin, 1953, 2 vols.

O Broin, Leon. *The Chief Secretary.* London, 1969.

O Broin, Leon. *Fenian Fever. An Anglo-American Dilemma.* London, 1971.

O Broin, Leon. *Dublin Castle and the 1916 Rising.* New York, 1971.

O'Cathasaigh, P. (Sean O'Casey). *The Story of the Irish Citizen Army.* Dublin, 1919.

O'Casey, Sean. *Autobiographies.* London, 1963, 2 vols.

O'Doherty, Katherine. *Assignment America: De Valera's Mission to the United States.* New York, 1957.

O'Donoghue, Florence. *No Other Law.* Dublin, 1954.

O'Faolain, Sean. *Constance Marciewicz.* London, 1934.

O'Hegarty, P. S. *A History of Ireland Under the Union, 1801–1922.* London, 1952.

O'Hegarty, P. S. *The Victory of Sinn Fein.* Dublin, 1924.

O Luing, Sean. *I Die in A Good Cause: A Study of Thomas Ashe.* Dublin, 1970.

O'Malley, Ernie. *Army Without Banners.* Boston, 1937.

Parmiter, Geoffrey de G. *Roger Casement.* London, 1936.

Pearse, P. H. *Collected Works: Political Writings and Speeches.* Dublin, 1924.

Pelling, Henry. *The Origins of the Labour Party, 1880–1900.* London, 1954.

Phillips, W. Alison. *The Revolution in Ireland.* London, 1923.

Plunkett, Sir H. *Ireland in the New Century.* London, 1904.

Reid, B. L. *The Lives of Roger Casement.* New Haven, 1976.

Rooney, William. *Prose Writings.* Dublin, 1909.

Ryan, A. P. *Mutiny at the Curragh.* London, 1956.

Ryan, Desmond. *The Rising.* Dublin, 1966.

Ryan, Desmond. *James Connolly.* London, 1924.

Ryan, Desmond. *The Fenian Chief.* Dublin, 1967.

Ryan, Desmond. *Remembering Sion.* London, 1934.

Ryan, Desmond. *The Phoenix Flame. A Study of Fenianism and John Devoy.* London, 1937.

Savage, D. C. "The Origins of the Ulster Unionist Party, 1885–6," *Irish Historical Studies,* 12, March, 1961.

Senior, H. *Orangeism in Ireland and Britain, 1795–1836.* London, 1966.

Shearman, Hugh. *Not an Inch. a Study of Northern Ireland and Lord Craigavon.* London, 1942.

Singleton-Gates, Peter and Maurice Girodias. *The Black Diaries.* New York, 1959.

Spindler, Karl. *The Mystery of the Casement Ship.* Tralee, 1965.

Stansky, Peter. *England Since 1867: Continuity and Change.* New York, 1973.

Stephens, James. *Insurrection in Dublin.* London, 1916.

Stewart, A. T. Q. *The Ulster Crisis.* London, 1967.

Street, C. J. C. *Ireland in 1921.* London, 1922.

Sullivan, A. M. *New Ireland.* London, 1877.

Tansill, Charles. *America and the Fight for Irish Freedom, 1866–1922.* New York, 1957.

Taylor, A. J. P. *English History, 1914–1945.* Oxford, 1965.

Taylor, Rex. *Michael Collins.* London, 1965.

Thompson, William I. *The Imagination of an Insurrection.* New York, 1967.

Thornley, David. *Isaac Butt and Home Rule.* London, 1964.

Tuchman, Barbara. *The Zimmermann Telegram.* New York, 1958.

Van Voris, Jacqueline. *Constance de Markievicz.* Amherst, Massachusetts, 1967.

Wade, Allan, ed. *Letters of W. B. Yeats.* London, 1954.

Ward, Alan. *Ireland and Anglo-American Relations, 1899–1921.* Toronto, 1969.

Ward, Alan. "America and the Irish Problem, 1899–1921," *Irish Historical Studies,* 16, March, 1968.

White, James R. *Misfit: An Autobiography.* London, 1930.

Whyte, J. H. *Church and State in Modern Ireland, 1923–1970.* New York, 1971.

Williams, Desmond, ed. *The Irish Struggle, 1916–1926.* Toronto, 1966.

Yeats, W. B. *Nine One-Act Plays.* London, 1937.

Yeats, William Butler. "The Rose Tree," *Collected Poems.* New York, 1944.

Younger, Calton. *Ireland's Civil War.* London, 1970.

Younger, Calton. *A State of Disunion.* London, 1972.

Zimmern, A. *The League of Nations and the Rule of Law, 1918–35.* London, 1936.

Bibliographical Note

The most recent edition, in either cloth or paperback, is cited for a number of the above titles since very often these will be more accessible to the reader.

Index

Abbey Theatre, 44, 56
Aberdeen, Lord, 122, 165
Act of Union, 5, 7
AE. *See* Russell, George
Agar-Robartes, W. G., 83
Allen, Fred, 118
American Association for the Recognition of the Irish Republic, 256
American Commission on Conditions in Ireland, 256
American Commission for Irish Independence: appointed, 223; purpose of, 224; visa question, 225; arrival in Paris, 226; activities in Dublin, 227; collaboration with Sinn Fein, 228; report on conditions in Ireland, 228; and President Wilson, 229; strife within, 229–230
American Committee for Relief in Ireland, 256
American-Irish, 8; support Land League, 21; and 1886 home rule bill, 27; response to executions (1916), 177; and Roger Casement's trial, 179; and Lloyd George, 184; and Woodrow Wilson, 191, 211–212; support Ireland's delegates to Peace Conference, 214–216; reaction to McCartan's declaration, 217; hold Irish Race Convention, 223–224; Lord Reading's analysis of, 225; as targets of British and Irish propaganda, 232
Amnesty Association, 17
Anglicans, 70
Articles of Agreement as signed on December 6, 1921, 290, 314–319
Asgard, 124–125
Ashbourne Act (1885), 25
Ashe, Thomas, 193
Asquith, Henry Herbert: becomes Prime Minister, 60; calls general election (1909), 61; and Parliament Bill of 1910, 64; introduces third home rule bill (1912), 67; and debate over third home rule bill (1912), 83; and George V, 85; and John Redmond, 85; proposes option for Ulster, 86; forces resignation of Gough, Seely, and Wilson, 88; reaction to Ulster gun-running, 90; meets with Carson, 91; attends conference at Buckingham Palace, 91; and Bachelor's Walk investigation, 93; and suffragettes, 98; and Ulster gun-running, 122; visits Dublin, 132; coalition government of (1915), 136–137; reaction to appeals for Casement, 179; visits Ireland (1916), 183, 188; replaced by Lloyd George, 185
Auxiliary Division: formation of, 274; engage in reprisals, 275; and the burning of Cork city, 278

Bachelor's Walk Incident, 93, 126
Bailey, Daniel, 155, 157, 167
Balfour, Arthur J., 34; Irish policies, 35; resigns (1905), 57; succeeded by Bonar Law, 76; and home rule, 85
Bannister, Gertrude, 178–179
Barry, Tom, 278
Barry, William, 248
Barton, Robert, 267, 287
Bethmann-Hollweg, Theobald von, 148, 149
Biggar, Joseph Gillis, 19
Birkenhead, Lord. *See* Sir Frederick Smith
Birrell, Augustine, 60, 122, 164, 165, 166; receives Nathan's telegram, 167; resigns, 174
Black and Tans, 262; augmented by the Auxiliary Division, 274; engage in reprisals, 275

Bloody Sunday, November 21, 1920, 277

Boer War, 36, 57, 260

Boland, Harry, 199; and de Valera's escape, 220; campaigns for Dail in America, 232; confers with de Valera in New York, 239

Bonsal, Stephen, 229

Boyne, Batte of the, 3, 81

British Trades Union Congress, 107, 108–109

Brugha, Cathal, 206, 207, 265, 287

Bryce, Lord, 233

Bull, Sir William, 83

Burke, T. H., 29

Butt, Isaac, 16–19

Campbell-Bannerman, Sir Henry, 57, 60

Carson, Sir Edward, 64; and Ulster Unionism, 72–74; address to Unionists, 75; reaction to Churchill's speech (1912), 77–78; signs Ulster Covenant, 81; and amendment to third home rule bill, 84; reaction to Asquith's proposal, 86; confers with Crawford, 89; meets with Asquith, 91; attends conference at Buckingham Palace, 92; reaction to Government of Ireland Act (1914), 95; and Ulster Volunteers, 97; and outbreak of World War I, 130–132; and Asquith's coalition government, 136–137; and Lloyd George, 184; becomes First Lord of the Admiralty, 185; reluctantly concedes to partition plan, 272

Casement, Sir Roger, 123–124, 127, 128; confers with Devoy, 144–145; Berlin mission of, 146; failure of German mission, 148–149; recruits Irish brigade, 150, 151; attempts to stop the rising, 155, 157–158; role as interpreted by Nathan, 167; trial of, 178–182

"Castle Document," 158, 159

Cathleen ni Houlihan, 42, 57

Cavendish, Lord Frederick, 29

Ceannt, Eamonn, 150, 176

Cecil, Lord Hugh, 64

Cecil, Robert, 284

Chamberlain, Austen, 284, 287

Chamberlain, Neville, 297

Chamberlain, Joseph, 32

Charles I (King of England), 2

Chichester-Clark, James, 306

Childers, Erskine, 124–125

Childers, Erskine Hamilton (President of the Irish Republic, 1973–1974), 302

Church of Ireland, 14, 15, 192

Churchill, Lord Randolph, 71

Churchill, Winston S.: Belfast speech (1912), 77–79; and third home rule bill (1912), 83–84; remarks on British Cabinet at outbreak of World War I, 94; and governmental post-war concerns, 201–202; and Sinn Fein boycott of Westminster, 209; and Sinn Fein prisoners, 218; urges Irish self-government, 284; and Anglo-Irish truce negotiations, 287; appeals for de Valera's support in World War II, 298

Citizen Army: formation of, 110–111; rebuilt, 111; conflict within, 112–113; during World War I, 136; size of (1916), 139; and I.R.B., 152; and Easter Rising, 169, 171

Civil Authorities (Special Powers) Act, 303

Civil Rights Association in Ulster. *See* Northern Ireland Civil Rights Association

Clan-na-Gael, 13, 20, 116, 117, 118; Casement asks for assistance from, 144–145; supports I. R. B., 145; supports Casement's Berlin mission, 146; and trial of Roger Casement, 179; and Friends of Irish Freedom, 214; at Irish Race Convention, 224; resents de Valera's involvement in American politics, 240

Clarke, Thomas, 117, 127, 150, 151, 176

Clemenceau, Georges, 213, 214, 230

Clune, Archbishop Patrick, 257n, 284

Cockrane, Bourke, 181, 253

Cohalan, Daniel, 214, 215; organizes lecture tour for de Valera, 239; and hatred for Britain, 240; *détente* with de Valera and Senate resolution, 241; promotes an alternative plank to de Valera's for Republican platform, 247; avoids Democratic Convention, 251

Colby, Bainbridge: urges British to characterize Sinn Fein as Bolshevik, 235

Collins, Michael, 194; background of, 195; and de Valera, 196; directs Volunteer's intelligence, 199; in Dail ministry, 206; and Democratic Programme, 208; and de Valera's escape, 220; urges de Valera to postpone American journey, 238; asked by Griffith to restrain I. R. A. violence, 260; and estimate of I. R. A. strength, 264; and intelligence network, 264–265; raises Dail Eireann national loan, 267; and Bloody Sunday, 277; elected to an Ulster constituency, 282; admits I. R. A. exhaustion at time of truce, 285; and the Anglo-Irish peace negotiations, 287–290; assassinated, 291.

Committee of Four, 213

Connolly, James, 100–102; joins Irish Transport and General Workers Union, 104; compared to Larkin, 104–105; arrested (1913), 107; emerges as labour leader, 110; need for a "blood sacrifice," 141; joins I. R. B. Military Council, 150, 152; meets with Pearse and MacNeill, 153; signs cease-fire, 172; executed, 176

Constitutional Proposals for Northern Ireland (White Paper), 306–307

Cork city: the burning of, 278

Cosgrave, Liam, 301–302, 308

Cosgrave, William T., 267, 294–295

Costello, John A., 299

Council of Four, 222, 229

Council of Ireland, 272, 308

Countess Cathleen, The, 44–45

Cox, James, 254

Craig, Sir James (later Lord Craigavon), 74–75; reaction to Churchill's speech (1912), 77–78; endorses arms smuggling, 89; elected Prime Minister of Northern Ireland, 282; excluded from de Valera-Lloyd George negotiations, 283; responds to de Valera-Chamberlain negotiations, 297; and unionist viewpoint, 303

Craig, William, 306

Craigavon, Lord. *See* Sir James Craig

Crawford, Major Fred, 86, 87, 89, 121

Croke Park, 277

Cromwell, Oliver, 2

Crooks, Will, 64

Crozier, General F. P., 274–275

Cumann na nGael, 54

Cummann na nGaedheal, 53

Curragh Incident, 87–88

Curzon, Lord, 185, 239

Cusack, Michael, 39

Dail Éireann: arrangements to convene, 204–205; first assembly of, 205; first executive session of, 206–207; disagreements over Democratic Programme, 207–208; and London Government, 209, 221–222; plans de Valera reception, 220; meets upon de Valera's return from America, 256–257; campaign against R. I. C., 260–261; introduces oath of allegiance for I. R. A., 265; meetings held during the Anglo-Irish War, 267; establishes own judicial system, 268; relationship with I. R. A., 269; publicly accepts responsibility for I. R. A., 269; boycotts trade with Ulster, 283; renounces Lloyd George's offer for dominion status, 286; accepts Anglo-Irish treaty, 290; passes the Republic of Ireland bill, 299; introduces bills to increase police power against I. R. A., 302

Daly, P. T., 107, 118

Dangerfield, George, 98

Davis, John W., 227

Davis, Thomas, 8, 9

Davitt, Michael, 8, 20, 21; calls for Parnell's resignation, 33; and collectivization, 99

Defenders, the, 5

Democratic Programme: ratified, 205; disagreement in Dail over, 207–208

Department of Agriculture and Technical Instruction, 50–51

Derby, Lord, 284

Derry, town of, 2. *See also* Londonderry

des Graz, Charles, 242

De Valera, Eamon: and the Easter Rising, 172; question of American citizenship, 177–178; Sinn Fein candidate, 190; at Sinn Fein convention (1917), 194; and Michael Collins, 195; background of, 195–196; and conscription conference, 197; and "German Plot," 199; appointed delegate to Peace Conference, 206; as potential Dail president, 206; as Dail president, 206–207; escapes Lincoln jail, 220; welcomes American Commission for Irish Independence, 228; three objectives in visiting America, 238; undertakes national tour, 239; scorns Clan-na-Gael's anti-British strategy, 240; *détente* with Cohalan and Senate resolution, 241; breaks with Cohalan over Irish plank for Republican platform, 247; and reception at San Francisco, 252; fails in his strategy at Democratic Convention, 252–253; seeks control of F. O. I. F., 254; establishes the American Association for the Recognition of the Irish Republic, 256; returns to Ireland, 256–257; reports to Dail upon arrival from America, 257; seeks to ostracize R. I. C., 261; appoints Lawrence Ginnell as Director of Propaganda, 266; elected to an Ulster constituency, 282; sets conditions for negotiations with Lloyd George, 283; deems Lloyd George offer of dominion status as unacceptable, 286; remains in Dublin during further Anglo-Irish negotiations, 287; rejects treaty and resigns Dail presidency, 290; imprisoned by Irish Free State, 294; released from jail and founds Fianna Fail Party, 295; heads Irish government and provides new constitution, 296; changes name of country to Eire, 297; succeeds in winning return of the treaty ports, 298; keeps Eire neutral in World War II, 298; elected President of the Irish Republic, 299; re-elected president, 300; dies, 302

Devlin, Joseph, 78, 197

Devoy, John, 117, 127, 128; confers with Casement, 144–145; asks for German arms, 153–154, 155; and trial of Roger Casement, 179; and Friends of Irish Freedom, 214, 215; confers with de Valera in New York, 239; and rivalry with de Valera, 240

Dillon, John, 33, 131, 132; reaction to Easter Rising, 175; and Lloyd George's partition plan, 184; allies Irish Party with Sinn Fein, 197; and conscription, 197–198

Disraeli, Benjamin, 16, 22, 26

Doheny, E. L., 245, 253

Doyle, Sir Arthur Conan, 233

Doyle, M. F., 179

Dublin Customs House, 267n, 278

Dublin Socialist Society, 100

Dublin Trades Council, 99–100

Dublin United Trades Association, 99

Dublin University, 15, 16, 60

Dublin University Magazine, 17

Duffy, Charles Gavan, 8

Duffy, George Gavan, 287

Duggan, E. J., 287

Duke, Henry, 187, 196, 198

Dungannon: civil rights demonstrations, 300

Dungannon Clubs, 115; and Sinn Fein, 116

Dunne, Edward F., 224, 227, 230

Dunraven, Lord, 85

Easter Rising: Britain fails to anticipate, 162–164; beginning of, 168–169; course of, 170–173; aftermath of, 173–178

Edward VII (King of England), 55, 63

Elizabeth I (Queen of England), 1

Emmet, Robert, 5–6

European Commission on Human Rights, 301

European Economic Community, 309

Ewart-Biggs, Christopher, 302

Faulkner, Brian, 306–309
Fenian Brotherhood, 9, 10, 12–13, 16; influence on Irish Land League, 24. *See also* Irish Republican Brotherhood (I.R.B.)
Fianna Éireann, 116
Fianna Fail, 295, 299, 301–302
Figgis, Darrell, 124, 125
Fine Gael, 299, 301–302
French, General Lord, 166–167, 175, 198; efforts to prevent insurrection, 198–199; as Viceroy, 209; and Sinn Fein prisoners, 218; memorandum regarding prisoners, 219–220; opposes de Valera's reception, 221; prerogatives of, 227; attempted assassination of, 270
Friends of Irish Freedom (F.O.I.F.), 214–215; prepares resolution for Republican Convention, 246; refrains from participation in Democratic Convention, 251; de Valera attempts to seize control of, 254; displaced by de Valera's American Association for the Recognition of the Irish Republic, 256

Gaelic American, 127
Gaelic Athletic Association (G.A.A.): founded, 39; Arthur Griffith and, 56, 116
Gaelic League, 39–40; Horace Plunkett and, 49; Sinn Fein and, 55; Arthur Griffith and, 56; and I. R. B., 82, 116; declared illegal, 199; suppressed in 27 counties, 269
Gallagher, Thomas, 215
Geddes, Sir Auckland: urges London to counter Irish propaganda, 245; recommends reply to Congressional protest, 246; expresses satisfaction with Republican Convention, 248; advises Lloyd George to appease Southern states, 250
George III (King of England), 6

George V (King of England), 63, 81, 85, 91, 94, 122, 282
Gerry, Peter, 242
Gibbons, James Cardinal, 177, 223; and German Catholic missions in the British Empire, 237
Ginnell, Lawrence, 266
Gladstone, William E., 12, 14–16; and land bill of 1881, 23; supports Irish home rule, 26; and first home rule bill, 27; resigns (1886), 28; and Parnell's resignation, 30–31; and home rule bill of 1893, 32
Glorious Revolution of 1688, 3
Gonne, Maud, 42, 118
Gough, General Sir Herbert, 88
Government of Ireland Act (1914), 95; restricted to twenty-six counties, 184; becomes law, 279
Grattan, Henry, 4
Green, Alice Stopford, 122–123
Greenwood, Sir Haman, 275, 278
Gregory, Lady, 43–44
Grey, Sir Edward, 94, 179, 181
Griffith, Arthur, 45, 52; founder of Sinn Fein, 53; dual monarchy scheme of, 54: and National Council, 55; personality of, 56, 57; denounces home rule bill of 1912, 68; and James Connolly, 110; and Erskine Childers, 125; and Easter Rising, 188–189; nonviolent views of, 193; defers to de Valera, 194; and conscription conference, 197; denounces alliance with Irish Party, 198; and "German plot," 199; appointed delegate to Peace Conference, 206; and de Valera's report on the Republican Convention, 248; intervenes to prevent I. R. A. violence, 260; elected to an Ulster constituency, 282; and the Anglo-Irish peace negotiations, 287–290; elected to succeed de Valera as Dail president, 290; dies of heart attack, 291
Gwynn, Stephen, 42–43, 203

Hall, Captain Reginald, 181
Harding, Warren G., 257
Harrell, W. V., 94
Healy, T. M., 58, 63, 198
Hearst, William Randolph, 245

Heath, Edward, 308
Heather Field, The, 44
Henry VIII (King of England), 1
Hobson, Bulmer, 115, 116, 119, 125;
  gun-running scheme of, 127–128;
  and Irish Volunteers, 140; and Devoy's opinion of Casement, 145;
  discovers plans for the rising, 158
Home Government Association, 18
Home Rule, 12; and Isaac Butt, 19;
  and Asquith, 60; and Protestant
  Unionists, 65–66, 71, 74; meeting
  in Belfast (1912), 77–79; and Ulster Covenant, 81; and Ulster
  counties, 86; delegation to Buckingham Palace 91–92; supported
  by trade unions, 100; British Government's indifference to, 137;
  Lloyd George initiates discussion
  of, 183; and Irish Convention,
  192; and conscription bill, 197. *See
  also* Home Rule Bill of 1886;
  Home Rule Bill of 1893; Home
  Rule Bill of 1912
Home Rule Act: suspended (1914),
  135
Home Rule Bill of 1886: introduced,
  27; defeated, 28
Home Rule Bill of 1893, 32
Home Rule Bill of 1912: introduced,
  67; provisions of, 67–68; reaction
  of Irish Parliamentary Party to,
  68; Irish Unionists and, 69; debate
  in Parliament over, 82–84; Carson's proposed amendment to, 84;
  reaction of U. V. F. and Ulster
  Unionist Council to, 91; amending
  bill for Ulster discussed, 91; passed
  (1914), 95
House, Colonel, 226
Hyde, Douglas, 40, 42, 43, 46, 51;
  and D. P. Moran, 52

Independent, 106
Industrial Workers of the World,
  101
Inglis, Brian, 180
Ireland Act of 1949, 299
Irish Agricultural Organization Soci-
  ety, 49, 50, 51
Irish Army mutiny of 1924, 294
Irish bond certificates, 243, 255

Irish Boundary Commission. *See*
  Royal Boundary Commission
Irish Citizen, 98
Irish Civil War, 290–291; costs and
  casualties, 294
Irish Congress of Trade Unions, 300
Irish Convention, 192
Irish Council Bill, 58–59
Irish Free State: receives official
  powers, 290; executes 77 rebels
  during civil war, 291; recognizes
  the boundary of Northern Ire-
  land, 292; and League of Nations,
  295; and Statue of Westminster,
  295
Irish Freedom, 56, 117, 119, 128
Irish Labour Movement: background of, 99–110; influence on
  Democratic Programme, 207
Irish Land League: founding of, 21;
  land war of 1879–1882, 22; outlawed, 24
Irish Literary Revival, 40–47
Irish Literary Society, 42
Irish Literary Theatre, 45
Irish neutrality, 298
Irish Parliamentary Party: founding
  of, 18; schism within, 32–33; reconciliation of factions (1900), 36,
  55; benefits from British Government's budget crisis (1909), 56; national convention of (1907),
  58–59; alliance with the Liberals,
  59, 60; and budget crisis of 1909,
  61; and election of January, 1910,
  62; supported by trade unions,
  100; and Irish Volunteers, 121;
  and Sinn Fein electoral chal-
  lenges, 190; credibility compromised, 191; at Irish Convention,
  192; allied with Sinn Fein, 197; alliance with Sinn Fein terminated,
  198; and election of 1918, 201,
  203. *See also* John Redmond
Irish People, the, 9, 10
Irish Race Convention, 223–224; analyzed by Lord Reading, 225
Irish Republican Army (I.R.A.): pro-
  claims Irish Republic, 205; adopts
  guerrilla tactics, 262; and British
  estimate of strength, 264; takes
  oath of allegiance to the Dail, 265;
  relationship to the Dail and Sinn

Fein, 269; mounts attacks against police in Ulster, 273; burns R. I. C. barracks, 275; and inadequate weapons, 276; and Bloody Sunday, 277; ambush, 278; attacks Dublin Customs House, 278; divided against itself during civil war, 291–292; factionalized by ideology in contemporary times, 293; and the border campaign, 299, 304; bombings shock opinion in the Republic, 301; and "official" and "provisional" branches, 302; rejects Northern Ireland Constitutional Bill, 307; and letter bombs, 308

Irish Republican Brotherhood (I.R.B.), 9, 12, 13, 16, 20; and Sinn Fein, 56; infiltrates Irish Volunteers, 82; renaissance of, 113–118; and World War I, 131; plans insurrection, 138–139; plans for a military victory, 144–145; establishes Military Council, 150; and Citizen Army, 152–153; and communication with Germany, 155–156; plan for the rising, 160–161; radicalizes Irish Volunteers, 187; infiltrates Sinn Fein and Irish Volunteers, 194; and the Irish Republican Army, 265. *See also* Fenian Brotherhood

Irish Review, The, 144

Irish Socialist Republican Party, 101

Irish Trades Union Congress, 100, 102; and Irish Transport and General Workers Union, 103–104

Irish Transport and General Workers Union (I.T.G.W.U.): objectives of, 103; affiliated with Irish Trades Union Congress, 104; and labour crisis of 1911, 105–106

Irish Unionism, 69–70

Irish Unionist Alliance, 71, 72

Irish Universities Act, 60

Irish Victory Fund, 255

Irish Volunteers: established, 82, 120–121; Ulster Volunteers military supremacy over, 90; gunrunning operation of, 92–93, 125–126; and World War I, 96, 97, 131; schism within, 97, 128–129; O'-Casey's opinion of, 112, Redmond

asserts control of, 126–127; and Citizen Army, 129; during World War I, 136; manipulated by I. R. B., 138–139; and I. R. B., 139–140; plans of Hobson and MacNeill for, 145; government policy towards, 165; and Easter Rising, 169, 171, 174; influenced by I. R. B., 187; de Valera becomes president of, 194; declared illegal, 199; and relationship between units and headquarters staff, 269. *See also* New Irish Volunteers; "Sinn Fein" Volunteers

Irish War for Independence, 11, 47; first blood shed in, 210

James I (King of England), 2

James II (King of England), 3

Johnson, Hiram, 246, 249

Johnson, Thomas, 207, 208

Joyce, James, 44

Kelly, Monsignor Francis, 237, 238

Kickham, Charles, 9, 10

Kilmainham Treaty, 23

Kitchener, Lord, 131–132, 133

Labour. *See* Irish Labour Movement

Labour in Irish History, 105

Lalor, James Fintan, 8

Land League. *See* Irish Land League

Lansdowne, Lord, 85, 92, 184

Lansing, Robert, 215, 216

Larkin, James: background of, 102, 103; and Irish Transport and General Workers Union, 103–104; and labour crisis (1911), 105; and tramwaymen's strike, 106–107; defeat of (1914), 108; tour of United States, 110; and Citizen Army, 111, 113

Law, Andrew Bonar, 76–77, 85, 86, 87; and Asquith-Carson meeting, 91; attends conference at Buckingham Palace, 92; and outbreak of World War I, 130–131; appointed to War Cabinet, 186; and conscription, 196; and de Valera's reception, 221; and American Commission for Irish Independence, 227, 229; responds to discussion in Commons over Sinn Fein activities in America, 243; opposes boundary realignment of Ulster, 291

Leader, the, 52

League of Nations, 211; Ireland claims admission to, 213, Covenant of, 222; seen by Clan-na-Gael as a British plot, 240; Wilson recommends referral of Irish question to, 252

Lemass, Sean, 299–300

Limerick, treaty of, 3

Lloyd George, David: proposes tax increase (1909), 61; attends conference at Buckingham Palace, 91; initiates home rule discussions, 183; partition plan of, 184; coalition government of, 185; releases Irish prisoners, 186; grants general amnesty, 190; pressured to reach an Irish settlement, 191; and Irish Convention, 192; and conscription, 196; introduces conscription bill, 197; post-war concerns of, 201, reaction to the Dail, 209; and Woodrow Wilson, 212, 225; and Colonel House, 226–227; and American Commission for Irish Independence, 227, 229; counters Ireland's bid for recognition at the Peace Conference, 230; receives Congressional protest regarding Irish prisoners, 245; introduces bill for two Irish parliaments, 271; and promise of post-war prosperity for the United Kingdom, 281; invites de Valera to enter negotiations, 283; warned by advisors on need to resolve Irish problem, 284; offers de Valera dominion status for Ireland, 285; promises a future readjustment of Ulster's boundaries, 288; ultimatum to the Irish delegation, 289

Local Government Act (1898), 35

Lodge, Henry Cabot, 243

Londonderry, 2, 300

Long, Walter, 72, 185

Lowe, Brigadier-General W. H. M., 172

Luby, Thomas Clarke, 9, 10

Lynch, Arthur, 203

Lynch, Jack, 301

Lynch, Jeremiah (Diarmuid), 177, 232

MacBride, Major John, 117–118

McCartan, Patrick, 117, 119; diplomatic offensive of, 216–217; envoy of the Irish Republic in America, 232

McCarthy, Justin, 33

McCullough, Denis, 114–115, 151

MacDermott, Sean, 82, 115–116, 127, and I. R. B. Military Council, 150; and I. R. B. Supreme Council, 151; as delegate to MacNeill, 159; executed, 176

MacDonagh, Thomas, 141, 142–143, 150; as delegate to MacNeill, 159; executed, 176

MacHale, Archbishop John, 7

MacNeill, Eoin, 82, 97, 119–120; and John Redmond, 127; and schism within Irish Volunteers, 129; and I. R. B., 138–139; underestimates I. R. B., 140; introduces Casement to Devoy, 145; meets with Connolly, 152–153; reacts to "Castle Document," 158; reaction to I. R. B. plans for the rising, 158–160; countermands Irish Volunteer parades, 167; in Dail Ministry, 206

McNeill, Ronald, 84

Macpherson, Sir Ian, 209; reports on Irish prisoners, 218–219; opposes de Valera reception, 221

Macready, General Sir Nevil: authorizes formation of B specials, 273–274

MacSwiney, Terence, 249n, 276–277

Making of Ireland and its Undoing, The, 123

Manchester Guardian, 230

Manning, Henry Edward Cardinal, 31

Markievicz, Countess, 42, 98; conflict with O'Casey, 111–112; and Fianna Éireann, 116; and Easter Rising, 174; spared execution, 177; settles industrial disputes, 267

Martyn, Edward, 44, 46
Maxwell, Major-General Sir John, 172, 174, 175, 176, 182, 187
Mellows, Liam, 232, 239
Midleton, Lord, 192, 227–228
Military Service Bill, 197
Milner, Lord, 185
Mitchel, John, 8
Monteith, Robert, 150, 154, 155, 157, 167
Moore, George, 42, 44, 46
Moran, D. P., 52
Mulcahy, Richard, 206
Murphy, William Martin, 106, 107

Nathan, Sir Matthew, 164–165; fails to anticipate Easter rising, 166–167, 168; resigns, 174
Nation, the, 7, 8, 9
National Being, The, 50
National Council, the, 54–55
National League: founded, 24
National Literary Society, 42
National University of Ireland, 60
National Volunteers: origin of, 97, 129
Nationality, 189
New Irish Volunteers: origins and nature of, 97, 129. *See also* Irish Volunteers: "Sinn Fein" Volunteers
Newman, Agnes, 178
"North Began, The", 119, 120
Northern Ireland Assembly, 307–308
Northern Ireland Civil Rights Association, 300, 305–306
Northern Ireland Constitutional Bill, 307
Northern Ireland Executive, 308–309
Nunan, Sean, 248–249

O'Brien, William (parliamentarian), 23, 58, 63, 64, 198, 203
O'Brien, William (trade unionist), 107, 207
O'Brien, William Smith (Young Irelander), 9
O'Casey, Sean: and Citizen Army, 111; conflict with Countess Markievicz, 111–113

O'Connell, Daniel, 6, 7
O'Connell, William Cardinal, 215
O'Connor, T. P., 186
O'Farrell, Elizabeth, 172
O'Hegarty, P. S., 42, 117
O'Higgins, Kevin, 267, 294–295
O'Kelly, J. J., 189
O'Kelly, Sean T., 206, 208, 213; letter to Woodrow Wilson, 222; at Peace Conference, 223; and American Commission for Irish Independence, 228
O'Leary, John, 9, 10
O'Mahony, John, 8
O'Neill, Terence, 300, 306
O'Rahilly, The, *See* Michael Joseph Rahilly
Orange Order, 4–5; founded, 71; re-emergence of, 70–71; and Ulster Volunteer Force, 79; and response to Sinn Fein threat in Ulster, 273; demonstrations and violence, 304; reaction to civil rights movement, 306
Orangeman's Day, 3
O'Shannon, Cathal, 207
O'Shea, Katherine (Kitty), 30
O'Shea, William, 30

Page, Walter Hines, 84
Paget, Sir Arthur, 87, 88
Paisley, Ian, 306
Pankhurst, Emmeline, 98, 99
Paris Peace Conference. *See* Versailles Peace Conference
Parliament Act of 1911, 65, 85
Parliament Bill of 1910, 63–65
Parnell, Charles Stewart, 8, 19–20; and Irish Land League, 21; and Land Act of 1881, 23; and Kilmainham Treaty, 23; promotes the National League, 24; reaction to 1886 home rule bill, 27; rise and fall of, 29–31; and Irish Parliamentary Party, 32–33; manifesto of 1890, 35; influences Irish writers, 43
Parsons, General Sir Lawrence, 133
Pearse, Patrick, 82, 124; romantic nationalism of, 141–142; and I. R. B. Military Council, 150; meets with MacNeill and Connolly, 153; confrontation with MacNeill,

158–159; announces establishment of provisional government, 171; surrenders, 172; executed, 176; burial of, 182
Peel, Robert, 7
Penal Laws, 3
Peep O'Day Boys, 5
Phelan, James, 215
Pigott, Richard, 29
Pitt, William, 6
Plantation policy, 2, 3
Playboy of the Western World, The, 45, 56
Plough and the Stars, The, 113
Plunkett, George Noble, Count, 189–190; delegate to Peace Conference, 206; in Dail ministry, 206
Plunkett, Sir Horace, 47–51; chairs Irish Convention, 192; writes of anti-British sentiment in America, 235
Plunkett, Joseph, 141, 143–144; Berlin mission of, 149–150; opinion of Casement, 150–151; executed, 176
Polk, Frank, 178
Power, John O'Connor, 19
Presbyterians, 2, 3, 70, 192
Protestant Reformation, 1
Protestants, Irish, 2, 3–4; and university question, 15; and the Irish Literary Revival, 46; and Irish home rule, 65–66; and Irish Unionism, 69; and Ulster Unionism, 70–72; and outbreak of World War I, 131; and war effort, 134. *See also* Ulster Protestants

Queen's colleges, 7
Queens University (Belfast), 60
Queen's University in Ireland, 7

Rahilly, Michael Joseph, 119–120, 124; and Irish Volunteers, 140; death of, 171
Reading, Lord, 225
Redmond, John, 33, 36; and Irish Council Bill, 59; and the Liberal Alliance, 59; and budget crisis of 1909, 61; and Liberal party, 62; and Lords' veto power, 63; and debate over Parliament Bill

(1911), 64; and home rule bill of 1912, 68; and Churchill's speech (1912), 78; response to Carson's amendment, 84; accepts Asquith's proposal, 86; attends conference at Buckingham Palace, 91–92; loses confidence of Irish nationalists, 92; pledges Ireland's support at outbreak of World War I, 94, 96–97, 130; reaction to Irish Volunteers, 121; reaction to Ulster gun-running, 122; meets with Casement and MacNeill, 124; asserts control of Irish Volunteers, 126–127; and schism within the Irish Volunteers, 128–129; advises British Cabinet, 131; and Asquith's visit, 132; campaigns for Irish brigades, 133; and Asquith's coalition government, 136–137; reaction to Easter Rising, 175; and Lloyd George, 184, 185; proposes Irish convention, 191; death of, 192. *See also* Irish Parliamentary Party
Republic of Ireland Bill, 299
Restoration of Order Act of August 1920, 276
Richardson, Sir George, 79
Rising of 1848, 8; veterans of, 9
Roman Catholics (Ireland), 2; and Glorious Revolution, 3; and Orange Order, 5; and Penal Laws, 6; and Church of Ireland, 14; and higher education, 15; and Isaac Butt, 17; and Dublin University, 60; driven from Belfast shipyards, 78; and World War I, 133, 134; and distinctive culture in Northern Ireland, 305
Roman Catholic clergy (Ireland): support Land League, 21; and tramwaymen's strike, 107–108
Roman Catholic hierarchy (Ireland): and Queens Colleges, 7, 15; opposes Fenians, 9, 13; and tramwaymen's strike, 107; censures I. R. B., 116; represented at Irish Convention, 192; reaction to conscription, 197; protests on behalf of prisoners' hunger strike, 275; influence upon the government of the Irish Republic, 309

Rooney, William, 53, 57
Roosevelt, Franklin D., 298
Rosebery, Lord (Prime Minister), 32; and Irish home rule, 33–34; breaks with Liberal Party, 57
Royal Boundary Commission, 288, 291, 292, 294
Royal Irish Constabulary (R. I. C.), 22, 139, 165; demoralized by ostracization of Irish people, 261; depleted forces strengthened with British recruits, 262
Royal University of Ireland, 60
Russell, George, 42, 43, 46, 49–50
Ryan, Michael J., 224, 227, 229

Salisbury, Lord Robert, 25, 28, 34
Saunderson, Colonel E. J., 72
Seely, Colonel J. E. B., 88
Sheehy-Skeffington, Francis, 173
Sheehy-Skeffington, Mrs. Francis, 98
Shortt, Edward, 198
Sinn Fein, 52, 53; founding of, 55; limited success of early initiatives, 55–57; doctrine of self-reliance, 56; anti-recruiting campaigns, 136; public image of, 188; develops as political force, 189–191; and Irish Convention, 192; factional disputes within, 193–194; Dillon allies Irish Party with, 197; alliance with Irish Party ends, 198; and "German plot," 199; declared illegal, 199; membership (1918), 200; and election of 1918, 201; election manifesto of 1918, 202; election campaign (1918), 203; election results (1918), 204; convenes Dail Eireann, 204–205; differences between principles and practice in, 207–208; Woodrow Wilson and, 211–212; reaction to McCartan's declaration, 217; prisoners released, 220; and American Commission for Irish Independence, 228; propaganda in United States denounced in House of Commons, 243; moderates regret need for guerilla war, 262; sweeps local elections, 267; suppressed, 269; prisoners on hunger strike in Mountjoy jail, 275; and propaganda abroad, 276; and Bloody Sunday, 277; and the May 1921 election, 282; agrees to an armistice, 285
"Sinn Fein" Volunteers: origins of, 129
Sinn Fein (Publication), 45, 55
Smith, Sir Frederick (Earl of Birkenhead), 77; and the trial of Roger Casement, 178, 180, 185; and advice to Lloyd George on Ireland, 284; and Anglo-Irish truce negotiations, 287
Smuts, General J. C., 284
Society of United Irishmen. *See* United Irishmen, Society of
Spindler, Captain Karl, 156–157
Spring Rice, Sir Cecil, 177, 181
Stack, Austin, 157, 287
Stephens, James, 8, 9, 10, 42
Stormont. *See* Parliament of Northern Ireland
Strange Death of Liberal England, The, 98
Suffragettes, 95–96
Sullivan, A. M., 180
Sunday Independent, 160, 167
Sunningdale conference, 308
Synge, J. M., 42, 44, 45–46, 56

Times (London), 29, 231, 249
Tobin, Liam, 265
Trinity College, 15, 16, 60, 282
Twisting of the Rope, The, 46

Ulster, 1–2; and Industrial Revolution, 6; Unionists in, 70, 79; and third home rule bill, 84, 85, 86, 92; importation of British troops into, 86–87; and Curragh incident, 88; gun-running in, 89–90; and amendment to third home rule bill, 91; reaction to Government of Ireland Act (1914), 95; and election of 1918, 203; and riots of 1920, 273; and the formation of the B specials. *See also* Ulster Protestants: Ulster Unionists: Ulster Volunteer Force
Ulster Covenant, 80–81
Ulster Liberal Association, 77, 78
Ulster Protestants: and Act of Union, 6; and Irish home rule, 65–66, 68;

and Irish Unionism, 69; and Ulster Unionism, 70–72; and Ulster Volunteer Force, 79; and Ulster Covenant, 80; and attacks on Catholics in Belfast shipyards, 273; and disinterest in self-government for Ulster, 279–280; vote in plebiscite to remain a part of Britain, 301; relieved by the failure of the Northern Ireland Executive, 308–309. *See also* Ulster: Ulster Unionists: Ulster Volunteer Force

Ulster Unionists, 70–79; and creation of Ulster Volunteer Force, 79–80; and Ulster Covenant, 80–81; attack home rule, 83; procure weapons, 86; and Army Act, 87; and British army, 88; condemned by British Liberal government, 90; and amendment to third home rule bill, 91; response to outbreak of World War I, 95, 130–131; postwar governmental influence of, 184; and Lloyd George's partition plan, 184; at Irish Convention, 192; and election of 1918, 203; suspicious of Council of Ireland proposal, 272; and May 1921 election, 282; respond to de Valera-Chamberlain talks, 297; guaranteed by Ireland Act of 1949, 299; perception of Northern Irish Catholics, 305; consider dominion status for Ulster, 306; refuse to participate in the Northern Ireland executive, 308. *See also* Ulster: Ulster Protestants: Ulster Volunteer Force

Ulster Unionist Council, 71, 72, 73, 75; and Churchill's speech (1912), 78; and Ulster Volunteer Force, 79, 81; and Ulster Covenant, 80; and arms procurement, 87, 89; pledge to create a provisional government, 91; reluctantly consents to partition plan, 272

Ulster Volunteer Force (U.V.F.): creation of, 79; organization of, 80; military preparations of, 81; and Irish Volunteers, 82; and procurement of weapons, 86, 89· mili-
tary supremacy over Irish Volunteers, 90; pledge to create a provisional government, 91; Eoin MacNeill and, 119; gun-running activities, 121–122; drills in response to Sinn Fein threat, 273. *See also* Ulster: Ulster Protestants: Ulster Unionists

Unionist Government (Ireland), 34–35

United Irishmen, Society of, 4

United Irishmen, The, 45, 53, 55

United Nations, 301

University bill, 15–16

Versailles Peace Conference: Sinn Fein manifesto and, 202; Dail delegates to, 206; London Government and, 210–211; petitioned by Dail delegates, 213; United States Congress and, 215–216; formal opening of, 218, 222; and Irish Race Convention resolution, 223; United States Senate and, 228; and Irish self-determination, 230

Von Bernstorff, Count, 146, 162–163

Walker, William, 102

Walsh, Frank P., 224, 226, 227, 230, 253

Walsh, Archbishop William, 107

Washington Times, 236

Westminster Gazette: de Valera interview, 240

White, Captain J. R., 111, 113

White Paper. *See* Constitutional Proposals for Northern Ireland

Whitman, Charles, 215

Willert, Sir Arthur, 244

William of Orange, 3, 81

Wilson, Harold, 306

Wilson, General Sir Henry, 88, 284

Wilson, Woodrow: receives demands of Irish-Americans, 191; and Sinn Fein, 211; and position on Irish demands, 212; refuses hearing to Irish delegates, 213; receives resolution endorsing Irish self-determination, 215; and Phelan resolution, 215; responds to O'Kelley, 222; and Irish-American

Committee, 224–225, 229; condemns Republican platform, 249; and December 1918 speech at Manchester, 281

Wimborne, Lord, 165, 166, 168; resigns as Lord Lieutenant, 174; replaced by Lord French, 198

Wolfe Tone, Theobold, 1, 4, 5

Worker's Republic, 101, 141, 152

World War I: outbreak of, 93–94; and Anglo-Irish differences, 130–131; Irish war effort, 131–134; Irish disaffection with, 135–138; British code-breaking during, 146–148, 156; conscription crisis in Ireland during, 196–198

Young Ireland, 7, 8, 16; members defended by Isaac Butt, 17

Yeats, William Butler, 41–42, 43, 44, 45; and Horace Plunkett, 49, 51; and Abbey Theatre riot, 56; and romantic nationalism, 141–142, 176

Zimmermann, Arthur, 148

PRINTED IN U. S. A.